Archaeological Survey

MANUALS IN ARCHAEOLOGICAL METHOD, THEORY, AND TECHNIQUE

Series Editors:
Charles E. Orser, Jr., *Illinois State University, Normal, Illinois*
Michael B. Schiffer, *University of Arizona, Tucson, Arizona*

ARCHAEOLOGICAL SURVEY
E. B. Banning

A Continuation Order Plan is available for this series. A continuation order will bring delivery of each new volume immediately upon publication. Volumes are billed only upon actual shipment. For further information please contact the publisher.

Archaeological Survey

E. B. Banning
University of Toronto
Toronto, Ontario, Canada

KLUWER ACADEMIC/PLENUM PUBLISHERS
New York, Boston, Dordrecht, London, Moscow

ISBN HB: 0-306-47347-X
PB: 0-306-47348-8

©2002 Kluwer Academic/Plenum Publishers, New York
233 Spring Street, New York, New York 10013

http://www.wkap.nl/

10 9 8 7 6 5 4 3 2 1

A C.I.P. record for this book is available from the Library of Congress.

All rights reserved

No part of this book may be reproduced, stored in a retrieval system, or transmitted in any form
or by any means, electronic, mechanical, photocopying, microfilming, recording,
or otherwise, without written permission from the Publisher, with the exception of any material
supplied specifically for the purpose of being entered and executed on a computer system,
for exclusive use by the purchaser of the work.

Printed in the United States of America

Preface

One of the questions that non-archaeologists often ask us is how we find archaeological sites. Today we often provide a pat answer about random or systematic sampling, or perhaps about fieldwalking. This does not do justice to what archaeologists actually do, or to the body of theory and methods we have built up.

After decades of carrying out surveys with intuitive designs, in the 1960s some archaeologists began to deal more explicitly with the design of archaeological surveys. Some seminal articles on aspects of archaeological survey design followed over the next two decades but, unlike excavation methods, archaeological survey has received no comprehensive treatment that could serve as a guide to survey practitioners. The main purpose of this book is to fill this gap.

In addition, most archaeologists have been reluctant to discuss aspects of survey other than sampling and a few of the factors that influence detection probability. They have also almost completely ignored the large body of literature on search theory that cognate fields have generated. In an attempt to put archaeological survey on a consistent theoretical and methodological basis, I have drawn on research in archaeology, mathematical earth sciences, and operations research. This will result, I think, in some surprises for archaeologists, who have sometimes struggled to identify and understand survey problems that other fields had already studied intensively.

My own interest in archaeological survey began more than 20 years ago, when an invitation to join the staff of a survey in southern Jordan quite quickly threw me into the midst of debates over sampling, discovery probabilities, site significance, site definition, and other issues. A few years later, I also had a hand in designing a survey in the eastern Nile delta of Egypt. I thank Burton MacDonald and Carol Redmount for providing those opportunities. These, and my own survey project, which I started in northern Jordan about that time, exposed me to survey in stony deserts, dune areas, plowed fields, and even dense oak scrub and forest (yes, there actually are forests in the Middle East). In addition, these seasons of fieldwork forced me to learn from my mistakes. It quickly became obvious that cookbook solutions that were popular at the time were quite ineffective for achieving my objectives. No longer would I design a survey the way I did in the early 1980s.

From 1985 to 1987, I divided a post-doctoral fellowship between the University of Virginia and the University of Arizona, where I was able to focus on some of the problems I had been encountering with survey design and evaluation, and benefited from discussions with Steve Plog and Mike Schiffer. I thank them and a number of archaeologists who responded to a questionnaire I circulated at that time, for helping me formulate my trial solutions to some of these problems, and the Social Sciences and Humanities Research Council of Canada for supporting my post-doctoral project.

I also thank Ron Farquhar for introducing me to the geophysical perspective on survey and remote sensing at the University of Toronto. My interactions with him while I served as teaching assistant in a course on archaeometry led me to try to find a unified theory for archaeological survey, as applicable to fieldwalking for lithic scatters as to magnetometry. Eventually, this experience, and a discussion with Dave Lasby, led to my discovery that such theories had long been available in the search literature of mathematical geology and operations research.

I would like to thank Tony Wilkinson and Michael Mathers for their helpful comments on content; Margaret Bateman and Jennifer Sharman for help with the bibliography, index, and proofing; and Mike Schiffer and Charles Orser for inviting me to contribute this book.

Knowing that part of my audience would be CRM surveyors, and that my own experience was focussed on the Middle East, I also sometimes relied on discussions with Steve Monckton, Ron Williamson, Paul Racher, Chris Watt, Dana Campbell, and Jeff Bursey for their impressions of the problems of CRM survey in the Great Lakes region of North America. Over the years, I have also benefitted from discussions about survey with Cesare d'Annibale, Max Friesen, Peter Dawson, Lou Levine, Bill Cavanagh, Sally Stewart, Alicia Hawkins, and Dave Lasby. I would also like to thank Mark Pearce at University of Nottingham for introducing me to W. G. Clarke's 1922 guide to fieldwalking.

The organization of this book reflects my belief that good archaeological survey design must both anticipate the factors that affect the detectability of archaeological materials and facilitate the surveys' objectives. Consequently, the main chapters following the introduction focus on influences on detectability and on three classes of survey that, I think, reflect the main goals that surveyors attempt to achieve. These are prospection, estimation, and the detection of spatial pattern. Certainly other classifications are possible, but I have found this a useful way to conceive of the differences between survey strategies and to resolve conflicts between site and "non-site," and sampling and "total" survey. Other chapters deal with practical matters that are common to all types of survey or (Chapter 8) to CRM surveys in particular.

The book is aimed at professional archaeologists and archaeological students who already have some familiarity with archaeological theory and methods. Some chapters explore mathematical aspects of survey design, but I would urge readers who find the mathematics tedious simply to focus instead on the substantive implications of the equations. Among these implications I would include:

1. It is indeed possible to find near-optimal geometries and distribution of effort for many kinds of survey.
2. Increases in survey effort often have diminishing returns.
3. Quantitative evaluation of a survey design and its results allows us to make realistic assessments about the proportion of targets the survey detected, about the extent of bias in their detection or in estimates of their parameters, and about the

places where targets probably will and will not occur in as yet unsurveyed regions.

I have also provided some simple examples to illustrate how some of the more important equations work in practical situations.

Students with less background in archaeology might want to focus on the more general Chapters 1 and 2, and on the more practical issues in Chapter 9, and to read the survey sections of general introductions to archaeological fieldwork, such as Brian Fagan's *Archaeology: A Brief Introduction* (1988), Jane McIntosh's *The Practical Archaeologist* (1986), or Robert Sharer and Wendy Ashmore's *Discovering Our Past* (1996).

Some of the approaches I advocate in this book, I am sure, will seem to some readers too theoretical, too counter-intuitive, or too much of a departure from years of practical experience. Yet part of my argument below is that the knowledge and intuition of experienced practitioners should be integral to the survey design process. In addition, I hope I can convince you that we should not satisfy ourselves with boilerplate surveys and cookie-cutter shovel-test intervals, just because they are easy for bureaucrats or developers to understand or because they provide a level playing field.

Modern development is rapidly altering forever the shape of the archaeological landscapes we hold dear. Let us find ways to explore those landscapes thoroughly, yet practically, while we still can.

Ted Banning
Toronto, Ontario

Contents

LIST OF FIGURES xix

LIST OF TABLES xxi

I.   INTRODUCTION 1
    1. A BRIEF HISTORY OF ARCHAEOLOGICAL SURVEY 2
       1.1 Early Archaeological Reconnaissance 2
       1.2 Fieldwalking in Britain 3
       1.3 Early Air Reconnaissance 4
       1.4 Surveys in Northwest Europe 4
       1.5 The Virù Valley Survey 4
       1.6 Diyala and Uruk Surveys, Iraq 5
       1.7 The Basin of Mexico Project 6
       1.8 Site Survey in the American Southwest 6
       1.9 Survey in North American Forests 7
       1.10 "Non-site Survey," and "Landscape Archaeology" 7
       1.11 Intertidal and Shallow-lake Survey 8
    2. SURVEY'S UNIQUE CONTRIBUTION TO ARCHAEOLOGY 10
    3. SURFACE DISTRIBUTIONS AND BURIED LANDSCAPES 11
       3.1 Models of Cultural Distributions 12
           3.1.1 The Monument Model 13
           3.1.2 The Earthwork Model 13
           3.1.3 The Uniform Distribution 14
           3.1.4 The Modal, "Bulls-eye," or "Fried-egg" Model 15
                3.1.4.1 Mathematical Models for Clusters of Artifacts 16
                3.1.4.2 Contagious Distributions 17
           3.1.5 The Palimpsest Model 18
           3.1.6 The "Off-site" or "Intersite" Model 19
           3.1.7 The Distributional or "Non-site" Model 20
           3.1.8 The Place Model 20
           3.1.9 The Paleolandscape Model 22
    4. RESEARCH DESIGN IN ARCHAEOLOGICAL SURVEY 22

II. THE GOALS OF ARCHAEOLOGICAL SURVEY 27
1. TYPES OF GOALS 27
1.1 Prospection 28
1.2 Statistical Survey 30
    1.2.1 Populations, Parameters and Estimation 30
    1.2.2 Estimating Densities of Sites 30
    1.2.3 Estimating Densities of Artifacts on the Landscape 31
    1.2.4 Estimating Proportions of Site Types 31
    1.2.5 Estimating Human Population Size or Growth Rate 32
    1.2.6 Estimating Proportions of Sites by Ecological or Land-use Zone 32
    1.2.7 Estimating Parameters of Artifact Attributes 32
    1.2.8 Estimating the Range or Diversity of Archaeological Materials 33
    1.2.9 The Relevance of Prospecting Tools 33
1.3 Surveying for Spatial Structure 34
    1.3.1 Detecting Settlement Lattices, Landscape Systems, and Communication Routes 34
    1.3.2 Mapping "Continuous" Distributions 34
1.4 Surveys with Multiple Goals 35
1.5 The Issue of Methodological Consistency 36
1.6 Summary 38

III. THE DISCOVERY OF ARCHAEOLOGICAL MATERIALS BY SURVEY 39
1. FACTORS AFFECTING ARCHAEOLOGICAL DETECTION 39
1.1 Method of Inspection 40
    1.1.1 Visual Inspection in Surface Survey 40
    1.1.2 Visual Inspection of Aerial Photographs with Groundchecks 41
    1.1.3 Survey by Test Pits, Divoting, Coring, or Augering (SST) 42
    1.1.4 Geophysical Survey 44
        1.1.4.1 Resistivity Survey 44
        1.1.4.2 Magnetometer Survey 44
        1.1.4.3 Electromagnetic (EM) Survey 44
        1.1.4.4 Seismic Survey 45
        1.1.4.5 Sonar or Acoustic Survey 45
        1.1.4.6 Ground-Penetrating Radar (GPR) 45
        1.1.4.7 Chemical Survey 45
        1.1.4.8 Thermal Survey 45
    1.1.5 Underwater Survey 45
1.2 Visibility 46
1.3 Obtrusiveness 48
    1.3.1 The Constituents of Archaeological Distributions 49
    1.3.2 Obtrusiveness of Artifact Scatters 49

Contents

    1.3.3 Constituent Removal by Chemical or Mechanical Destruction 54
    1.3.4 Obtrusiveness in Aerial Reconnaissance 54
    1.3.5 Obtrusiveness in Geophysical Survey 55
    1.3.6 Obtrusiveness in Chemical Survey 55
  1.4 Distance from Target to Sensor 56
    1.4.1 The Law of Clean Sweep or Definite Detection 57
    1.4.2 Inverse-cube Law 58
  1.5 Geometry of Sites or Artifact Clusters 59
  1.6 Intensity or Density of Effort 60
  1.7 Resolution 62
  1.8 Coverage 63
  1.9 Accessibility 63
  1.10 Crew Training, Experience, and Motivation 65
    1.10.1 Training and Briefing Team Members 66
    1.10.2 Team Composition 66
    1.10.3 Team Motivation 66
    1.10.4 Accounting for Variability 67
  1.11 Data Units 67
  1.12 False Targets 67
2. ESTIMATING DISCOVERY PROBABILITIES 68
3. POST-DEPOSITIONAL FACTORS THAT AFFECT SPATIAL PATTERN 72
  3.1 Artifact Displacement or Sorting by Erosion 73
  3.2 Artifact Removal by Erosion 73
  3.3 Artifact Displacement or Removal by Bioturbation 73
  3.4 Artifact Removal by Chemical or Mechanical Destruction 73
  3.5 Artifact Displacement by Plowing 73
4. SUMMARY 74

IV. UNITS, SAMPLING FRAMES, AND EDGE EFFECTS IN ARCHAEOLOGICAL SURVEY 75

1. THE SPATIAL DISTRIBUTION OF MATERIAL CULTURE 75
2. BOUNDARIES OF THE SURVEY AREA 76
  2.1 Physical-Geographical Boundaries 77
  2.2 Historical-Political Boundaries 78
  2.3 Estimated Political-Economic Boundaries 78
  2.4 Catchment Boundaries 78
  2.5 Oversize Boundaries and Group Territories 79
  2.6 Edge Effects 80
    2.6.1 Edge Effects in Nearest Neighbor Analysis 80
    2.6.2 Edge Effects on Rank-Size Analysis 80
3. TYPES, SHAPES, AND ORIENTATION OF UNITS 81
  3.1 Sites 81

3.1.1 Site Size, Shape, and Orientation 82
3.2 Geometrical Spatial Units 83
    3.2.1 Edge Effects on the Detection of Sites 83
    3.2.2 Edge Effects on Parameter Estimates 85
    3.2.3 Cost Effects of Unit Size 86
3.3 Non-geometrical Spatial Units 86
3.4 Arrangement of Units 88
    3.4.1 Regular Grids 88
        3.4.1.1 Arrangement of Point Samples 88
    3.4.2 Transects 89
        3.4.2.1 Parallel Transects 89
        3.4.2.2 Intersecting Transects 90
        3.4.2.3 Undulating Transects 91
        3.4.2.4 Retiring-square Pattern 92
    3.4.3 Unconventional Arrangements 92
    3.4.4 Nested Arrangements 94

4. SCALE EFFECTS IN ARCHAEOLOGICAL SURVEY 94
4.1 Size of Units 95
4.2 Optimal Arrangements, Sizes, and Spacing 96
    4.2.1 Optimizing the Arrangement of Systematic Point Grids 97
    4.2.2 Optimizing the Arrangement of Continuous Parallel Transects 100
    4.2.3 Optimizing the Arrangement of Polygons 100
    4.2.4 Optimizing the Spacing of Systematic Point Grids 101
        4.2.4.1 Optimal Spacing of Point Grids at a Fixed Cost 102
        4.2.4.2 Optimal Spacing of Point Grids Taking Cost and "Value" into
              Account 102
    4.2.5 Optimizing the Spacing of Parallel Transects 105
        4.2.5.1 Optimal Spacing of Transects Taking Costs and "Value" into
              Account 106
        4.2.5.2 Spacing Transects within Polygons 107
        4.2.5.3 Retiring-square Pattern 108
    4.2.6 Optimizing the Size of Quadrats and Other Spatial Units 108
        4.2.6.1 Optimizing Polygon Size for the Variance of Estimates at a
              Fixed Cost 108
        4.2.6.2 Balancing the Costs and Benefits of Polygon Size 109
        4.2.6.3 Optimizing the Size of SSTs for Artifact Density 109
4.3 Influences on Detection of Spatial Pattern 110
4.4 Influences on Parameter Estimates 110

5. CONCLUSIONS 112

V. SAMPLING SPACE: STATISTICAL SURVEYS 113

Contents

1. **SAMPLING DESIGNS** 113
   - 1.1 Basic Sampling Designs 113
     - 1.1.1 Random Sampling 113
     - 1.1.2 Stratified Sampling 115
     - 1.1.3 Systematic Sampling 116
   - 1.2 Complications in Geometric Spatial Samples 117
     - 1.2.1 Systematic, Stratified, Unaligned Sampling 117
     - 1.2.2 Transects Nested in Quadrats 117
     - 1.2.3 Cross-cutting Stratification 118
     - 1.2.4 Adaptive Sampling 118
   - 1.3 Cluster Sampling and Element Sampling 119
   - 1.4 Sampling with Point Samples 121
   - 1.5 Sampling Geomorphic and Cultural Features or "Places" 122
2. **SAMPLE SIZE AND ESTIMATION** 124
   - 2.1 Sample Size and Sampling Fraction 124
   - 2.2 Fixed-sample Designs 124
   - 2.3 Optimal Allocation for Stratified Samples 126
     - 2.3.1 Neyman Allocation 127
     - 2.3.2 Minimizing Variance on a Fixed Budget 128
     - 2.3.3 Minimizing Cost for a Fixed Variance 129
   - 2.4 Sequential Sampling 130
3. **USING SAMPLES** 130
   - 3.1. Estimating the Density of Archaeological Materials 130
   - 3.2. Estimating the Number of Archaeological Sites 131
   - 3.3. Estimating the Proportions of Archaeological Occurrences by Type or Period 131
   - 3.4 Estimating the Proportions of Sites in Different Environments 131
   - 3.5 Estimating Changes in Regional Population or Settlement Area 132
   - 3.6. Creating Locational Models 132
4. **CONCLUSION** 132

VI. PURPOSIVE SURVEY: PROSPECTION 133

1. **PROSPECTING** 134
   - 1.1 Surveying for Historically Documented Sites 134
     - 1.1.1 Location of Upper Creek Villages in Alabama 135
     - 1.1.2 Search for *La Navidad* 135
     - 1.1.3 Nautical Survey for *The Monitor* 135
     - 1.1.4 Search for the Submerged City of Helike 136
   - 1.2 Using Aerial Photography or Satellite Imagery 136
   - 1.3 Exploiting Structure in Landscapes 137
   - 1.4 Exploiting Structure in Target Interrelationships 138

1.5	Exploiting Exposures of Buried Deposits	138
1.6	Using Predictive Models and GIS	138
	1.6.1 Early History of Predictive Modelling	139
	1.6.2 Assumptions of Predictive Modelling	140
	1.6.3 Steps in the Use of Inductive Predictive Models	141
	1.6.3.1 Creating Primary and Secondary Coverages	141
	1.6.3.2 Creating the Model	142
	1.6.3.3 Testing the Model	142
	1.6.3.4 Applying the Model	143
1.7	Using Geophysical Remote Sensing	144
1.8	Adaptive Sampling Strategies	145
2.	**PROSPECTION TO TEST MODELS OR HYPOTHESES**	**145**
3.	**BAYESIAN PROSPECTION AND OPERATIONS RESEARCH**	**146**
3.1	Search Patterns	147
	3.1.1 Search for the Chesapeake Flotilla	148
3.2	Optimal Allocation	149
	3.2.1 Simplified Examples of Optimal Allocation	150
3.3	Incrementally Optimal Searches	152
4.	**GAME THEORY AND LINEAR PROGRAMMING IN OPTIMAL SEARCHES**	**152**
4.1	Discrete Search Games	153
4.2	Continuous Search Games	153
	4.2.1 Exponential Spiral Search Trajectories	154
5.	**CONCLUSIONS**	**154**
VII.	**SURVEYING FOR SPATIAL STRUCTURE**	**155**
1.	**WHAT IS SPATIAL STRUCTURE?**	**155**
1.1	Settlement Patterns and Settlement Systems	156
1.2	Central Places and Settlement Lattices	157
	1.2.1 The Central Place Model	157
	1.2.2 Hunter-gatherer Land-use Models	158
	1.2.3 Site-catchment Models	158
	1.2.4 Optimal Location Models	158
	1.2.5 Settlement-lattice Models	159
	1.2.6 Rank-size Models	160
1.3	Dendritic and Other Networks	161
1.4	Earthwork Patterns	163
1.5	Trend Surfaces, Clustering, and Isopleth Maps	164
1.6	Distributional Archaeology	165
2.	**"THE CASE FOR TOTAL SURVEY"**	**167**
2.1	The Definition of "Total Survey"	167
2.2	The "Presampling" and Large-site Bias Arguments	168

Contents

- 3. How to Survey for Spatial Structure ... 168
  - 3.1 Determining the Scale of Survey ... 168
    - 3.1.1 Surveying with Central Place Models ... 168
    - 3.1.2 Surveying for Settlement Lattices ... 169
    - 3.1.3 Survey for Rank-size Analysis ... 170
    - 3.1.4 Surveying Dendritic Networks ... 171
    - 3.1.5 Landscape Survey ... 172
  - 3.2 Selecting Effective Search Patterns ... 172
    - 3.2.1 Surveying with Central Place and Site-catchment Models ... 173
    - 3.2.2 Surveying for Settlement Lattices ... 173
    - 3.2.3 Survey for Rank-size Analysis ... 174
    - 3.2.4 Dendritic Networks ... 174
    - 3.2.5 Landscape Survey ... 175
- 4. Conclusion ... 175

VIII. Cultural Resource Management and Site Significance ... 177

- 1. What is Cultural Resource Management? ... 177
  - 1.1 The Objectives of Cultural Resource Management ... 178
  - 1.2 The Responsibilities of CRM Professionals ... 178
    - 1.2.1 Responsibility to the Client ... 178
    - 1.2.2 Responsibility to Archaeological and Other Heritage Resources ... 179
    - 1.2.3 Responsibility to the Public ... 179
    - 1.2.4 Legal Obligations ... 179
    - 1.2.5 Responsibility to Personnel ... 179
- 2. Regional Impact assessments by Field Survey ... 180
  - 2.1 Goals of Impact Assessment ... 180
  - 2.2 Satisfying Clients and Regulations ... 181
  - 2.3 Use of Predictive Models in Phase I Assessment ... 181
    - 2.3.1 What Are Predictive Models and Sensitivity Models? ... 182
    - 2.3.2 Do Sensitivity Models Create Bias? ... 183
- 3. Assessing Significance ... 183
  - 3.1 Kinds of Significance ... 184
    - 3.1.1 Scientific or Scholarly Significance ... 184
    - 3.1.2 Public, Recreational and Educational Significance ... 185
    - 3.1.3 Historical Significance ... 186
    - 3.1.4 Economic Significance ... 186
    - 3.1.5 Ethnic Significance ... 187
    - 3.1.6 Significance in Land Claims ... 187
  - 3.2 Measuring Significance ... 188
- 4. Administrative, Ethical, and Legal Aspects of CRM ... 189
  - 4.1 Government and Institutional Regulation of Surveys ... 190

    4.1.1 US Federal Legislation and State Guidelines 190
    4.1.2 English Legislation 191
    4.1.3 Canadian Legislation 193
    4.1.4 Summary 193
  4.2 Professional Organizations and Self-regulation 194
    4.2.1 The American Cultural Resources Association (ACRA) 194
    4.2.2 The Register of Professional Archaeologists (RPA) 194
    4.2.3 The Institute of Field Archaeologists (IFA) 195
    4.2.4 The Canadian Association of Professional Heritage Consultants (CAPHC) 195
  4.3 Development Pressures on Surveys 195
  4.4 Reporting Requirements 196
5. CONCLUSION 196

IX. SURVEYING SITES AND LANDSCAPES 197

1. FIELDWALKING AND SURFACE SURVEY 197
  1.1 Locating Transects and Staying on Course 198
  1.2 Intertidal Surveys 199
  1.3 Facilitating Evaluation of Survey Results 199
2. COMMON ATTRIBUTES OF SITES 200
  2.1 Site Size 200
  2.2 Site Function and Site Hierarchies 201
  2.3 Site Chronology 201
  2.4 Site Features or Topography 201
  2.5 Site Environment 202
  2.6 Site Preservation 202
3. EXAMINING SITES AND COLLECTING OR RECORDING ARTIFACTS 203
  3.1 Estimating Site Size 203
  3.2 Site Chronology 204
  3.3 Documenting Site Features 206
  3.4 Sampling or Stratifying the Site 207
  3.5 To Collect or Not to Collect 208
  3.6 Test Excavations 209
  3.7 Cleaning Intertidal Deposits 209
4. DOCUMENTING "NON-SITE" OR "OFF-SITE" MATERIAL CULTURE 210
  4.1 Artifact Discovery 210
  4.2 Quadrat Mapping 211
  4.3 Artifact Recording 211
  4.4 Recording Geographical Information and Formation Processes 212
  4.5 Recording Influences on Visibility and Detectability 212
5. INTERTIDAL SURVEYS 213

Contents xvii

    6. CONTROLS AND DATA QUALITY 213
      6.1 Control for Artifact Detection 214
      6.2 Control for Accuracy of Artifact Attributes 215
      6.3 Control for Accuracy and Precision of Site and Spatial Attributes 215
    7. CONCLUSION 216
X. EVALUATING SURVEYS 217
    1. ASSESSING DETECTION PROBABILITIES 217
      1.1 Estimating Detection Probabilities of Systematic Surveys 217
      1.2 Assessing the Impact of Visibility, Intensity, and Other Specific Factors 218
      1.3 Estimating Detection Probabilities of Informal Surveys 219
    2. ASSESSING THE "EXHAUSTION" OF A REGION 220
    3. EVALUATING THE EFFECTIVENESS OF SAMPLING 223
    4. ASSESSING THE RELIABILITY OF CREW OBSERVATIONS 224
    5. ASSESSING BIAS IN THE CHARACTERIZATION OF FINDS 226
    6. ASSESSING VARIATIONS IN COLLECTION METHOD 227
    7. CONCLUSION 227
XI. SURVEYING THE FUTURE 229
    1. SURVEY'S EXPANDING ROLE 229
    2. INVESTIGATING "HIDDEN" AND NEGLECTED LANDSCAPES 230
      2.1 Subsurface Survey and Geoarchaeological Approaches 230
      2.2 Wetland Survey 231
      2.3 Marine Survey 231
    3. SURVEY METHOD AND TECHNOLOGY 232
    4. MATHEMATICAL APPROACHES TO SURVEY THEORY AND EVALUATION 233
      4.1 Optimizing Surveys 233
      4.2 Evaluating Survey Results 233
    5. CONCLUSION 234
APPENDIX 1. HEALTH, SAFETY, AND PRACTICAL MATTERS IN FIELD SURVEY 235
    1. HEALTH AND SAFETY IN FIELD SURVEY 235
      1.1 Notifying Landowners and Relevant Authorities or Agencies 235
      1.2 Educating Team Members 236
      1.3 First-Aid 236
      1.4 Communication 236
      1.5 Preparation for Weather 236
      1.6 Risk of Encountering High-voltage Lines, Toxic Waste, or Explosives . 237
      1.7 Risks from Animals or Disease 237
      1.8 Risk from Hunters or Military Activity 237
      1.9 Insurance 238

2. OUTFITTING THE SURVEY CREW 238
2.1 Personal Gear and Bad-weather Gear 238
2.2 Mapping and Recording Instruments 238
2.3 Sampling Equipment and Supplies 239
2.4 Safety Equipment 239
3. CREW TRAINING AND ORIENTATION 239
BIBLIOGRAPHY 241
INDEX 265

List of Figures

Figure 1. The "bullseye" or "fried-egg" model.. 16
Figure 2. The Palimpsest model 19
Figure 3. Repeated discard over "satisfactory" spaces on the landscape 21
Figure 4. A spatial sample of 100 quadrats superimposed on a hexagonal-lattice settlement pattern 35
Figure 5. Poisson distribution for $\lambda = 2$ 51
Figure 6. Models for the effect of lateral range on probability of detection 57
Figure 7. The ability of an observer to see an object on a distant surface 59
Figure 8. Diminishing returns of increasing search time 61
Figure 9. The probability that point grids will intersect a circular target 69
Figure 10. Relationship between sites' discovery radius and their probability of detection 71
Figure 11. The effect of site size on the probability of site detection by transects 83
Figure 12. Effective areas of a square and a transect of equal area 84
Figure 13. Variation in the detection of sites per unit area with transects, squares, and hexagons 85
Figure 14. Transects, each divided into 1 ha sections, nested within a polygonal survey unit 87
Figure 15. Arrangement of points on square, isoceles, and equilateral triangular grids, superimposed on circular sites 89
Figure 16. A selection of search geometries for parallel straight and wavy transects and two passes by transects oriented 45° 91
Figure 17. Expanding-square or retiring-square search over a target with a circular normal probability distribution 92
Figure 18. Positions of nine units, each 3 mi long, in a stratified random sample of the Cache and Bayou de View channels in northern Arkansas 93
Figure 19. Variation in intersection probability with size of survey unit 96
Figure 20. The largest circular site that can escape detection for the square and equilateral triangular grids 97
Figure 21. An easy way to establish points on an equilateral triangular grid 99
Figure 22. Eliptical targets at optimal orientations centered at the corners of isoceles (a), equilateral (b), square (c), and rectangular (d) grids 101
Figure 23. Estimating optimal transect spacing with respect to the "values" or mitigation costs of sites 104

Figure 24. The effect of quadrat size on the identification of dot clustering 111

Figure 25. Four ways to define the "neighborhood" of an initial sample element in adaptive sampling 118

Figure 26. Example of adaptive sampling in a systematic survey by shovel tests or augering. 119

Figure 27. The population of main and branch canals of the Seleucid-Parthian period in the lower Diyala basin, Iraq 123

Figure 28. Selecting a perpendicular transect to search for a circular enclosure 144

Figure 29. A model of the network of Mississippian settlement in the Middle Mississippi Valley 162

Figure 30. Chronological relationships among field boundaries 164

Figure 31. Smoothing a set of artifact counts by averaging over a neighborhood to allow isopleth mapping 166

Figure 32. Survey regions defined by one- and two-hour walks from a known settlement site, as defined by walking radially arranged transects. 170

Figure 33. Density distribution of medieval pottery in plot H145 of the 1986 East Brittany Survey 212

Figure 34. Map of Glueck's probable routes of survey in 1942, overlaid on the survey universe of the 1981 Wadi Ziqlab Survey 219

Figure 35. Increases in number and diversity of known sites in Wadi Ziqlab suggest that the region is not exhausted 221

Figure 36. Intersection probabilities of circular and elliptical targets with centers at varying distances from an observation point 222

Figure 37. Exhaustion map for elliptical targets 800 m x 400 m in Glueck's 1942 survey within the boundaries of the Wadi Ziqlab drainage 223

Figure 38. Number of lithic artifacts collected in each meter square at Dakhleh locality 216TP, Egypt, by different collectors 224

List of Tables

Table 1. Point intervals on square, rectangular, isoceles (rhombic), and equilateral (hexagonal) grids to minimize the size of the largest circular target that could escape detection within a survey rectangle of length L and width W 98

Table 2. Sample statistics (with standard deviations) and population parameters for the density of Seleucid-Parthian sites (sites per segment) along a population of canal segments in the lower Diyala valley, Iraq 123

Table 3. Examples of allocations to three spaces with unequal areas, proportional, equal and unequal probabilities, and different amounts of total survey effort 151

Chapter I

Introduction

Archaeological survey is often the first stage of a long-term archaeological project. At other times it is the principal method for studying some aspect of the past. Survey allows archaeologists to discover sites they may wish to excavate, to assess potential damage to archaeological resources from construction, road-building or other development, and to assess aspects of past settlement systems and regional economies. Survey can range from very informal exploration to detailed and explicit prospection or sampling strategies designed to maximize the probability of detecting sites or artifacts over a region, or to provide representative samples of cultural materials. It also ranges from visual inspection of fairly obvious features and artifacts on the modern surface, sometimes called "fieldwalking," through dispersed excavations ("shovel testing"), to geophysical remote sensing of buried materials.

Survey is not simply a poor substitute for archaeological excavation, or meant only to discover sites for us to excavate. In fact, it is uniquely able to address some research questions that excavation alone will never answer. Only regional survey is capable of producing the data we need to investigate prehistoric use of landscapes, settlement hierarchies, and human behaviors that were dispersed in space instead of concentrated within the more obvious kinds of "sites."

This book will introduce concepts and methods relevant to investigating archaeological phenomena at the regional scale. It will deal with some of the common goals of regional archaeological survey, the characteristics of archaeological remains that surveys are meant to discover or document, and how these and the way we design a survey affect the survey's results. It will not specifically address survey at the smaller, site-specific, scale, although some of the same concepts are applicable to both regional and intra-site survey.

We will begin with a brief history of archaeological survey, including some case studies that will help to emphasize points in later chapters. A discussion of the role of regional survey in archaeology will follow. The next section will deal briefly with models or assumptions of the ways cultural material can be distributed in space, and on exposed surfaces or in buried deposits. Then a brief section on general aspects of research design in archaeological surveys will set the stage for later chapters.

1. A BRIEF HISTORY OF ARCHAEOLOGICAL SURVEY

1.1 Early Archaeological Reconnaissance

European curiosity about the visible remnants of past civilizations led to documentation of archaeological landscapes from at least the 16th century. In the United Kingdom, the Ordnance Survey began to include antiquities on its detailed maps as early as 1801, and the *Gentlemen's Magazine* published articles on discoveries of English archaeological sites in the 18th century.

Leaders of some early archaeological surveys did not explicitly conceive of them as such. Often archaeological observations were only adjuncts to geographical exploration, as in early Russian expeditions to Siberia, or even military expeditions, such as Napoleon Bonaparte's in Egypt. Even so, some of these explorers laid the ground-work for methods that archaeologists have used ever since. At first, these were usually explorations by Europeans in non-European parts of the world; indigenous people, after all, already had long familiarity with their ruined monuments and had oral traditions about their significance. In some cases, as in 18th-century expeditions to relocate and study ruined cities in Central America, the European antiquarians relied on guides and porters to take them to sites that were already well known locally.

As the United States expanded its frontier westward, its settlers found considerable prehistoric monuments. One of the major questions was the origin of the "mound builders." Expeditions by Squier and Davis (1848) and later the Bureau of American Ethnology (Thomas, 1894) devoted considerable time to exploration and survey of these mounds. Exploration of the American Southwest also led to study of both contemporary Hopi villages and the ruined pueblos that preceded them (e.g., Cushing, 1890).

Other Europeans and Americans turned to exploration of the antiquities of the Holy Land. The earliest of these were mainly itineraries by pilgrims to the Middle East's holy places, such as accounts by Theodericus (ca. 1172), Frescobaldi (ca. 1390), Gucci (ca. 1390), and Bertrandon de la Broquiere (1457). There were also similar early accounts by Arab writers, such as Ibn Jubayr (1185). Later and more influential 19th-century surveys of Ottoman Palestine, Syria, Transjordan, and Arabia included ones by Buckingham (1821; 1825), Burckhardt (1822; 1829), Conder (1889), and Robinson (1856). These documented mainly quite obtrusive sites, such as Roman ruins, and tried to identify them with historical or biblical place-names, usually on the basis of their modern Arabic names. At the time, there was no way for them to date sites except in the rare instances when inscriptions were visible, and the sites they discovered were ones already quite well known locally.

1.2 Fieldwalking in Britain

One of the first authors to describe the methods of archaeological survey, and possibly the first specifically to address methods for surveying artifact scatters, was W. G. Clarke (1922:24-32), in a guide to amateurs interested in prehistoric lithics. Although he does not discuss any explicit research design, he does give good advice on fieldwalking for surface scatters, and notes the importance of fire-cracked rock as evidence of prehistoric cooking activity.

> An examination of an arable field in a suitable district, a sufficient time after it has been ploughed for the soil to have settled and a considerable proportion of the stones to be lying on the surface, will disclose a perplexing quantity [of lithics] (Clarke, 1922: 25).

In describing one day's survey in southwestern Norfolk, he notes that, while walking over a heath, surveyors could only find artifacts where the burrowing of moles and rabbits had thrown them up (Clarke 1922: 30). In a newly plowed field, by contrast, their method was as follows.

> Following our usual practice we walked across the middle in each direction, trusting to get some indication of the best portion of the field. Scattered flakes occurred in all parts, but were much thicker at one place than others, and to this spot we returned and endeavoured to delimit the area which would best repay detailed searching. This was soon revealed by a careful inspection and a systematic search was then made, almost every yard being scrutinised (Clarke, 1922: 31).

In this he employs an assumption that archaeologists continued to use for decades: that high-density clusters of artifacts on the surface are somehow more important or more likely to correspond with the places where prehistoric activities were concentrated. He notes that in some areas lithic densities are so high that selective collection is "inevitable" and provides advice on how to recognize culturally produced flakes and to detect retouch quickly in the field. He also provides recommendations on recording provenience:

> On arrival home, surface implements such as these are washed and scrubbed, and the locality in which each flint was found either indicated by a number, corresponding to that in a register, a gummed label with parish and collectors's initials printed thereon, or a written locality. A method by which the particular field in which the implement was found can be ascertained is to be recommended, as variations in the industries of sites only a few hundred yards from each other, are thus made obvious (Clarke, 1922: 32).

1.3 Early Air Reconnaissance

One of the great boons to archaeological survey was the advent of aerial reconnaissance during the First World War. Archaeologists were quick to apply this new technology to archaeological discovery in regions ranging from England (Crawford, 1929; 1953) to Syria (Poidebard, 1934). Not only was it easier to discover earthworks and detect patterns in their distribution by viewing landscapes from the air in raking light, sometimes buried ditches and building foundations were detectable in vegetation patterns called "crop marks" (Bewley and Rackowski, 2001; Dassié, 1978; Deuel, 1969; Kennedy, 1995a, 1995b; Kennedy and Riley, 1990).

1.4 Surveys in Northwest Europe

Northwest Europe has long had a tradition of landscape archaeology, focussed largely on the distribution of small farms, villages, burial monuments, pathways, field walls and ditches. Since the 1920s, "fieldwalking" has benefited from aerial reconnaissance and amateur documentation.

One of the interesting features of the European tradition of survey is its treatment of whole landscapes, and especially evidence for agricultural land use, and not only of settlement sites. Even before, but especially after aerial reconnaissance became available, European archaeologists noticed traces of old fields at different orientations than the modern ones. Some of these old fields also had distinctive shapes, such as the "Celtic fields," and sizes, corresponding, for example, to the traditional field unit of an "acre." Some were bounded by parallel heaps of stone, called "reaves," or by "lynchets," sediment that naturally accumulated on the downslope edges of fields plowed for many years.

Some early research in British field archaeology dealt with the formation of lynchets and "ways" or tracks (Clay, 1927), others with "Celtic fields" and other kinds of field systems (e.g., Curwen, 1927), and still others with evidence from crop marks over buried roads and buildings (Crawford, 1929).

In Scandinavia, archaeology had close links with natural history even in the late 19th century, and this sometimes led to a more ecological perspective on site distributions. By the first quarter of the 20th century, regional settlement archaeology had become more common (e.g., Almgren, 1914; la Cour, 1927), and later regional settlement surveys by Therkel Mathiassen (1948; 1959) used large numbers of amateurs to help search out sites in Denmark.

1.5 The Virù Valley Survey

Gordon Willey's classic study of the ancient Virù Valley in Peru took archaeogical survey well beyond the simple prospecting for interesting sites. With some resemblance to the European fieldwalking surveys, it focussed on "settlement pattern," which Willey defined as

... the way in which man disposed himself over the landscape on which he lived. It refers to dwellings, to their arrangement, and to the nature and disposition of other buildings pertaining to community life. These settlements reflect the natural environment, the level of technology on which the builders operated, and the various institutions of social interaction and control which the culture maintained (Willey, 1953:1).

This definition's emphasis on the distribution of sites and buildings on the landscape, without explicit reference to how it "reflects" human behaviour, does not do justice to the actual research Willey and his colleagues conducted. Willey concerned himself, not merely with the distribution of sites in space, but with site functions, population sizes and sociopolitical organizations. This survey and other studies of settlement patterns in the 1950s had already begun to address the identification of "community patterns" with temporal, functional, ecological and social components in addition to the spatial one (Willey, 1953).

This survey had a profound influence on Americanist archaeology, leading to the kinds of spatial samples and environmental orientations that were particularly common in surveys of the 1970s, and eventually even to the kinds of landscape archaeology that became popular in the late 1980s.

1.6 Diyala and Uruk Surveys, Iraq

Surveys in the Diyala and central Euphrates floodplains of Iraq inspired a whole generation of archaeologists in the Near East (Adams, 1965; 1981; Adams and Nissen, 1972). From 1956 until 1975, these surveys' designs were based on

the premise that in a semiarid country like ancient Mesopotamia settlement would have been possible only where water was available — along rivers and canals. Where the settlements of a period showed linear patterns, it could be assumed that the lines reflected the water-courses upon which the settlements depended (Jacobsen, 1981:xiii).

In addition, traces of canal levees visible in aerial photographs provided a framework for finding less obtrusive sites, which could be assumed to occur along these canal routes. In the aerial photographs, often "a pattern of linear discolorations emerged, generally consisting of the faint traces of ancient levees" (Adams, 1981:28). Since a major goal of these surveys was to document changes in agricultural land use in the region, linking the survey so explicitly to the most limiting agricultural resource — water — was a highly effective strategy. We will return to surveys of this type in discussion of purposive survey, sampling frames, and the detection of spatial structure in chapters 4, 6 and 7.

1.7 The Basin of Mexico Project

Surveys by the Basin of Mexico Project were also quite influential. The project had the ambitious goal of 100% coverage by pedestrian survey over a region some 600 km^2 in area to document changes in residential distributions and people's interactions with their social and natural environments since 1000 BC. Methods changed over the period from Sanders's and Parson's surveys of the Teotihuacan Valley of 1960-1966, through Blanton's work on the Ixtapalapa region, Sanders's and Santley's survey of the Cuautitlan region, and surveys by Parsons and Hrones and Parsons in the Texcoco, Chalco, Xochimilco, and Temascalapa regions up to 1975, but shared some principles to protect the data's consistency (Sanders et al., 1979:11-15, 20).

This was a site survey, with inferred settlement locations as its basic units of observation and analysis. The surveyors argued that settlements were places "where people had spent enough time to leave some obvious, enduring physical traces on the present ground surface" (Sanders et al., 1979:15). Their definition of "site" required that survey teams recognize fairly discrete clusters of surface artifacts to which they could assign boundaries, apparently where density dropped off to "empty space." They recognized the possibility that some of these clusters were palimpsests of several overlapping occupations, and strove to separate these. They thought they could estimate what type of settlement some sites represented, and occasionally even used artifact densities to estimate sites' numbers of residents. Importantly, they recognized the importance of ensuring "that a blank on the settlement map for any particular time period was the product of a lack of settlement rather than a lack of survey" (Sanders et al., 1979:16-17).

Their survey initially used modern fields, identified on air photos, as observation units, rather than arbitrary geometric units. This presented problems in uncultivated areas or where field boundaries had shifted since the air photos were taken. Later surveys involved fast reconnaissance of broad transects, survey on and around known sites, and systematic pedestrian transects with intervals typically around 50 m but varying between 15 m and about 75 m. This variation depended on "common sense considerations of topography, drainage, vegetation, modern occupation," and other factors (Sanders et al. 1979:24). Except for small sites whose boundaries were fairly obvious, definition of site boundaries awaited analysis of the transect information, which showed where survey teams had recorded "on-site" artifact densities.

1.8 Site Survey in the American Southwest

The American Southwest has a long tradition of archaeological exploration, and work there has had a strong impact on theory and method in archaeological survey.

The earliest archaeological exploration, from about 1870, concentrated on documenting very obtrusive pueblos and cliff-dwellings. Surveys by John and Richard Wetherill (Pepper, 1902), Guernsey and Kidder (1921) expanded the coverage to cave sites and earlier "basketmaker" remains.

Introduction

But the Southwest was also a testing ground for the "New Archae
1960s, and this had an impact on archaeological surveys there. Fred Plo
survey by the Southwest Archaeological Expeditions of the Field Museum of Natural
History of the Upper Little Colorado River region in 1967 and 1968, and especially the
Hay Hollow Valley, to test a number of hypotheses concerning demographic change,
site differentiation, social integration, and technological developments. More generally,
he used these in an attempt to demonstrate the power of positivist explanatory frameworks that were beginning to become common in North American archaeology. Along
the way, Plog explicitly dealt with such problems as classifying sites on the basis of
activity sets, indirect measures of human population size (based on room numbers) and
ways to correct these for site longevity and rates of room abandonment.

Another influential survey in the Southwest was the Black Mesa Project (Gumerman
and Euler, 1976; Plog, 1978; Plog and Powell, eds., 1984). The project began with a
pipeline survey on the lease of a coal company in northeastern Arizona, but expanded in
scope to investigate many research hypotheses and to explore both theoretical and practical issues surrounding archaeological survey.

These and other surveys in the Southwest led to development of many of the theoretical concepts that will be discussed in later chapters.

1.9 Survey in North American Forests

In parts of North America where forest cover and leaf litter are major impediments
to the surface visibility of sites, archaeologists have devoted considerable effort to developing methods of subsurface survey. As we will see in later chapters, this work also
led to important theoretical advances in the detectability of archaeological materials
(e.g., Alexander, 1983; Kintigh, 1988; Krakker et al., 1983; Lightfoot, 1986; 1989; Lovis,
1976; Lynch, 1980; McManamon, 1980; Nance, 1983; Nance and Ball, 1986; Shott,
1985).

1.10 "Non-site Survey," and "Landscape Archaeology"

Prior to about 1980, most surveys in North America and the Old World concentrated
on the documentation of "sites." There was not much consistency in the definition of
sites, but generally these were concentrations of material culture, sometimes involving
traces of architecture, that archaeologists tended to assume marked the locations of ancient settlements, workshops, and so on.

Over the last 25 years, however, archaeologists have shown growing interest in the
residues of dispersed activities that did not necessarily occur in settlements or other
kinds of "sites." This trend began with surveys that used very minimal definitions of
"site;" sometimes discovery of a single artifact was sufficient. Increasing recognition
that hunter-gatherers conceived of landscapes as consisting, not of sites and empty space,
but of fishing holes, hunting grounds, pathways and portages, accelerated the pace of
this development.

In the late 1960s, David Hurst Thomas began a project that was to be very influential in the rise of "non-site" surveys. He worked in the Reese River Valley of central Nevada in an attempt to test Julian Steward's ethnographic model of Great Basin hunter-gatherer adaptation on archaeological evidence (Thomas, 1972; 1975). Rather than survey for sites in the environmental zones associated with different economic activities in Steward's model, Thomas measured attributes of artifacts found in 140 spatial units, each 500 m x 500 m in size, distributed across those zones. Thomas assumes that individual artifacts or cultural items, rather than sites, are his minimal units, but actually uses spatial units.

In the Amboseli Basin of Kenya, Robert Foley's research also led him toward what he calls an "offsite" approach (Foley, 1977; 1981a; 1981b). Foley noted that, like plant ecologists, archaeologists were interested in the distributions of small items, usually artifacts rather than plants, and that, in the Amboseli Basin, these artifacts were distributed in a virtually continuous manner. Unlike most of the archaeologists who had conducted surveys up to that time, he explicitly considered the site-formation processes that would have affected those distributions, and began with models that would guide his field research and data interpretation. With these models he conceived of sets of overlapping distributions, created by a variety of processes (see below, pp. 18-19). Consequently "sites," as defined by elevated densities, are only anomalies in the continuous spatial distribution of artifacts, and not necessarily the locations where habitation or other activity was concentrated at any particular time in the past. Although this conclusion has often led to the assumption that artifacts, rather than sites, are our basic units of analysis, Foley's approach, like Thomas's, actually leads us to a method based on the analysis of spatial units, such as quadrats (see chap. 4).

Some people object to some kinds of non-site survey because of the relatively high cost per unit area. However, Ebert (1992:170-171) argues that they may nonetheless offer lower costs per unit of information, as evidenced by comparison of his Seedskadee Survey results with the data found in the site-based records of the Intermountain Antiquities Computer System. He suggests that the Seedskadee data is equivalent to the information from a site-based survey with 528 sites/km^2.

1.11 Intertidal and Shallow-lake Survey

One type of survey that has only recently begun to receive the attention it deserves is the survey of intertidal zones and lake-bottoms revealed by falling water levels. Changes in sea levels, erosion of coasts, the excellent preservation of organic remains, and the human tendency to make use of coastal areas all combine to make it extremely important to survey the surfaces that receding waters briefly expose.

The archaeology of foreshores or intertidal zones, which lie between the high- and low-tide levels of sea coasts, has a much longer history than one might expect. William Borlase (1753; 1756) was a natural philosopher who, on a visit to the Isles of Scilly west of Cornwall in 1752, saw boulder walls forming enclosures in the islands' broad intertidal zone and recognized them as the remains of field walls and houses. He concluded that the islands had sunk over time, finding the alternative hypothesis — that sea levels

Introduction

had risen — too implausible. Naturalists and amateur archaeologists of the 18th and 19th centuries took considerable interest in traces of submerged forests, and sometimes archaeological sites, that coastal construction or storms periodically exposed along English coasts (e.g., Boyd Dawkins, 1872; Codrington, 1869; Cox, 1894). In the early 20th century, archaeologists' attention turned to intertidal remains related to the submerged "Lyonesse surface" along the Essex coast (Crawford, 1927; Smith, 1955; Warren et al., 1936).

It was only in the late 1970s, however, that intertidal archaeology began to depend regularly on survey, rather than chance exposures. Philip Hobler (1978) demonstrated the importance of the intertidal zone to the early prehistory of British Columbia, when sea levels were as much as 5 m lower than they are today, in a survey of Moresby Island. Wilkinson and Murphy (1986) discussed the problems and potential of intertidal survey on the basis of work along the Essex coast of England that represented the resurgence of this approach in the United Kingdom. Shortly thereafter, the Severn Estuary Levels Research Committee began extensive research in the intertidal zones of the Severn River (Allen and Fulford, 1986; Bell, 1993; Bell et al., 2000). More recently, English Heritage and Historic Scotland have devoted considerable attention to intertidal archaeology (e.g., Ashmore, 1994; Fulford et al., 1997; Historic Scotland, 1996). Intertidal survey is now a growing component of archaeology and heritage assessment in the United Kingdom (Aberg and Lewis, 2000; Wilkinson and Murphy, 1995), Ireland (O'Sullivan, 2001), northwestern North America (Fedje and Christensen, 1999; Langdon, 1987); and the South Pacific (e.g., Felgate, 2002; Reeve, 1989; Sheppard and Aswani, 1997; Wickler, 2001).

Intertidal surveys pose unusual practical problems, notably in the timing of fieldwork (see pp. 47, 65, 165), but also have great rewards, particularly in the excellent preservation of wooden and other organic remains that often pertains. They also yield unparalled evidence for watercraft, bridges, piers, fish weirs, salt pans, duck-decoy ponds, and other material culture associated with coastal and wetland economies.

Surveys of surfaces that emerge when lake levels are low are very similar in some respects to intertidal surveys. The most famous early examples involved discovery of the "Lake Villages" of Switzerland and parts of France, Italy, and Germany during the dry spell of 1853-54 (e.g., Keller, 1866), but some reports of wooden structures in shallow lake waters are even earlier in Ireland (e.g., Lewis, 1837), and further work on *crannogs* (lake dwellings) in Ireland, Scotland and the Continent closely followed (e.g., Munro, 1882; 1890; Wood-Martin, 1886). As with intertidal survey, there has been a recent resurgence of work on shallow and receding lakes, including survey along the shores of Lake Tiberias in Israel (Nadel, 1993), and survey of *crannogs* and other sites in Irish lakes (Buckley and Sweetman, 1991; O'Sullivan, 1998).

2. SURVEY'S UNIQUE CONTRIBUTION TO ARCHAEOLOGY

Many archaeologists are skeptical about the value of the data from regional surveys for addressing archaeological problems, leading Bowden et al. (1991) to ask whether survey is "skimming the surface or scraping the barrel." For example, Prag (1984:66) suggests that only botanical remains from excavated sites are of any use to document changes in agricultural economy. Other critics, even champions of survey as a valuable archaeological tool, focus on problems with the use of data from surface or plow-zone contexts that allegedly make them inferior to excavation data (e.g., Hope-Simpson, 1983; 1984). While many of the skeptics' concerns about existing regional databases are legitimate, and the processes that create and modify the distribution of material culture on the landscape are complex, to respond with dismissal of data from regional surveys betrays a failure to recognize the unique potential of archaeology's spatial dimensions.

Existing survey data do suffer from biases and unevenness in survey coverage, from inconsistency in methods and definition of analytical units, from the attrition of evidence through erosion, construction, burial and other processes, from differences of visibility, from a lack of good fit between some surveys' goals and methods, and from lack of adequate publication. The distributions that surveys detect furthermore concern the population of archaeological materials that persist and are accessible in the present, rather than the population of those that existed in the past. Yet most of these problems are just as damaging to excavations (Cherry, 1984; Dunnell and Dancey, 1983). In most cases, the problem lies not with survey generally, or with survey sampling in particular, but with the failure to design surveys to meet a particular set of goals in particular cultural and geomorphological circumstances, or to recognize what "target" the survey is really investigating. Poor research design is not unique to survey.

Furthermore, regional survey data are not merely "poor cousins" of data from excavations. Regional survey is uniquely capable of providing some categories of data that quite routine archaeological research often requires (Ruppe, 1966). For example, problems concerning agriculture and pastoralism in antiquity are inherently rural. It is doubtful that plant remains or animal bones from large towns would be reliable indicators of the structure of regional subsistence systems. Pre-industrial central places could have drawn on large agricultural and pastoral hinterlands, potentially populated by small settlements, camps and farm outbuildings that excavations have typically underrepresented. As Sullivan (1996) notes, for example, infering Anasazi diet in the American Southwest on the basis of botanical and faunal remains from large pueblo sites has probably led to substantial bias.

Only regional data that reflect the spatial organization of rural activities will inform us in detail about the economic basis of ancient agricultural societies. The spatial distribution of rural material culture was created, in part, through cumulative decisions about agricultural and pastoral production, harvesting, storage, and transport. The distributions of carbonized seeds from excavations in village or town sites, meanwhile, originate in a complex combination of decisions about food selection, processing, storage, use, discard and post-depositional disturbance; they are just as subject to attrition and bias. It is unwarranted to assume that isolated botanical remains from a few excavations, even from primary storage contexts, are necessarily superior sources of evidence for subsistence systems than are patterns in the spatial distributions of material culture in agricultural fields and pastures. We should expect survey data to provide the bulk of our evidence for rural behavior, supplemented by the record of plant and animal remains from a few excavations, even though that evidence is incomplete.

Similarly, for hunter-gatherers, only regional data from base camps, temporary camps, quarries, food-processing and kill sites, or even from dispersed, off-site activities, that reflect the spatial organization of a variety of hunting and gathering behaviors will help us reconstruct and interpret prehistoric economies. As among the Shoshoneans who inspired Thomas's model of resource use in the Reese River Valley, one should expect some of the most important economic activities to have been dispersed on the landscape, rather than concentrated in particularly obtrusive "sites." Survey strategies that do not focus on sites have made substantial contributions over the past 25 years to our understanding of extensive hunting-and-gathering activities on landscapes. A combination of regional survey and small-scale excavations is one way to obtain data relevant to different scales and kinds of hunter-gatherer activity.

3. SURFACE DISTRIBUTIONS AND BURIED LANDSCAPES

Debates in the literature over the value of survey, or over the relative merits of "site-based" and "non-site" surveys, often result from failure to recognize that archaeologists on opposite sides of the debate have completely different goals or perceive of archaeological remains with completely different models.

One of the long-standing debates in archaeology has been over the usefulness of surface or plow-zone distributions of material culture relative to buried distributions (Haslegrove et al., 1985; O'Brien and Lewarch, 1981; Schofield, 1991). It has been common for archaeologists to assume that surface remains are only distorted traces of prehistoric cultural distributions, and to favor excavation as a way to sample allegedly undistorted buried distributions. Other archaeologists, however, have pointed out that virtually all archaeological materials once lay on surfaces, only some of which have become buried through the actions of various geomorphological or site-formation processes. It has become clear that the distributions of buried remains are potentially just as subject to distortion by these processes as those of remains currently exposed on the modern surface. Furthermore, it is now recognized that a congruence between surface remains and sub-surface ones is not necessary for the former to be considered valid archaeological evidence (Synenki, 1984). We should no more expect the spatial distribution of material culture on the modern surface to "mirror" that below than to expect the remains in one layer of a stratified site to "mirror" those of an underlying layer (Dunnell, 1988). Only experimental work and study of site-formation processes will help us understand the relationship between surface and subsurface remains (Ammerman, 1985; Sullivan, 1998).

Another debate has been over the status of "sites" as units of analysis. After decades in which archaeologists neglected the study of low-density artifact scatters and other evidence for ancient activities that were dispersed in space, many recent archaeologists now discount the site altogether or even refer to "antisite survey" (e.g., Ebert, 1992). Their position that past activities that left material evidence took place over whole landscapes with varying intensity and at various scales, and not only at places we might recognize as "sites," is unassailable. It does not follow, however, that "sites are never discovered during survey," as Ebert (1992:69) claims. "Sites" are not always arbitrarily bounded clusters of high artifact density. Some, such as caves, are bounded in a very concrete way. Settlement sites in some regions are bounded by substantial fortifications. This does not mean that all activities, or even the ones of greatest archaeological interest, took place in these caves or walled settlements, or that these types of settlement are appropriate units of analysis in a particular case. For some archaeological goals, however, "sites" of these and similar types constitute perfectly legitimate target populations. Furthermore, "non-site" or distributional survey might be poorly suited to the accomplishment of some of these goals. Thus, the debate over the appropriate way to survey archaeological distributions resolves into differences in research goals and perception of archaeological phenomena.

Although we will return to some aspects of these debates in more detail in later chapters, it is useful to consider some of the models for the distribution of material culture, implicit or explicit, that archaeologists have employed in designing their surveys.

3.1 Models of Cultural Distributions

Even surveys that appear to have had no explicit research design employ models of how cultural remains are distributed in space and relative to the modern surface. It would be naïve to suppose that these models had no effect on the results of those surveys. The following presents some highly simplified and idealized models on which many survey designs appear to have been based, even when the designs were far from explicit. The list is not exhaustive, and some archaeology involves combinations of two or three of these simple models. In addition, the way the models are conceived here often mixes models for ancient behavior (discard, etc.) with models for post-depositional processes and models for the final product of these processes. Arguably it would be better to separate these, but I think the treatment here at least approximates the conception of such models in archaeological literature. What archaeologists survey are the products of processes, some of which happened in the distant past, but it is important to think about how those products formed if we are ultimately to learn anything about the past.

The order of models is not intended to imply any value judgements, and only roughly reflects historical order in the use of these models. Note that I have somewhat arbitrarily assigned names to these models that are not always equivalent to those used by their authors. Terms such as "off-site," for example, have been applied to more than one of these, and I have attempted to be more consistent in usage.

Introduction 13

Some of the models discussed below can be expressed mathematically. It is important to note that the formal, mathematical versions of these models are often modelling probabilities, rather than actual artifact densities, chemical concentrations, or the like (Buck et al., 1996:255-291; Kintigh, 1988:691-692). In other words, if the model for a "site" is flat-topped (a "uniform distribution"), this does not mean that artifact density or phosphate values, for example, will be exactly the same all across the site; it only involves a simplifying assumption that all parts of the site have an equal probability of having some density or phosphate value (the mean for on-site values). Debates over whether it is appropriate to use the Poisson model (e.g., Nance and Ball 1989; Shott 1989), for example, are sometimes lost over this point. Mathematical models can be extremely useful in helping us design effective surveys or evaluate their results, and it is worthwhile even for readers who do not consider themselves very adept at mathematics to try and follow the discussions of mathematical modelling when they occur in subsequent chapters.

3.1.1 The Monument Model

The oldest surveys appear to have been based on the assumption that the archaeological population consists of a set of discrete "sites" or "monuments" that are quite obvious on the modern surface. These include fairly large urban centers with traces of substantial architecture, artificial mounds and cairns, monuments built of standing stones, ditch-and-mound enclosures, standing stone or brick buildings, and even culturally-modified trees. Later, as artifact scatters became defined as sites, archaeologists at first conceived of them as discrete concentrations with boundaries that we could at least approximate (see section 3.1.3).

This model, however, is not simply a historical curiosity no longer relevant to archaeological work. It still fits any situations where the "target" of survey is a discrete object, such as a shipwreck, burial mound, or historic fort. In addition, modern Global Positioning Systems (GPS) now allow some archaeologists to use individual features, such as caches, as the basic unit of survey (e.g., Stewart et al., 2000).

In the search for a discrete entity of the monument type, however, we can often model the probability of finding it in various locations with a continuous probability model, similar to the "fried-egg model" (below, section 3.1.4). In these cases, the models that naval and search-and-rescue experts have developed are potentially applicable (Koopman, 1980; Morse and Kimball, 1951; Stone, 1989; Washburn, 1981).

3.1.2 The Earthwork Model

Archaeological authors from North America sometimes forget that a major class of archaeological survey, especially after aerial photography became available, has been based on the recognition of large-scale physical traces on landscapes, such as those left by roads, trails, ditches, mounds and house foundations. Thus, it is a kind of "off-site" archaeology that precedes the recent resurgence of landscape archaeology by many decades. In a sense, however, it is a more extensive variety of the monument model in that it emphasizes constructed landscape features, such as mounds. It is important to recognize, however, that it also depends to a large degree on inadvertent traces of repeated or prolonged activities. For example, "lynchets" are the mounds that accumulate along the downhill edge of fields as a result of repeated plowing. Thanks largely to this accidental result of agricultural activity, some European landscapes preserve microtopographic traces of several overlapping field systems (e.g., Bowden, 1999; Curwen, 1927).

Archaeologists who pursue this type of archaeology tend to work at the scale of whole landscapes, conceiving of those landscapes as sets of earthworks and crop-marks that mark a series of events. Somewhat as with stratigraphy within sites, these landscape archaeologists attempt to decode the sequence of events by studying the apparent relationships between landscape features. In field systems, this type of survey takes advantage of the fact that these features often work together; the individual ditches, mounds and walls are just the components of a field system that was created effectively as a unit. We will return to this type of research in chapter 7.

3.1.3 The Uniform Distribution

As mentioned in section 3.1.1, archaeologists for many years conceived of some kinds of sites, such as settlements, as relatively discrete concentrations of artifacts, chemical residues, and other remains, much higher in concentration than a "background" of off-site values of natural origin or due to much more dispersed human activity.

For practical reasons, archaeologists sometimes still use this fairly simple model to help them design surveys, evaluate their results, or detect the "edges" of sites through spatial analysis. The mathematical version of this model is the uniform distribution, in which every part of the site has an equal probability of having an artifact or a particular chemical composition, and the expected artifact density or chemical value is the mean (or average). Meanwhile, all spaces in the background also have an equal probability of containing artifacts or yielding some chemical signature, but the mean is quite different. For example, the mean artifact density on the site might be 2 artifacts/m^2, while the mean artifact density off-site might be less than 0.02 artifacts/m^2.

This does not mean that the actual values will be constant across the site or the background, only the probabilities or mean values. In fact, most archaeologists have assumed that actual distributions of artifacts and other observations within the site and the background are either random or clustered ("patchy"). Where it is reasonable to assume that discrete objects, such as artifacts, are randomly distributed, and we are counting the artifacts found in a number of spatial units of equal area, we can model them with the Poisson distribution (see below, pp. 50-53). Where we would expect artifacts to be distributed in a "patchy" way, we might estimate the degree of clustering (clustered distributions have variance larger than the mean) and use the negative binomial distribution (below, p. 53) to model the distribution of artifacts within sites (Kintigh, 1988:694-695; Nance, 1983:329).

One application of the uniform model is in the evaluation of surveys by shovel-testing, augering, or coring, where the object is to estimate the likelihood that the tests will encounter artifacts. The uniform model for sites, combined with a normal, Poisson or negative Binomial model for the distribution of artifacts within sites, provides a useful and fairly simple framework for evaluating these kinds of surveys. As we will see below, however, there can be better models for this type of evaluation.

Buck et al. (1996:260-291) use a uniform model and a Bayesian approach to image analysis to clarify the boundaries of phosphate anomalies. In this model, the natural logarithms of "on-site" phosphate levels are assumed to be normally distributed around a high mean value, and the natural logarithms of "off-site" phosphate values are also assumed to be normally distributed, but around a lower mean. They idealize the boundary between "on-site" and "off-site" areas as quite abrupt, and use image segmentation to partition a gridded map into regions that probably belong to the "on-site" and "off-site" classes. The same methods would be applicable to artifact densities.

3.1.4 The Modal, "Bulls-eye," or "Fried-egg" Model

A somewhat more sophisticated model than the monument and uniform ones is based on the recognition that cultural remains can be nearly continuous in space,[1] but takes the view that concentrations of remains on the modern surface or in the plow zone (i.e., modes of relatively high artifact densities) represent places where repeated or continuous human activity has accumulated material culture (figure 1). As with the uniform model, many users of this model perceive of the low-density scatters around the modes as "background" or "noise," a perception to which we will return in chapter 3. Those who employ this model tend to assume that there is a nearly one-to-one association between artifact concentrations and the locations where concentrated human activity took place, and that the composition and diversity of the assemblages have predictable relationships with the kinds of activities that took place there. A few explicitly recognize that both cultural and non-cultural processes make the association with human activity tenuous, but still tolerate the model as an approximation at least of discard activity. Some archaeologists employing this model further assume that there is a reasonably close relationship between surface or plow-zone assemblages and any buried assemblages that might exist. This is an assumption that is reasonable in some circumstances, but depends on the site-formation processes that have created and modified those assemblages. For example, in the Great Lakes region of North America, areas with anomalous, high densities of artifacts sometimes correspond only with the midden areas of large, Iroquoian villages, which could lead to underestimate of site size. Similarly, concentrations of lithics in Ethiopia have at best a poor relationship to past settlement sites (Gallagher, 1977).

---

[1] Although archaeologists frequently regard artifact distributions as "continuous," they actually consist of sets of discrete objects separated by spaces. Unlike the spatial distribution of magnetic intensity, for example, we cannot confidently interpolate between two measured values of artifact density, while the shape of the density distribution depends, much as with histograms (Whallon, 1987), on the interval and location of the grid we impose to measure density. Consequently, drawing isopleth maps, the density analogues of contour maps, usually requires us to "smooth" or "filter" the data from our grid, or to apply Kriging methods (Zubrow and Harbaugh, 1978).

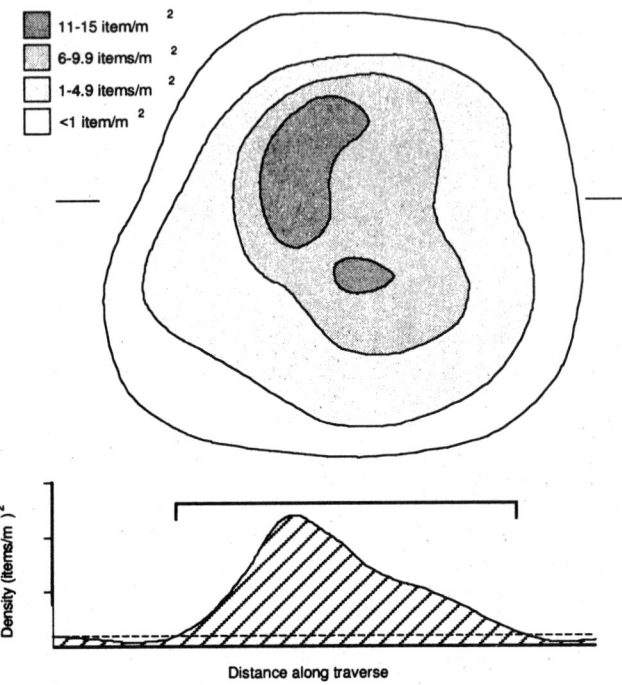

Figure 1. The "bullseye" or "fried-egg" model, which allows density to fall off in some way from one or more modes of high density. If we assume that the "site" occurs wherever density exceeds the "background" indicated by the dashed line in the lower part of the figure, the ticked bar represents the width of the site.

This is also a model that can be applied to chemical surveys. "Sites" are expected to correspond with anomalies of high phosphate concentrations, for example, on a "background" of phosphates derived from the local geology.

3.1.4.1   Mathematical Models for Clusters of Artifacts

As Kintigh (1988:692) has noted, archaeologists can choose among a number of potential mathematical models for the intuitive "fried-egg" model. This choice depends on our perception of how artifacts tend to be distributed on the site, and especially on what we think happens near the edges of sites. Unlike the uniform model, which has very abrupt edges, these models share the assumption that artifact densities, chemical signatures, and other important "site constituents" change fairly gradually towards the edges of sites, eventually merging with the background values.

Introduction

The hemispherical distribution provides a somewhat more realistic picture of reality than the uniform distribution, while retaining somewhat abrupt edges. This model has artifact density, phosphate concentration, or other values only gradually diminishing away from the site's center until, near the edges of the site, they fall off increasingly rapidly.

The conic distribution models sites as having extremely high values at the site center that decrease in a linear manner away from the center. It is a relatively poor candidate for modelling most types of sites, as there is usually no strong reason to expect site constituents to be so highly concentrated in the site's center.

A more appealing mathematical version of the "fried-egg" model for cases where "sites" represent the loci of highly localized activity is a sinusoidal distribution. A useful version of this type of model is the bimodal normal distribution with mean coordinates $(\bar{x}, \bar{y})$ centered on the scatter or chemical anomaly. This can also be used to model the probability of finding discrete targets, such as monuments or shipwrecks, on a landscape or the sea floor prior to beginning a search (see chapter 6).

Note that for many types of sites, and especially large, complex ones, the bimodal normal model is probably too simplistic because it involves the assumption, as with the conic model, that densities are likely to be substantially higher at the site center. For most large sites, it is a more reasonable assumption that densities and other measures are equally likely to take some value over a large area, and tail off only near the site edges. This involves something like a combination of the uniform and sinusoidal distributions, or at least a very flattened sinusoidal distribution.

3.1.4.2 Contagious Distributions

Statisticians and ecologists have researched processes that can lead to clusters of items that are analogous to the clusters that interest archaeologists. "Contagious distributions" can result in a number of ways, but typically from the growth of clusters around centers that are themselves distributed randomly by a Poisson process. Contagious distributions include the negative Binomial and Neyman type A distributions (Bartlett, 1954; 1960; Cliff and Ord, 1973; Hodder and Orton, 1976:86-88; Moyal, 1962; Neyman, 1939; Neyman and Scott, 1958; Paloheimo, 1971; Thompson, 1954; 1955). It is also possible to model patchy distributions with a doubly stochastic Poisson process (Bartlett, 1963; 1964; Matérn, 1960; Paloheimo, 1971).

For cluster processes, there are cluster centers distributed according to the Poisson distribution with a particular density, λ, and the locations of these centers are assumed to be independent. A probability function generates the number of individuals to be found in each cluster, while a density distribution generates the locations of these individuals around their respective centers, as in the models discussed in the last section. For example, the "offspring" points could be distributed around each center by the circular normal distribution.

Doubly stochastic Poisson processes result in a set of randomly placed clusters, or discs, within each of which individual items are distributed randomly according to a Poisson distribution.

3.1.5 The Palimpsest Model

Another site-based model attempts to account for the possibility that the spatial distributions on ancient and modern surfaces have accumulated through prolonged cultural activity, so that an archaeological "site," here defined as a high-density cluster of cultural remains, does not necessarily correspond with a discrete ancient or prehistoric settlement or other locus of activity. Instead, it presents the "site" as a set of overlapping distributions, each representing a different activity or set of activities at different times (figure 2; e.g., Dancey, 1998: 9). As site areas constitute the union of the areas of several or even many hundreds of small settlements and work areas occupied or used at different times and with slightly different centers, and even casual discard events, they should not be used to estimate settlement size.

For example, in Wadi al-Hasa of southern Jordan, the plateaux overlooking the canyon were virtually paved with lithic scatters that sometimes extended, nearly continuously, for more than a kilometer. Although artifact densities were higher in some parts of these scatters than in others, it was impossible to delineate sites in the conventional sense, and site numbers were assigned to the denser localities just for the sake of labelling the provenience of collections. It seems likely that these extensive scatters resulted from the cumulative discard of millions of artifacts on the landscape over hundreds of thousands of years, and wind has eroded the sediments away to collapse the artifacts onto a single, deflated surface (Banning, 1988).

Users of the palimpsest model may also try to account for post-depositional processes, such as plowing, that may have affected the relationship between the original distributions and the modern surface distributions (e.g., Odell and Cowan, 1987; Wandsnider and Camilli, 1992).

One of the interesting implications of this model is that "sites," in the sense of elevated artifact densities, can occur where there was no mode of cultural activity at any time in the past, simply because the peripheries of several clusters overlap there (figure 2). Robert Foley (1981a) demonstrates that our perception of sites depends on the processes that form the archaeological record over long periods of time. Only some of these processes are human behaviors, and only some human behaviors concentrate debris in locations we would typically recognize as "sites." Discard is a continuous process, sometimes over hundreds of thousands of years, and archaeologists see the cumulative result of this process (Foley, 1981a: 159). Patterning in the way discarded artifacts are exposed (by erosion), moved, or destroyed can also result in clusters that the "fried egg" model would classify as "sites."

As in the last section, it is possible to model the processes that can lead to such palimpsests. One way is with contagious distributions that are allowed to overlap. For example, we can generate a random distribution of centers, and then generate a cluster of points around each center. If the density of centers is reasonably high, and we make no effort to restrict the distances between them, some of the resulting clusters will overlap, thus generating palimpsests with elevated densities of points in the regions of overlap.

Introduction

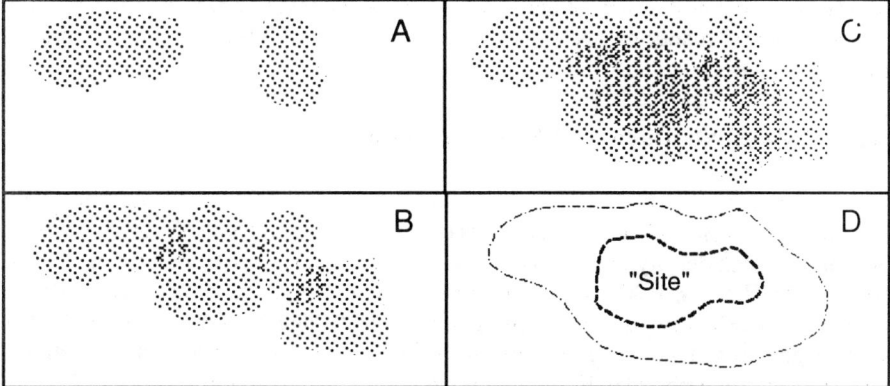

Figure 2. The Palimpsest model. Over time newly deposited scatters overlap with older ones, or older ones are revealed by erosion, creating a single dense scatter that looks like a "site."

Some archaeologists employing the palimpsest model prefer the term "locality" over "site" to emphasize that a cultural scatter does not necessarily correspond with any settlement or discrete activity area.

3.1.6 The "Off-site" or "Intersite" Model

The term "off-site" archaeology has been used for various approaches to survey that do not focus only on sites. Here I use the term, in contrast to "non-site" archaeology, to describe surveys employing a model in which the spatial distribution of material culture consists of both reasonably discrete sites and inter-site debris.

Users of this approach to not necessarily dismiss the importance of high-density clusters of archaeological remains, often including traces of architecture, because these are often clearly identifiable as settlement locations. In some regions, including the Near East and central Asia, persistent settlement at favored locations has often left clear evidence for the places where people lived, worked, worshipped, and interacted socially. It would be perverse in such instances to ignore this evidence.

However, users of the off-site model recognize that such persistent settlements provide only part of the picture. Even in urban societies, many activities, especially those pertaining to agriculture, pastoralism, raw-material procurement, and sometimes waste disposal, take place away from settlements. Low densities of debris in the spaces between sites may be evidence for such off-site activities. Patterning in intersite densities may then preserve information about which fields were used for intensive agriculture, for example.

One example of the use of this model is Wilkinson's (1982;1989) survey in the northern Jazirah of Mesopotamia. Here there are "sites" that show evidence, including high artifact densities, of having been settlements. In addition, sherd densities on the order of 0.2 to 0.3 artifacts/m² in the fields around and between sites may have resulted from agricultural manuring and diffuse activities that were probably mainly agricultural.

3.1.7 The Distributional or "Non-site" Model

A relatively recent approach, as we saw in Section 1, has been to assume that spatial variation in aspects of all cultural materials is important, and not only the distribution of "clusters" of high density (e.g., Dunnell and Dancey, 1983; Ebert, 1992; Foley, 1981a; Isaac, 1981; Thomas, 1975). In effect, these surveys assume that background artifact density is zero. Their focus is on variation in the density, degree of clustering, and other assemblage parameters over space, or on the effect of various environmental parameters, such as soil type or landform, on the probability that cultural remains will occur. The model against which distributions are compared is usually a spatial Poisson model, with artifacts and the behaviors with which they were associated randomly distributed in spaces that have varying probabilities of having attracted those behaviors. The goal is to detect and understand the ways in which the observed record deviates from this model of randomness, such as the scale of clustering.

As with the palimpsest model, however, archaeological formation processes over long periods of time make any pattern that results a cumulative one (figure 3). Gradually, repeated discard activity over spaces that satisfy the criteria for settlement, resource procurement and other behaviors builds up the density of debris over broad swaths, while spaces unsatisfactory for these purposes do not accumulate significant densities (Foley, 1981:159-61). Consequently, even though the resulting clusters of high density do not correspond with any specific settlements at any point in the past, they do correspond with preferrred habitats over some length of time and may allow us to infer the resources and other factors that attracted humans to those places.

Many users of this model claim that they have substituted the individual artifact for the "site" as their basic analytical unit. In fact, most "non-site" archaeology uses some geometrical spatial unit, such as a square quadrat, as its basic analytical unit, and the densities of artifacts or statistics of their attributes are measurements on those units. As it happens, this has the advantage of avoiding cluster sampling by making the sampling units and analytical units identical (Banning, 2000:82-83).

3.1.8 The Place Model

An underappreciated version of the landscape model is one by which the cultural landscape is conceived as a set of "places" with varying probabilities of attracting settlement or other cultural and economic activities, such as fishing or setting game ambushes (Schlanger, 1992). For example, Binford (1982) conceives of hunter-gatherer space as consisting of a residential base, a foraging radius from which the group extracts resources on a daily basis, and a logistical radius that the group exploits more rarely or through special task groups. In addition, these task groups may use logistical bases while away from the residential base, some of which may occur at the sites of aban-

Introduction

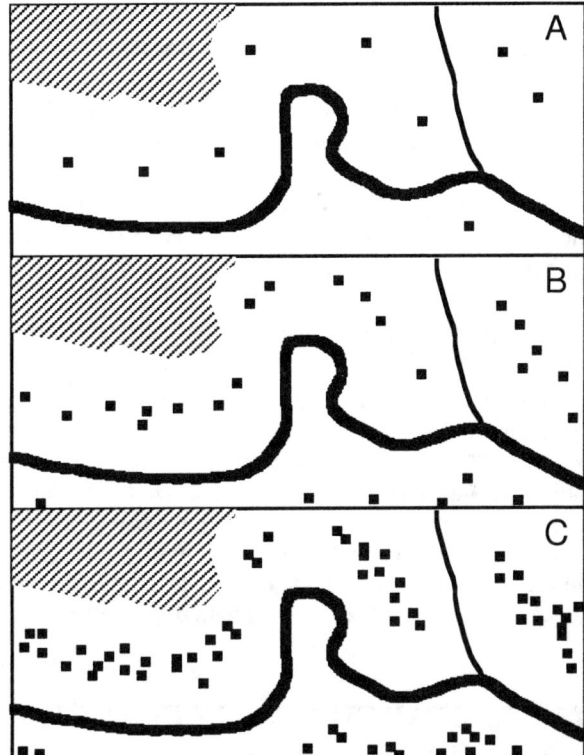

Figure 3. Repeated discard over "satisfactory" spaces leads to elevated densities in parts of the landscape so that, by time C, there appear to be distinct bands, in this case along alluvial plains (cf. Foley, 1981:160).

doned residential bases. Some kinds of activities may be concentrated in residential bases, logistical camps, or both, but others are dispersed over the foraging and logistic territories.

Because the settlement systems Binford is trying to model are ones with a high degree of mobility, the model must be a dynamic one, and we should expect considerable overlap of bases, camps, and foraging and logistic territories over a period of time. Consequently, as with the palimpsest model, artifacts found in any part of relevant space will have resulted from the cumulative activities of very many separate camping, resource-extraction, and tool-maintenance events, as well as other site-formation processes.

However, it is reasonable to conceive of the places used in this or other ways as consisting of relatively distinct topographic phenomena, or "landscape elements" (Schlanger, 1992; Stafford, 1995). People do not typically camp randomly on landscapes, nor are flint outcrops or fruit-bearing plants distributed unpredictably. Certain kinds of topographic features, such as stream terraces, hilltops or rockshelters, are typically conceived as appropriate for certain kinds of camps or settlements. In the Reese River survey, for example, surveyors considered places that satisfied at least five environmental criteria as "potential loci of habitation" (Williams et al., 1973:231). Other kinds of features are likely to have been used as routes for travelling between regions, as places to ambush game, or as fields for particular kinds of crop.

Consequently, it is possible for us to model the landscape as sets of topographic or geographical units, each with different probability of having been used for particular kinds of settlement, resource extraction, defence, communication, or even symbolic meaning. As we will see in later chapters, we can then either sample these features as members of a sampling population or survey them in a way that allows us to test particular hypotheses about their past use.

3.1.9 The Paleolandscape Model

This is a geoarchaeological approach that goes a step further by using subsurface and geomorphological evidence to define a series of changing landscape surfaces, each of which has its own distribution of cultural remains (Stafford, 1995). The paleolandscapes are conceived as sets of landforms, each of which has a particular probability of having cultural material. Unlike many of the other models, this one does not involve the assumption that remains on the modern surface have any predictable relationship with buried remains. In fact, it depends on the fact that the density and other attributes of those remains varies with depth and geomorphological context.

4. RESEARCH DESIGN IN ARCHAEOLOGICAL SURVEY

One of the central points of this book is that no archaeological survey should proceed before there is a research design. A research design is an explicit plan for accomplishing research objectives (Binford, 1964; Boismier, 1991; Goodyear et al., 1978; Redman, 1973). It begins with identifying general research problems or hypotheses, followed by reviewing past work on and method and theory relevant to those problems, as well as the context in which the research will take place. The resulting information is used to generate the "problem domains" of the research: more specific research questions and a range of methods and data that might help to answer them in the specific context of the proposed project. The research design also involves reviewing the kinds of data analysis that could prove useful, and selecting those that are appropriate given the limitations of the research context, the questions we are asking, and the kinds of data we expect to be available.

The context of the research has a significant impact on the research design. Even if the general research problem is similar, both the research questions and the most effective methods in a research design for a survey in the eastern desert of Jordan will be very different from those in a survey in upper New York State because the research context is so different. Some kinds of data available in one area will be rare or absent in the other, or differences in natural and cultural site-formation processes or the visibility of material culture will call for entirely different research designs.

Introduction 23

Reviewing past archaeological work as well as information that can be gleaned from geological and soil surveys, from historical documents, including maps, from ethnographic or ethnohistoric sources, and from long-time residents of the area to be surveyed is a critical aspect of research design. This research reveals "gaps" in knowledge that the survey might be able to address and also, quite importantly, can help with modelling the cultural distributions of interest. In short, one can design much better surveys with a clear idea what to expect on the ground.

Problem domains specify the research problems in ways that allow us to evaluate them with the kinds of data we can expect in the context of a particular project. For example, if a research problem involves tracking changes in some attribute, such as site size, over time, there is no point in specifying this problem in terms of very short time intervals if we can only expect to date survey results to rather long time intervals. Or, if we had hoped to identify site hierarchies through differences in the proportion of decorated pottery, but background research shows that "pot hunters" have seriously depleted the decorated sherds at some of the sites, we may have to consider a different approach.

Problem domains often specify indirect measures for phenomena we cannot observe directly, such as measuring the proportion of decorated pottery as an indirect way of assessing a site's place in a settlement hierarchy. Another example, if the research problem involves changes in the size of human populations or in human population density in settlements, would be to specify some "proxy" for human population size, perhaps based on site area or numbers of sites (assuming a site-based survey) or calculated from the area and probable productivity of identifiable agricultural fields. Generally, estimates based on such indirect measures have fairly large errors (Banning, 2000:14-17).

The stage of problem domains also involves trying to identify or construct models that might account for aspects of the data. For example, Hayes (1991) generates a series of models for the expected effects of rubbish disposal, manuring, and several varieties of mixed farming, specialized farming, and pastoralism on the distributions of artifacts on the landscape. In some situations, it might be useful to model the distribution of artifacts with the Poisson distribution, a mathematical model for the random distribution of countable items in units of space or time (pp. 50-53), or model the distribution of "on-site" and "off-site" phosphate levels for a chemical survey with a uniform distribution (pp. 14-15). The models help us refine our research questions and focus attention on the kinds of data necessary to distinguish between different processes that may have generated patterns in space.

Specification of problem domains should include estimating such factors as the expected density of archaeological targets, their expected degree of aggregation, their expected association with resources or landscape features and with each other, the expected distribution of constituents within sites or clusters of archaeological remains, the size, shape, and obtrusiveness of sites or clusters, and variations in the visibility of archaeological targets across the landscape (Wobst, 1983:60). Are there non-archaeological features (false targets) that could be difficult to distinguish from archaeological ones? There are also many other factors, discussed in chapter 3, that the problem domain should address.

Problem domains guide the selection, not only of what data to collect, but of the methods and strategies to collect them. For example, is a probability sample necessary and, if so, what should the population, sample element and sample size be? Is it reasonable to depend on visible surface remains in plowed fields, or necessary to use shovel-testing or geophysical remote sensing? How will will the survey account for the factors that affect the probability of detecting archaeological materials, such as visibility?

Having selected methods, surveyors need to assess the capability of sensors, whether they are simply surveyors' eyes or various geophysical devices. How does their capability of detecting targets decrease with distance? What is the relationship between the amount of effort invested in survey and the probability that the sensors will detect materials of interest? How readily can the sensors distinguish these materials from false targets?

The research design also specifies analytical procedures, such as how to classify or group data for analysis, what kinds of quantitative or qualitative analysis to carry out, and how to map results. It is important to select procedures that are appropriate to the data one can expect.

Another important aspect of research design is to determine how much effort to invest in ensuring the reliability of results. What is the probability that a particular survey plan will succeed in finding materials of interest or acquiring a representative sample of the correct population? How precise do measurements of attributes or estimates of parameters need to be? How much difference will omission of some sites or kinds of material make? What is the best way to test the accuracy of measurements? Although ensuring a high level of data quality may be costly, it would also be wasteful to spend time and money on a survey whose results fail to accomplish basic goals. In that case, it might be better to spend the money on some other project.

This leads us to the issue of cost. Surveys always have costs, even when they are run with volunteers, and some can be very costly indeed. Especially when there is so much competition for funds and time, it often pays to minimize these costs as long as the survey can accomplish its goals and does not compromise the archaeological evidence. Research design usually involves a trade-off between the competing demands of achieving results, ensuring reliability, and keeping cost under control. Once a survey plan is complete, it is necessary to estimate its costs and adjust the plan if its cost is excessive. Chapters 5 and 6 will discuss some quantitative ways to achieve this trade-off.

Many surveys have a "multi-stage" research design (Redman, 1973; Redman and Anzalone, 1980), in which a preliminary or pilot stage helps to refine the research questions or methods and provides a more accurate idea of the data one can expect and the costs of acquiring them. Some authors (e.g., Ebert, 1992:52-53) object to research designs that change part-way through a project because they may result in a lack of consistency in or comparability of evidence, or because they are biased in favor of denser or more clustered archaeological materials. In most cases, however, it is both possible and desirable to adapt research designs to conditions and information that only become apparent during the course of survey. One can always continue to collect data with the original procedures as well, as a way to assess the changes' effects. Meanwhile, it makes no sense to retain a research strategy that is clearly flawed or inappropriate just for the

Introduction

sake of consistency. In some cases, admittedly, it may be necessary to resurvey parts of a region with the new strategy to ensure consistency. Furthermore, adaptive methods that incorporate "memory" of previous solutions or results can guide research into optimal designs.

A very basic "multi-stage" approach is to use a pilot study or reconnaissance survey to help in the design of a more thorough survey. It is one of the paradoxes of surveys (and of sampling, more generally) that we can always make a better survey design once the survey is over. A small, cheap survey, however, can often collect enough information to permit a good estimate of the amount of variation in the targets and their environments, and to allow sensible decisions about sample size, survey frame, sensing method, density of effort, and basis for stratification. It can also guide practical decisions or allow tests of recording procedures. For example, it might turn out that categories on a recording form are ambiguous or do not fit the materials at hand, or that the plan does not budget enough for travel time between survey units (Orton, 2000:29).

For purposive survey (chapter 6), some survey designs are "incrementally optimal." In these, survey takes place in stages, each designed to allocate survey effort with the help of information acquired in the previous stage (or background research, in the case of the first stage). This is a good example of multi-stage research.

Finally, an important but sometimes overlooked step in research design is evaluation. Following the survey, it is important to assess its success at detecting materials of interest and achieving its other goals (chapter 10).

The following chapters will deal with some of these aspects of survey design, beginning with the objectives the survey is intended to achieve.

Chapter II
The Goals of Archaeological Survey

It is easy to think of examples of surveys that failed to detect the sites of greatest interest, that provided biased estimates of a site's date or importance, or that yielded none of the contextual information or economic evidence needed to investigate a particular research problem. Most failures of archaeological survey, however, are due to inappropriate survey design and especially to failure to tailor that design to the survey's objectives.

The results of any archaeological survey depend heavily on the objectives it was designed to achieve. No one should expect a survey to be good at discovering small, open-air campsites if it employs methods suitable for finding caves or large town sites. Nor should methods that preferentially discover certain kinds of site at the expense of others be useful for estimating the proportions of site types on an archaeological landscape. Surveys designed to discover highly clustered material culture, such as sites, cannot be expected to be effective for helping detect or understand ancient human activities that were dispersed on the landscape. Furthermore, surveys designed to provide representative samples of populations, a very common design in archaeology, are not at all effective at finding rare materials or detecting some kinds of spatial structure. It is essential that the strategies and methods for implementing a survey are consistent with the survey's goals.

1. TYPES OF GOALS

These goals are not self-evident, as indicated by the commonly held and often uncritical assumption that all surveys aim to produce representative samples of populations (e.g., Lewarch and O'Brien, 1981:298; Schiffer et al., 1978:1). In fact, archaeological surveys fall broadly into three categories. Sometimes a survey's goal is simply to find archaeological materials of a particular type or age, or that can be used to test very specific hypotheses. Survey of this kind is "prospection." Quite commonly, surveys are designed with the goal of estimating the number or density of sites or artifacts, identifying the range of site types in a region, the proportion of each type, or the proportions that satisfy certain environmental or cultural conditions. More generally, their goals involve estimating parameters of some archaeological population or populations, testing some statistical hypothesis, or generating some predictive model. Achieving these goals does indeed require samples representative of a population, and projects of this type are thus "statistical surveys." Other surveys aim to identify spatial structure in the distribution of archaeological materials. The kinds of pattern they may seek can include the way settlements are arranged relative to their nearest neighbors, or relative to roads and waterways, as well as whether archaeological materials are clustered or evenly dispersed or how the probability of cultural remains being present varies over space. I propose calling survey of this type "structural survey," although some authors favor such terms as "total survey," "siteless survey," "off-site survey," or "non-site survey" for some surveys of this type.

Some survey designs satisfy more than one of these goals. For example, a survey might be suitable for determining the proportions of several site types and also to find at least one example of a type of site that is so rare that it would not likely turn up in a statistical sample.

The goals of archaeological assessment, as in Cultural Resource Management, typically are of the statistical type, as the managers of cultural heritage usually need to know what kinds of archaeological materials are under their care and how they are distributed. They are also concerned with the construction and use of predictive models for the distribution of archaeological and other heritage occurrences. However, identifying and protecting rare and significant sites is also typically in their mandate, making prospection quite useful. Furthermore, there is no reason why cultural resource managers should not also show interest in the relationships among sites, one kind of spatial structure, or how "non-site" materials are distributed. Assessing the significance of archaeological entities and using predictive models are issues to which we will return in chapter 8.

1.1 Prospection

Although prospection is common in archaeology, there is sometimes a tendency for archaeological prospectors to use methods more appropriate for statistical surveys, probably out of fear of seeming "unscientific." The common answer to the question of how to find archaeological sites is to use a statistical sample. Yet a statistical survey is actually a very poor way to discover specific, and especially rare, kinds of archaeological materials because it is explicitly designed to find mainly the typical and common ones (Asch, 1975; Cowgill, 1975; Redman, 1974:22). Only an extremely large statistical sample can dependably include observations of rare phenomena, and detecting rare classes of material culture by this means is very wasteful of resources. More generally, sampling is not meant to optimize the discovery of archaeological materials, but rather to make generalizations about them. Prospection is the type of survey involved in *finding* sites.

Well designed prospection, often called "purposive survey," takes advantage of any information available that may improve the chances of discovering the archaeological remains of interest, or the "target." For example, if previously discovered Paleoindian sites in a survey region have all occurred on fossil beach ridges, in spite of attempts to find them elsewhere, to ensure very thorough inspection of all the fossil beach ridges would be prudent (e.g., Storck, 1978; 1982; 1984). If the goal is to find lithic quarrying sites, surveyors should consult geological maps to concentrate inspection in areas where suitable lithic raw material was likely to occur at or near the surface. In some cases, furthermore, a survey's objective may be to find the raw material sources themselves, and not "sites" as conventionally defined. If the goal is to locate and map Roman roads, meanwhile, it might make sense to concentrate effort on strips of land between known Roman cities, with particular attention to topographic features, such as mountains and rivers, that probably affected roads' locations.

Prospecting concerns the recovery of archaeological data ('recovery theory,' Sullivan, 1978), with particular emphasis on optimizing the probability of detection. Most archaeologists will be surprised to learn that there is a large body of literature on how to do this. Research on how to detect targets quickly and efficiently was intense as long ago as the Second World War, and today informs search-and-rescue operations, mineral exploration, optimization of computer disk drives, and even internet searches (Banning, 2002). This body of theory is also applicable to archaeological searches.

Typically, a well designed prospection combines a wide range of background information to determine which locations are most likely, and which only somewhat probable, to contain the type of archaeological evidence we seek. Surveying only locations where the probability of detecting such materials is high makes the results of survey inappropriate for generalizations about whole populations; such generalizations require statistical survey instead. Yet generalization is not the goal of prospection, and informed search of the most likely locations is the most efficient way to detect the evidence of interest. Objecting to prospection on the grounds that its results are biased is like objecting to search-and-rescue missions that detect lifeboats rather than open sea.

In fact, some archaeological surveys have the goal of locating very specific targets, such as a particular shipwreck or a particular colonial outpost known only from historical records. In these cases, archaeologists can not only take advantage of clues in the historical evidence, they can sometimes exploit the extensive theoretical literature on optimal search (e.g., Koopman, 1980; Stone, 1989).

In addition, as Cowgill (1975) has emphasized, testing some kinds of archaeological hypotheses requires what he calls "selection," rather than statistical samples. For example, a predictive model for the distribution of archaeological materials in the Reese River Valley that is based on Steward's ethnographic observations is testable by intensive search of locations where the model predicts materials should and should not occur (Thomas 1972; Williams, et al., 1973). Survey of random spaces in this valley would be at best an inefficient way to test the model. This is a situation that clearly calls for prospection instead.

Modern prospection can take large amounts of information into account by using Geographic Information Systems (GIS) to classify areas on a map by their probability of yielding archaeological remains of the type specified, once a GIS model has been built on the basis of previous knowledge. "Groundchecks" — survey targeted at the predicted locations and a sample of places where the models predict none should occur — serve to test the GIS model and recover relevant data.

1.2 Statistical Survey

Surveys with the goal of estimating population parameters, building predictive models, or testing probabilistic hypotheses are usually achieved through sampling designs (chapter 5). In these cases, it is not necessary to detect all archaeological materials, or to find specific sites. Instead, a survey can satisfy its goals as long as it recovers a sample that is representative of the population of interest, and is of sufficient size for estimates to be reasonably precise and accurate. Sampling rather than examining whole populations reduces the cost of fieldwork and analysis while also, in some cases, preserving unsurveyed parts of the archaeological record for future generations. This is the type of survey that many archaeologists today regard as standard. In fact, even among statistical surveys there can be great variety in both goals and methods.

1.2.1 Populations, Parameters, and Estimation

It is useful to review briefly the difference between the archaeological population or "universe" of interest and samples, which are what archaeologists actually study. Whether or not archaeologists employ sampling theory, their analysis is based on only a subset of the evidence that could, in principle, be studied or could have existed in a study area. For example, one could define a population as all the prehistoric artifacts lying within a "universe" bounded by the Reese River Valley's watershed, while the sample might consist of only a few thousand artifacts found at various locations within this universe. More commonly, the population consists of a set of spatial units, such as square quadrats, and the sample is a subset of these units. When archaeologists use statistical inference, statistics of the sample, such as average artifact density, serve as estimates of *parameters* of the population, which are unknown. Many archaeological surveys aim to estimate such parameters as the number of Archaic sites, the proportion of Hohokam sites larger than 0.5 ha, or the density of Neolithic artifacts.

1.2.2 Estimating Densities of Sites

A common goal for a survey of a previously unexplored region is to estimate the number or density of all archaeological sites of each major period, cultural type, or technocomplex. As long as estimated site density is accurate, estimating the number of sites simply involves multiplying the density by the area of the survey universe. If, for example, a well designed sample of 500 m x 500 m quadrats has allowed estimate of the density of Iron Age farmsteads as 0.15 ± 0.05 sites/km^2, the number of such farmsteads in a survey universe 40 km^2 in area would be about 6 ± 2.

McManamon's (1981) survey of the Cape Cod National Seashore, Massachusetts, is an example of this type of survey. Its goal was to facilitate management and interpretation of the region's archaeological resources by allowing estimates of their location, frequency and some of their characteristics. In effect, locations were classified as belonging to one of four environmental strata in a stratified sample, and in each stratum McManamon attempted to estimate site frequency, or density (average number of sites per sample unit).

1.2.3 Estimating Densities of Artifacts on the Landscape

Today it is increasingly common for surveys' goals to require information on whole archaeological landscapes, and not just on the clustered remains associated with "sites." Although the ultimate goal of most such surveys is to decipher the structure of material culture in space (see section 1.3), some of them concentrate on estimating the densities of material culture in different environmental zones. The underlying assumption of these surveys is that elevated densities in particular kinds of geographical contexts reflect repeated or persistent use of these places as prefered locations for settlement or as favored resources (see chapter 1, 3.1.5). In some instances, the densities are in space-time, rather than only in space, in order to account for the fact that more artifacts can be expected to accumulate over long periods than short ones (Foley, 1981:176). Rather than simply number of artifacts per hectare, for example, it might be better to estimate number of artifacts per hectare-century.

Survey of the Amboseli Basin in Kenya (Foley, 1980) is an example of a project in which the goal was to use the densities of material culture to identify preferred habitats and infer aspects of prehistoric subsistence behavior. To accomplish this goal, it is not strictly necessary to measure artifact density continuously over large landscapes, but only to measure it at locations in a stratified sample. The subpopulations or strata correspond with different kinds of habitats and significant differences between the subpopulations in artifact density would help us identify the ones where human use or occupation was persistent, repeated, prolonged, intensive or produced unusual amounts of refuse.

1.2.4 Estimating Proportions of Site Types

Many surveys have as their principal aim the estimate of the proportions of sites that belong to different size classes, chronological periods, cultural taxa or functional type. This was a major component of the first attempts to reconstruct ancient settlement systems (e.g., Willey, 1953; Adams, 1965).

A common goal of survey is to document site hierarchies. The ratio of different site types to one another can even help us infer the structure of a settlement system, although to demonstrate its existence would require further survey of a different type. For example, a distribution that included approximately 12 small settlements and two or three medium-sized settlements for every large one might hint at a hexagonal settlement lattice, but would not be sufficient to demonstrate it (see chapter 7).

An even more common goal is to determine the proportions of sites belonging to each time period. This information may be essential for Cultural Resource Management. Often archaeologists view these proportions as having at least a crude relationship with changes in regional population size.

1.2.5 Estimating Human Population Size or Growth Rate

Some archaeological research requires estimates of the number of people who inhabited a large region at some time in the past, or estimates of population growth rates over a number of centuries. Surveys carried out in pursuit of this information typically use the average size and density of sites to create indirect measures of human population size. Although such estimates are always based on indirect measures, and require many assumptions, surveys designed to estimate changes in the density of settlement (settled area divided by total surveyed area) are usually more useful than ones that focus only on the number of "sites."

Such attempts are complicated by the fact that we really need to know the density of settlement, not just in space, but in space-time. Even in the unlikely event that there was a simple and constant relationship between settlement area and number of people across sites, we must account for the probability that not all the sites existed simulataneously. Archaeological periods tend to be at least a century long, and some new settlements could have been founded over their duration, while others disappeared. Sites that were only seasonally occupied, in particular, would tend to exaggerate population estimates unless they take this effect into account.

1.2.6 Estimating Proportions of Sites by Ecological or Land-use Zone

An extremely common goal of archaeological surveys has been to identify patterned relationships between site locations and environmental or land-use zones. Such studies depended on the assumption that people would tend to settle where they could minimize the distance to the resources they used the most or that were most critical in their economy. For example, Zarky (1976) tried to find non-random relationships between the locations of Formative sites and a variety of environmental zones in part of Guatemala as clues to economic changes over time.

Although they use a variety of methods, the essence of such studies is to estimate the number, density, or, most commonly, proportion of sites in each of several spatial zones and compare these with the values we would expect if there is no pattern at all. A random or patternless distribution occurs when the distribution of sites is simply proportional to the distribution of the environmental zones. If loess soils cover 20% of the region of interest, for example, we would expect 20% of the sites to occur on loess soils if there is no patterned relationship between site location and soil type.Today GIS provides sophisticated tools for this kind of analysis.

1.2.7 Estimating Parameters of Artifact Attributes

Although less common than surveys that focus on the number, density or proportions of archaeological materials, surveys aimed at estimating parameters of tool assemblages and the like are growing in importance.

For example, the "non-site" survey of the Reese River Valley was used to estimate characteristics of the population of lithics on the landscape, such as edge angle, in the hope of relating these to the distribution of economic activities with which the tools were involved (Thomas, 1972).

As with the densities of artifacts, it is not strictly necessary to measure these throughout the landscape in order to associate attributes with one another or with kinds of geographical contexts. A sample, such as a stratified sample, will suffice for us to document these associations and measure their strength and the confidence we can place in them.

1.2.8 Estimating the Range or Diversity of Archaeological Materials

Sometimes archaeologists may be interested in how diverse some aspect of the archaeological record may be in a region. One simple measure of diversity is *richness*, which is simply the number of categories represented in the population. The number of site types, for example, may have some relation to the complexity of a settlement system. Higher than usual artifact diversity in some parts of a survey universe, meanwhile, may reflect the greater range of activities at or more persistent use of those places. However, estimating diversity on the basis of samples is quite difficult because it is so sensitive to sample size. Clearly we should expect a greater number of site types or artifact types to appear in a large sample than in a small one, and accurate estimates of richness require us to correct for this effect (Kintigh, 1989; Ringrose, 1993). If measuring some kind of diversity is an important goal of survey, it is critical to ensure that the survey can accomplish this.

1.2.9 The Relevance of Prospecting Tools

Because one of the first steps of a statistical survey is to define the population of interest, the statistical survey can seem to overlap with prospection. Anyone who defines this population in a very specific way, rather than as "all sites" or "all 100 m x 100 m spaces" in a region, for example, might need to use some prospection techniques to ensure that he or she is sampling the right population. For example, if the target population is all pioneer homesteads of the Red River settlement founded prior to 1830, it would make sense to consult historical records and maps to ensure that the survey samples the places such homesteads are likely to be found, and not areas that are irrelevant to the research problem. Otherwise the survey is not only likely to be inefficient, it is likely to provide biased estimates of the population's parameters. In addition, some tools, and especially remote sensing, that are typically associated with prospection can sometimes be useful either to guide design of a sampling frame or to ensure adequate inspection of the units included in a sample.

1.3 Surveying for Spatial Structure

Investigation of many spatial phenomena that interest archaeologists would be ill-served by most kinds of statistical survey (Asch, 1975; Kowalewski, 1990). Because spatial samples omit large areas of the landscape, while the areas that are inspected are typically dispersed, it is usually impossible for them to detect spatial patterns larger than the basic sampling unit (chapter 4). For example, in a spatial sample of 100 scattered squares, each 250 m x 250 m in size, it is highly unlikely that anyone could recognize a hexagonal organization of sites, all arranged an average 1600 m from their nearest neighbors (figure 4).

1.3.1 Detecting Settlement Lattices, Landscape Systems, and Communication Routes

The goals of many surveys, however, require us to make precisely this kind of recognition. Archaeological applications of Central Place Theory, discovery of settlement lattices, and understanding networks of roads or trade routes all require that the data include, not merely a random sample of sites, but all the sites in a contiguous portion of space. Omitting more than a very few sites might hopelessly confuse interpretation of the pattern. Furthermore, understanding irrigation networks or agricultural field systems requires documenting their traces extensively and continuously, not in a patchy way. Chapter 7 will deal with these kinds of survey in detail.

1.3.2 Mapping "Continuous" Distributions

In addition, some types of spatial analysis require regular, or systematic, measurement of archaeological phenomena over space. For example, producing an isopleth map that shows how the density of artifacts varies over a survey region, rather than simply a map with dots to show individual concentrations of artifacts (or "sites"), is difficult or impossible with a random scatter of observations. Instead, it is more practical to divide the survey area systematically into a grid (rectangular, triangular or hexagonal), measure or estimate the density of artifacts at each and every grid unit, and then shade the units on the map to indicate their densities, show a three-dimenional histogram, or smooth the resulting matrix of data to produce an isopleth map that looks similar to a topographic map. Isopleth maps and similar maps showing the ratio of one artifact type to another can be a good way to define sites where their boundaries are not particularly obvious, or to recognize spatially dispersed activities. Technically, the kind of survey used to produce this type of data often relies on a particular kind of sampling, which produces a spatially systematic sample (chapter 5), yet it is a "total survey" in the sense that there must be an observation at every grid unit, even if only a portion of each unit is used as the basis for observation.

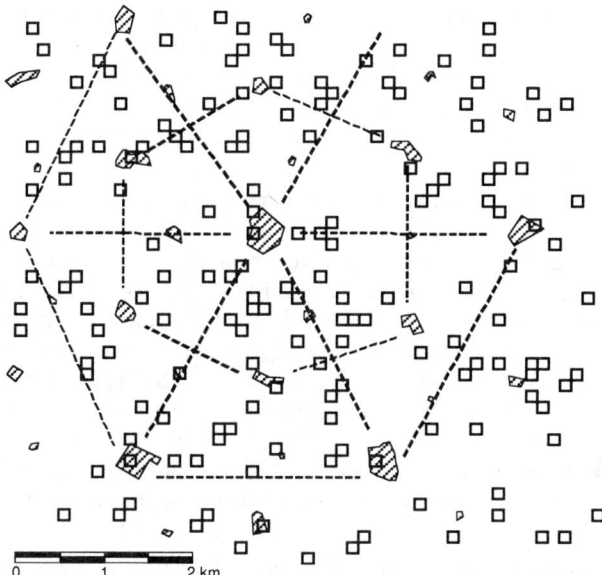

Figure 4. A spatial sample of 100 quadrats superimposed on a hexagonal-lattice settlement pattern. Note that few of the quadrats intersect sites (hatched) and it is unlikely that the pattern would be detectable.

1.4 Surveys with Multiple Goals

The previous discussion may give the impression that the three basic kinds of survey are incompatible. Yet it is not uncommon for surveyors' goals to require both generalization about populations and detection of spatial structure or identification of particular kinds of sites or candidates for future excavation.

The most common combination is prospection and statistical survey. Cultural resource assessments, for example, often have the goal of identifying the range of archaeological resources in a region, or the proportions of resources of various types. A statistical sample is very effective at accomplishing this for the most common kinds of archaeological materials but, unless the sampling fraction is very large, very poor at detecting, let alone estimating the abundance of, rare materials.

One way to combine prospection and statistical survey is simply to budget some time for each. This is almost like doing two separate surveys. One involves defining the sampling frame for a population and then sampling it to obtain a representative set of archaeological materials. This can provide the basis for estimates of the density or proportion of these materials or for estimating other parameters. The other involves using available information about rare materials of interest to target the locations where surveyors are most likely to find them. Because this involves investing extra effort in making these rare observations, they are not usable for parameter estimates, but it can help put limits on the abundance of rare sites or other archaeological remains. For example, the statistical sample may indicate that the density of some rare site type is less than 0.05 sites/km^2, with a certain range of uncertainty. A purposive survey, meanwhile, may suggest that about half the places that are likely locations for the rare materials in fact contain them. If such target locations occupy some 2% of the survey area, one might then conclude, albeit with a large margin of uncertainty, that the rare sites occur with a density somewhere near 0.01/km^2.

Perhaps a more common way to combine prospection and statistical survey is to carry out the statistical survey first, in the usual way, and then follow it with purposive survey meant to fill in "gaps" in the statistical sample. For example, certain kinds of places that prehistoric people probably favored for settlement might only constitute a very small portion of the sample that results from the statistical survey. In that event, it is possible to add observations in such places in the time remaining. In addition, the results of the statistical survey might provide hints as to the likely location of materials that it did not actually detect. Low densities of artifacts in locations where geomorphological processes could have redeposited them from higher ground, for example, might suggest searching an adjacent hilltop for signs of settlement. Note that any sites discovered outside the sample areas should not be included in calculations of parameter estimates, as this would lead to bias (Redman, 1975:154).

Combining statistical survey with search for spatial structure is arguably more difficult because a typical sample leaves too many gaps in space while some kinds of structure would be undetectable by anything less than an enormous cluster sample. There are some instances where such a combination is possible, however.

For example, the high obtrusiveness of large settlements, such as towns or cities, sometimes allows us to record almost all the surviving examples of such settlements in a large survey area, and then to use a small sampling fraction to document the lower levels of the settlement hierarchy. In fact, the distribution of the large sites not only allows us to infer the spatial structure of this level of the settlement system, but can be used as the basis for stratifying the statistical sample (see chapter 7).

Another possible combination is prospection and spatial structure. One way this might be carried out is to use purposive survey to prospect for a base camp or urban site, and then intensive survey with 100% coverage in the space adjacent to this site with the aim of understanding activities that took place off-site. Another might be to use a model for spatial structure as the tool with which to predict the locations of settlements, and then to test the model by purposive survey at those locations. GIS provides a useful framework for accomplishing this.

1.5 The Issue of Methodological Consistency

Clearly, there are advantages in using methods that are consistent from case to case if we plan to compare these cases, yet insistence that surveys should all employ the same strategies and methods can only ensure mediocre results.

Any attempt to pool the results of several surveys to compare human population densities or document population change over time is undermined if the surveys use substantially different methods or define "sites" or settlements in different ways. One survey, for example, might have a design that favors the discovery of large settlement sites, and very rarely detects small settlements, such as camps or farmsteads, and leads to small underestimates of population size. Another, that employed a sample of very small quadrats, totalling 20% of the sampling frame, and simply did not include very many of the largest sites, might underestimate human population even more. Differences in the way the surveys defined "site" or whether they even used sites as observational units will also be a factor, while failure of any of these surveys to determine the length of time each settlement was occupied would make the comparison even more tenuous. Consistency in these aspects of the surveys' designs, however, would allow comparison of the *relative* magnitudes of differences in population between survey areas or between time periods.

In Cultural Resource Management, there are usually regulations dictating at least some aspects of survey design, such as minimum sampling fractions or shovel-test intervals (see chapter 8). Arguably, it is essential for managers to have at least minimal standardization of the information in their databases. In addition, such standards set a level playing field for archaeologists bidding on CRM contracts.

Ebert (1992:47, 52) argues for methodological consistency in archaeological survey, and then offers his own strategy of "distributional archaeology" as the solution. He claims that it is impossible to compare data from surveys carried out with different field strategies or units. Certainly there are many cases where such comparisons would have many "apples-and-oranges" complications.

Yet Ebert unwittingly undermines the argument for standardized research strategies because distributional archaeology is only one example of a strategy that would be ineffective or unsatisfactory in many contexts. His insistence that "sites" do not exist simply would be unacceptable in parts of the world where they are quite evident, sometimes to the point of having substantial fortification walls marking their boundaries, as in many parts of the Old World. Although archaeologists can agree that not all human behavior took place in these well demarcated settlements, it would be perverse to ignore their existence. Furthermore, Ebert's method ignores chronology. This may be acceptable in projects that seek to document and understand persistent use of certain places over very long periods, or where the evidence simply makes chronological distinctions impossible. Yet for projects with research objectives that include understanding change over time, chronological distinctions are essential. Clearly, there will never be a single set of methods that will satisfy all research objectives.

In addition, it is incorrect to claim that all kinds of methodological variety lead to incommensurate results. Although it is not meaningful to compare demographic estimates based on densities of sites with ones based on artifact densities in quadrats, for example, it is entirely reasonable to compare artifact densities in a survey by square units with those in a survey that used hexagonal ones. Both survey frames will yield statistics of artifacts per square meter and statistical errors on those statistics that allow good estimates of artifact density in the population. Even varying the size of the sampling units will affect mainly the size of the error and the degree of clustering, not the estimate of density, except in poorly designed or very unlucky samples. Methodological inconsistency in survey design makes some observations incommensurate, but not all.

The pressures for standardization in CRM regulations, although understandable, do not encourage the most elegant solutions to archaeological problems. Strict adherence to these guidelines may involve investing inordinate proportions of survey effort in areas where survey is unproductive or may reinforce previous biases. Yet these regulations often only enforce minimum standards, and do not necessarily prevent more inventive strategies as long as they are reasonably cost-effective. Some regulators may even welcome creative proposals for innovation.

What, then, is the solution? Archaeologists should design surveys to satisfy the specific research questions they have or help in the decisions that cultural managers must make. Inevitably, this will lead to quite different survey designs in different circumstances. Where one can reasonably anticipate the need for inter-project comparisons, there should be efforts to make these comparisons possible with as little distortion as possible. In many cases, this will involve standardizing some kinds of data recovery as minimal procedures, but should not prevent anyone from going beyond the standards to meet the objectives of the research. Perhaps most important is the need to document exactly what our strategies and methods are. As long as there are detailed, published descriptions of these procedures, including maps showing the exact routes of transects or locations of sub-surface tests, and any deviations from them due to human error or chance opportunities, other researchers can attempt to account for methodological effects on the survey's results. It is also important to evaluate the effectiveness of surveys, and to make others aware of any deficiencies in the results that we may find. Such details allow us to determine the *detection functions* of the surveys, and thus correct for many kinds of bias or differences in discovery probability. As noted in chapter 10, it is even possible in some instances to map the "exhaustion" of a region to depict the probability that cultural resources escaped detection in different parts of the map.

1.6 Summary

There is an inescapable relationship between the design of a survey and the results we can expect it to yield. Consequently, it is important to design each survey to produce the kinds of results its designers require. Broadly speaking, surveys are designed either to optimize recovery of specific kinds of archaeological materials (prospection), to allow us to estimate parameters of a population on the basis of a sample (statistical generalization), or to enable us to detect and identify spatial structure (pattern recognition). Although most surveys combine aspects of at least two of these goals, subsequent chapters will deal with the methods suitable for each in turn, following chapters on concepts common to all surveys.

Chapter III
The Discovery of Archaeological Materials by Survey

Once we have identified the goals of an archaeological survey and decided on the general type of survey most appropriate to those goals, we need to identify specific factors that may affect the survey strategy's effectiveness at intersecting, detecting and recognizing the archaeological materials we seek. Characteristics of those materials and of the environments in which they are found are among these factors. Others are post-depositional factors that affect patterns in the distribution of those materials, or are inherent in our methods or sensors and the way we deploy them.

Careful consideration of these factors can lead to advantageous survey designs, as well as furnish grounds for evaluating the surveys' effectiveness and accuracy.

1. FACTORS AFFECTING ARCHAEOLOGICAL DETECTION

In the 1970s, a rapid expansion of archaeological survey activity, in part fueled by the growth of Cultural Resource Management, led to detailed consideration of some of these factors and new terminology to describe them. Summary papers on archaeological survey design by Ammerman (1981), Cherry (1983), Schiffer et al. (1978) and Plog et al. (1978) helped to standardize this terminology. Subsequently, a number of authors investigated some of the factors affecting detection by particular methods, notably subsurface testing (e.g., Kintigh, 1988; Krakker et al., 1983; Lynch, 1980; McManamon, 1980; Nance, 1983; Nance and Ball, 1986; Shott, 1985; Stone, 1981; Wobst, 1983). Here we will deal with these concepts as well as some others and their relationship to similar concepts found in geophysical remote sensing, search-and-rescue, and Operations Research (e.g., Kolesar, 1982; Koopman, 1980; McCammon, 1977; Stone, 1989).

Many of the factors that archaeologists have studied concern the probability that a particular survey will *intersect* archaeological materials. However, archaeologists have recognized for a long time that intersecting a site or any other item of interest does not by any means guarantee that it will be detected.

As geophysicists, mineral prospectors, and experts in search-and-rescue and naval operations have known for a long time, the factors that affect detection of a "target" can be classified as ones that depend on the properties of the target, ones depending on the type of signal that communicates information about these properties, ones that depend on the medium of signal propagation, ones that depend on the kind of sensor or method of inspection, and, quite importantly, ones that affect our ability to recognize the signal and correctly identify it.

All of these collectively contribute to *detectability* (Shennan, 1997:390-93; Thompson and Ramsey, 1987; Thompson and Seber, 1994; 1996). Detectability involves the possibility of failing to notice the target even when it is included in an observation. For example, an archaeologist might intersect an archaeological site with an auger hole, but still not find anything in the sediment that the auger removed to indicate that the site is present, either because there is no artifact in the sediment or because the archaeologist did not notice or recognize it (Krakker, et al., 1983; Lovis, 1976; McManamon, 1980; Nance, 1979; Nance and Ball, 1986; Stafford, 1995; Shott, 1989).

1.1 Method of Inspection

One of the more obvious influences on the probability that a survey will detect particular kinds of archaeological materials is the method of inspection. Most archaeological surveys are based on visual inspection of the surface while walking across the landscape, but other methods, such as ones that use aerial reconnaissance or geophysical remote sensing, are better at detecting some kinds of materials in some situations.

More generally, method of inspection involves at least two interacting factors. One is the type of signal that communicates information about some material of interest, including the target. Another is the sensor with which we detect this signal and its sensitivity to variations in signal due to the contrast between a target and its environment. For example, the signal could be visible light and the sensor could be a person's eyes. In that case, successful detection depends on the ability of surveyors' eyes (and associated visual processing in the brain) to distinguish the subtle differences in patterns of light reflected from various surfaces.

Whatever method or methods a survey employs, it is important to evaluate the capabilities of sensors, and particularly their ability to deal with anticipated challenges to visibility and the way in which their ability to detect materials of interest decreases with distance (see sections 1.2 and 1.4). Both these factors affect the choice of method and the desired spacing of observations.

1.1.1 Visual Inspection in Surface Survey

Survey by visual inspection is what archaeologists normally mean by "archaeological survey." Older archaeological surveys typically entailed searching visually for archaeological remains on horseback or from a motor vehicle (so-called "windscreen surveys"). In some regions with dense bush, it has been common to survey streambanks or lakeshores by canoe or boat. Although such surveys continue, at least for preliminary reconnaissance, it is now much more common for visual inspection of the surface to be accomplished through pedestrian survey.

Discovery of Archaeological Materials

In pedestrian survey (Department of the Environment, 1980; Fasham et al., 1980), team members typically distribute themselves across space in such a way as to inspect some geographical unit systematically. That is, they are spaced approximately an equal distance apart, with each team member responsible for searching some subset of the target space. Most commonly this is done by dividing the space into long narrow transects, perhaps 3 m or 10 m apart, with each team member walking the length of one transect to search for traces of material culture on the surface before beginning another such transect. By walking back-and-forth across a field or quadrat in this way, the team hopes to detect all archaeological traces (usually potsherds or lithics) that happen to be visible on the surface. Sometimes they arrange to have fields plowed before the survey begins as this removes vegetation and churns up artifacts in the plow zone, thus improving archaeological visibility.

One variation on this type of survey involves walking meandering or zig-zag paths instead of straight transects (Mortensen, 1979; Rupp, n.d.), or walking each unit a second time in a different direction than the first. In search-and-rescue at sea, a second search pattern is optimally oriented 45° to the first (Koopman, 1980:218), a practice that might be useful in archaeological cases as well. The purpose of these variations is to improve the likelihood that survey of a given space will indeed detect all material culture traces on the surface (much as to optimize the search for a life raft). Small overlaps between adjacent meandering transects or intersecting straight ones add a small amount of redundancy, while changing the searchers' viewpoint relative to incident light and minimizing the chance of merely duplicating previous survey work. A second search pattern at 45°, meanwhile, also maximizes inspection of previously untraversed space (Koopman, 1980:219).

An important variation is necessary when it is likely that archaeological materials could be buried by colluvium or alluvium. In these cases, we have little reason to expect archaeological materials to be visible on the modern surface except where some process, such as gullying or modern construction activity, has cut down into buried deposits. Surveys that give special attention to eroded surfaces, gullies, animal burrows, ditches, road cuts, wells, and construction sites will be much more successful at detecting buried sites (typically including the oldest sites), than ones that only inspect the surfaces of fields. Not only the cut itself, but also any spoil heap of sediment removed from it, may exhibit artifacts.

1.1.2 Visual Inspection of Aerial Photographs with Groundchecks

The use of aerial reconnaissance to detect archaeological sites was pioneered in the years following the First World War (chapter 1), but has growing potential in some parts of the world. In addition to aerial inspection in visible wavelengths of light, modern survey can employ infrared, ultraviolet and even radar, and satellites and space shuttles now supplement airplanes and balloons as observation platforms (Bewley and Rackowski, eds., 2001; Dabas et al., 1998; Dassié, 1978; Deuel, 1969).

Aerial reconnaissance in visible light works particularly well in either deserts or where large expanses of pasture and agricultural fields with shallow soils experience seasonal water stress. In deserts, the lack of dense vegetation, high perspective, and the shadows that result from even tiny topographical variations in raking light, found in early morning or late afternoon, make certain kinds of sites much easier to recognize than they would be to an observer standing on the ground (see p. 66, figure 7). Traces of roads and stone or brick walls, even if they are buried, often appear clearly as linear traces. Low mounds with phosphate-rich, artifact-rich or ashy sediments will often appear quite different in color than their surroundings. In agricultural fields and pastures in western Europe, variations in the color and height of vegetation can be even more important than the "microtopography" of the surface. When it has not rained for a few weeks, for example, vegetation growing above buried ditches and pits will be greener and higher than surrounding vegetation, while vegetation above buried stone walls, by contrast, will be stunted. The combination of color difference and shadows in raking light can make some kinds of sites, especially those where stone foundations have been built or large ditches dug into underlying chalk, quite obvious. Even details of architectural plan are sometimes quite obvious. These kinds of traces in vegetation are called "crop marks."

Targets detected by aerial survey require confirmation by groundchecking. Simply put, it is necessary to visit anomalous features seen in the aerial photos to find out if they are archaeologically significant and, if so, what they are. Groundchecking is likely to include searching for artifacts on the surface, and therefore may employ some of the same techniques as pedestrian survey. The main difference is that surface inspection focusses on particular landscape features or their relationship to other features, rather than arbitrary spatial units.

1.1.3 Survey by Test Pits, Divoting, Coring, or Augering (SST)

Sometimes either the leaf-fall from forests, grass cover, or overlying soil and sediment make it impossible to detect archaeological remains on the modern surface (see *visibility*, section 1.2). Furthermore, the paleolandscape approach (Stafford, 1995) requires information on both buried and surface archaeological remains. In these cases, it is usually necessary to employ a more intrusive form of visual inspection, which involves either digging sets of test pits or using a coring tool or an auger to extract material from below the surface, and then examining the removed sediment for artifacts or other archaeological traces.

In the interest of clarity, it is necessary to define some terms, as much confusion has resulted from using terms for these methods interchangeably (Stein, 1991). Coring is the removal of a continuous and relatively undisturbed column or cylinder of sediment or rock with a tool that resembles a hollow tube and has a straight bit. Augering, by contrast, uses a tool with a screw or helical bit that digs out sediment and pushes it into a cylindrical bucket for removal in relatively small increments, and thus disturbs the integrity of the sediment. Most archaeologists use the terms, "sub-surface testing" (SST), "test-pitting," and "*sondages*" to describe manual excavation of relatively small (e.g., <

1 m x 1 m) areas to reveal buried deposits. Divoting is a variety of sub-surface testing that involves cutting a small, shallow square of sod or forest leaf-mat with a spade and turning it over to look for artifacts (Lovis, 1976). Manual execution of any of these can be hard work, especially where sediments are compacted or very stony, and in many contexts mechanical versions are an excellent investment. Stein (1991:142) notes that many CRM companies now routinely use truck-mounted hydraulic corers or augers to extract long cores or large-diameter auger samples in large numbers. In some parts of the United States and Canada, similarly, CRM archaeologists use series of trenches excavated by backhoes or peel off large areas of plow zone or sod with mechanical graders. In the former cases, crew members then check the walls of the trenches for stratification and signs of features, such as house-pits, while in the latter they look for the tops of pits, signs of post-molds, and artifacts on the newly exposed surface. Even firebreak plows have seen service in archaeological survey (Bloemaker and Oakley, 1999).

Where we use test pits, divots, cores or auger holes to prospect for or sample archaeological remains, the density and size of the probes is a major factor in the probability of site detection (Krakker, et al., 1983; Lovis, 1976; McManamon, 1980; Nance, 1979; Nance and Ball, 1986; Stafford, 1995); Shott, 1989). Clearly, a large number of closely-spaced auger holes is more likely to hit sites than a smaller number of widely spaced ones. This is a problem of *resolution*, which exploration geologists have investigated in detail and to which we will return in in section 1.7. Also, a 2 m x 1 m trench is more likely to intersect a site than is an auger hole with a diameter of 15 cm. What is less obvious is that we have to consider the probability of actually recognizing a site if we hit it, a problem of "detectability." Unless the artifacts or other "site constituents" on a site are very dense or nearly continuous, it is fairly likely that most cores or auger holes, even if they pierce the site's deposits, will not detect artifacts or other materials associated with cultural activities. Artifact density and clustering are aspects of the site's *obtrusiveness*. We will return to some of these issues below and in chapter 5.

Artifacts are not the only kinds of traces that can help us detect archaeological deposits in test pits or auger holes. In some cases, and especially in test pits of reasonable size (i.e., at least 1 m^2), there may be stratification visible in the pit's section that appears to be cultural. For example, there could be a thin, dark or ashy layer that has a high probability of being a living floor or "anthropic soil horizon" (Valentine, et al., 1980). One kind of trace that has been useful in some contexts is chemical content (Bakkevig, 1980; Cavanagh, et al., 1988; Cook and Heizer, 1965; Eidt, 1973; 1977; Heidenreich and Konrad, 1973; Heidenreich and Navratil, 1973; Proudfoot, 1976; Provan, 1971; Sjoberg, 1976; Woods, 1977). For example, because much of the rubbish that people discard on and around settlements, and particularly bone, is high in phosphate, their decay can elevate the phosphate level of the sediment substantially. However, anthropic soils and chemical anomalies may not be as ubiquitous as artifacts in sites, while chemical anomalies can also result from variations in bedrock (McManamon, 1984; see "chemical survey," section 1.1.4.7).

1.1.4 Geophysical Survey

Remote sensing is survey that depends on the transmission of information about buried materials to a detector, generally by means other than visible light. For most remote sensing methods, we are indebted to geophysics, which uses them to investigate the structure of the Earth's crust and to detect mineral or petroleum deposits.

Although this is not the place to discuss these methods in detail, the following lists some of the methods more commonly used in archaeology, with brief assessment of their archaeological potential and limitations. For more comprehensive information about these methods, consult texts on archaeometry and remote sensing (Aikens, et al., 1977; Aitken, 1974; Dabas et al., 1998; Ebert, 1984; Ebert and Lyons, 1976; Lyons and Avery, 1977; Remote Sensing Society, 1984).

1.1.4.1 Resistivity Survey

This type of survey uses variations in the voltage of electrical currents flowing through the ground to detect buried objects or features that are either better or worse conductors than the surrounding sediment. Results vary with the pattern and spacing of electrode array, and it is important to convert the voltage and current data into estimates of *resistivity* (a characteristic of the material through which the current flowed) as distinct from the *resistance*. Generally, where there is appropriate electrical contrast, resistivity is greater where buried stone walls interrupt the path of current and lower where there are buried metal objects or pit features that contain topsoil or retain moisture.

1.1.4.2 Magnetometer Survey

This type of survey detects tiny variations in the Earth's magnetic field that result from the proximity of magnetic (principally iron) objects and from variations in the magnetic susceptibility of iron-containing soils and sediments. It is particularly effective for detecting remanently magnetized features, such as large kilns that were weakly magnetized when they cooled in the Earth's magnetic field after their last firing. Magnetometry is commonly used in terrestrial archaeological surveys, but can also be useful in detection of shipwrecks if the ships either had steel hulls or cladding or had iron guns. The magnetometer is towed some distance behind a ship. One unusual aspect of magnetic survey is that the magnetic anomaly is only centered over the target in polar and equatorial regions. At intermediate latitudes there are both positive and negative anomalies associated with each target, and the offset varies with magnetic latitude.

1.1.4.3 Electromagnetic (EM) Survey

This type of survey uses a coil to induce electrical currents in the ground, which, in turn, induce magnetic fields in buried objects or features. A second coil detects these magnetic fields. As with resistivity survey, therefore, it is good for detecting contrasts in conductivity.

Discovery of Archaeological Materials

1.1.4.4 Seismic Survey

This type of survey uses sharp impacts or small explosions to transmit seismic waves through the ground, some of which are reflected by interfaces between deposits of different density.

1.1.4.5 Sonar or Acoustic Survey

This type of survey similarly uses sound waves reflected from surfaces to detect objects, especially underwater. Sonar is frequently used in survey for shipwreck sites (e.g., Linden and Shurer, 1984).

1.1.4.6 Ground-Penetrating Radar (GPR)

This type of survey uses an antenna to detect radio waves reflected from interfaces between deposits of different density.

1.1.4.7 Chemical Survey

In cases where most traces of archaeological materials have decayed away, sometimes they have left a chemical signature in sediment. Human habitation and refuse disposal sometimes concentrates phosphates, nitrogen, and heavy elements, such as lead or copper, in archaeological sediments. Chemically analysing small soil samples taken at intervals provides the basis for detecting areas of unusually high concentration (Eidt, 1984; Schlezinger and Howes, 2000). It is also possible to combine chemical analysis with analysis of the soil samples' magnetic susceptibilities (e.g., Clark, 1977), as habitation or burning may also elevate the maghaemite levels in the soil.

1.1.4.8 Thermal Survey

A relatively little-known technique in archaeology is thermal survey, which includes both aerial infrared thermography and direct-contact thermography (Bellerby et al., 1992). This technique detects temperature anomalies associated with buried features under the influence of diurnal or other periodic shifts in surface heat. It is based on the principle that a buried body with thermal properties different than its surroundings will disturb the temperature "wave" associated with the Fourier-series harmonics of variations in surface temperature.

1.1.5 Underwater Survey

As compared with aerial and especially pedestrian survey, survey for underwater sites poses quite difficult problems. Sometimes, when sites lie in shallow water, aerial reconnaissance methods are quite effective. For example, the wooden posts of Neolithic and Bronze Age villages in France, Germany, Italy and Switzerland can sometimes be seen in shallow lakes from vantage points in the air (e.g., Arnold, 1986). As we have seen in the last section, sonar and magnetometry can also be used to detect shipwrecks.

Yet some kinds of underwater survey still depend on close visual inspection, much as with pedestrian survey, and even survey by magnetometer or sonar requires a plan for making transects across the region to be inspected and "ground checks" by divers.

To allow a ship towing a magnetometer or using sonar to follow a predetermined search path accurately, and to ensure accurate placement of any anomalies that might be shipwrecks or other sites, surveyors can use beacons, buoys or GPS. A radio beacon set up on shore next to the search area can serve to keep the search ship on course, or the ship can make traverses between carefully placed, anchored buoys that mark the ends of transects. A GPS system on board can use satellites to track its position almost continuously and with considerable accuracy.

Where divers survey by visual inspection, visibility is often quite poor, and divers attempt to maintain course and spacing between them by holding onto lines.

1.2 Visibility

Visibility is a characteristic of the environment in which archaeological materials may be found that can make it relatively easy, or more difficult, for archaeologists to detect them (Schiffer et al., 1978). This aspect of detectability (Shennan, 1997:390-93) depends on the media of signal propagation. Exactly the same materials, such as a scatter of pottery sherds, may be highly visible in some situations and very difficult to detect — virtually invisible — in others.

Poor visibility is often the result of some relatively opaque material interposed between a surveyor and the items of archaeological interest that acts as a filter, or even a barrier, to diminish a particular sensor's ability to detect it. For example, a layer of sediment, vegetation cover, or both, may make it difficult for someone to see a scatter of sherds or stone tools. Yet the visibility factor also depends on the method of detection. A layer of sediment that is opaque to visible light, making it impossible for us to detect buried artifacts visually, is at least somewhat transparent to magnetic fields, radar, sound waves and other physical phenomena capable of transmitting information about some kinds of buried objects to a sensor above the ground. Most archaeological surveys employ visual inspection exclusively, so that visibility is obstructed by anything that restricts the transmission of visible light, but archaeologists should specify their method of inspection when they talk about visibility. In some instances optical visibility is so poor that it is necessary to use one of the methods of remote sensing discussed in section 1.1. In others, plowing fields before survey makes more artifacts visible at the surface.

Sediment and vegetation cover are not the only things that can reduce visibility by visual inspection, although they are very common. Sediment cover is a particular problem in areas that have been subject to substantial colluviation or alluviation, as in major river valleys and at the foot of slopes. In major river valleys, alluvium can sometimes bury even substantial site mounds (Brooks, et al., 1982). In some instances, archaeological sites of interest are buried so deeply that they are virtually undetectable except by accident or where they are intersected by erosion gullies. At the bottom of hill slopes, colluvium can cover a large proportion of archaeological occurrences (Allen, 1988; Allen, 1991; Bell, 1983; Chapman, 1981; Mills, 1985a; Mills, 1985b), even a single season of landslides sometimes having a remarkable effect on site visibility (Banning, 1996; Field and Banning, 1998). Consequently, attention to the geomorphology of the survey area, including attention to road cuts, gullies and other opportunistic sections, is critical in hilly or alluvial areas to assess the extent of erosion and deposition and their probable impact on site distributions. Sand dunes, meanwhile, have the additional complication that they may shift their position over time. Consequently, they can completely cover a site at one time that is completely exposed at the surface some decades later.

Vegetation cover is a serious impediment to visibility in tropical, temperate and subboreal forests, as the litter of fallen leaves, as well as the living vegetation, tends to obscure archaeological remains on the surface. Except for the most obtrusive sites (see section 1.3), these kinds of situations usually call for methods other than simple visual inspection by fieldwalking, such as test-pitting or shovel-testing and geophysical remote sensing. Other types of vegetation cover, such as grass and agricultural crops, vary in their effect on visibility of archaeological remains. In some cases, they may even increase detectability, when viewed from the air, by varying their height or color in response to buried archaeological features.

Sediment load in the water is a frequent impediment to visibility in underwater survey by visual inspection. Often visibility is so poor that surveyors cannot even see each other and need to be guided carefully by lines.

Intertidal survey poses unusual visibility problems. Water recedes from the target areas for no more than a few hours and only intermittently. Sediments washed in during each high tide obscure materials that archaeologists had cleaned off during the previous low tide.

Construction is an increasingly common impediment to visual inspection by fieldwalking. Pavements and structures that are more recent than the archaeological remains of interest can cover them so completely as to render them completely invisible by visual inspection. In some cases, however, the construction activity may inadvertently have redeposited more ancient material on the modern surface. Because the sites favored for ancient settlement are often also favorable locations for modern construction, this can be a difficult problem unless more invasive (test-pitting) or geophysical methods are feasible.

Impediments to visibility are not only opaque coverings, however. Archaeologists have long recognized that variations in lighting and whether or not it has rained affect the success of the search for archaeological material by visual inspection (Hirth, 1978; Wills, 1929; 1932, cited in Allen, 1991:39).

Nor should we forget that some circumstances, rather than obscuring archaeological materials, actually improve visibility. Processes that concentrate artifacts on the surface, such as sheetwash, that churn up buried artifacts, such as plowing, or that make them easier to see, such as rain or favorable lighting, may improve visibility during visual inspection of surface remains. In winter, early mornings or late afternoons, shadows are long and detection of some artifacts and features may be easier. Walking toward or away from the sun, however, will also have a substantial effect on detection, so walking transects in different directions may be advantageous. In some contexts, surveying on overcast days may improve artifact visibility and will lead to greater consistency in recovery.

Although most surveys today at least record factors that we can expect to have an effect on visibility, some surveys explicitly attempt to quantify visibility, and may even use a visibility score to "calibrate" their results (Ammerman and Bonardi, 1981). In the Hvar Survey in Croatia, for example, Gaffney et al. (1991) adjusted the measurements of artifact density on their transects by a visibility factor scored from 0 to 10. In this way they attempted to account for the effect of visibility on their data set. In the Cecina Survey in Italy, nominal visibility score and computer simulation of visibility effects led to a correction based on the ratio of sites to the proportion of site neighbourhoods with high visibility (Terrenato, 2000; Terrenato and Ammerman, 1996).

We should not fail to note that visibility is an issue for non-visual inspection methods as well, where the medium of propagation — air, soil, or water, for example — can have a substantial effect on the strength of a signal and our ability to discriminate it. In most of these cases, the strength of signal decreases with distance. In fact, many detecting techniques follow the inverse-cube rule: detectability decreases as function of the cube of the distance (see section 1.4, below).

Nance (1983) has dealt extensively with the effect of differential visibility on estimates of population characteristics, but it also affects discovery probabilities and our recognition of spatial pattern.

1.3 Obtrusiveness

Obtrusiveness is arguably the principal contributor to detectability. Conventionally, archaeologists consider obtrusiveness, unlike visibility, a characteristic of the archaeological materials, and not of their environment (Schiffer et al., 1978). Some archaeological remains, such as well preserved stone architecture, are inherently easier to detect by a given surveying method than are others, such as diffuse scatters of lithic debitage. As with visibility, however, we cannot consider obtrusiveness without reference to sensing method and environment. Objects that are difficult to see with the unaided eye may still have pronounced magnetic or radar signals, for example, that make them quite obtrusive to magnetic or radar survey. A rusted iron pipe or canonball lying partially revealed at the surface of the ground might be very difficult to detect visually, but would produce an enormous magnetic signal. Most importantly, obtrusiveness depends on the target object's *contrast* with its environment, and not only on its intrinsic properties.

Contrast is a measure of how much something "stands out." An archaeological artifact or site stands out and gets noticed because it differs from its environment. A scatter of predominantly grey lithics is much more visible on a background of dark brown, plowed soil than on a beach or desert pavement covered by grey pebbles, when visual inspection is the survey method. It is also easier to detect artifact clusters when there are almost no artifacts in the space between clusters, thus creating contrast in density. In magnetic or electromagnetic survey, a pit containing iron-rich sediment is only detectable if the surrounding sediment is lower in magnetic susceptibility or electrical con-

Discovery of Archaeological Materials

ductivity. "Crop marks" above buried ditches or stone foundations are only noticeable in aerial photographs if there is contrast in the color or height of vegetation on and off the buried features. These, in turn, depend on contrasts in the availability of water and nutrients. Consequently, surveys for crop marks tend to be timed to coincide with periods of water stress.

There is a long history of research into the characteristics of targets that make them detectable by the human eye on various backgrounds. These include luminance, reflectance, texture, contrast, and target size (Koopman, 1980:324-332). For non-visual methods, the principal measure of obtrusiveness is the *signal-to-noise ratio* (see below, pp. 55).

1.3.1 The Constituents of Archaeological Distributions

The most important aspect of obtrusiveness is the material that makes up the distributions in which archaeologists are interested. Lithics, pottery and other portable artifacts are only the materials that have historically attracted most interest. Bone, charcoal, chemical residues, sediments with anomalous magnetic susceptibilities or electrical conductivities, facilities and features can also be important targets for survey. In some regions, highly obtrusive architectural features may even occur. McManamon (1984) describes all these as "site constituents," but they are equally the targets of "non-site" or "off-site" survey.

All of these constituents vary in their obtrusiveness to a given inspection technique in a given environment. To ensure an effective survey design, we should assess the likelihood that particular constituents are present in local archaeological distributions, and characterize the sediments and other environmental contexts with which those constituents must contrast in order to be detectable. Then we can determine which inspection methods will allow the constituents to "stand out" in those environments.

For example, where a survey must detect low-density scatters of flakes made from an ubiquitous flint material, on surfaces that are covered with naturally broken, as well as cultural flint, detecting the flakes visually during a quick traverse over the landscape is far from foolproof. Because the flakes' visual contrast with their flinty environment is poor, reliable detection of flakes may require repeated inspection of each survey quadrat, under different lighting conditions, walking in different directions, or using different personnel.

1.3.2 Obtrusiveness of Artifact Scatters

For artifact scatters, the most commonly encountered type of survey evidence, obtrusiveness of "sites" by visual inspection depends on the density and clustering of artifacts, and the ability of surveyors to see the artifacts when they occur. Whether we use test pits or augering, or simply visual inspection of the surface, it is easier to detect dense clusters of artifacts than diffuse artifacts at very low density. However, it is easier to detect sites when the artifacts within them are distributed more uniformly than when they are concentrated in clusters that our transects or tests might miss (Kintigh, 1988:696).

It is also easier to detect artifact clusters when the space around the clusters exhibits very few artifacts, a "background" of very low density analogous to noise (figure 1). Even though this "background" may owe its origins to diffuse cultural activities, many surveys do aim to identify clusters of more intense or more prolonged activity, while some "background" originates in non-cultural, geomorphological processes. Some survey designs have involved the assumption that settlement sites correspond with higher artifact densities than "background" scatters from such activities as manuring (Wilkinson, 1982; Wilkinson, 1989). In "non-site" and "off-site" surveys, however, the diffuse activities that low-density scatters may represent are not background, but the focus of inquiry, particularly where there are indications that refuse disposal and other discard activities left the majority of artifacts off-site or where the site concept, itself, is not very useful (Ebert, 1992).

It is worth noting that any measurement of obtrusiveness that is based on artifact density requires us to define what we mean by "artifact." In most cases, this is a matter of size. If we do not explicitly decide the minimum size of an "artifact," the measure of artifact density is meaningless, while including all artifacts, even microscopic ones, might lead to effectively infinite densities. Archaeologists should cite a minimum size for the artifacts they count, such as 1 cm^2. This does not prevent anyone from collecting or recording some artifacts smaller than this, if it seems warranted; however, for the sake of consistency, it is necessary to exclude these smaller examples from the counts used to estimate densities. In some instances, it is also necessary to specify whether lithic chips and chunks, as distinct from flakes, or probable fire-cracked rock qualify as "artifacts." Whether or not these are included could have a substantial impact on estimates of artifact density.

We can model random scatters of artifacts with the Poisson distribution. With a space partitioned into quadrats of equal area, the mean density of artifacts in that space will be equal to the total number of artifacts divided by number of quadrats. But the distribution of actual numbers of artifacts per quadrat will not be symmetrical about the mean if densities are fairly low. In part, this is because no quadrat can have less than 0 artifacts, but it is also because some quadrats could, in principle, have surprisingly large numbers of artifacts. If this were not the case, we would never be able to distinguish "sites" from "background."

The mathematics for the Poisson distribution are not difficult, and can be illustrated with an example. Suppose that someone has surveyed a space in units that are 1 m^2 in area. If the artifacts are randomly distributed, the probability that any given unit will contain a particular number (x) of artifacts is

$$p(x) = \frac{e^{-\lambda}\lambda^x}{x!} \text{ for } x = 0, 1, 2, ...$$

This means simply that the probability of getting x artifacts depends on the parameter λ (the mean or expected number of obsidian tools per unit) and e (= 2.718...). If $\lambda = 2$, then the probability of finding exactly two artifacts in a unit is

$$p(2) = \frac{e^{-2}2^2}{2!} = \frac{(2.718...)^{-2}4}{2*1} = \frac{0.541}{2} = 0.271$$

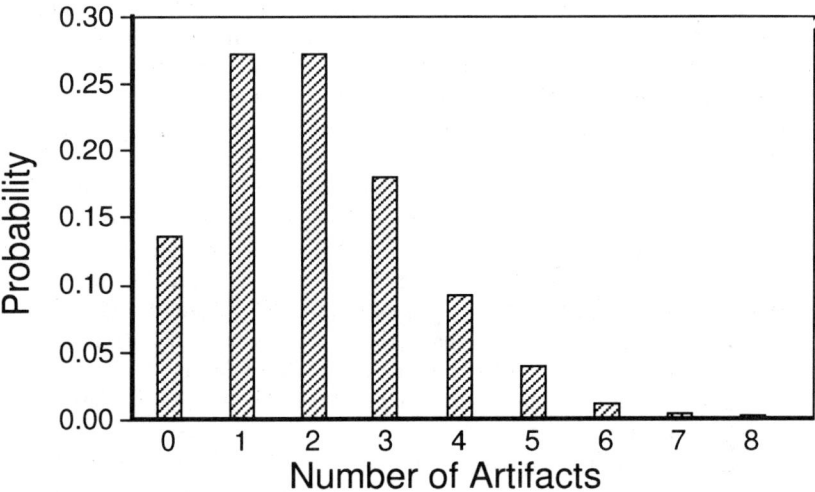

Figure 5. Poisson distribution for $\lambda = 2$ (values above 8 omitted).

Calculating this for other values of x yields the distribution in figure 5. Although the graph does not show bars for values higher than 8, this is only to save space. In fact there is a real, although very low, probability of getting more than ten artifacts in any 1 m^2 quadrat, and one could theoretically find dozens of them. The graph shows us that we would not expect that to happen very often, however.

One property of the Poisson distribution is that its variance is equal to its mean (λ). This turns out to be a useful property.

There are two reasons that the Poisson distribution is important for survey design. First, it provides a simple model that allows us to estimate how likely it is for any given observation unit in our survey to encounter artifacts or other discrete archaeological objects, such as sites, if their distribution is random. If we can even approximately estimate the likely density of archaeological materials in a survey area, we can use this information to help us ensure that survey methods are thorough enough to detect them. This information is particularly important for deciding the *resolution* of survey and the size of observation unit (see below). Second, it helps surveyors conceive of the difficulty of distinguishing denser clusters of archaeological material, such as sites, from "background" scatter of artifacts off-site, one way to conceive of their obtrusiveness (see figure 1). Although archaeologists do not actually expect cultural distributions to be random, the Poisson model allows us to estimate how difficult it could be to distinguish between clustered and random observations when we only have a sample, while also providing a kind of standard from which we might expect "sites" or clusters to stand out. For example, some surveys assume that sites will have densities of at least 5 artifacts/m^2. The graph in figure 5, however, shows us that even in "background" areas where the mean artifact density is 2 artifacts/m^2, we would expect to find more than 5 artifacts/m^2 in a significant number of instances. Meanwhile, on a "site" with $\lambda = 10$ we should expect to find no more than 4 artifacts/m^2 5% of the time.

Nance and Ball (1989) have criticized the use of Poisson distributions in this context. Although they are right that most archaeological distributions are probably clustered, rather than random, the Poisson distribution and many other mathematical models are still useful, although idealized, standards with which to compare real distributions. In some instances, the Poisson distribution may be a conservative, or alternatively a somewhat optimistic, approximation. In cases where distributions are highly clustered, meanwhile, it is still important to recognize that they are *clustered at a particular scale*. At other scales they could still be random, and this characteristic is the basis for some analytical procedures, particularly those based on the variance-to-mean ratio, in distributional archaeology (Ebert, 1992). It is also useful, in some situations, to model the clusters as disks or ellipses of contagious distributions that are themselves distributed according to a Poisson model. In that case, we may assume a Poisson process that generates the centers of clusters, and then a secondary process that establishes the number of items in each cluster and their distribution around the center (e.g., Bartlett, 1964; Moyal, 1962; Paloheimo, 1971).

As we will see later in discussion of the size of observation units, a simple way to ensure that most quadrats show artifact counts closer to the mean is to adjust the scale of observation. For a Poisson distribution and density of 10 artifacts per square meter, the mean for 2 m x 2 m units would be 40 ± 6.3 artifacts, the distribution would be more symmetrical about the mean, and the probability of finding less than 20 artifacts would be only 0.0000000000037. Thus, the larger observation unit makes it less likely that we will mistake a "site" for "background," and the Poisson distribution helps us decide what the optimal unit size should be. In many instances, however, increasing the size of the observation unit to this extent would simply be impractical. More usefully, if we also use the Poisson distribution to model the "background," we can test observations against this standard to see if they differ enough to be considered "sites; " are the artifact densities so high that it is extremely unlikely that they could occur in background areas?

The discussion so far has been on the assumption that sites exhibit a uniform distribution, that is, that the parameter λ is constant everywhere on the site. As mentioned in chapter 1, some models for sites assume hemispherical or sinusoidal distributions of artifact densities. In those instances, the Poisson distribution can still be useful, but it is necessary to vary the value of λ as a function of distance away from the center of the site (see Kintigh, 1988:692-694).

Even this, however, does not consider the potential for rather "patchy" clustering on site, or the scale of clustering. A survey to detect a buried site by augering, for example, might fail to find it even when artifact density is fairly high if the artifacts are clustered into small patches that predominantly fall between the auger holes. In such cases, the Poisson distribution provides only a rather optimistic model for site discovery (Shott, 1989:398). Where such uneven artifact distributions are likely, it would be wise to consider the resolution of survey very carefully, and attempt to minimize the chance that such clusters will "fall between the cracks." In that case, it is necessary to consider the distribution of the clusters, which might itself be approximately random, and not only of the artifacts.

Because cultural behavior, and even natural processes, are patterned, we should often expect clustered distributions of archaeological material. Although such clustered distributions do not conform to the Poisson predictions, the latter still provide limits that help us anticipate the likely character of the sites and non-sites we will encounter. Where artifacts have clustered distributions, rather than random ones, observations of less than 5 artifacts would be even more common than the 5% predicted above for Poisson distributions with $\lambda = 10$. The Poisson distribution also gives us a way to measure the degree of clustering. Because the variance of a Poisson distribution is equal to its mean, a variance-to-mean ratio substantially greater than 1.0 indicates a highly clustered distribution at the scale of the observation unit (e.g., 1 m² quadrats). A high degree of clustering will only increase obtrusiveness if the resolution of survey (see section 1.7) is a good match to the scale of clustering. Where resolution is a poor match, clustering will *decrease* obtrusiveness.

One strategy takes the degree of clustering explicitly into account. One way to do this is to take advantage of the relationship between variance and mean to measure the degree of clustering, assume a uniform distribution for the mean artifact density on a site, and then model artifact distribution within the site with the negative binomial distribution (Kintigh, 1988:694-695).

An alternative to the variance-to-mean ratio for measuring the degree of clustering is the parameter k, which ranges between very small positive values for highly clustered distributions, through very high values for cases that are nearly Poisson:

$$k = \frac{\bar{x}^2}{s^2 - \bar{x}} \quad \text{for } s^2 > \bar{x}$$

Where the variance, s^2, is only slightly greater than the mean, meaning that it is approximately Poisson, and where the density is fairly high, as happens when we have large spatial units, k is very large. Meanwhile, where density is low or variance much greater than the mean, k is much less than 1.0.

The probability of there being no artifacts in an observation unit when that unit has actually intersected a site can then be modelled with the negative binomial distribution (Kintigh, 1988:695):

$$p(0) = \left[\frac{k}{k + \bar{x}}\right]^k$$

The probability that any observation unit will contain at least one artifact is $1 - p(0)$.

These models deal with the probabilities that an observation unit, whether a quadrat or transect on the surface or the contents of a shovel-test or auger bucket, contains artifacts. If it does, we must rely on some archaeologist or archaeologists to detect these artifacts (Kintigh, 1988: 696-697; Krakker et al., 1983:478-479). Whether or not they do depends on the size of the artifacts, whether or not the sediment is screened and by what screen size, lighting conditions, and even how tired or attentive the archaeologists are. To a large extent, this is a matter of obtrusiveness of site constituents for a given technique (visual inspection). Small artifacts much the same color as the sediment in which they are found are clearly less obtrusive than large ones or ones whose color contrasts with their surroundings. If we do not take into account the probability that a survey crew member will actually recognize an artifact that is included in a test unit, our estimates of the probability of detecting sites will be over-optimistic.

1.3.3 Constituent Removal by Chemical or Mechanical Destruction

The removal or destruction of artifacts and other archaeological materials can diminish obtrusiveness by visual inspection and most remote sensing methods to the point that formerly dense scatters are perhaps detectable only by their phosphate signatures, by the densities of microscopic particles (e.g., microdebitage), or by high magnetic susceptibilities.

Constituents such as bone and shell are particularly susceptible to destruction in some environments. Bone has both organic and inorganic components, and conditions favorable to the preservation of the former tend to be destructive to the latter, and *vice versa*. Where surveyors hope to encounter identifiable bone fragments, preservation of the inorganic component is more important. Where preservation of collagen for radiocarbon dating or some other purpose is important, conditions conducive to the survival of the organic component are crucial. Sediment pH is one of the most important factors.

Poorly fired pottery can also suffer destruction in adverse environments (e.g., Schofield, 1989). The low firing temperatures of some Neolithic pottery, in combination with wet-dry cycling and trampling by livestock, may account for the rarity with which surveys identify Ceramic Neolithic sites in some regions, such as semiarid parts of Southwest Asia.

Chemical and magnetic anomalies can suffer from disturbance processes that mix deposits, thus blurring the edges of anthropic layers or features and reducing contrast. Bioturbation, such as that caused by earthworms, is a common impediment to clear chemical and magnetic contrasts.

1.3.4 Obtrusiveness in Aerial Reconnaissance

In aerial reconnaissance, as we saw above, obtrusiveness depends on contrasts in the color or intensity of light emitted from the surface of the ground or from the plants growing on it. Contrast in light intensity depends on the casting of shadows, so sites with microtopography that hints at buried features, and especially linear or other geometric features, are more obtrusive. Sites whose constituents (phosphate content, water content, stone content) likewise vary in non-random, culturally structured ways are also more likely to show recognizably cultural patterns when viewed from the air during parts of the growing season or when vegetation cover experiences water stress. Plants growing over more favorable sediments, such as water-retaining ditches or high-nutrient middens, will be taller, leafier or greener than ones growing over stone walls or hard clay close to the surface. These will sometimes translate into differences in tone or texture that are recognizable in aerial photos.

1.3.5 Obtrusiveness in Geophysical Survey

In geophysical survey, obtrusiveness involves not only the strength of the signal emitted by the buried object or feature, but how it contrasts in magnitude with the signals from its surroundings. It is useful to consider this contrast in terms of a signal-to-noise ratio. Exactly the same feature, with the same physical properties, will be much more obtrusive when it contrasts substantially with its surroundings in a key characteristic (e.g., conductivity, magnetic susceptibility, or density) than when it contrasts only a little.

For example, a prominent magnetic anomaly may occur over a buried ditch cut into iron-poor rock or soil, but filled with sediment rich in iron minerals, such as magnetite or maghaemite. The anomaly occurs because there is significant contrast in the magnetic susceptibility of the ditch's contents and its surroundings.

However, one cannot simply say that culturally significant features will occur wherever there are anomalously high (or low) values in magnetic field, electrical conductivity or acoustic signals. The interpretation of geophysical remote sensing is more complicated than this. In mid-latitudes, the magnetic anomaly associated with a buried pit, for example, will consist of twinned positive and negative peaks. If the buried feature has higher magnetic susceptibility than its surroundings, the positive peak will be south of the negative one if the site is in the northern hemisphere. Only at the poles and in equatorial regions will the anomaly be centered over the buried feature. Resistivity survey also produces bimodal or other complex anomalies in some situations.

Furthermore, these anomalies occur at the scale of individual features and even artifacts, rather than the scale of whole sites or buildings. Consequently, most varieties of geophysical remote sensing are better at detecting spatial structure within sites than in the detection of sites or clustered material culture in regions. In any case, most of these methods would require a very high resolution of observations, making them costly at the regional scale, much as with effective augering and chemical surveys.

1.3.6 Obtrusiveness in Chemical Survey

McManamon (1984) has reviewed the usefulness of chemical signatures for regional survey. Although anomalously high values of carbon, nitrogen, sodium, potassium, sulphur, calcium, copper, lead, and magnesium have all been considered as possible evidence for the decay of cultural waste, most research has focussed on phosphates. Cook and Heizer (1965), for example, initially considered values more than two standard errors above the mean for non-cultural soils in their study region to indicate culturally modified sediments. In other words, two standard errors were taken to represent significant contrast from the natural environment. There are several problems with this attempt to define chemical obtrusiveness, most of them sampling problems. They used a single observation of chemical concentration from each site, rather than the mean of many observations, and thus should have defined obtrusiveness with the standard deviation, rather than the standard error. Furthermore, the mean values for off-site observations are from a large area rather than from the immediate vicinity of sites where soils could be expected to have the same parent material. Cook and Heizer addressed these problems in other work by using standard deviations and off-site samples close to the sites (Cook and Heizer, 1965:29-39).

However, most studies continued to define sites as areas with chemical, and especially phosphorus, levels in the upper 5% or 2.5% of the probability distribution for off-site locations (i.e., above the one-tail or two-tail, 95% confidence interval). As McManamon (1984:239) points out, this is a problem because samples from within sites defined on other grounds (e.g., artifact scatters) often have chemical signatures well below this cut-off. In Cook and Heizer's (1965:40-61) study, for example, 38% of sites showed no significant difference from off-site soils. This is, in part, a sampling problem, as a small sample of sediments or soils from either site or off-site locations is unlikely to represent the full complexity of the population of sediments and soils (Carr, 1982). It should not be any more surprising to find places within sites that have low phosphate values than it is to find parts of sites with low artifact densities or no artifacts at all. Consequently, modelling similar to that discussed in section 1.3.2 would be beneficial in chemical survey as well.

But the problem is also due to the focus on central tendencies and extreme values, rather than on identifying boundaries. It is important to note that absolute values of any of these chemical abundances are meaningless as indicators of clustered cultural materials. In other words, we cannot simply say that phosphorus values greater than 0.20, for example, indicate "sites." Instead, it is only the contrast between *some* high phosphorus values within the boundaries of "sites" and the "background" values outside those boudaries that allow us to define areas likely to correspond with the clustered deposit of cultural materials. The absolute values depend too much on the chemistry of parent rock and various geomorphological and climatic factors. They can also be expected to vary considerably within sites as a result of spatial variety in the processes that deposited various kinds of waste.

Cavanagh et al. (1988), by contrast, use a Bayesian approach to search for the most probable chemical discontinuities in a spatial sample of soils and sediments. They used the uniform distribution to model these discontinuities. Theirs appears to be a productive approach because it focusses on the contrasts that define obtrusiveness. The large sample sizes required, however, can be relatively costly, making it more feasible for defining the boundaries of sites already known or suspected to exist than to prospect for completely unknown sites.

1.4 Distance from Target to Sensor

Detection depends on the propagation of a signal from materials of archaeological interest to a sensor, such as eyes, through some kind of medium, such as sediment or air. Not surprisingly, this signal is attenuated with distance, or *range*. For many kinds of survey, it is useful to define the range as the perpendicular distance away from a transect (Koopman 1980:57); here we will distinguish this by the term, *lateral range*. For many kinds of geophysical prospection, however, we also need to consider attenuation with depth from the sensor.

Discovery of Archaeological Materials

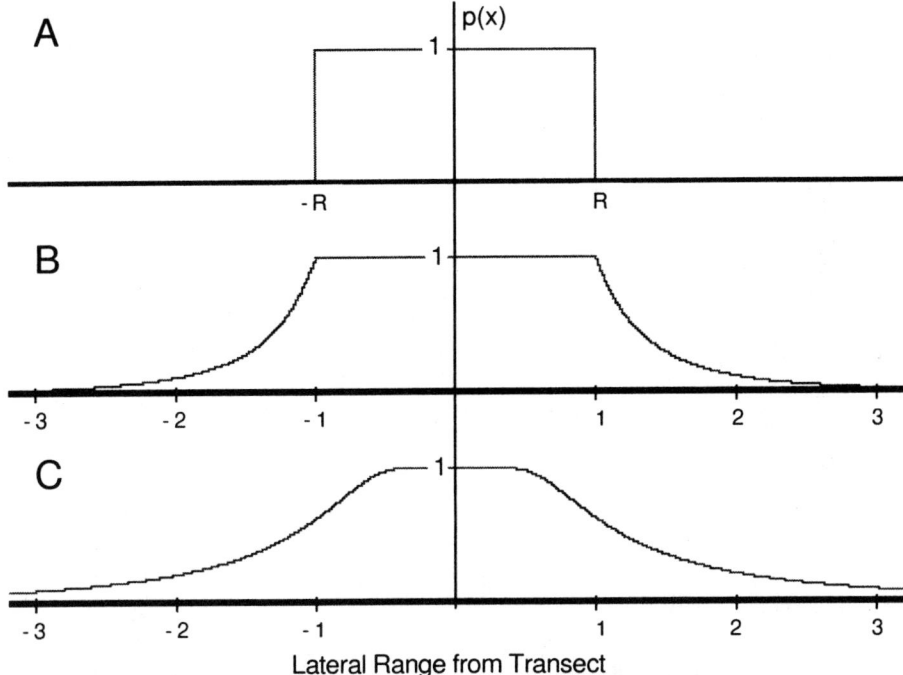

Figure 6. Models for the effect of lateral range on probability of detection: A, definite detection within range R, B, inverse-cube detection, and C, exponential detection (after Koopman, 1980).

In some cases, the simplifying assumption that a target will be detectable within a certain lateral range, but undetectable outside it, is fairly reasonable. These cases fit the *definite range law*, or *law of definite detection*. This law simply states that detection is assured as long as the target is within the lateral range, R (Koopman, 1980:57, 82-83). Figure 6a models this situation with a graph of the instantaneous probability of detection against lateral distance from the target.

1.4.1 The Law of Clean Sweep or Definite Detection

For some surveys, it is important to ensure that search is sufficiently intensive to guarantee that transects or observation points will actually detect, or at least intersect, a specified target if it occurs in the area surveyed. For example, an archaeologist might want to space auger holes closely enough to ensure intersection of at least one auger with any site greater than a particular size.

It is possible to generalize this problem as an aspect of the definite range law, which provides a simple model whereby the target is certain to be detected if it comes within the range, R, of a survey observation. For sets of parallel transects, for example, specifying a transect interval of 2R allows surveyors to "sweep clean" some portion of the survey area. In other words, we will be able to say that, if they do not find any targets in that area, then no targets exist there:

> A law of "definite detection" or "clean sweep" is an idealized search that detects all targets within a particular region R and none outside. Any detection system is said to be "equivalent" (under stated conditions) with a particular definite detection law if each detects the same expected number of targets in a uniform random distribution (Koopman, 1980:83).

For point grids, each observation point can be considered as the center of a circle of radius R (the range) and, for an optimally spaced set of observations, these circles become packed, and somewhat distorted (to something like hexagons). In that case, the region **R** of definite detection has a total area of npR^2, where n is the number of observation points and R is the range.

For transects, the area swept clean **R** is a function of the transect length, L, and double the range, $2R = W$.

Note that the law of definite detection only applies to situations of excellent visibility and obtrusiveness. For many kinds of survey, some targets can remain undetected even when intersected.

1.4.2 Inverse-cube Law

In many instances, especially when the range is large relative to sensor height, the probability of detecting a target decreases approximately as the cube of the range. This is known as the *inverse-cube law*. We can summarize this relationship for visual inspection of the surface as

$$\gamma(r) = \frac{kh}{r^3}$$

where $\gamma(r)$ is the "instantaneous conditional probability of detection by one glimpse," given that a target is present at a range of r, r is the horizontal distance to the target, h is the height of observation above the surface, and k is a factor combining the other influences on detectability (Koopman, 1980:59). Although the mathematics for continuous searching, rather than individual glimpses is more complicated, $1/r^3$ will still approximate one factor. In a survey that involves searching for artifacts while walking widely spaced transects, the probability of artifact detection would then fall off with distance from the transect's center line somewhat as in figure 6b. For visual inspection, this inverse-cube effect is due to the fact that an object of given size occupies a smaller solid angle (product of the vertical and horizontal angles) of the visual field as distance increases (figure 7). If the target is a rectangle of length, l, and width, w, at a range, r, and the observer or detector is a height, h, above the ground, then the distance between observer and target is s, and the solid angle is $\alpha\beta = lwh/s^3$. This means that the probability of seeing the object is proportional to the object's size (lw) and the observer's dis-

Discovery of Archaeological Materials

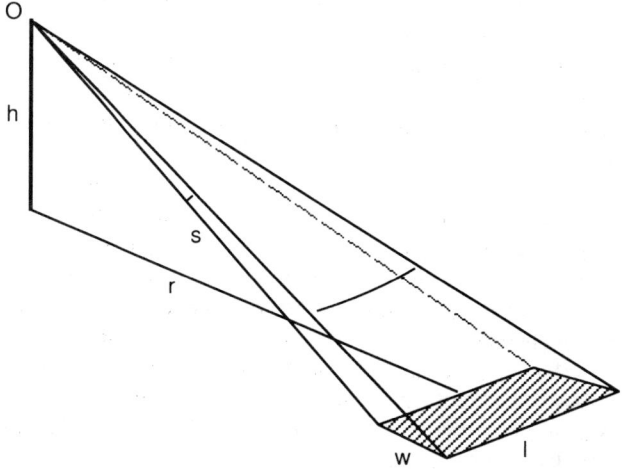

Figure 7. The ability of an observer (O) to see an object (shaded rectangle) on a distant surface is inversely proportional to the cube of the distance (s) because of the solid angle that the target occupies in the viewing field (after Koopman, 1980).

tance above the ground (h), but inversely proportional to the cube of the distance (s^3). Where h is very much smaller than r, s and r are nearly equal, so that we can say that this probability is approximately inversely proportional to the cube of the range.

For geophysical methods, such as magnetic and electromagnetic survey, a similar inverse-cube relationship may apply, although for different reasons, while in others attenuation with distance may be slightly better or much worse. Doubling the distance between a proton magnetometer's detector and the target, for example, may decrease the size of a magnetic anomaly by a factor of about eight. In most situations, that will make the target much more difficult to detect. For resistivity survey, the maximum effective depth of detection is a function of inter-electrode spacing. The usual rule of thumb is that this depth is roughly 1.5 times the distance between electrodes. Although in most resistivity surveys the resolution of survey and inter-electrode distance are identical, this does not have to be the case. For example, a Wenner array of electrodes spaced one meter apart can be moved in half-meter steps to get a higher resolution, while still detecting to depths of 1.5 m.

1.5 Geometry of Sites or Artifact Clusters

Many attempts to estimate the probability of site detection under various circumstances make the simplifying assumption that sites or other targets of archaeological survey are circular (e.g., Krakker et al., 1983:470). In fact, both the size and the shape of sites have a substantial impact on the probability of their discovery (Shott, 1989).

Archeologists have long recognized that the probability that a survey will intersect a site is directly proportional to site size.

What surveyors recognize less often, however, is that the shapes of sites are quite important. Simply put, a long, narrow site is more likely to be intersected by some kinds of survey, and especially by transects, than a circular site of the same size. If there are differences in typical site shapes over time, furthermore, this will affect your estimates of site abundances by period, and thus of changes in settlement intensity.

Where previous experience has shown that elongated elliptical sites, rather than near-circular ones, should be common — for example, settlements may be strung out along watercourses — it may be worthwhile to model this situation in the design of a survey. Clearly, the best strategy for optimizing discovery in such cases is for continuous transects to be perpendicular to the most probable axis of elongated sites. For discontinuous observations, such as test pits, things are more complicated (see chapter 4), especially if there are advantages to intersecting the site more than once. Estimates of site density and similar parameters, meanwhile, will be biased unless the survey design takes the site shape factor into account.

The shape of artifact clusters can even affect some kinds of "non-site" survey. Failure to consider the possibility of elongated clusters could lead to inaccurate evaluation of the scale of clustering or artifact density, particularly if there is an unlucky interaction of this effect with the size or shape of sample units.

1.6 Intensity or Density of Effort

Intensity is the term that archaeologists have used to refer to the density of effort that went into searching a given space. It can be measured in the number of person-hours of inspection per hectare, the total area of test pits per hectare, or by the number of auger holes per hectare, for example. The more observations per area, or the smaller the spacing between transects, the greater the thoroughness, or intensity, of the survey. Intensity is positively correlated with both cost and, for a given crew size, search time. Operations Research typically describes intensity as *density of search effort* (Koopman, 1980:140-142).

Search time obviously has a relationship with the probability of detecting a target, and one way to measure intensity of effort is in the total amount of search time devoted per unit area, as in person-hours per hectare. What is not as obvious, however, is that for visual surface survey the relationship between search time and detection probability is not linear, but exponential (Koopman, 1980:55, 71-74, 329). In many instances, the search time, t, and probability of detection, $p(t)$, in that time, conform to the law of random search,

$$p(t) = 1 - e^{-kt}$$

where k is a factor that combines the effects of contrast, target size, search area, visibility, and other factors (see under 1.4, Distance). What this means is that, holding other factors constant, increasing the search time of a single observer will increase the probability of detection, but with diminishing returns (figure 8). Only experiments in particular field conditions will allow estimate of k, and thus to determine how much time

Discovery of Archaeological Materials 61

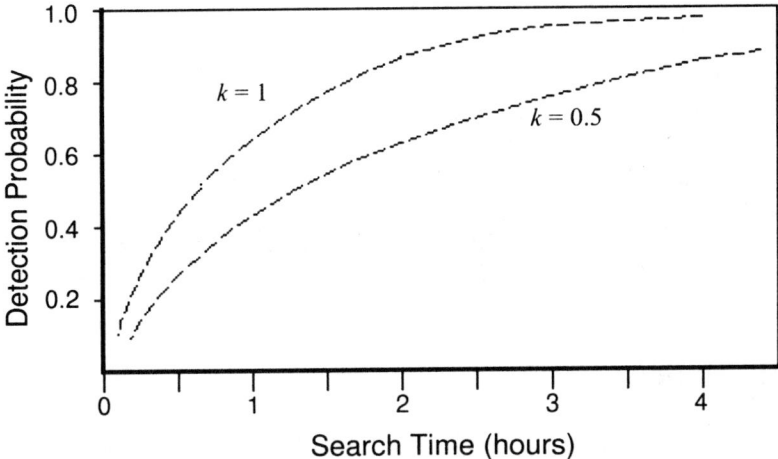

Figure 8. Diminishing returns of increasing search time, under different conditions (k) (after Koopman 1980).

each crew member should devote to searching each quadrat, transect or other search unit. The results of these experiments would then allow good estimates of survey intensity in person-hours per unit area.

In surveys that use a sampling frame of quadrats or other geometrical spaces, it is easy to estimate intensity simply by dividing the number of spatial elements or data units that were examined by the total number of such units in the whole sampling frame (see chapter 4 and 6). This spatial version of the density of effort is the one most commonly found in Operations Research. However, it is important to account for edge effects (chapter 5) that can cause the actual area within which sites are detectable to be greater or less than the areas of the survey elements. Some archaeologists describe intensity measured in this way as "coverage," as in "total coverage surveys." In section 1.8, I will attempt to avoid the confusion this may cause by employing an older definition of coverage.

Because measurement of intensity in this way is a proportion, we can also consider it a probability. In a site-oriented survey designed to have 20% intensity, ideally the probability that any individual site in the survey area will be detected would be 0.20. If this were actually the case, we could then estimate the number of sites in the whole region, a useful population parameter, simply by multiplying the number of sites we found by five. In reality, this is only one of the probabilities that would contribute to the overall probability of discovering a target; one would have to multiply this 0.20 by the probability of intercepting targets within the surveyed units and by the probability of correctly identifying the targets intercepted.

For informal surveys that do not employ a regular sampling frame, it is only possible to estimate intensity by estimating the area covered and dividing by the survey region's total area (see chapter 10).

It is much easier to estimate the intensity of surveys that employed formal sampling frames, but the important point is that these estimates are not exactly equivalent to the probabilities of site detection because they never recover all of the archaeological information in the area covered.

Deciding on an appropriate intensity of survey effort is very important, particularly as it has such a direct impact on the cost of survey. Chapters 5 and 6 include guidance on the optimal allocation of search effort for stratified samples and purposive survey. Chapter 10 will discuss intensity's role in the evaluation of completed surveys.

Although some archaeologists indicate intensity by the spacing of observations, typically over a regular, systematic grid of some kind, I prefer to describe this as "resolution."

1.7 Resolution

Most of us are already familiar with the concept of resolution as it applies to television screens, computer monitors, and laser printers. In those cases, typical measures are the number of pixels per inch across the horizontal, the number of pixels in each of the x- and y-axes across the screen, or "dots per inch." In effect, these are measures of the density of data points.

When designing an archaeological survey, archaeologists must decide the spacing and arrangement of data points. In many, but not all, cases, they employ a survey design based on a regular grid of such points, a design called "systematic survey." This is particularly common in surveys that employ geophysical remote sensing techniques, such as resistivity survey or magnetic survey, but it is also a common arrangement for visual inspection of the surface, augering and shovel-testing. Clearly, a closely-spaced net of such data points will result in a more thorough survey, and be more likely to detect small clusters of cultural remains, than a much more dispersed one, but only at considerably greater cost in time and energy. Selecting an appropriate resolution, then, is not a trivial decision, and the subject of arbitrary 30m intervals in some state assessment regulations has generated considerable discussion among the practitioners of Cultural Resource Management in the United States.

Particularly when searching for small clusters of material culture, such as small campsites, it is better to search with high resolution, with many observations per unit area. However, the costs of greater resolution increase exponentially. For example, to dig a small test pit every 10 m along transects spaced 10 m apart, rather than one every 30 m along transects 30 m apart increases the number of test pits by a factor of nine. Thus, it takes about nine times as long or requires nine times as much personnel to accomplish. Budgetary constraints might well make such resolution impossible. However, the cruder resolution makes it less likely that the survey will find any kind of archaeological remains, and not just small scatters. We will return to this problem in chapter 5.

Deciding on the appropriate resolution involves an interplay between the cost of data collection (principally in time and labor in the field), the probable size and density of archaeological entities (e.g., sites), their degree and scale of clustering, the size of the

Discovery of Archaeological Materials 63

area to be surveyed, and the probability that a data point that intersects an archaeological entity will be recognized as such. This last point is related to obtrusiveness. For example, as mentioned in Section 1.3, even if a meter-square test pit were to intersect a site with a mean artifact density of 10 artifacts per square meter, the probability that the test pit has less than five artifacts is 0.05. The probability of getting less than two artifacts is 0.0005. That means that one time in twenty, a test pit that intersects the site might not yield enough artifacts for us to realize that a site is present. For an auger hole with an area substantially smaller than a square meter, or for sites with lower artifact densities, the probability of failing to recognize the site is much higher. The same problem applies when we are talking about mean chemical signatures or mean magnetic susceptibilities.

Operations Research considers resolution in terms of the "spacing" of transects or (in petroleum exploration) bore-holes. We will return to the issue of resolution while considering coverage in section 1.9 and scale issues in chapter 5.

1.8 Coverage

Like intensity, resolution, and method of inspection, coverage is one of the factors under the control of archaeologists, and concerns how much area we subject to survey.

Typically, archaeologists have considered coverage to be equivalent to *sampling fraction* (see chapter 6), or the proportion of the target elements (defined as quadrats, sites, visible features, or surface artifacts) that the survey detected and recorded. For example, many archaeologists assume that if they walked over 20% of a region with reasonably high resolution, they will have detected 20% of the sites, and have 20% coverage.

However, this traditional, archaeological definition of coverage differs little or not at all from density of effort (section 1.6). The following instead employs the meaning of coverage used in Operations Research. There a survey's coverage is "the extent of target positions exposed to its detection" (Koopman, 1980:19). It is not a percentage or probability, but the total area in which we could expect to detect targets, and only the first step in calculating density of effort. One sums the areas of all the surveyed units (accounting for edge effects) to arrive at coverage, and then divides coverage by the total area of the survey universe to arrive at density of effort. Because of edge effects, however, coverage for small or unobtrusive targets will be lower than for large or obtrusive ones.

1.9 Accessibility

One should not overlook the possibility that some parts of a survey area may simply be inaccessible. Landowners may refuse permission to walk across their fields or may simply not be at home, prisons, border zones or military bases may be off-limits, and toxic waste facilities may be too hazardous. Even dense undergrowth, thistles or dense forest can make some kinds of survey virtually impossible, either by making crew too uncomfortable or by interfering with the layout of a grid. In intertidal survey, the areas to be surveyed are only accessible intermittently, during low tides, and then only for a few hours at a time. Limits on accessibility can be particularly problematic for statistical surveys and "total" surveys intended to reveal some aspect of spatial structure.

Inaccessibility would not be such a serious problem if it were at least independent of the archaeological resources that interest us. However, there is often a strong relationship between inaccessible land and places that contain important archaeological materials. Military bases are often built at strategic locations that were also strategic in the past. In fact, they often include historic forts. In the Middle East, important archaeological sites are often large mounds, called tells, which in otherwise flat terrain are likely locations for military communications towers, radar dishes and missile launchers. Landowners are sometimes fully aware of archaeological materials on their land, and sometimes are concerned that archaeologists will prevent them from developing the land, or even that the land will be expropriated. In that event, their cooperation with archaeologists who want to survey the land is unlikely. Furthermore, the nutrient-rich sediments and stony impediments to plowing that often occur on archaeological sites can encourage the growth of dense stands of thorny vegetation.

Archaeology is not unique in having this problem, however, and social scientists have found some ways to deal with it. For example, pollsters making telephone surveys must account for people who are not at home or decline to be interviewed, a problem they call, "non-response." Most of the time they try to alleviate this problem by calling back or provide incentives for people to cooperate, or the bias that results is small enough to be tolerable. Sometimes, however, the non-response rate leads to such large bias that the results are ruined (Deming, 1950:33-36). Some statisticians would recommend replacing the non-responding elements of the sample with a judgment sample, carefully selected in the hope of representing the kinds of elements that tend not to respond. An archaeological analogy might be replacing a hilltop that we could not sample because an army outpost occupied it with another similar hilltop that has no military presence. It would be best not to do this too often, however, and to evaluate the reliability of the samples that result as though they are judgment samples.

In archaeological survey, it is sometimes possible to avoid the most obvious problems of inaccessibility through careful definition of the sampled population or the survey boundaries. In cases where the goal is to estimate population parameters and there is no *a priori* reason to suspect that excluding an inaccessible region, such as a military base, would have any effect on the accuracy of those estimates, the simplest solution is to define the sampling frame in such a way as to avoid it. Of course, this is only an option when it is possible to know in advance where inaccessible places are, a rather rare occurrence.

In other instances, surveyors only discover that a particular space they intended to survey is inaccessible when an uncooperative landowner, a soldier on guard duty, or a hostile dog bars access. In these cases, the simplest solution is to have a data-recording category for inaccessible survey units. The record should include any suspicion surveyors may have that exclusion of those units might create bias in parameter estimates or omit sites from a settlement lattice or site hierarchy. In that case, they might also attempt to substitute survey of the nearest accessible space or the nearest place with comparable

Discovery of Archaeological Materials   65

topography. Because of spatial autocorrelation, the adjacent space might give results closely similar to those that would have obtained in the inaccessible unit, or allow observations, such as the presence of a low-density scatter extending away from it, that provides hints about the area surveyors were unable to view directly.

In regions where older archaeological research has preceded a new survey, or there are historical records, old photographs, or travel itineraries, it is sometimes possible to make fairly reliable inferences about archaeological remains in inaccessible spaces. In a survey I once conducted, for example, I was fortunate that a fairly important archaeological site to which a military officer politely refused access had already been documented, albeit in a cursory manner, in the 1940s. Although the published record of this site was not as detailed as I would have liked, it saved me from omitting from analysis a site that was probably fairly high in an Iron Age settlement hierarchy. Topographic maps and my observations around the forbidden base, furthermore, gave me a fairly good idea of the site's size and environmental characteristics.

In intertidal survey, accessibility is limited temporally. This is less problematic than in some of the cases mentioned above, but does require a lot of planning. Surveyors need to time surveys for periods when low tides are as low and prlonged as possible, but ideally also when they correspond with long periods of daylight. To make such surveys cost-effective, it is also useful to plan lab work or terrestrial survey to occupy the lengthy periods between low tides (Tyson et al., 1997:84). In addition, areas of the foreshore nearest the low tide level are accessible for the shortest periods of time, while the upper foreshore is available for study much longer.

Another increasingly important influence on accessibility is the designation of wildlife areas. In some of these areas, survey will not be allowed during the breeding seasons of protected species or other times when disturbance is undesirable (e.g., Allen et al., 1993:1).

1.10 Crew Training, Experience, and Motivation

As much as archaeologists like to assume that their survey methods are "objective," the composition of survey teams and even their members' moods can affect the likelihood that they will detect archaeological remains and the measurement of the attributes of those remains. There are ways to ensure that this variation does not render survey results meaningless, however.

This source of variation may be most noticeable in surveys by visual inspection of the surface, when each member of the team is expected to spot scatters or individual artifacts on the ground. Different people tend to see things rather differently. Some people have a sharp eye for lithics but tend to miss pottery. Others may tend to overlook lithics but have an amazing ability to spot small objects, such as beads or coins. But variation between teams and team members can occur in other field methodologies as well.

1.10.1 Training and Briefing Team Members

We should not expect any team member to carry out survey properly without adequate instruction and background. For survey by visual inspection or test pits, for example, all team members should be familiar with the kinds of materials they might conceivably encounter, such as lithics, pottery, glass, beads, tile, brick, corroded coins or nails, and fragmentary animal bone. They should be competent in the survey's methods, including remote sensing methods where those are used, and there should be some attempt to ensure consistency in the way those methods are carried out. For example, training crew to scan the surface the same way and at the same speed, or to insert the electrodes for resistivity survey to the same depth, will help ensure more consistent results. Crew should also be briefed on the topography, geology and major landmarks of the area they will survey each day, have compass and map or GPS, and know how to use them. Many authors have noted that detailed familiarity with a region has a substantial effect on a surveyor's ability to notice subtle features, such as a low mound or a shallow depression, that could be cultural in origin. Briefing of crew members should include expectations about visibility, possible site characteristics, safety precautions, and how to deal with bad weather.

1.10.2 Team Composition

Survey teams should always have a minimum of two members, and it is helpful to arrange teams so that their members complement one anothers' strengths and weaknesses. For pedestrian survey with visual inspection, the team might include people with backgrounds in lithics, pottery, and geomorphology, for example. It should also include at least one member with considerable experience in the research area or the project. In some surveys, it may be necessary to ensure that at least one member of each team speaks a local language, so as to be able to explain their presence to landowners or soldiers. In many countries, the conditions of an archaeological permit may also specify that each team include a member from a governmental agency, such as a national department of antiquities.

1.10.3 Team Motivation

Clearly, the survey team's morale and motivation can have a significant impact on the survey's results. A happy crew of well-rested people who are excited about the work will be more dedicated, more thorough and more productive than a team of underfed, tired, unpaid, and poorly briefed people who have little or no stake in the survey's results. To keep team morale up, make sure that the survey is well organized, that people know what is going on, that everyone is properly clothed for bad weather, that there is sufficient "down-time," and that food and housing are as comfortable as circumstances will allow.

Discovery of Archaeological Materials

1.10.4 Accounting for Variability

Although we must accept that individuals and teams will differ in their perceptions of the archaeological evidence, so that two teams visiting the same site or field could record rather different artifact densities or site sizes, for example, that does not mean we cannot rely on the data they collect. We can account for this problem through checks on measurement error and data quality (see chapter 10).

1.11 Data Units

The influences on site detection over which we have most control are the size, shape and distribution of the grids or observation units we use to organize our search for and documentation of archaeological materials. Surveys can be designed to ensure detailed, high-resolution examination of circular areas, square quadrats or long transects, or the basic unit of investigation could be sites or potential sites identified in aerial photographs, for example. Decisions about what data units to use have a significant impact on the probability of detection, and thus also on the accuracy of estimates and success at detecting spatial patterns. When sites are the basic survey units, for example, large sites, other things being equal, have much greater likelihood of being detected than small ones (see chapters 4 and 5).

1.12 False Targets

Most of the factors discussed to this point, if a survey design does not deal with them adequately, can lead to failure to detect archaeological materials. Sometimes, however, the problem with a survey is that it seems to detect something of interest when, in fact, it is not there. A "false target" is any object that could be mistaken for the target, or object of interest.

Many detection methods are sensitive to the problem of false targets. Even visual discrimination of artifacts from non-artifacts on the surface is imperfect, but in archaeology the problem of false targets is of greatest concern in surveys that employ geophysical remote sensing. For example, the signals from natural geological features, modern metal trash, or buried pipes or cables may be difficult to distinguish from archaeological features in magnetic or electromagnetic surveys.

In surveys where false targets can be a problem, survey designs may employ two stages. The first involves detection of a signal, or "contact," but its detector is unable to tell whether the contact comes from a target or a false target. This stage is called a "broad search." The second stage, or "contact investigation," involves use of methods that allow discrimination of the target from false targets, but that may not be practical for use in a broad search. In many instances, broad search can continue as contacts are marked for later investigation; in others, contact investigation is immediate. Planning a survey so that contact investigation continues until targets are distinguishable from non-targets with certainty — identification and not only detection — is called a "conclusive contact investigation policy" (Stone, 1989:136-139).

Surveying for artifact clusters by subsurface testing (SST) provides an example of the need to deal with false targets. Most discussions of the problems with this type of survey have focussed on the problem of failing to detect a "site" even when cores or augers intersect it because artifacts are unlikely to occur in such small sample volumes. It is perhaps less obvious that the presence of an artifact in a single core or auger sample does not guarantee that it has intersected a site, unless the survey uses a very minimal definition of "site" (one artifact). One way to deal with this problem is to follow an initial broad search with a large sampling interval with a contact investigation that places additional cores, shovel tests, or auger holes with smaller intervals in the vicinity of the initial contact. Discovery of more artifacts in at least some of these additional samples would confirm the presence of a site or artifact cluster. In fact, as long as the additional sediment volumes can be treated as samples representative of the cluster, they can be used to estimate the spatial density of artifacts in it. Another, usually more expensive, means of contact investigation is excavation in the vicinity of the initial contact.

In some instances, it is reasonable to assume that false targets will be distributed randomly and independently, and therefore to model them with a Poisson distribution with the single parameter, "false-target density" (Stone, 1989:140-145). In other cases, false targets may have patterned or clustered distributions. In those cases, sometimes detection and identification of one false target provides information that can make it easier to anticipate and distinguish later false targets. For example, buried cables and some geological outcrops have linear distributions. Adaptive survey plans make use of this kind of information.

A key consideration when surveyors can expect false targets is the amount of time it will take to investigate them. Obviously this could lead to substantial cost increase in some instances, but it is possible to estimate this cost as long as we can estimate the expected number of false targets (Stone, 1989:141).

2. ESTIMATING DISCOVERY PROBABILITIES

As noted above, intensity and intersection probability are poor measures of the probability that a survey will discover various kinds of sites. To get a more realistic estimate of this probability, surveyors must attempt to account simultaneously for the factors that affect site discovery. The following represents one possible approach that can be used when sites are the units of interest, and survey employed transects, clusters of transects, or a regular grid of observations (see chapter 4).

For surveys that employ shovel-testing, test excavations, augering, divoting or chemical sampling, as long as the sample is systematic and we know the sampling interval, the shape of the array, and the size of the observation unit, it is easy to estimate the probability that any given array of points (auger holes, for example) will intersect a target of given size (figure 9). For square grids and circular sites with diameters less than the interval, this intersection probability is

$$p(i) = \frac{\pi r^2}{i^2}$$

Discovery of Archaeological Materials 69

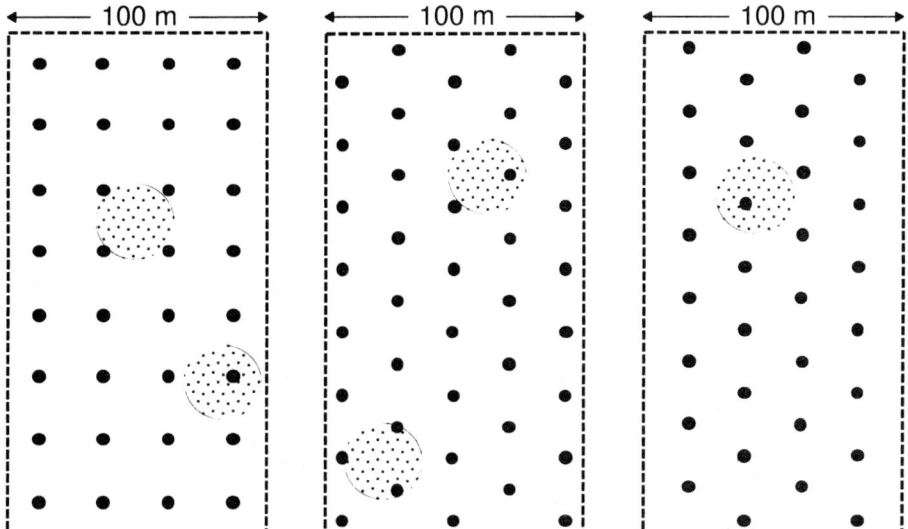

Figure 9. The probability that points on square (left), "offset" or isoceles (center), or equilateral triangular grids will intersect a circular target is a simple function of the target's size (radius) and the distance between the points (i).

where *p(i)* is the probability of intersection, r is the site radius and i is the interval between tests (Shott, 1985:461). Similarly, for small elliptical targets and any systematic arrangement of points, the probability of intersection is simply the ellipse area divided by the area enclosed by the nearest four points in the grid. The probability of any single point intersecting an ellipse is given in chapter 4, section 3.1.1.

The more difficult problem is that the probability that any auger hole or test pit intersecting a site will actually detect that site is less than 1.0. This is the problem of obtrusiveness (Section 1.3), and the estimated probability of detection depends on the model we use for the distribution of artifacts on the site. By combining the probability of intersecting a site with the probability of detecting and recognizing site constituents, it is possible to construct a graph that shows how the probability of site discovery varies with site size (Kintigh, 1988; Krakker et al., 1983; Nance, 1979; 1983). To simplify, most archaeologists have made the assumption that sites are circular, although research in petroleum exploration allows us to estimate the probabilities of discovering elliptical sites as well (e.g., Savinskii, 1965; Singer, 1975; see also chapter 5).

A similar approach is applicable to surface survey by visual inspection. Some of the factors affecting the probility of discovering sites, particularly site size and obtrusiveness, can be summarized by a single statistic, the range or *discovery radius, R*. This is the estimated distance at which we would expect a particular site to become detectable (see the *definite range law* in section 1.4, above). Some kinds of site, such as low-density artifact scatters, are usually not detectable by visual inspection until we actually walk on them. In these cases, the estimated discovery radius is half the diameter of the site (assuming circular sites), and it is exactly the same as the radius for intersection by sub-surface testing (above). Large sites with low obrusiveness have higher probabilities of detection than small ones, simply because it is more likely that one or more transects will intersect them. More obtrusive sites, such as those with traces of architecture at the surface, however, differ from the case of subsurface testing. Even a small, obtrusive site might be visible at a distance of 100 m, unless trees, for example, reduce visibility. For these obtrusive sites in areas of good visibility, the discovery radius would then be half the site's diameter plus 100 m. Although this approach is exactly analogous to the use of intersection probabilities for subsurface testing, in these cases, a transect does not need to intersect the site itself for the site to be detected. The transect only needs to intersect the circle represented by the site's discovery radius, or the *discovery region* of the site. Consequently, small, obtrusive sites can have as much probability of being detected as large, unobtrusive sites because their discovery radii are similar (Banning, 1985; 1988). Although it is often convenient to assume that discovery regions are circular (and indeed in many cases they are), it is also possible to have elliptical and even irregular discovery regions. For example, in hilly terrain, it may be possible to see a site from a long distance from a vantage point on a hilltop, even though the site may not become detectable from a valley floor until it comes within quite a short range. Today viewshed analysis in GIS makes such modelling a more realistic possibility.

Although it is convenient to define the discovery radius as defined by the definite range law (figure 6), for visual survey of the surface it may instead be governed approximately by the inverse-cube law (see above, section 1.4). It can also be shown that it is proportional to the angle that the target occupies in the visual field (figure 7). Consequently large objects that are close or are viewed from a roughly perpendicular direction (i.e., from above) are easier to see than the same objects far away or viewed obliquely (see Koopman, 1980:58-59). In that case, rather than assuming that a target will be detected as long as it is within range R, we might instead try to determine the range within which some high percentage of targets, say 90%, will be detectable.

For any survey design that employs transects, or some other geometrical sampling frame, as with the subsurface tests, it is easy to calculate the relationship between discovery radius and probability of site detection as long as we know the survey spacing, or resolution. If the distance between transects is not constant, as happens in subsampling when transects are bundled into quadrats, for example, the slope of this function will change at least once. For example, in the Wadi al-Hasa Survey (figure 10), the slope changes because bundles of transects 30 m apart were separated by 200 m and sets of four such bundles occurred as sub-samples in each of a sample of 1 km^2 quadrats (Banning, 1988).

One problem with this approach is that it only estimates the detection probabilities for sites with visibilities greater than zero. If the detection method is restricted to visual inspection of the surface, buried sites, for example, will have detection probabilities of 0, but will not be included in the graph. Consequently, even these estimates of discovery probability will be biased if there are sites of very low visibility, perhaps to the extent that a different detection technique, such as augering, may be necessary. The resulting estimates are at least more conservative than assuming uncritically that spatial intensity is equivalent to discovery probability.

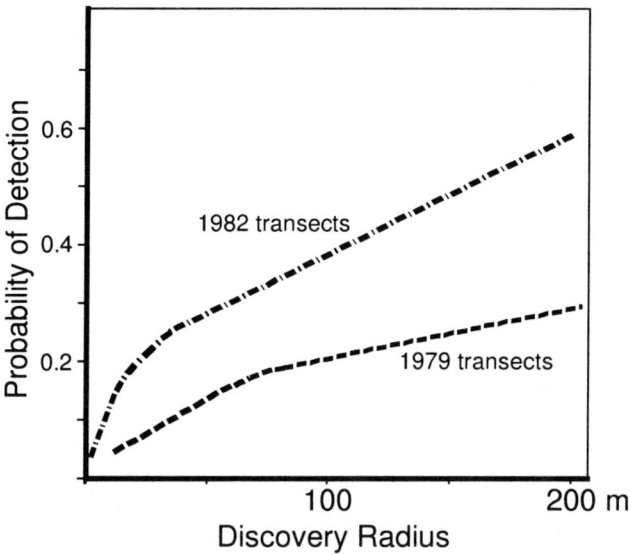

Figure 10. Relationship between sites' discovery radius and their probability of detection on the Wadi al-Hasa survey, Jordan, during 1979 and 1982 (after Banning, 1988:22-23).

As Krakker et al. (1983:479) note, the overall probability of detecting a site is the product of the probability of intersection, the conditional probability of encountering artifacts given intersection, and the conditional probability of recognizing the artifacts given that they occur. In fact, more generally, we can combine the probabilities of intersecting archaeological materials with estimates of the probabilities for any of the factors that affect detection of those materials once intersected. For example, the resolution and intensity of a surface survey might lead to a probablity of 0.15 that transects will intersect a particular type of site, but previous experience in the region might suggest that approximately 60% of such sites are buried under colluvium, so that they have 0 visibility by visual inspection of the surface. The probability of a site being visible on these landforms is therefore 0.4, and the combined probabilities of intersecting and detecting a site there are 0.15 * 0.40 = 0.06. Alternatively, in a survey by augering designed so that the probability that one auger will intersect a particular size of site is 0.6, while the probability that an auger-hole intersecting a site will contain at least one artifact is 0.6, and the probability that a crew member will detect this artifact is 0.9, then the probability that the survey will actually find the site is 0.6 * 0.6 * 0.9, or only about 0.32. Note that the probability of noticing artifacts might vary from crew member to crew member or among different kinds of artifact.

What is perhaps less obvious is that combining these probabilities has a substantial impact on the error of any measurements based on the survey results. As Shennan (1997:391-393) points out, not only do detectabilities less than 1.0 lead to larger variances on the estimates of population parameters, such as the density of a particular kind of site or artifact, but the detectability estimates also have errors. Because the variances are cumulative, taking detectability into account makes a big difference to any estimate of the measurement's precision. This is true whether we explicitly estimate detectability and errors or not, so it pays to take this effect seriously.

Estimating detection probabilities is not only important at the planning stage, but also in the post-fieldwork evaluation of archaeological surveys (see chapter 10).

3. POST-DEPOSITIONAL FACTORS THAT AFFECT SPATIAL PATTERN

Whether or not varying densities of surface artifacts are the basis either for identifying "sites" or for reconstructing and interpreting past use of landscapes, research designs should consider the post-depositional effects on the spatial structure of sites and artifact scatters, and not only the human behaviors that may originally have deposited them. These are simply a subset of site-formation processes (see Schiffer, 1987).

Although most researchers who have considered this problem have focussed on the post-depositional distortion of patterns formed during the deposit of archaeological materials, it is important to consider ways that transformation, transport, and destruction of deposits can also *create* patterns (Foley, 1981:162-63; Taylor, 1973). Recent land use and other factors that affect visibility, for example, can actually create false patterns: "the same underlying real pattern of sites can generate an infinite number of apparent ones, depending on the visibility encountered at the time of the survey" (Terrenato, 2000:66).

In parts of the southern Levant, for example, erosion has removed sediment from hilltops, often concentrating artifacts and exposing architectural remains or previously buried surfaces there. Meanwhile, downslope sediment transport has often buried archaeological materials downslope, or carried artifacts from above. As a result, there is a tendency for archaeologists' maps of settlement pattern to show a strong association between sites and hilltops, with empty space on valley floors and perhaps some sites near the foot of slopes. In addition, the interaction between this effect and real differences in settlement pattern over time can make sites of some periods seem much rarer than they actually are, or make them appear clustered in areas where in fact they were no more common than in other areas that simply have lower preservation or visibility (Banning, 1996).

Furthermore, many kinds of physical landscapes, such as dissected valleys and coasts, have changed quite radically over the centuries, often preserving only small remnants of surfaces belonging to some periods, or none at all. If we do not take these landscape changes into account, the patterns in the distributions of sites will reflect only the pattern of landscape attrition and burial, rather than the structure of ancient settlement.

Many site-formation processes have important effects on survey results. The following is only a sample, and readers should consult Schiffer (1987) for further details.

Discovery of Archaeological Materials

3.1 Artifact Displacement or Sorting by Erosion

The shape of artifacts has a significant impact on their probability of being carried downslope by erosion. Allen (1991) describes an experiment in which equal numbers of natural flints, and struck flint flakes and blades were scattered in a strip on an 11° slope, 10m above a trap. After just two small rainstorms, 87% of the flints that were found in the trap were thin and flat, and 94% of these were blades. After four years, more than 60 flints had moved into a second trap 50 m downslope, and 80% of these were struck flakes and blades. Water flow can also carry artifacts and concentrate them into "sites" with varying degrees of integrity (Petraglia and Potts, 1994).

One of the more extreme cases of artifact displacement may be on coasts, where wave action can eat into coastal sites and leave their artifacts scattered in the intertidal zone.

3.2 Artifact Removal by Erosion

High-energy erosion has the ability to remove some kinds of artifacts completely from an original concentration. Again, artifact shape is significant in influencing which artifacts the erosion is most likely to remove.

3.3 Artifact Displacement or Removal by Bioturbation

Bioturbation can have both positive and negative impacts on survey. On the one hand, burrowing animals can bring buried material up to the surface, thus increasing visibility. On the other, earthworms and other organisms can cause certain artifacts to settle deeper in the soil profile, or may bury them with earth and leafmould (Darwin, 1882). Blackham (2000) has shown that Middle Eastern mole rats, for example, can move a tremendous volume of artifacts, including sherds of considerable size.

3.4 Artifact Removal by Chemical or Mechanical Destruction

Destruction of many site constituents, such as bone and even (poorly fired) pottery, can be due to trampling, wet-dry cycling, salt damage, pH of sediments, and other factors (see section 1.3.3).

3.5 Artifact Displacement by Plowing

Archaeologists have conducted considerable research on the effects of plowing on surface and plowzone distributions of artifacts (Dunnell, 1988; Roper, 1976; Schofield, 1989; 1991; Yorston, et al., 1990). Although the effect is real, fortunately this displacement appears to be a smaller effect than many archaeologists once feared.

4. SUMMARY

As the foregoing demonstrates, the probability that any kind of survey will successfully detect archaeological materials or distinguish cultural from natural clusters of them depends on numerous factors. Some of these are inherent in the archaeological materials, or constituents, that are the survey's targets and the extent to which the constituents' physical characteristics contrast with those of their environments. These contribute to the *obtrusiveness* of the archaeological materials. Others are environmental factors that tend to obscure various signals from the cultural remains of interest. These have to do with *visibility*. In both cases, it pays to research the likely nature of archaeological materials and their environments in order to design effective surveys. Obtrusiveness and visibility jointly contribute to the *detectability* of those remains. Many other factors, fortunately, are under archaeologists' direct control. These include the techniques used for detecting archaeological materials, which surveyors should select so as to take advantage of the kinds of materials expected and the types of signals most likely to show contrast between cultural and non-cultural phenomena in the local environment. They also include the composition and training of survey crews, the boundaries of the survey area, the shape and kind of observation units, and the *resolution* and *intensity* of observations. Still others are generally outside our control, and are not always predictable, such as refusal of access. In addition, a variety of non-cultural processes can concentrate or selectively remove archaeological remains in ways that mimic archaeological "sites."

Survey design involves a careful interplay of all these factors. The following chapters will focus on some of the important factors over which we have most control.

Chapter IV
Units, Sampling Frames, and Edge Effects in Archaeological Survey

It is possible to survey a region with no more explicit attention to spatial units than to define the region's boundaries. For probability samples, however, it is necessary to partition the archaeological landscape into a set of units of which the sample will be a subset. Other kinds of survey also usually employ some standardized spatial unit of observation and analysis. This chapter will explore archaeologists' grounds for defining and arranging these partitions in particular ways, some of the effects of employing those definitions, and ways to optimize their arrangement in space. Generally the characteristics we must consider involve the shape, size, edges, spacing, and arrangement of units. Because surveys are costly, it makes sense to take advantage of these effects to make more efficient surveys that give us the best results at a particular cost, or that minimize cost for a particular result.

1. THE SPATIAL DISTRIBUTION OF MATERIAL CULTURE

Ideally, procedures for partitioning the archaeological landscape should be sensitive to how material culture is distributed on it (see chapter 1, section 3.1).

Archaeologists have most often conceived of archaeological distributions as sets of discrete sites, which could in principle be the basic units of analysis at the regional scale. Although their definitions of these sites vary, generally they think of them as clusters of former human habitation and activity, the analogues of campsites, villages, towns, quarries, industrial complexes and so on. In practice, sites are often defined by anomalous densities of artifacts encountered during survey. Some surveys instead set an absolute threshold of artifact density, defining a site, for example, as any location where the local density of artifacts on the surface is at least five artifacts per square meter. Others have defined sites on the basis of as little evidence as two co-occurring artifacts in a survey unit.

As some authors have pointed out, however, the density of cultural items varies in a nearly continuous way over space, and even fairly high densities of artifacts sometimes arise through cultural and natural agencies that transport them considerable distances from settlements and other places where they were originally deposited. Erosion, fluvial transport, and use of archaeological sediments as fertilizer in modern agriculture can all distribute artifacts across the landscape. Furthermore, human activities are not restricted to discrete spaces such as settlements, and prolonged human use of a landscape can result in considerable accumulation of artifacts casually dropped during dispersed activities. One way to model this last process is with the Poisson distribution, which describes the random distribution of discrete, countable items (such as artifacts) in units of space or time (see chapter 3). These factors have led some archaeologists to conceive of the archaeological landscape as more continuous, with clusters of higher density (departures from the Poisson model) that could result from more intense or more persistent activity in those areas, as well as spaces with low densities representing less intense or more sporadic activity. Some authors refer to surveys based on this model as "non-site survey" or "siteless survey" (Dunnell and Dancey, 1983; Thomas, 1975; Wilkinson, 1982; 1989;Williams, et al., 1973).

Although the distribution of material culture in a region may seem nearly continuous, recording and analysis usually require that we impose a system for partitioning this continuum into units. Where the units are equal in size, this facilitates measurement of densities (the number of observations per unit) and survey resolution. Although many projects claim to use the artifact as the basic unit of survey and analysis, most of these actually use some spatial unit, such as a quadrat, as a survey unit, and measure or count the number of items found in each. Section 3 will deal with these kinds of spatial partitions within the boundaries of survey regions.

2. BOUNDARIES OF THE SURVEY AREA

Most explicit survey designs begin with defining the boundaries of the region to be explored. This is not strictly necessary in a simple prospection for sites. In that case, one could even survey outward from a given point until finding the target of interest, rather than arbitrarily restricting the search area. All surveys that employ sampling theory, however, require definition of the population to be sampled (see chapter 5), and so usually require well-defined boundaries. In addition, agencies that grant archaeological permits or the clients in Cultural Resource Management may require formal boundaries or impose particular boundaries. Inaccessibility of some spaces for lack of landowners' cooperation or because of military security can also force surveyors to bound their search area in particular ways.

The selection of useful, rather than completely arbitrary, boundaries can be difficult, especially for survey projects with wide-ranging goals. For probability surveys, the ideal would be a population, and therefore a survey area, that was culturally meaningful. But the portion of space that enclosed the territory of an Archaic band would probably be quite different than the territory of a Late Woodland village in the same region. Designing a survey to draw meaningful conclusions about both the Archaic band and the Woodland village would consequently be complicated even if there were some way of knowing what those territories were likely to be.

In fact, archaeologists almost never know such boundaries in advance. Only for periods with historical documentation is it reasonably straightforward to estimate the position of culturally meaningful boundaries. Instead, archaeologists often settle for natural geographical boundaries of some type in the hope that these had at least some effect on past cultural boundaries. We can expect large rivers and high mountains, for example, to have influenced the rate of flow of people and information between communities on either side, and consequently these may make fairly reasonable survey boundaries for a variety of time frames. Many archaeologists have used the drainage basin of a small or medium-sized watercourse as their survey area, its boundaries defined by the watershed or by arbitrary lines that are close to it. In some cases, this may approximate the territory of small cultural groups whose settlements clustered along the stream or river. Rarely is it possible to assess how well such boundaries have worked until after the survey, as well as surveys in neighboring drainage basins, are complete. We must also be mindful that landscapes do change over the time scales that archaeologists use, so that rivers and other such boundaries existing today may not have existed, or have been in different locations, in Palaeolithic France, or in Archaic Pennsylvania.

Commonly, the boundaries of a survey area are at best an approximation of some natural geographical unit. That is because of the need, in some kinds of survey, for the survey area to consist of a set of equally-sized spatial units that are usually defined by partitioning the survey area with a grid.

2.1 Physical-Geographical Boundaries

The most common survey boundaries in archaeology, with the exception of those that clients impose in Cultural Resource Management, are ones conforming to natural geographical features, such as watersheds, rivers and cliffs.

The rationale for using such boundaries is that they may correspond, at least loosely, with the boundaries of some group's economic territory. No doubt the exceptions to this correspondence are numerous, but often there are few other options for determining reasonable boundaries prior to fieldwork. Some geographic features, such as high mountains, clearly are impediments to communication and, where military security may have been a factor, have strategic importance as well. River drainages, meanwhile, facilitate communication, so that it is not unreasonable to expect a cultural group to have taken advantage of the whole of a small drainage basin. Islands provide the least controversial boundaries of this type.

The principal problem with using a physical-geographical boundary is that it probably encloses only a portion of a group's territory. Hunter-gatherers and pastoral nomads may often have ranged well beyond individual drainage basins. In fact, their economies often depend on exploiting a range of physiographic regions in different seasons. State societies, too, will often have had much larger territories. Only small-scale sedentary communities are likely to have been limited to individual drainages or islands, and even then probably had extensive trade and communication networks. Furthermore, uncritical use of physical-geographical boundaries can sometimes lead to circular reasoning in the identification of spatial and seasonal patterning (Sampson, 1988:13).

2.2 Historical-Political Boundaries

In fortunate circumstances, historical evidence may be available with which to reconstruct meaningful cultural boundaries with some confidence.

For example, archaeologists interested in surveying the *ager* of the Roman colony of Cosa could take advantage of the fact that the boundaries of Cosa's territory were reasonably certain. A land survey of AD 1508-1510 made use of historical information from the medieval and Roman periods, providing historical continuity in the documentation of boundaries that we can rarely match (Cardarelli, 1924; 1925; Dyson, 1978). Consequently, their survey universe constituted a meaningful political entity that could contain a meaningful population of sites.

2.3 Estimated Political-Economic Boundaries

Rarely is history as cooperative as in the example from Cosa. In cases of surveys of state-level cultures, and where the locations of the largest settlements are already known, however, it may be possible to approximate the political boundaries between central places with Thiessen polygons or with polygons adjusted to physical-geographical features.

In ordinary Thiessen polygons, the boundaries are straight line segments that mark points of equal distance between the nearest two (or three at corners) central places. They are easy to determine, as they are simply perpendicular to a line that runs between any two neighboring places, and occur at the halfway point along this line (Hodder and Orton, 1978:59-60).

A variation that results in polygons that might be a little more realistic attempts to account for the possibility that large central places had larger territories than small ones. In this case, rather than always placing the boundaries at the halfway points between settlements, the distance to each is weighted by the sites' relative sizes (Hodder and Orton, 1976:78, 188-190).

A final variation is to begin with Thiessen polygons and then adjust them to geographical features. For example, if one boundary between two Thiessen polygon occurs very close to a river, there is a good chance that the actual boundary between them was at the river itself.

Occasionally, previous finds of coins or other artifact types that can be expected to circulate mainly within a political-economic boundary can provide evidence for the likely location of borders (Kimes et al., 1982).

2.4 Catchment Boundaries

Another possible approach to the problem of defining survey boundaries that have cultural relevance again requires knowledge of at least one settlement's location. In that case, the known settlement serves as the center of the survey universe. The settlement's catchment can then be defined by a three-hour walk, or some other time thought to approximate foraging or agricultural range, radiating in all directions from the center. The resulting survey universe will be a deformed circle that takes travel time to resources into account. It is even possible to design such a survey without defining the *spatial* boundaries of the catchment in advance, by instead sampling *in time* while walking transects that radiate from the central site. A simple but less satisfactory approach is to approximate the catchment as a circle with a radius assumed to approximate the settlement's foraging or agricultural range. Yet another approach that could be helpful in some instances is to depend on evidence of resources found at the central settlement, especially if it has been excavated (Flannery, 1976). If the sources of these materials are known or can reasonably be anticipated, they can be used to help define, or at least refine, the boundaries of the catchment for the purpose of survey.

2.5 Oversize Boundaries and Group Territories

One solution to the problem that meaningful hunter-gatherer territories are not known in advance is to postpone final boundary placement until after the survey. For example, Sampson (1985; 1988) makes the discovery of such boundaries one of the goals of his survey. To do this he begins with a survey universe that is much larger than the expected annual range, or even lifetime range, of any of the bands he expects to occur in the Upper Seacow valley and, in fact, uses the valley's watershed to delineate most of his initial boundaries. There is good reason to expect these boundaries to contain several bands' annual ranges, the areas within which various families belonging to the same band were likely to range in a single year.

Sampson then assumes that styles will show different discard rates in different territories, and uses spatial patterning in the stylistic characteristics of bushman pottery in an attempt to detect the territories of each style group, corresponding with regions of high density for that style.

Assuming that these style regions correspond with band territories — at a minimum they should have some cultural meaning — we can then use survey data from each territory to make inferences about meaningful populations.

In a similar vein, the distribution of coins, which have symbolic and economic connections with the territories that issued them, can sometimes suggest the locations of political boundaries in societies with money economies. Often, coins are worth less, or are required to be exchanged for local currency, when they travel outside the territory of their issuing states. In that case, we would expect a marked fall-off in their frequency outside their usual boundaries. For example, smoothed density plots of the distribution of Celtic coins attributable to various tribes in southern Britain suggests tribal territories that are consistent with the locations of Celtic temples (Hodder, 1975; Hodder and Orton, 1976:80, 158). In this case, however, the data for coin spots took many years, not just one or two surveys, to accumulate.

2.6 Edge Effects

The choice of exactly where to place the boundaries of a survey region has a number of effects. Some of these are called *edge effects*: sources of bias that are caused by the interaction of the distributions that interest us and the (usually arbitrary) boundaries that we impose on those distributions. Some edge effects affect whole survey regions; section 3.2 refers to the edge effects of quadrats and other observation elements.

2.6.1 Edge Effects in Nearest Neighbor Analysis

Nearest Neighbor Analysis (NNA) is one kind of analysis on which the selection of survey boundaries could have a significant effect.

NNA detects the degree of clustering or evenness in a scatter of objects in space. It is based on the observation that in an evenly spaced distribution of dots on a map, the distances between neighboring dots is maximized, while in clustered distributions, the distance between each dot and its nearest neighbor is quite small (Hodder and Orton, 1976:38-51). In random distributions, the nearest neighbor distances lie between these two extremes.

Once there are boundaries on a map, however, it is likely that the nearest neighbors of some of the dots will lie outside those boundaries. Consequently, any attempt to measure the distance from these dots to their nearest neighbors will actually be measuring the distance to the second-nearest or even third-nearest neighbor. As a result, the estimated average distance to nearest neighbor will be biased — it will tend to overestimate this distance — and the analysis could fail to detect clustering or even incorrectly suggest an evenly-spaced distribution (Hodder and Orton, 1976:41-43).

One way to control for this problem is to use nested survey areas. Even a rough idea of the average distance between sites, perhaps based on measurements in the center of the survey area, can suggest the placement of a second boundary inside the one actually surveyed, offset by a little more than the expected distance to nearest neighbor. Counting only the sites within this smaller area, but checking the larger area for nearest neighbors, substantially reduces the risk of missing the nearest neighbor of any site in the more restricted data set, and will result in more accurate estimates of mean distance to nearest neighbor. However, this is somewhat costly, as it requires surveying an area larger than the one that will be the focus of analysis.

2.6.2 Edge Effects on Rank-Size Analysis

In a similar way, the placement of a boundary can affect the shapes of rank-size distributions (Johnson, 1980; Zipf, 1949). In particular, whether a fairly large site occurs inside or outside the boundary can sometimes make the difference between a "convex" and a "concave" distribution. This effect is particularly pronounced when the site in question would be the second-largest site if it were included, and when the third-largest site is considerably smaller. Omitting the site (thus "promoting" the third-ranked site to the second rank) would convert a convex to a concave distribution.

3. TYPES, SHAPES, AND ORIENTATION OF UNITS

Whether archaeologists conceive of archaeological distributions as sets of discrete sites or as nearly continuous scatters of material culture, they almost always begin an archaeological survey by partitioning space geometrically. Even if sites are the phenomena of interest, generally we do not know, in advance, where these sites are, and can only organize a search for them by reference to space. Partitioning space provides a framework for survey. The most common framework, or *sampling frame*, for archaeological survey consists of a set of equal, rectangular quadrats defined by a grid. Frames that consist of a set of long, parallel transects (essentially long, narrow rectangles) are also fairly common. Less common are sets of circlular areas. In principle, the sampling frame could be a grid of hexagons, triangles, or any other shape that seems useful or convenient (Wobst, 1983). It is important to realize that it could even consist of non-geometric spatial units. In addition, some kinds of survey employ a version of point sampling, in which observations are made at the corners of rectangular or triangular grid frames or at intervals along a transect.

Although many archaeologists seem to default to square quadrats either $1 km^2$ or 1 ha (100 m x 100 m) in size, the shape, size and arrangement of these spatial units warrant explicit attention because they all affect the survey's outcome.

Generally, the target elements of an archaeological survey consist of sites, landforms, or more arbitrary spatial elements, each of which can be defined in a number of ways.

3.1 Sites

Where sites are the element of interest, it is important to define them carefully. The textbook definition of a site as "any locus of past human behavior" or the like is generally not very useful in the context of archaeological survey (McManamon, 1984:226). It is a definition in the past, dynamic, behavioral realm, while the survey can only be expected to find materials in the present archaeological record (Schiffer, 1987). We need to have specific criteria for identifying localities that *may have been* loci of past human behavior, and cannot always be certain that "sites" were not created by some natural phenomenon or by modern activities. Furthermore, at least in some regions of the world, it is likely that every part of the landscape has been a locus of human behavior at some time or other. That is one reason that some archaeologists favor "non-site survey."

As previously mentioned, some surveys define sites by some arbitrary threshold of artifact density, such as 5 artifacts/m^2. In others, sites are defined as distinct clusters of material culture, or by contrasts in density with the "background noise" around them (figure 1; Banning, 1985). In still others, there is no general definition of "site," but loci are recorded as sites as long as they satisfy the definition for one of several site types, such as pueblos, lithic scatters, cave sites, and so on.

A major problem with using sites as the fundamental spatial unit of survey is that we rarely know where they are in advance of survey. It is impossible to construct a sampling frame that consists of the set of unknown sites until after the survey is over, which poses particular problems for surveys of the sampling type. Sites are more useful as survey elements in cases where the survey consists of ground-checking observations on aerial photographs, or where someone simply wants to revisit sites discovered in previous surveys. However, it is still common to use sites as units of analysis while using one of the other spatial units, discussed in following sections, as the unit of discovery. This either involves cluster sampling (see chapter 5) or prospecting (chapter 6).

3.1.1 Site Size, Shape and Orientation

When sites are the target of survey, their size and shape have considerable impact on discovery probability. Most kinds of survey are always more likely to intercept large targets than small ones (figure 11). For example, a random or systematic distribution of auger holes has a higher propability of "hitting" a large than a small site.

Most archaeological treatments of discovery probability have varied site size, but assumed that sites are circular. It is usually more realistic to think of them as elliptical. In that case, it is necessary to consider both their length/width ratios (the most obvious measure of shape) and their orientation. Some kinds of site, such as roads or field walls, are effectively linear. Furthermore, it is not uncommon to have L-shaped or irregularly-shaped sites, but it is difficult to quantify the effects of such shapes.

In general, and when the orientation of elongated targets is unknown, the probability of intersection for any search pattern is highest for circular targets and lowest for linear ones. Assuming that sites are circular, then, provides a rather optimistic view and may cause overestimate of a survey's success at finding them.

We can determine the probability of intersecting elliptical targets in cases where all orientations of the ellipse are equally likely (Singer and Drew, 1976: 643). Where a is the semimajor axis of the ellipse and b is the semiminor axis, intersection will occur with certainty whenever an observation falls within b of the ellipse's center and intersection will not occur at all outside of a. Observations at distances greater than b, but less than a will have intermediate probabilities of intersection, depending on the angle of orientation. Where r_d is the distance between a point observation and the ellipse's center, the angle f represents the range of orientations in which it is possible for points at distance r_d from the center to intersect the ellipse; such points will miss the ellipse at all other orientations. Drew (1966) determined that the probability that a point, D, will intersect the ellipse equals the arc length of the possible "hit" orientations, f, divided by all orientations (180°):

$$p(D) = \frac{2\tan^{-1}\frac{b}{a}\sqrt{\frac{a^2 - r_d^2}{r_d^2 - b^2}}}{180} \text{ for } a > r_d > b$$

This treats the ellipse as the target's area and assumes that intersection equals detection. To take the other influences on detectability into account, however, there may be cases where the target's discovery region is effectively elliptical, allowing the same means of estimating its discovery probability. Small but obtrusive targets could have

Units and Sampling Frames

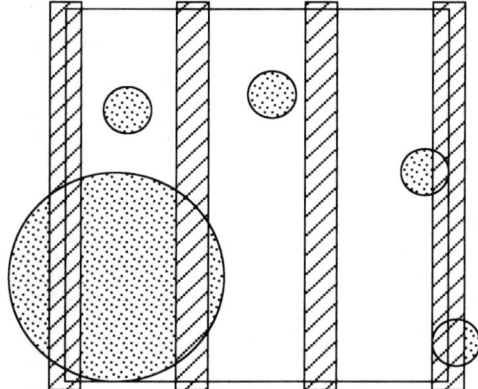

Figure 11. The effect of site size on the probability of site detection by pedestrian transects (hatched rectangles). Note that some small sites (small circles) lie completely between transects, while larger sites always intersect at least one.

relatively large, elliptical discovery regions. At the other extreme, where intersection does not guarantee detection, one would need to multiply $p(D)$ by the target's estimated detectability.

3.2 Geometrical Spatial Units

In modern surveys, the most common target elements are arbitrary units of space with square, rectangular, circular or other geometrical shapes (Wobst, 1983).

Most of these elements are quadrats, transects, or points, although other configurations are possible. Quadrats, the most common units employed in modern archaeology, are usually squares defined by a rectangular grid framework imposed on a survey area. It is also possible, and advantageous in some contexts, to have grids of elongated rectangles or rhombuses. Even other polygons, such as hexagons or triangles, are quite useful, although these have been used less often in archaeology. Transects are essentially very elongated rectangles, which gives them a high edge/area ratio. This results in a much higher probability of intersecting clustered archaeological materials (below). Point elements are usually actually circles or small squares, their centers defined by coordinates selected systematically or randomly. In geophysical remote sensing, however, data are usually collected at coordinates that are effectively points on a grid.

3.2.1 Edge Effects on the Detection of Sites

As Plog et al. (1978:397-402) point out, geometrical survey units with long edges are more likely to detect sites than ones with relatively short edges.

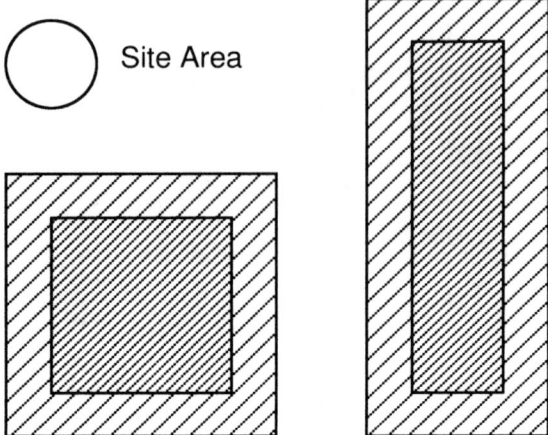

Figure 12. A square and a transect of equal area (closely hatched), but with effective area (lightly hatched) that is greater for the transect than for the square. The edge effect equals the radius of the circular site (after Plog et al., 1978:399).

When a survey's goal is simply to discover sites or clustered archaeological phenomena, crew members would include even those observations that do not lie completely within the quadrat or other spatial unit we surveyed. Survey along the west edge of a square quadrat, for example, might encounter a site that lies mostly outside the quadrat, only its eastern third jutting into the square. This has the effect of discovering more sites (especially large ones) than would lie strictly within the sample of spatial units. The longer the total edge of a spatial unit, therefore, the more likely it is to encounter sites and the greater the total number of sites we may expect to encounter.

Basic geometry determines that some shapes of spatial unit have greater edge length for a given size. A quadrat 100 m x 400 m is the same size as one 200 m x 200m, but the former has 1000 m of edge while the latter has only 800 m of edge. Consequently, the long quadrat is more likely to intersect sites than the square one. As Plog et al. (1978) indicate, it is useful to think of the edges as creating an *effective* site detection area that is larger than the actual area of the quadrat (figure 12). The size of this effective area is determined both by the length of edge and by the size or obtrusiveness of the sites or features to be detected (or *range* of detection). When the goal is to detect sites, clearly elongated survey units are more efficient than square or hexagonal ones (figure 13).

In addition, because the the edge effect has the same absolute width (the discovery radius) no matter what the size of the survey unit, edge effects are more pronounced for small units than for large ones. The effective site detection area for a circular target with a radius of 25 m is 302,500 m^2 for a 500 m x 500 m quadrat, but 22,500 m^2 for a 100 m x 100 m quadrat, and 4900 m^2 for a 20 m x 20 m quadrat. Thus, the ratio of effective detection area to quadrat area in these cases varies from 1.21, through 2.25, to 12.25. Clearly, when the goal is to detect as many sites as possible, elements with small areas lead to much higher intersection probabilities.

Units and Sampling Frames

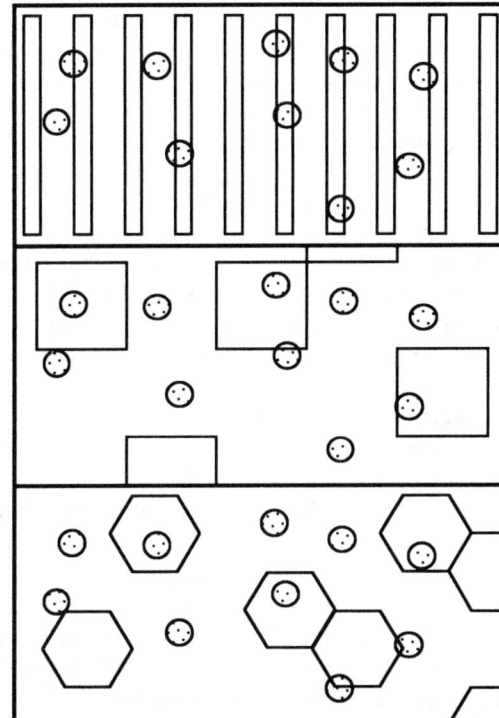

Figure 13. Variation in the detection of sites per unit area with survey units that are transects (top), squares (middle), and hexagons (bottom). Of the ten circular sites, the transects detect seven (1.5 per unit area), the squares detect four (1.1 per unit area), and the hexagons detect five (1.3 per unit area).

When, however, estimation rather than detection is our goal, we need to consider ways to avoid or account for the bias that these edge effects would bring to our estimates.

3.2.2 Edge Effects on Parameter Estimates

One of the problems archaeologists encounter when they attempt to estimate population parameters, such as settled area or even number of sites, is what to do with observations that sit on the borders of our quadrats or other spatial units, or whose centers actually lie outside our sample elements. Should they be included, or only if at least half their areas lie within the quadrat? Or should only the part that lies within the quadrat be included? Decisions on this matter have an important effect on estimates.

As just seen, edge effects allow detection of sites only small portions of which lie strictly within the units of survey. Simply counting all the information from these sites toward estimates of site density, site size, and so on, would lead to bias. Specifically, it would overestimate the density of archaeological material, the amount of settled area and, because large sites are more likely than small ones to intersect quadrat edges, average site size.

One fairly obvious way to avoid this problem is simply to exclude from any statistics sites whose centres lie outside the sample elements. It is still possible to describe and report archaeological evidence from edge areas, but they should not be allowed to affect the estimates of population parameters. This approach also requires attention to cluster sampling (see chapter 5).

Perhaps a better approach in some situations, which also avoids cluster sampling, is to use the survey unit itself as both the sampling element and the analytical element, and to treat the area of each site that falls within the sampling element as a measurement on that element. For example, one 100 m x 200 m quadrat might intersect part of a site that has an estimated area of 9000 m^2, but only 3500 m^2 of that site actually falls within the quadrat boundaries. Possibly another smaller site, with an area of 200 m^2, falls completely within the same quadrat. Rather than counting two sites, we could count 3700 m^2 toward the total site area for that quadrat or, if the two sites differed in ways considered important, count 3500 m^2 toward one site type or period and 200 m^2 to another. When, for example, the goal is to estimate ancient population or population growth on the basis of settled area, this would probably be the better approach. In cases where average village size is of interest, however, it would not be helpful.

3.2.3 Cost Effects of Unit Size

As later chapters will show, there are sometimes advantages to survey units that are small, but large in number. For example, this has the effect of increasing sample size and decreasing variance for many samples. However, the decision to use small units can increase cost substantially, because cost is not a simple function of the units' total area.

There are some fixed and nearly fixed costs associated with laying out survey units irrespective of their size. It is necessary to locate each unit in space, whether by map or GPS, and it may be necessary, for example, to document the survey unit's environmental circumstances, or to place stakes or pin-flags to mark unit corners or the ends of transects. The cost of these activities may be little different for long transects and short ones.

The major cost effect of decreasing the size, and thus increasing the number, of survey units, however, is travel time. Surveys of a small number of fairly large units devote a larger proportion of their time to the work of survey. Having many, small units scattered across a large region requires a large investment of travel time between units.

3.3 Non-geometrical Spatial Units

Although most archaeologists partition space geometrically, and especially into rectangular quadrats or transects, there is no *a priori* reason for this to be the best approach. In some instances, non-geometrical spatial units make more sense as the basic elements of survey.

For example, in a survey designed to discover sites in caves and rockshelters, it would not be efficient to partition a map into square quadrats and then search some number of these quadrats for possible cave sites. Caves and rockshelters do not occur

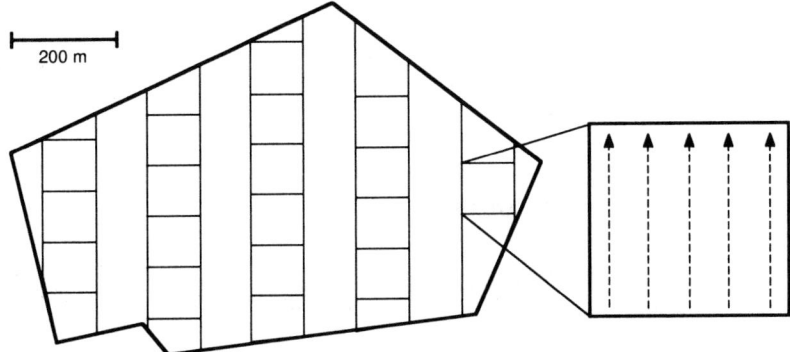

Figure 14. Transects, each divided into 1 ha sections, nested within a polygonal survey unit in Bohemia (after Kuna, 1998).

randomly on the landscape, but in areas where particular kinds of rock outcrop on the surface, and especially where rock has been exposed in canyons and other deep valleys, or where limestone has been subject to karstic processes. A better survey design in such a situation would be to use geological maps to determine which spaces potentially could contain caves, and then to explore all or a sample of these spaces to search for caves and rockshelters and try to determine if they contain cultural remains. Such spaces would probably be irregular in shape, corresponding to the boundaries of rock outcrops or cliff faces.

Some archaeologists now embrace this approach by using "landscape elements" as their fundamental observational unit (e.g., Schlanger, 1992; Stafford, 1995). Landscape elements are minimal homogeneous portions of the landscape, as defined in terms of some combination of landform, surface geology, soil type, vegetation, slope, aspect, or other environmental attributes.

Although far from abandoning the site concept, Binford's (1982) reference to topographic locations where people periodically paused and carried out actions also lends itself to the use of landscape elements as analytical units.

The kinds of non-geometrical spaces, or "places," that could be the elements of a survey include the vicinity of springs (particularly in arid regions), stream terraces in meandering, deeply-incised valleys (Banning, 1996), segments of rivers or canals between confluences (Stafford, 1994), or individual fields in ancient field systems visible in aerial photographs (Banning, 1996).

The Czech-British project, Ancient Landscape Reconstruction in North Bohemia, provides one example of using field systems as the basis for a sampling frame. This survey used "polygons" — normally modern fields — as the sampling elements, although these were selected by randomly locating points in space to see which polygons the points intersected, rather than randomly selecting the polygons themselves. This has the effect of giving large polygons a higher probability of being included in the sample than small ones. As long as the polygons could be recognized in recent aerial photographs, they could just as easily have been numbered and formed the sampling frame for a simple random or stratified sample, thus avoiding this bias. The polygons were then subsampled by transects made up of smaller polygons, most of which were squares 100 m on a side, so that half the area of each field was collected (figure 14; Kuna, 1998:80).

3.4 Arrangement of Units

Once they have decided what type of survey unit they will use to organize a survey, archaeologists usually also need to decide on its arrangement. This is especially true of geometrically-shaped units.

3.4.1 Regular Grids

The most common arrangement is the grid. The set of spatial units is typically imposed on a map in such a way as to "tile" some region, such as a drainage basin or an area expected to suffer impact from development. In order to make the units fit reasonably closely to a preconceived boundary, the boundary sometimes has to be distorted or appears quite jagged. A fairly common variation on the grid of squares is a grid with quadrats twice as long as they are wide. Hexagonal and other kinds of geometrical grids are less common, but are perfectly acceptable and even have advantages in some situations (see below). In all these cases, one has to decide on the grid interval, which determines the size of the quadrats (see section 4). Probability surveys entail intensive examination of a subset (or sample) of the quadrats in this grid (see chapter 5). Prospection can entail allocating survey resources unevenly among the grid units in order to optimize the recovery of archaeological evidence.

3.4.1.1 Arrangement of Point Samples

Geophysical surveys and surveys by by coring, augering or other subsurface tests (SSTs) typically use the coordinates of grid corners to define a set of data points, and the number of points per unit of space constitutes the resolution of survey. The sample units (points, circles or small squares) are typically arranged in a square or triangular pattern (figure 15). Archaeologists and others have studied the effect of various geometrical arrangements of points on the probability that they will intersect circular targets (see below, section 4).

Using a grid arrangement entails selecting, not only a particular kind of grid and its interval, but also its orientation and origin. Many archaeologists decide, quite arbitrarily, to orient the grid to geographic North or to grid North on some easily available map series. In some instances, however, it pays to consider grid position quite carefully. In rough terrain, arbitrarily orienting the grid to true North could result in units that crosscut natural features, such as cliffs and rivers, in rather awkward ways, potentially adding considerable field time to the survey or posing some physical danger to survey crew. In addition, an unlucky selection of grid orientation might even cause bias in the detection and interpretation of archaeological materials. This problem is more common in the

Units and Sampling Frames

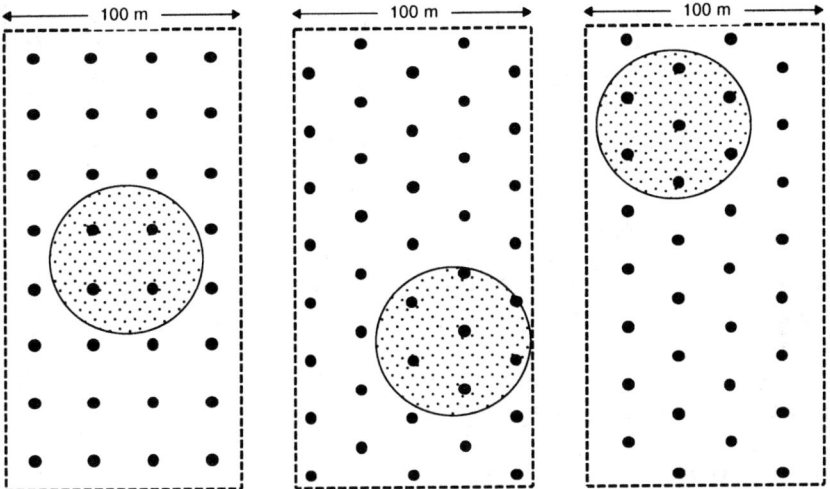

Figure 15. Arrangement of points on square (left), isoceles triangular (center), and equilateral triangular (right) grids, superimposed on hypothetical, circular sites.

survey of settlements than in regional survey. The classic examples are those where the ancient inhabitants, like the modern archaeologists, chose true North to orient their street system and an inter-house spacing very similar to the archaeologists' sampling interval; the archaeologists' grids then systematically missed every single house (Flannery, 1976a:49-50). Where this is a possibility, it would be a mistake to orient the grid to the cardinal points or to any architectural features that might be visible. Pick a random orientation or a non-rectangular grid instead. However, it is also true that natural topography can influence the orientation of elongated sites; where this is likely, consider the most likely site orientation in arranging a grid. One can take advantage of this information to improve the likelihood of encountering sites or, alternatively, to correct for bias in estimates (see section 4.2.1).

3.4.2 Transects

3.4.2.1 Parallel Transects

Another common arrangement is to cover a survey area or unit with a series of parallel transects (figure 16). Again, it is necessary to decide on the spacing and orientation of these transects. The spacing is based on assessment of the risk that archaeological remains of interest might be overlooked between adjacent transects (see below, section 4.2.5). As mentioned above, transects result in high detection probabilities. They also have the tendency, which could be an advantage in some situations, to intersect a variety of landscapes. However, walking long transects in rough terrain, especially if the transects cross-cut canyons or high ridges, can be very difficult and there may be other practical considerations mitigating against the use of long transects. For example, unless the team includes a driver who will drop other team members off at the beginning of a long transect and pick them up again at the other end at the end of the day, it may be better to use pairs of shorter transects so that team members can walk up one and down the other in a single work day. As with quadrats, probability surveys that employ transects select only a sample of transects for thorough investigation, so that most of the transects surveyed will be non-adjacent (i.e., there will be unsurveyed space between them). Systematic (i.e., equally spaced) transects are very common in terrestrial and marine surveys and geophysical surveys. In the case of the last, the transect usually actually consists of a linear arrangement of equally-spaced points where measurements were made.

Some survey designs employ purposive or random arrangements of transects instead of parallel ones. A common way to select random transects is to number intervals around the boundary of the survey area and select pairs of random numbers to determine the endpoints of each transect. This strategy typically results in transects that vary considerably in length, which could have negative effects on the practicality of survey. Some transects may be too long for a survey team to cover effectively in one day. As with parallel transects, there may be difficulties with transects that cross-cut steep or inaccessible terrain. They may also be somewhat inefficient if there are many intersections of transects, leading to repeated survey of the same spaces, although this might be a good way to check on the thoroughness of the previous search. It is possible, however, to restrict the selection of coordinates on the survey boundary to prevent frequent intersections by stratifying the survey area into bands and randomly selecting a transect terminus at each end of each band. Note, however, that this creates bias in sampling surveys, as the central area of each band would have a higher probability of being surveyed than other parts. Some archaeologists position transects purposively to follow approximately the lines of watercourses and mountain ridges or, in geophysical survey, orient linear arrangements of data points to detect known or suspected linear and geometric features, such as roads, canals, and circular enclosures, more efficiently.

3.4.2.2 Intersecting Transects

Archaeologists are well aware that a single pass by a set of transects is unlikely to lead to 100% detection of archaeological materials in most instances. Consequently, some have opted for repeating the survey of each space with a second set of transects oriented differently from the first one.

In surface survey or distributional archaeology (Ebert 1992), a second set of transects is often at right angles to the first, the rationale being that repeating the survey from a different angle (and with different lighting conditions) will reveal some artifacts missed in the first pass. In mineral and petroleum exploration, it is also common to use a second set of transects at right angles to the first one (e.g., McCammon, 1977:373-376). This has some practical advantages in that a rectangular grid is easy to set out, and the target intersection probabilities are published.

Units and Sampling Frames 91

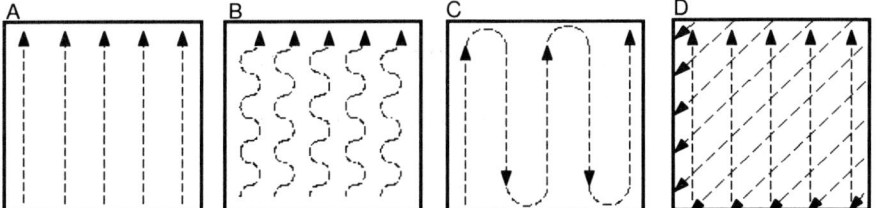

Figure 16. A selection of search geometries for parallel straight (A, C) and wavy (B) transects and two passes by transects oriented 45° (D).

However, rectangular grids of transects are not the most efficient option. Because of basic geometry, it is optimal for a second set of transects to be diagonal to the first (fig. 16d), rather than at right angles, because it maximizes the area of new ground covered. In search-and-rescue, 45° is the recommended orientation of the second pass (Koopman, 1980:218).

3.4.2.3 Undulating Transects

Recognizing that the probability of detection falls off rapidly with distance away from a transect, some archaeologists have attempted to deal with this problem by using very narrow transect intervals, while some others have tried "wavy" transects to conduct surface survey by visual inspection (figure 16b). The rationale behind these is that wandering back and forth within transect bands might decrease the systematic omission of observations that might otherwise lie between transects (e.g., Mortensen 1974; Rupp n.d.). They also have the advantage of forcing fieldwalkers to examine the ground from different directions, presumably in somewhat different light.

However, there are some disadvantages to this approach too. First, wavy transects make it more difficult to evaluate detectability, as there is no obvious way to measure the way it drops away from the path each crew member walks. In fact, it is difficult even to measure the length of each transect, which probably varies from one crew member to another. These problems would not be as serious if we could at least be certain that the wavy transects accomplished their objective of locating all the artifacts on the surface within each transect band. However, unless the transect spacing is very narrow, this is unlikely. Furthermore, where the transect spacing is fairly small, there is likely to be some overlap of coverage. On the one hand, this helps to improve detectability by examining some surface areas more than once; on the other, it is less efficient because repeated or prolonged search in the same space has diminishing returns. There are also practical problems in keeping crew members on course.

Consequently, this search pattern is more rarely used than the more easily evaluated straight transects.

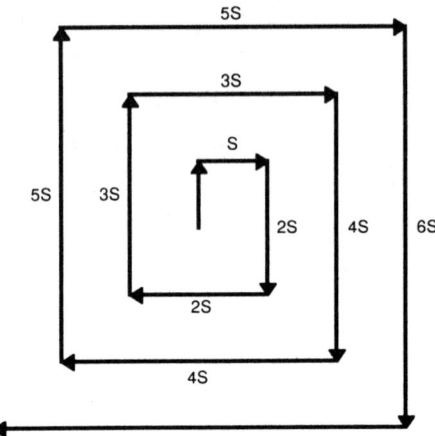

Figure 17. Expanding-square or retiring-square search over a target with a circular normal probability distribution, and with transect spacing of S. A repeat search would orient the second square at 45° to the first (after Koopman 1980:214-221).

3.4.2.4 Retiring-square Pattern

One arrangement of transects that is unfamiliar to archaeologists, but common in search-and-rescue (Koopmans, 1980: 214-227; Richardson and Discenza, 1980), is the retiring square or expanding square. This is a transect that spirals out from a "point of fix" at the place with the highest prior probability of containing some specific target. Where the search is repeated, the second expanding square is optimally oriented 45° from the first one, to maximize new area covered.

Because this pattern is only applicable to prospection, full discussion of this survey plan will be found in chapter 6, section 3.1.

3.4.3 Unconventional Arrangements

Even quadrats, however, are sometimes arranged without reference to a grid. For example, in cases where it is likely that ancient settlement focussed on streams or coastlines, positioning rectangles at intervals along these features so that one axis of each rectangle is perpendicular to the beach or stream can be advantageous. For less than 100% coverage of these rectangles, one can systematically or randomly select a sample of them. In a survey of Cape Cod, McManamon positioned the short edges of rectangles that were 100 m x 200 m in size so that their long axes were perpendicular to the stream (McManamon, 1981). In the Cache River survey, House and Schiffer (1975a), divided the Cache River and Bayou de View into nine segments, each 24 miles long, and selected a single 3-mile subsegment from each (figure 18). The resulting units were centered on the river and extended 1000 feet to either side.

Units and Sampling Frames

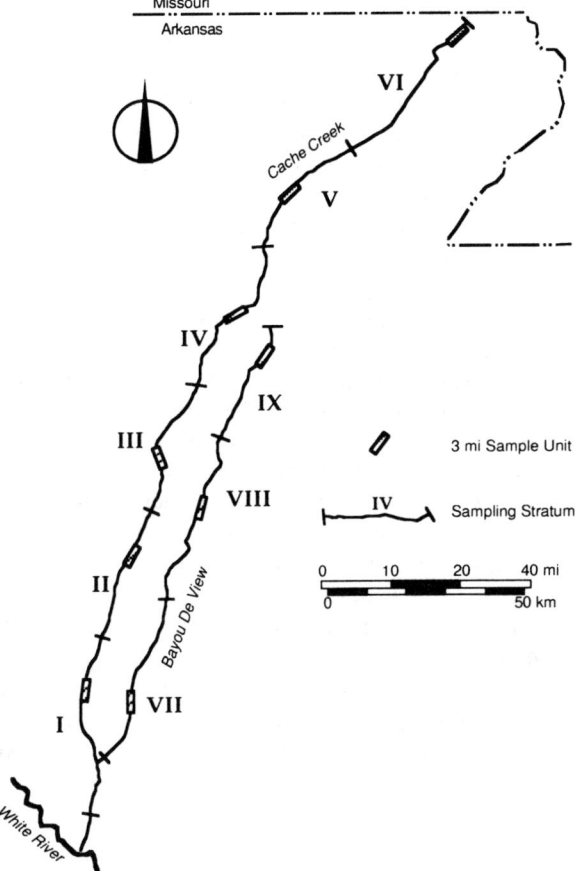

Figure 18. Positions of nine units, each 3 mi long, in a stratified random sample of the Cache and Bayou de View channels in northern Arkansas (after House and Schiffer, 1975a: 46). Unit size is not exactly to scale, and Roman numerals are stratum labels.

In other cases, it can be useful to arrange transects, quadrats or wedge-shaped units radially around known sites or highly clustered resources, such as springs. A survey aimed at finding small satellite sites and special-purpose sites around a village or base camp, for example, might involve intensive investigation along eight or more transects radiating from that site. Walking such transects would have the added advantage, incidentally, of allowing the surveyors to estimate travel time from the site to nearby resources and landscape features, providing more realistic estimates of the site catchment (Higgs and Vita-Finzi, 1972) than arbitrary circles would provide. Alternatively, it could involve selecting the centers of circular or quadrat-shaped units by randomly selecting compass directions and distances away from the central site.

3.4.4 Nested Arrangements

A large proportion of surveys employing regular grids of some kind actually involve a combination of quadrats and transects or quadrats and points. For example, survey begins by selecting a sample of fairly large quadrats within the survey boundaries. Then the surveyors either walk a series of transects across each quadrat or place a number of subsurface tests within it. Unless the transects or SSTs are so closely spaced as to guarantee that they will miss no archaeological materials, this is a type of subsampling, a sample within a sample.

The Czech-British project, Ancient Landscape Reconstruction in North Bohemia, is an example of subsampling. Its designers first randomly selected points on the landscape. Then they selected polygons (fields) that these points intersected as sample elements. Then they divided the polygons into sets of transects 100 m wide (figure 14), and collected artifacts found within each 1 ha section of alternate transects (Kuna, 1998:80). Still smaller transects within the 1 ha collecting units are assumed to have small enough spacing (20 m) to ensure discovery of all artifacts within them. Since they probably missed some material on these transects (how much depends on the detection function), it is possible to conceive of this as yet another level of subsampling.

For a variety of practical reasons, it is quite common for surveys to employ two or more levels of subsampling. This is often a good compromise between intensity and scale of survey as long as the surveyors and those who use their results recognize that subsampling has taken place.

However, subsampling does create statistical complications, which archaeologists have often ignored in favor of statistics that are appropriate for simple random designs, but make inaccurate parameter estimates for subsamples. As with any kind of cluster sampling, it is important to use the correct estimators for the mean and variance (see Drennan, 1996:247-253).

4. SCALE EFFECTS IN ARCHAEOLOGICAL SURVEY

Because archaeological surveys usually employ a frame of spaces, rather than artifacts or sites, it is important to consider carefully the way that the size and spacing of these spaces affect survey results (e.g., Matson and Lipe, 1975).

Most archaeological surveys employ equally-sized, rectangular spatial units, called quadrats, while others use triangles, auger-holes, transects, or "points" that are regularly spaced. Varying the size of these quadrats or the spacing of other units can have quite dramatic effects on discovery probabilities, perception of spatial patterns, and estimates of population parameters.

4.1 Size of Units

Whenever a sampling frame consists of some arbitrary spatial unit, such as quadrats, the size of that unit has a substantial impact on the survey's results.

In general, a large number of small units is better than a few large units from the statistical point of view, but this is also usually more costly. In addition, where detection depends on the discovery of artifacts on the surface or in auger-holes or test-pits, too small a unit may make it impossible to distinguish sites or other targets from their surroundings or from false targets. There are also scale effects on the probability of detecting targets of various sizes or obtrusiveness. Consequently, the selection of unit size is a trade-off.

There are two main reasons why small units have statistical advantages. One is that, for the same amount of area covered, the small units result in a larger sample size and this, in turn, results in a smaller standard error on any estimates of population characteristics (see chapter 5). The other has to do with spatial autocorrelation. Things that are close together in space are likely to be similar to each other (i.e., have similar soil, geology, elevation, rainfall, distance to water sources, etc.), so a large spatial unit will not sample a very large variety of geographical circumstances. The same area spread over a larger space is more likely to sample this variety, and thus result in more accurate estimates of the space's characteristics. Orton (2000:31-32) demonstrates this by imagining the larger units as clusters of the small ones. In sample units made up of four contiguous small squares, these squares are likely to be correlated with each other. Dismantling the clusters and spreading the small squares across the space provides essentially four times as much information about the space.

However, using the smaller units also increases the cost of fieldwork (Cochran, 1963:245). Some of the cost increase is due to the increased travel time and set-up time associated with using a larger number of smaller units. Simply locating the observation units accurately, even with GPS, can take considerable time. Section 4.2 deals with ways we can take these costs into account in planning surveys.

Furthermore, as mentioned in chapter 3 (pp. 49-54), it may be harder to recognize archaeological targets in smaller units if recognition depends on intersecting scattered objects, such as artifacts, that occur at low densities. In a small unit, the expected frequency of artifacts in a unit may be 0, while larger units distributed over the same space might have expected frequencies of 10 or more. Assuming for simplicity that artifacts within sites or artifact clusters are distributed approximately by the Poisson distribution facilitates selecting a unit size that has a reasonably large expected frequency, λ, and reasonably low probability of failing to intersect materials on site areas.

In addition, because survey by quadrats to discover sites involves the intersection of two types of spatial units — unobtrusive sites are discovered if part of their surface area intersects the surface area of a quadrat — varying the size of quadrats affects the probability of detecting sites (figure 19).

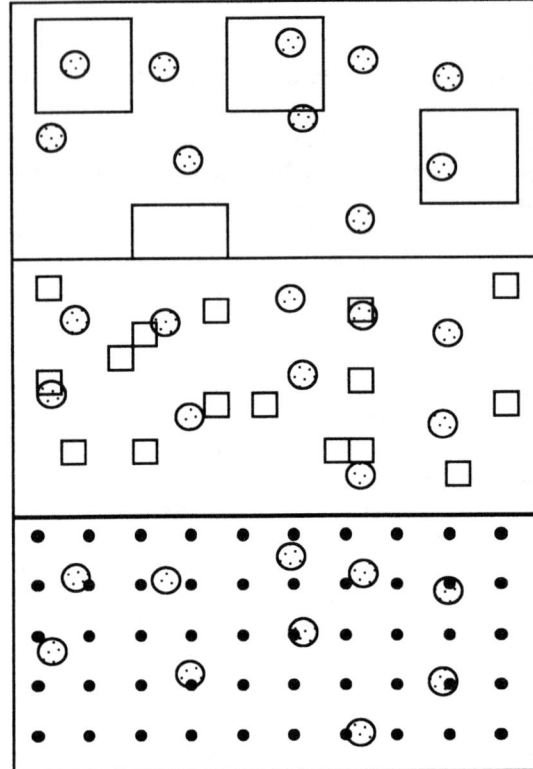

Figure 19. Variation in intersection probability with size of survey unit. Because edge effects are more pronounced for small units, the small squares and auger holes (middle and bottom) intersect more sites relative to their areas (0.19 and 0.9 sites per unit area, respectively) than do large squares (0.07 sites per unit area, top).

When quadrats are very small, approaching the size of point samples, there is a very strong relationship between intersection probability and the size of targets. It is quite probable that more than one quadrat will intersect each large site, while small sites are highly unlikely to be "hit" by even one. Most small sites, in fact, will not be intersected at all. In addition, the relationship between site size and edge effects is more pronounced for small units than for large ones.

4.2 Optimal Arrangements, Sizes, and Spacing

In any regular geometric grid with systematic spacing, it is possible to design it in ways that help achieve particular goals, such as minimizing the risk of missing targets, or minimizing the variance of estimates on a fixed budget. Some aspects of optimization that involve sample sizes and distribution of effort appear in chapters 5 and 6. The following will concentrate on the optimal arrangement and spacing of grids.

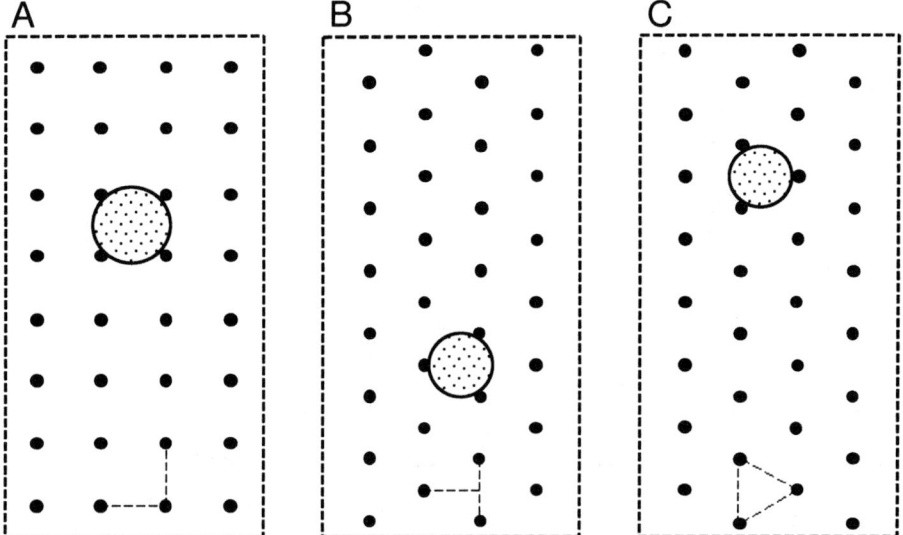

Figure 20. The largest circular site that can escape detection is largest for the square grid (a) and smallest for the equilateral triangular grid (c), with spacing interval i *represented by the light dashed line segment. The "offset" or isoceles triangular arrangement (b) is intermediary.*

4.2.1 Optimizing the Arrangement of Systematic Point Grids

There is considerable literature on the optimal arrangement of point grids for exploration, most of it generated in exploration geology. The archaeological literature has focussed mainly on the problem of intersecting and detecting circular targets with shovel tests, cores or augers.

Krakker et al. (1983) note that square arrays of points are not as efficient at the detection of circular targets as triangular arrangements. The largest circular site that a square array will fail to intersect has its center exactly equidistant from four points (figure 20a) and has a radius equal to the sampling interval (i) divided by $\sqrt{2}$ (table 1). Consequently, the square array will intersect every site with a radius greater than $i/\sqrt{2}$. The probability of intersecting smaller sites is a function of the ratio between their radius and the sampling interval, and only approaches 1.0 for sites with radii close to $i/\sqrt{2}$. The probability of intersecting as site whose radius is only half the grid interval is 0.78, while for still smaller sites we can calculate the intersection probability as the simple ratio of the circle's area divided by the area of the square of length i:

$$p(i) = \frac{\pi r^2}{i^2}$$

where p(i) is the probability of intersection at a given interval, i, and r is the site radius.

	Ratio of $\frac{i}{s}$	Spacing (s)	Edge (e)	Largest Missed (d)
Square Grid	1	i	$\frac{s}{2}$	$i\sqrt{2}$
Rectangular Grid	specified	$\frac{W}{t}$	$\frac{s}{2}$	$\sqrt{s^2 + i^2}$
Isoceles Grid	1	$\frac{W}{t - 0.25}$	$0.375s$	$1.25i$
Isoceles Grid	specified	$\frac{W + \sqrt{W^2 + ti^2}}{2t}$	$\frac{4s^2 - i^2}{8s}$	$s + i^2/4s$
Equilateral Grid	$\frac{2}{\sqrt{3}}$	$\frac{3W}{3t - 1}$	$\frac{s}{3}$	$\frac{4s}{3}$

Table 1. Point intervals on square, rectangular, isoceles (rhombic), and equilateral (hexagonal) grids to minimize the size of the largest circular target that could escape detection within a survey rectangle of length L and width W. The interval between points in a row is i, the spacing between rows is s, and the number of rows is t (after Kintigh, 1988:688).

A simple improvement is to offset alternate rows in a square array to convert it into an array of isoceles triangles with the spacing, i, the same along each transect, and the distance between transects is also i, but with alternate transects offset by $i/2$ (figure 20b). This arrangement, called rhombic in the geological literature, leads to substantial increases in the probability of intersecting a circular target of given size. For a site with a radius equal to half the spacing interval, for example, the intersection probability is now 0.94 instead of the 0.78 for the square array with the same interval (Krakker et al., 1983:472). Note that the resulting isoceles triangles have one side equal to i and the other two equal to $(i\sqrt{5})/2$.

An arrangement of equilateral triangles (often described as "hexagonal" in the archaeological literature and simply "triangular" in the geological literature) is even more efficient for the intersection of circular targets (table 1). Here, all sides of the triangle whose corners are sampled are equal to i (figure 20c).

Archaeologists more accustomed to laying out rectangular grids might object that ones consisting of equilateral triangles are difficult to lay out accurately. Trying to lay out parallel transects with an inter-transect spacing of $(i\sqrt{3})/2$ would seem awkward, but this is actually unnecessary. Especially for survey crews with two or three members, it is much easier and much more accurate to take advantage of the equilateral property and simply stretch three tapes out to measure the equal sides of a large triangle with sides some multiple of i in length, mark the corners and intervals of i along those sides with stakes or pinflags, and then use two tapes stretched from two of the previously marked corners to repeat the process for the next large triangle (figure 21).

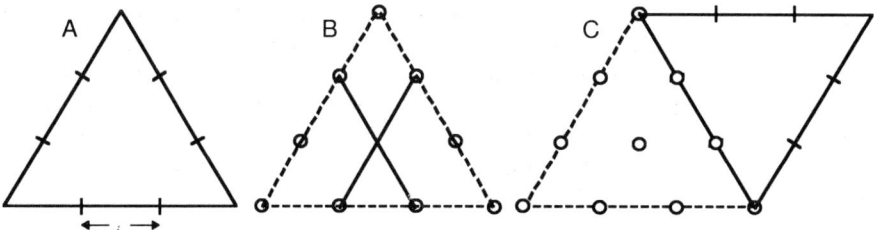

Figure 21. An easy way to establish points on an equilateral triangular grid is first to lay out a large triangle with three tapes so that each side is an equal multiple of i (a), then pull two tapes across the triangle to find its center (b), then repeat the process for an adjacent large triangle (c).

Although the "hexagonal" array is optimal in the sense of minimizing the size of the largest circular target that could escape intersection, it is not necessarily optimal in other ways. Generally all point arrangements are equally efficient whenever the intersection probability is fairly low, as happens when the interval is too large for any target to be intersected more than once (Drew, 1979:228). In that case, the probability of detection is simply the target area divided by the area enclosed by a polygon (rectangle or rhombus) joining the nearest four points, which is identical for all shapes when the density of points is fixed (figure 22).

While archaeologists have focussed on point arrangements for circular targets, mathematical geology has investigated them for circular, elliptical, and linear targets for many years (e.g., Drew, 1979; Savinskii, 1965; Shurygin, 1976; Sinclair, 1975; Singer, 1972; 1975; 1976; Singer and Wickman, 1969). Generally, unless we have advance information about the likely orientation of elongated targets, our point grids are less likely to intersect ellipses and especially lines than to intersect circles. In other words, assuming that targets are circular provides only rather optimistic estimates of intersection probabilities.

Just as Krakker et al. (1983) later determined for circular sites, Slichter (1955), Celasun (1964), Drew (1966), and Singer (1975) determined that equilateral triangular arrangments of points are more efficient for intersecting targets when we have no information about the likely orientation of elongated ones, or when their orientation is random.

When prior information about ellipse orientation is available, however, it is generally most efficient to use a rhombic (isoceles triangular) arrangement with the long axis of the rhombus parallel to the long axis of the ellipse (figure 22a; Mickey and Jespersen, 1954). However, an arrangement of rectangles oriented 26° to the long axis of the ellipses is equally efficient in many cases (figure 22; Drew 1979), although no arrangement is ever more efficient than the rhombic one. For square and rhombic arrangements of points, Singer (1975) has shown that their efficiencies vary with their orientation relative to the long axis of the ellipse. Interestingly, their relative efficiencies for getting one or more intersections are reversed when the criterion is getting two or more intersections.

Fortunately, many archaeological situations allow reasonable guesses about the orientation of archaeological targets. For example, some kinds of sites along riverbanks tend to have their long axes parallel to the watercourse. It is also fortunate that even fairly large errors in estimates of this orientation only have a small adverse effect on the intersection probabilities for a rhombic pattern (Mickey and Jespersen, 1954; Schlichter 1955). However, the effect of error in the specification of site orientation is more pronounced the more elongated the targets are.

4.2.2 Optimizing the Arrangement of Continuous Parallel Transects

There are both practical and geometric aspects to the placement of transects. In rugged terrain orienting the transects roughly parallel to ridges and valleys may increase the ease of survey, while orienting them to cross-cut environmental zones may allow faster reconnaissance of the survey region's variety. The geometry of the transects only affects the probability of intersecting targets, however, when those targets are elongated (Chung, 1981).

McCammon (1977) provides guidance on the intersection probabilities for survey frames that consist of systematic parallel transects and grids of orthagonal and oblique transects (see also Wignall and De Geoffroy, 1987). To simplify the problem, he looks at the extremes, such as cases where the target is circular or linear, and assumes that most real cases will be intermediary (e.g., elliptical targets). However, he only treats the situation in which the orientation of elongated targets is unknown, so that transect orientation is not that important.

When there is reason not only to suspect that targets of interest are elongated, but also that they are oriented in a particular way, we can take advantage of that information (Nance, 1979:175). For example, along rivers, coasts, or roadways, it is common for settlements to be elongated, thus maximizing access to water or communications. In that case, and if anticipated detectability is reasonably high, continuous parallel transects that are perpendicular to the most likely orientation of the targets' long axes have the highest probabilities of intersecting and detecting the targets, or of intersecting them more than once. For discontinuous transects (such as rows of test pits) or for poor detectability perpendicular transects are not optimal because a single intersection might not lead to detection, or the target may be narrow enough to fall between observation points. An orientation that makes it more likely for two or more discontinuous observations to hit the target is optimal. As noted in the last section, an angle of 26° between the ellipse's axis and the transect is optimal in this situation.

4.2.3 Optimizing the Arrangement of Polygons

As in the case of transects, the optimal arrangment of polygonal survey units, such as quadrats, has both practical and mathematical aspects. From the practical point of view, it is often advantageous to arrange units with respect to natural topography, so as to make fieldwalking easier or to reduce travel time between areas that need to be sur-

Units and Sampling Frames 101

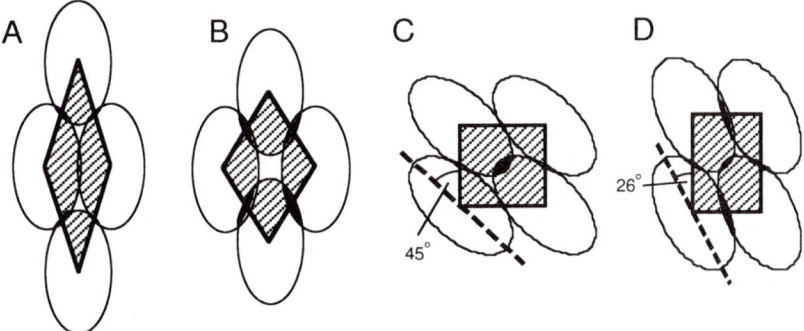

Figure 22. Eliptical targets at optimal orientations centered at the corners of isoceles (a), equilateral (b), square (c), and rectangular (d) grids to illustrate the areas of no intersection (white), one intersection (hatched), and two intersections (black)(after Drew, 1979:227). For smaller ellipses, the probability of one intersection equals the ellipse's area divided by the area (hatched) that the nearest four points enclose.

veyed. From the mathematical point of view, however, it is optimal to orient the polygons to maximize their probability of intersecting targets. As with point grids, this is important in cases when we can expect elongated targets to have a preferred orientation.

One can evaluate the relative efficiencies of different shapes of polygons and their orientation relative to the axis of ellipses with reference to the edge effects mentioned in section 3.2. For an ellipse of given size and length/width ratio, what combination of orientation and polygon shape gives the highest ratio of "effective discovery area" to polygon area? Estimating this involves overlapping the area of the polygon with the area in which targets intersect the polygon edges, with extremes at the corners.

As with the point grids, the optimal shapes and orientation in this situation are either rhombic with long axes parallel to the expected orientation of elliptical targets or long rectangles oriented 26° to the target ellipses (figure 22). Where it is necessary to use square quadrats, the optimal arrangement, when targets are both elongated and have an expected orientation, is 45° to the target axes.

4.2.4 Optimizing the Spacing of Systematic Point Grids

Optimizing point grids is a problem not only of point arrangement but also of spacing. The optimal interval between points might minimize the size of the largest target that could be missed by a fixed density of points (fixed cost), or might find the optimal balance between survey cost and results.

The obvious solution to preventing a survey on a point grid from missing targets is to increase resolution — the density of points — until at least one point will intersect even the smallest targets of interest. However, the diminishing returns associated with increased search effort make it unreasonable to increase resolution unduly. This is something that archaeologists have appreciated intuitively, but have rarely explicitly addressed.

If resolution is the proportion of pixels or quadrats in the survey area in which there are direct observations, a/A (the sampling fraction or density of search effort), then the relationship between detection probability and resolution in a random search is

$$p(t) = 1 - e^{-ka/A}$$

where $p(t)$ is the probability of detection in a time interval t, A is the total survey area, a is the area of the observation points or quadrats, and k is a variable that combines other factors that affect probability of detection, including visibility, obtrusiveness, target size, and so on (Stone, 1989:24-25). Just as for search time, the diminishing returns of higher resolution are pronounced.

Most archaeological surveys, however, employ systematic rather than random search. Here, too, we expect diminishing returns on the detection of sites that vary in size. This will happen because, at low resolution, the points will intersect sites of various sizes but, as resolution increases, there will be an increasing tendency for the points to intersect targets more than once, unless they are very small. Such redundancy may help with the recognition of sites and elimination of false targets (see chapter 3, sections 1.1.2 and 1.12), but will not increase the probability of at least one intersection.

4.2.4.1 Optimal Spacing of Point Grids at a Fixed Cost

Kintigh (1988) summarizes formulas for determining the optimal spacing of points on square, rectangular, isoceles (rhombic), and equilateral (hexagonal) grids for a given number of rows and data points. Thus, he takes the cost of survey as given. These solutions are optimal in the sense of minimizing the size of the largest circular target that could escape intersection (table 1). To similarly optimize point spacing for elliptical targets, the probability of intersection by at least one of the points is equal to the ellipse area divided by the area of the smallest quadrilateral polygon (square or rhombus) that the points will define (Drew, 1979).

When the cost of survey is fixed, optimizing the spacing of points then involves simply calculating how many points can be placed (or how many in each stratum — see allocation in chapter 5, section 2.3), and then using the formulas in table 1 to distribute the points optimally.

4.2.4.2 Optimal Spacing of Point Grids Taking Cost and "Value" into Account

In addition to the problem of diminishing returns, increasing the resolution of a point grid has a dramatic effect on the cost of survey. Halving the interval between points increases cost roughly by a factor of four. Consequently, it makes sense to consider optimum spacing of points as a balance between cost and anticipated benefit, unless the cost is already fixed.

The cost of survey actually has several components (Wignall and De Geoffroy, 1987:38-39). The most obvious one is the cost of making each observation. This is the cost of digging test pits, augering to a particular depth, or taking resistivity readings, for example. This source of cost increases as the square of any increase in survey resolution. A second cost includes the establishment of the control grid or, for surveys that do not use regular grids, simply establishing the location of each observation point. A third one is travel time between observation points plus any setup time that is necessary to make observations.

Several authors in mathematical geology have dealt with the optimal spacing of point arrays for intersecting circular or elliptical targets. They have also explicitly dealt with the goal of optimizing the balance between the cost and payoffs of different point intervals. Whether the search is for minerals, oil, or archaeological evidence, it is easy to measure the costs of search in terms of the number of points, the number of person-hours required to execute the survey plan, or the monetary equivalent of these person-hours.

Because geologists are interested in profitable mineral or petroleum exploration, however, they also evaluate the benefit of a survey plan in the dollar value of targets' contents. This is very convenient, but not an appropriate measure of benefit in the context of archaeological research. Consequently, we need to find some other measure for the values of targets (see chapter 8, section 3.1.4). For CRM archaeology, one possibility is the estimated cost to developers to conduct mitigation of a site that construction activity unexpectedly encounters. The reason for considering this a benefit is that knowing the site is there in advance provides the option of modifying the development plan to avoid the site or minimize impact on it. For example, Schiffer (1987:353) notes a case when the failure of a survey to detect a major pueblo site led to substantial and unexpected mitigation costs. Excavation cost is mainly a function of the site's surface area, allowing estimate of the "values" of sites as the product of their areas and excavation cost in person-days per square meter or dollars per square meter, with some adjustment for the fixed costs of mitigation. Another possibility would be the estimated value of sites for tourism or recreation, although this is a measure that most archaeologists resist (see significance, chapter 8, section 3). For grant-funded research, a possible valuation would be the amount of funding that could typically be expected to excavate sites of various kinds and sizes, or this amount weighted by the probability that a grant proposal is funded. These are undoubtedly crude measures of target value, and have the serious disadvantage of making large sites more "valuable" than small ones, but do provide a basis for justifying particular intensities of survey, and may help convince developers and planners that there are benefits to spending more money on survey. Other measures of value would depend on the survey's goals, and are more difficult to make commensurate with costs. For example, lower variance or standard error is a benefit when the goal of survey is to estimate population parameters, but it is difficult to compare the benefit of halving the standard error with the cost of quadrupling the survey effort. Normally, this would instead be dealt with as an allocation problem (see chapter 5, section 2.3), and the spacing would then be determined for a fixed number of points, as in the last section.

In most cases, archaeologists can only determine the optimum spacing for a fixed cost. They have a certain budget for survey that allows them, for example, to insert 40 test pits in each sample quadrat of 100 m x 300 m (Kintigh, 1988:688). In that case, solving for s for an equilateral pattern with four rows (table 1) results in a spacing between rows of $s = 27.27$ m, with the sides of the triangles of $i = 31.49$ m, and the largest circular target that the pattern might fail to intersect is 36.4 m in diameter.

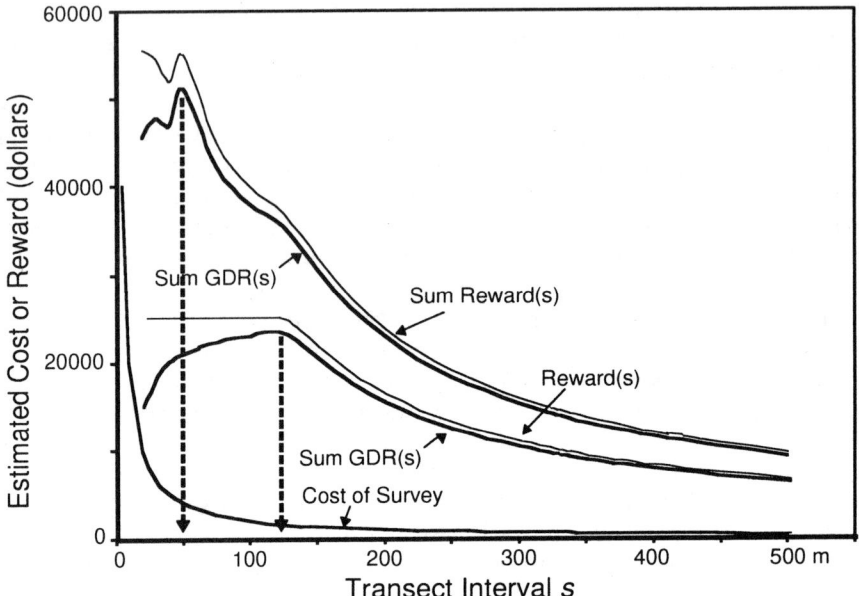

Figure 23. Estimating the optimal transect spacing for a case in which it is reasonable to compare survey costs with the rewards or "values" of sites based, for example, on their mitigation costs. The lower lines show the case of elliptical targets predicted to be 160 m x 60 m, with a probability of occurrence of 0.1, and the optimal spacing is 125 m. The upper lines are for a mix of four site sizes and yields an optimum spacing of 50 m.

Where it is possible for costs and benefits to be commensurable, however, the optimum spacing (s) is the value of s that maximizes the payoff or expected gross detection return (*GDR*), which Drew (1979:236-245) defines as the expected reward minus the absolute cost:

$$GDR(s) = P(s) * V - C(s)$$

where $P(s)$ is the probability of detecting the target with a spacing of s,[2] V is a measure of the target's value, and $C(s)$ is the cost of carrying out a survey with an interval of s. Because the probability of intersection, $P(s)$, drops off exponentially for spacings greater than those that assure intersection, but are a constant 1.0 for all of the smallest spacings, *GDR(s)* will rise sharply and then fall off exponentially. The optimum spacing is where the *GDR(s)* curve peaks (figure 23). This method is applicable to single targets, a known number of multiple targets, or the most realistic case, potentially multiple unknown targets. In this last instance, it is necessary to modify gross detection return as

$$GDR(s) = \sum_{i=1}^{n} g_i P(s) * V_i - C(s)$$

---

[2] $P(s)$ is actually the product of the probability of intersection and the probability of recognizing the target, given that we intersect it (typically a function of artifact density and clustering), but for simplicity, here we only consider the probability of intersection.

where g_i is the *a priori* probability that the *i*th target occurs in the search area and *n* is the *a priori* estimate of the number of targets (Drew, 1979:243-245). Previous surveys in similar or adjacent regions could serve for estimating the probabilities that various kinds of targets are present in the survey area. The result is robust even with rather rough estimates of the probabilities and values, so one need not worry too much about errors in these estimates.

Although Drew subtracts the absolute cost from the value to calculate *GDR(s)*, an alternative is to weight the cost by the probability of failing to detect targets (Wignall and De Geoffroy, 1987:40, 171). However, this has the undesirable effect of making highly intensive surveys seem costless!

The following section will include an example of using *GDR* to estimate optimal spacing, but for transects.

4.2.5 Optimizing the Spacing of Parallel Transects

Clearly, for circular targets, intersection by parallel transects is assured as long as the spacing *s* is less than the target diameter, 2*r*. As with the point grids, then, it is simple to determine a spacing that will intersect all targets greater than a particular size. Thus, a spacing only slightly less than *s* = 2*r* is generally effective (but see Krakker et al., 1983:473-474 for the problem of intersecting sites at their edges).

However, as with the point grids, there is no need to assume that targets are circular or larger than the spacing interval. In the case of continuous parallel transects, the probability of intersecting a target is generally proportional to the ratio, *l/s*, where *l* is the greatest dimension of the target (the length of lines and ellipses, or diameter of circles) and *s* is the spacing between transects (Agocs, 1955; McCammon, 1977; Wignall and De Geoffroy, 1987:129). More exactly, the probability of intersection for linear targets of random orientation, for cases where *l < s*, is,

$$P(s) = \frac{2l}{\pi s}$$

Thus, using the pessimistic scenario of linear sites ensures intersection of all targets greater than a particular length, regardless of their shape. In that case,

$$s = \frac{2l}{\pi}$$

Linear targets longer than the interval, *s*, could intersect transects more than once. Consequently, their probability of intersection (Wignall and DeGeoffroy, 1987:129) is

$$P(s) = \frac{2l}{\pi s}\left[1 - \sqrt{(1 - \tfrac{s}{l})^2} + \tfrac{s}{l} * Acs(\tfrac{s}{l}) \right]$$

For circular targets, orientation is immaterial and the probability of intersection is simply,

$$P(s) = \frac{l}{s}$$

for cases where the diameter is less than the interval, *s*, and *P(s)* = 1.0 otherwise.

Ellipses have P(s) intermediate between these two values (McCammon 1977:372), which depends on the shape ratio, simply the ratio of width to length, b/l (Wignall and De Geoffroy, 1987:129-130). For any transect spacing, the intersection probability for an ellipse, P_e, is the sum of the probabilities for lines (P_l) and circles (P_c), each weighted by the shape ratio as follows:

$$P_e = (1 - \frac{b}{l})P_l + (\frac{b}{l})P_c$$

These formulas not only allow determination of the value of s that guarantees intersection of targets above a particular size, but also of the probabilities and confidence intervals for detection of smaller sites or larger spacings.

4.2.5.1 Optimal Spacing of Transects Taking Costs and "Value" into Account

Determining the optimum balance between survey cost and benefit then works in the same way as in section 1.1.4, by finding the peak in gross detection return, $GDR(s)$.

To illustrate this, imagine a situation in which the estimated prior probability that a survey area of 5 km by 2 km contains one elliptical Iroquoian village on the order of 30,000 m² in area, about 160 m long and 60 m wide, is $g_1 = 0.1$. For simplicity, let us ignore other effects on detectability here and assume that intersection equals detection; in real examples, we would multiply these two probabilities together. Let us also suppose that the unanticipated mitigation of such a village would cost a developer $5,000 for mechanized earth removal, approximately 30 person-months or $75,000 for archaeological excavation, $150,000 in penalties for delay in the completion of the development project, and $20,000 for post-excavation analysis. Thus the "value" of the site to the developer is estimated at $250,000. Further, the estimated cost of surveying transects by walking level, plowed fields, and each crew member covering 10 km per day, is $200 per day (including breaks, travel time between transects, and time lost locating transects). Thus, if we only consider this one site, the gross detection return for this site is

$$GDR_1(s) = g_1 P1(s) V_1 - C(s) = 0.1 * P_1(s) * 250{,}000 - C(s)$$

Figure 23 compares the expected reward, $P(s) * g * V$, with the cost of survey and GDR for various spacings. The highest value of $GDR(s)$ in this example occurs at a spacing of $s = 125$ m, where GDR is $23,400. We can also express some uncertainty about the dimensions of the anticipated site by, for example, recalculating $GDR(s)$ for probabilities based on the lower and upper confidence limits on site size.

A more realistic survey would consider a variety of sites, most of which are considerably smaller and more difficult to find than this large Iroquoian village. Assuming the possibility of three smaller site types, in addition to this large one,

$$GDR(s) = \sum_{i=1}^{4} g_i P_i(s) V_i - C(s)$$

Units and Sampling Frames

Assuming that previous experience in similar nearby areas suggests a prior probability of 0.2 of containing a site of about 10,000 m² and 80 m long, of 0.4 of containing a site of about 3140 m² area and 40 m long, and of 0.8 of containing a site of about 625 m² and 20 m long, there are four expected site types of varying size and probability of occurrence. For the sake of simplicity, let us further assume that the "value" of the smaller sites is in the same proportion to their area as the large Iroquoian village (actual costs of mitigation might include fixed costs). Adding these estimates leads to an estimated optimum transect interval of 50 m (figure 23).

A few words are necessary to explain these results. The "optimum" spacing is not to be construed as one that will find all the targets, if they exist, and certainly not all the very small ones. Clearly, the only way to be reasonably certain of finding all the sites 20 m long, even given perfect detectability, would be to use the more pessimistic formula for the probability of intersecting linear targets, and the spacing would be $s = 40/p = 12.73$ m. However the cost of such a spacing would be about four times as much as for the 50 m spacing, while only marginally improving the probability of finding sites, and not improving the probability of finding the larger sites at all. The goal in this section was not to find all the sites, but to find a balance between survey cost and results. We can also use the survey results to estimate the number of small sites the survey missed with the "optimum" spacing (see chapters 5 and 10). Where it is absolutely necessary to avoid missing sites, and not merely to estimate how many we missed, clearly the smaller spacing is appropriate, as long as it does not mean omitting other survey spaces with similar probabilities of containing large and small sites.

4.2.5.2 Spacing Transects within Polygons

Whenever archaeologists employ transects to subsample or prospect quadrats or other spatial elements by visual inspection of the surface, a different approach to optimum spacing is called for. In this case the goal is to find artifacts, whose areas are extremely small relative to the quadrat size and, probably, transect spacing. In such instances, the targets are so small that edge effects are negligible, we would not expect transects to intersect artifacts exactly, and range effects are much more important influences on the probability of detection. Consequently, it is important to evaluate the way the probability of detection declines with distance from the center of a transect (see chapter 3, section 1.4).

Archaeologists who have considered this problem have tended implicitly to use the definite detection model. In other words, they have assumed that fieldwalkers in pedestrian survey by visual inspection will detect all artifacts exposed on a plowed field that lie, for example, within 2 m of their path, and have ignored the possibility of detecting artifacts at greater distances. In this scenario, a transect spacing of $s = 2R$ (4 m in this case) "guarantees" detection of all artifacts that are visible on the surface. This spacing is known as the "sweep width," $W = 2R$ (see chapter 3, section 1.4). Similarly, this approach assumes that a spacing of $s = 4R$, for example, would lead to recovery of 50% of the artifacts.

A more realistic assessment would use an exponential or sinusoidal detection function (see chapter 3, section 1.4) to estimate the spacing that would yield some expected percentage of the artifacts, such as 80%. For example, the "effective visibility" of the detector, E, is half the sweep spacing that results in a detection probability of 0.5 (expected 50% of artifacts). For definite detection, $W = E$, but for inverse-cube detection, $W = 1.076E$ (Koopman 1980: 76-77, 217). Archaeologists need to conduct experiments to estimate the value of E for their crew members.

4.2.5.3   Retiring-square Pattern

In prospection, it is also possible to optimize the spacing between the concentric squares of the expanding-square pattern (see chapter 6, section 3.1). When definite detection applies, the optimal spacing, s, can be calculated from

$$s = 0.65\sqrt{W\sigma}$$

where W is the "sweep width" (normally twice the range of definite detection — see chapter 3, section 1.4) and σ is the standard deviation of a circular normal probability distribution centered on the point of fix. Where it is not reasonable to assume definite detection, however, we can substitute the "effective visibility" (E) of the detector. The spacing interval is then

$$s = 0.75\sqrt{E\sigma}$$

4.2.6 Optimizing the Size of Quadrats and Other Spatial Units

It is often advantageous for quadrats and other areal survey units to be larger than the anticipated scale of the clustering of archaeological materials, unless the goal is to measure that scale, as in distributional archaeology (see below, pp. 165-166). When the goal is simply to maximize the probability of intersecting targets, generally edge effects make small polygons more efficient than large ones. Recognizing targets that are intersected, however, often requires larger polygon areas, as in SSTs.

4.2.6.1   Optimizing Polygon Size for the Variance of Estimates at a Fixed Cost

Using a larger number of smaller survey units results in a larger sample size than a small number of large units with the same total area. Consequently, for sampling surveys, the smaller units lead to estimates with smaller standard errors. Once the optimal sample size for estimation of some important parameter and a given level of confidence has been determined (see chapter 5, section 3.2), then the optimum unit size is simply A/n, where A is the total area of survey that the budget allows, and n is the optimal sample size.

However, the variance is itself a function of the polygon size. Larger units, on average, will contain more items or will show internal autocorrelation, resulting in lower variance. Consequently, polygon size is trade-off.

4.2.6.2 Balancing the Costs and Benefits of Polygon Size

The solution in the last section assumes that survey cost is a linear function of survey area, but this is generally not true because the costs of unit setup and travel between units are not proportional to area. One way to evaluate the effects of grid setup and between-quadrat travel time on cost will be familiar to readers interested in Optimal Foraging Theory, even if the optimal solution for surveyors is quite different from that for foragers.

In essence, survey polygons are like the patches in a foraging patch-use model, and surveyors are trying to optimize their allocation of time to each patch with reference to the productivity of that patch. Given a small number of fairly large survey units, surveyors can expect to spend a higher proportion of their time surveying within them and recording or collecting artifacts. As the number of survey elements increases, while their size decreases so as to keep total survey effort constant, the amount of time spent on set up and other fixed costs grows, but the average distance between units is shorter so that travel time decreases, once there are enough units to allow survey of more than one per day. Meanwhile, the amount of time spent discovering sites is mainly a function of "patch" area. Consequently, graphing the ratio of time spent on travel and setup to the time spent searching for artifacts or sites against the number of survey units would result in a curve that falls at first and then rises as the increasing effect of the fixed costs becomes dominant. The point where the lowest proportion of time is invested in unproductive travel and set up — the trough in the curve — marks the optimal number of units, and unit size would then be A/n.

4.2.6.3 Optimizing the Size of SSTs for Artifact Density

Section 1.1.4 dealt with optimizing the spacing of SST points, so as to maximize the probability of target intersection under the constraint of cost. However, intersection does not guarantee detection; usually detection of buried targets by SST depends on the interaction of artifact density with the area or volume of each SST. A number of authors have discussed this problem (Kintigh, 1988; Krakker et al., 1983; Lynch, 1980; Nance, 1983; Nance and Ball, 1986; Shott, 1985; Stone, 1981).

A simple approach is to find the area or volume that will lead to some reasonable probability of encountering some minimum number of artifacts. The simplest way to do this is to assume that the artifacts have a Poisson distribution, although various authors have criticized this assumption on the grounds that artifacts often have clustered distributions. Nonetheless, where we can make a reasonable guess at artifact density, but do not yet have information on the degree of clustering, the Poisson distribution can provide useful, albeit somewhat optimistic, guidance in the selection of SST size. As noted already in chapter 3 (section 1.3.2), the Poisson distribution has a single parameter, λ, and the probability of finding x artifacts in a unit of a given size is

$$p(x) = \frac{e^{-\lambda} \lambda^x}{x!}$$

Given that the Poisson distribution is rather optimistic in archaeological contexts (Nance and Ball, 1989), this expression demonstates that the probability of finding artifacts in, for example, small-diameter auger holes, is depressingly small in most situations. For example, on a site where the artifact density is as high as 4 artifacts/m^2, even shovel tests 50 cm x 50 cm have an expectation of only one artifact ($\lambda = 1$), and the probability that one test will find no artifacts at all in this situation is 0.37. Auger holes with a diameters of 9 cm, meanwhile have $\lambda = 0.0254$ and the probability that any given auger hole will find no artifacts is 0.975! Since the probability of finding one or more artifacts is simply $1 - p(0)$, then this is 0.63 in the former but only 0.025 in the latter case. One way to decide on the size of SSTs, then, is to find the size that yields an estimated probability of finding one or more artifacts of, for example, 0.5. In the case of an artifact density of 4/m^2, that would have an area of 0.17 m^2. Where expected artifact densities are quite a bit lower than this, such an approach could call for test units quite a bit larger than is typical. Yet it is pointless to use units that are regularly too small to detect targets of interest even when they intersect them.

4.3 Influences on Detection of Spatial Pattern

Sometimes a survey's goal is to determine whether sites, buildings or artifacts are clustered, evenly spaced, randomly distributed in space, or conform to some other pattern. The fact that patterns can occur at different scales means that the scale of the quadrats used has a large effect on the chances of detecting them.

For example, selection of unit size could determine whether a distribution of artifacts or sites appears clustered, random, or evenly spaced. In figure 24, there are clear clusters of dots, yet small polygons give the impression of a random or slightly clustered distribution, while large ones suggest an even distribution (all units have the same density of dots). Only when the survey polygons are close in size to the clusters do we notice the strong contrasts in density that would lead us to detect clustering, and even there unlucky positioning of the polygon borders could blur this effect.

Similarly, the size of quadrats or the spacing between point-observations has a marked effect on the shape of stepped statistical surfaces or isopleth maps. This is analogous to what happens when the interval on histograms changes (Whallon, 1987:144-147). This effect is so great that it usually calls for smoothing or "filtering" the data, or the use of "Kriging," to provide a realistic impression of how densities or other values vary over space (see Orton, 1980; Zubrow and Harbaugh, 1978).

4.4 Influences on Parameter Estimates

The shape, size and arrangement of spatial units also affect estimates of population parameters, such as estimated site size or density, degree of clustering of artifacts, and proportion of sites or artifacts belonging to a particular type or period.

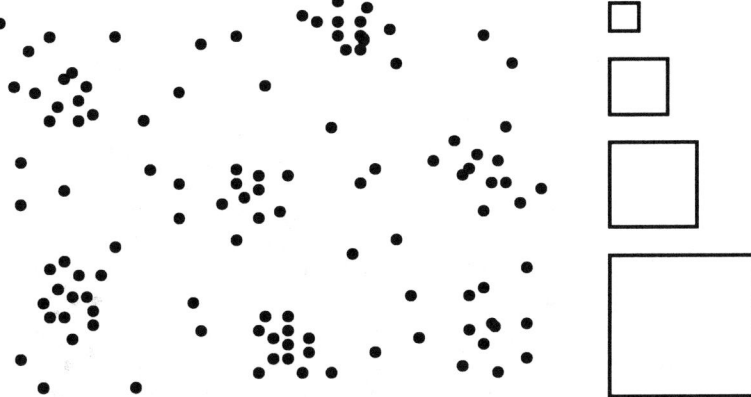

Figure 24. A dot pattern with several obvious clusters would probably apear only slightly clustered in a survey using the smallest quadrat, strongly clustered with quadrat that comes closest to the size of clusters, and evenly distributed with the large quadrat (cf. Hodder and Orton, 1976:37).

As noted above, edge effects make it more likely that long spatial units, such as transects, will intersect clustered phenomena than would circular or near-circular units. A consequence of this is that they will also return higher estimates of the number and density of artifact clusters or sites, unless we correct for this effect.

One way to compensate is to count only those sites whose centers lie within the boundaries of the survey element when enumerating the sites for that element (record sites whose centers lie outside but omit them from the quadrat statistics). Another is to avoid measuring the intensity of occupation within the quadrat by its number of sites, and instead measure the total site area that occurs within the quadrat or other spatial element. That way, only the portions of sites that properly occur within the sample are counted toward statistics, thus avoiding cluster sampling. A third way, which also avoids cluster sampling, is to use "non-site survey," and observations such as artifact density for the quadrat, rather than for any "site" within it.

Because the edge effect is more pronounced for the intersection of large sites than for small sites or features, it will also affect estimates of the proportions of site types whenever these tend to vary in size. A sample of long rectangles is therefore likely to overrepresent large Late Woodland villages relative to small Archaic camp sites, for example.

Some kinds of transect frames can result in biased samples of space. For example, in a selection of transects with endpoints at random loctions along the two sides of a rectangle, spaces near the center of the rectangle have a much higher probability of being intersected by transects than do spaces near the rectangle's ends. It is better to minimize this problem as much as possible, either by stratifying the survey area into relatively narrow, parallel bands, or by removing the restriction on the endpoints of the transects.

5. CONCLUSIONS

Deciding on effective shapes, sizes, spacing, and arrangements of survey units depends on a survey's goals and the nature of the archaeological material and region of interest.

Defining the "universe" or the study area is usually the easiest step unless it is critical for it to conform to a real cultural unit whose boundaries are usually unknown. It is sometimes outside our control altogether, as in many cases of Cultural Resource Management. It is important to realize, however, that a sampling frame does not need to be a regular grid. In some cases, a population of topographic units might be more effective at achieving the survey's goals.

Deciding on the type and arrangement of spatial elements requires the most thought. A predilection for square quadrats oriented to geographic North is too often without any substantive basis. When geometric grids are appropriate, it makes sense to anticipate the likely character of targets to help with decisions about the grids' shapes, orientation, and intervals (e.g., McCammon, 1977; Singer and Wickman, 1969). Elements based on natural geographic partitions, such as lengths of streams delimited by confluences, or arbitrary geometric units positioned along geographical features, are often more effective than grids whenever those features are relevant to ancient cultural behaviors. Finally, even if there has been no attempt to optimize the framework for survey, it is important to evaluate what effect the survey frame may have had on detection probabilities and other results (see chapter 10).

Chapter V
Sampling Space: Statistical Surveys

Sampling is appropriate whenever the goal is to make economical estimates of the characteristics (parameters) of a population, to test *statistical* hypotheses about populations, or to construct some kinds of predictive models. Although it is a truism that all archaeological observations constitute samples in some sense, here by "sampling" I mean the use of samples selected by reference to probability theory.

As mentioned briefly in chapter 2, sampling depends on the concepts of population and sample. The population is the set of artifacts, sites, clusters of material culture, or spatial elements (quadrats, transects, etc.) of interest. The sample is a subset of the population and, if the sample is well designed, it should be representative of the population from which it was selected. This means that any statistics of the sample should be close approximations of parameters of the population. Parameters of interest typically include the proportions of archaeological material belonging to various categories or associated with various environmental circumstances.

As other parts of this book emphasize, sampling is not the appropriate method for all archaeological problems, or even for all kinds of hypothesis testing. In some cases other approaches, especially prospection, are much more economical, efficient, and effective.

1. SAMPLING DESIGNS

Most archaeologists are familiar with the basic varieties of sampling designs: random, stratified and systematic. More complicated surveys are usually based on combinations of these three basic designs.

1.1 Basic Sampling Designs

1.1.1 Random Sampling

A simple random sample is one in which each element of the population has an equal probability of being selected.

In random sampling *with replacement*, the simplest kind of sampling, this is true at each and every selection, which means that some elements could be selected twice or even three times. In practice this does not mean that it is necessary to resurvey the unit (unless to check on consistency between survey teams, for example). It only means that the data for the units selected twice receive double weight, and those selected three times get triple weight.

In archaeology, it is more common to find random sampling *without replacement*. In this case, at the first selection, all elements have an equal chance of being selected. But once the first element is removed from the pool, the other elements have a second chance to be selected from a slightly smaller pool, and so on until the last element to be selected has perhaps had many chances to be selected and an increasing probability of selection at each draw. For example, if the population contains 100 elements, at the first selection all elements have a probability of 1/100, or 0.01, of being selected. On the second selection, all the remaining elements have an additional probability of 1/99 of being selected, or a probability of 1/100 + 1/99 of being selected in the first two draws. By the fifth drawing, the probability will be 1/100 + 1/99 + 1/98 + 1/97 + 1/96, and so on. Fortunately it turns out that, because one element is as likely as any other to be drawn early or late, sampling without replacement provides unbiased estimates of parameters. Furthermore, for small samples sampling without replacement is more efficient, meaning that variance on the parameter estimates is small relative to sample size. However, these nuances of probability do mean that you should be using slightly more complicated equations to calculate variance or confidence intervals than when you sample with replacement. Make sure you use the correct equations.

A random sample of sites would be possible in cases where the locations of all the sites in the population were known in advance. We could simply number the sites and randomly select a set of numbers to choose the sample of sites. The known site locations might come from aerial photographs, for example. It is rarely possible, however, to sample sites in this way because their locations are unknown. Alternatively, the population could consist of a large number of landforms on which sites might be located. In that case, numbering the landforms would permit random selection of a sample on which to search for sites.

In spatial contexts, an archaeological random sample more commonly consists of a random selection of quadrats from a gridded population. A surveyor need only assign a unique number to each quadrat, and then randomly select numbers. The number of selections (including the number of repeated selections if sampling with replacement), constitutes the sample size, n. The sampling fraction is n/N. An alternative to numbering all the quadrats, if we are using a regular grid, is to number increments along the x and y axes and then select pairs of random numbers as the x- and y-coordinates of the quadrats in our sample.

Random samples are simple and unbiased, but are not always the best choice for a survey design. Spatial random samples sometimes leave large areas of the map unsampled, which could result in omission of important information or entire topographic or geographical zones. They also have larger variance than some of the other sampling designs.

Sampling Space: Statistical Surveys   115

1.1.2 Stratified Sampling

In stratified random sampling, the population is subdivided into subpopulations, called *strata*, and a random selection takes place in each stratum. In effect, this helps avoid one of the problems of simple random sampling — the possibility of omitting important parts of the map — and ensures that the sample represents important aspects of a diverse population.

Stratified sampling takes advantage of prior information that may be relevant to the parameters a surveyor plans to estimate with the sample. For example, if some of these parameters have to do with site size, and there is reason to expect that the largest sites will be in river valleys while a variety of small site types will occur in the surrounding hills, the estimated variety of site sizes, as well as mean site size and total site area, would be inaccurate if most information came from the valley floors. Stratification is effective in cases where the individual strata are internally homogeneous but differ from other strata in some relevant respect. In other words, variance in relevant variables should be smaller within strata than between strata.

The report on a survey that employed stratified sampling should include clear justification for the selection of strata and demonstration that the parameters of interest indeed vary by stratum. It is not enough simply to say, "we stratified the population by soil type," as though the purpose of this strategy were self-evident. If there is reason to believe that soil type influenced the distribution and type of archaeological materials, perhaps because of varying agricultural potential, it is necessary to justify this claim. One of the greatest failings of surveys that have used stratified samples is that many of them offer no justification for the selection of strata. Typically the strata are large and default to some geographical variable, such as soil type or elevation. As Wobst (1983:59) points out in the case of Massachussets, this is in spite of the fact that site densities do not vary with the variable used as the basis for stratification. Clearly, this calls for the use of some other basis that the surveyors can justify.

Stratified sampling is also common at the scale of individual sites. In that instance, the best strategy is to use strata that may correspond with relevant variation across the site. For example, topographic breaks, such as terracing or the slope change between a high mound and a lower mound, might mark the boundary between a citadel or elite area and a common domestic or industrial area, or between site components that differ in their age (e.g., Portugali, 1982). Traces of large architectural features, such as possible fortifications or ditches, or traces of a street system, might also permit partitioning of the site into strata that are probably meaningful. In the absence of such criteria, a common approach is simply to partition the site into four quarters, but the arbitrary orientation of the quarters to the cardinal points, although the most common choice, is unlikely to produce well differentiated and internally homogeneous strata.

Stratified samples can be proportional or disproportional. In a proportional stratified sample, the sampling fraction for each stratum is the same as in the whole population. In other words, if stratification of the population is by soil type, and 10% of the survey area has brown stony soils, 10% of the sample would come from the stratum with brown stony soils. This is the most common approach in archaeological applications except where stratification is by "sensitivity." Sometimes, however, it is better to have larger sampling fractions in some strata than in others. For example, if one of the strata is very small, even a sample size of one for that stratum might constitute a larger than average sampling fraction, and obtaining a reasonably large sample size for the stratum might require a significantly larger sampling fraction than that of the largest stratum. A disproportional stratified sample is also useful in cases where some strata have markedly different means and variances than others. A common practice today is to use disproportionate sampling of strata defined by "sensitivity," or the probability that they will contain sites (see chapter 11). Unless these strata are very well justified, however, this practice can lead to such minimal sampling in areas of perceived "low potential" that it will amplify biases in our understanding of archaeological distributions (Wobst, 1983). Another justification for disproportional stratified sampling is to minimize the overall variance of estimates, a form of optimization (see section 2.3).

Because a well-designed stratified sample takes relevant information into account to ensure that the sample provides useful information on different segments of the population, it can be a very efficient design. That means that it has less sampling error (lower variance on estimates) than simple random sampling. For detailed discussion of stratified sampling, see Som (1973). For sample size issues, see section 2.

1.1.3 Systematic Sampling

A systematic sample employs a regular "spacing" rule to ensure that sample elements are evenly distributed across a population.

For sampling objects that are numbered in sequence, for example, a sampler decides on an interval and then randomly selects the first element. Once it is selected, all the other members of the sample are determined by the spacing rule. For example, if the interval is five and the randomly selected element was numbered 18, the sample would include the elements (3, 8, 13, 18, 23, 28, ...). Systematic sampling is not random sampling because only one selection is random; all the others are strictly determined by the spacing rule. Depending on where they fit in this spacing, the other elements have a probability of either 1.0 or 0 of being selected, once the first element has been chosen.

Most archaeological uses of systematic sampling, however, involve even spacing of quadrats or, especially, transects or point-like units. In principle, this involves partitioning the survey universe into a sampling frame consisting of a grid or a set of transects, randomly selecting the first quadrat, point, or transect, and then taking all the other quadrats, points, or transects that satisfy the spacing rule. For example, if we have selected an interval of four, and randomly select the seventh transect, then our sample would consist of the transects numbered 3, 7, 11, 15, 19, and 23. In practice, however, most archaeologists using systematic sampling do not select any of the transects randomly, but instead arbitrarily select transects that lie on the boundaries of quadrats predetermined by existing topographic maps. As long as the map grid is independent of the distribution of targeted material culture, such an arbitrary selection of the starting transects may be just as good as a random selection. However, in a survey for historic sites in a region where 19th-century roads were surveyed along these same grid lines, it would be better to use a different spacing and orientation of transects to avoid bias. In addition, the existing grid may be far from optimal in its fit to the scale of the archaeological observations that the surveyors expect to make, and a more thoughtful attention to the size, shape, and orientation of units is preferable (see chapter 4).

Note that one reason that archaeologists have tended to favor spatial systematic samples is that they combine some of the best aspects of sampling and prospecting. In particular, their simple geometries make it easy to estimate the likelihood that the survey has missed sites of any shape and size (see chapter 4), and thus to take this into account in estimates of population parameters.

1.2 Complications in Geometric Spatial Samples

Many archaeological examples of spatial sampling involve combinations of the basic sampling strategies.

1.2.1 Systematic, Stratified, Unaligned Sampling

A common archaeological survey strategy, especially at the scale of individual sites, aims to avoid random sampling's pitfall of leaving large areas unexamined. It employs a grid of large quadrats that serve as the strata of a stratified sample. A single, small sample element (usually a quadrat or circle) is randomly selected in each of the large quadrats, so that the resulting sample of small quadrats is fairly evenly spread across the map. There is no reason why this strategy could not also be used at the regional scale, but it would usually make more sense to stratify by some more meaningful criteria than arbitrary squares (see section 1.1.2).

1.2.2 Transects Nested in Quadrats

Another common archaeological survey strategy involves a random selection of relatively large quadrats, followed by a systematic sample of transects or point-like elements within them. This more complicated design constitutes subsampling if the transects or points are spaced far enough apart that we can expect them to intersect only some of the archaeological materials or sites in each quadrat, or if detectability is imperfect. Subsampling complicates both calculations of parameter estimates and the relationship between discovery probability and site size or discovery radius (chapter 3).

This strategy can have some practical advantages. For example, grouping of transects can create time savings in the field and the regular spacing of transects within the quadrats allows us to estimate intersection probability.

However, use of this strategy can lead to biased estimates if its practioner is not careful to consider spatial autocorrelation and to account for cluster sampling, where necessary (see section 1.3).

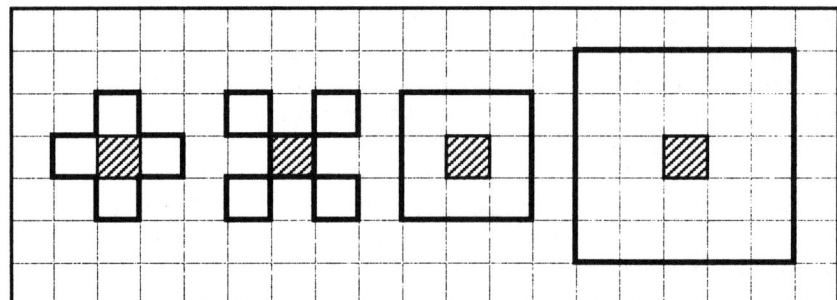

Figure 25. Four ways to define the "neighborhood" (dark outline) of an initial sample element (hatched) in adaptive sampling.

1.2.3 Cross-cutting Stratification

Sophisticated sampling designs sometimes use more than one criterion to stratify the population into a fairly large number of subpopulations and obtain very precise and accurate estimates of parameters. For example, in a region with steep mountains and broad valleys oriented predominantly north to south, there might be reason to believe that the characteristics of a population of sites varied both by elevation, and from north to south. Cross-cutting the elevation zones and the latitudinal zones would result in a set of relatively small strata defined by the intersection of criteria.

Effective stratification, whether inside or outside of archaeology, is often based on cross-cutting several relevant variables in ways that lead to very precise estimation of population parameters.

1.2.4 Adaptive Sampling

Archaeologists are generally less familiar with adaptive sampling than with the more traditional strategies. Adaptive sampling adds new sample elements in response to information gathered in previously surveyed elements (Orton, 2000:34-38, 93-98; Thompson and Seber, 1996:94-95).

In spatial sampling, a typical application of adaptive sampling involves adding sample elements adjacent to any of those that contain sites, artifacts, or features. The added elements are described as the "neighborhood" of the original element, and can be defined in a variety of ways (e.g., figure 25). When no more elements can be added, because none of the most recently surveyed units meets the condition for adding its neighborhood (e.g., they contain no artifacts), the process stops. The result is a number of clusters of sample elements that meet the condition, each cluster, or "network," surrounded by a kind of buffer zone of elements that do not.

One application of adaptive sampling is in subsurface testing (SST) and contact investigation (figure 26). Whenever an initial transect of shovel tests or auger samples at, perhaps, 20 m intervals yields an artifact in one SST, surveyors would add SSTs to its

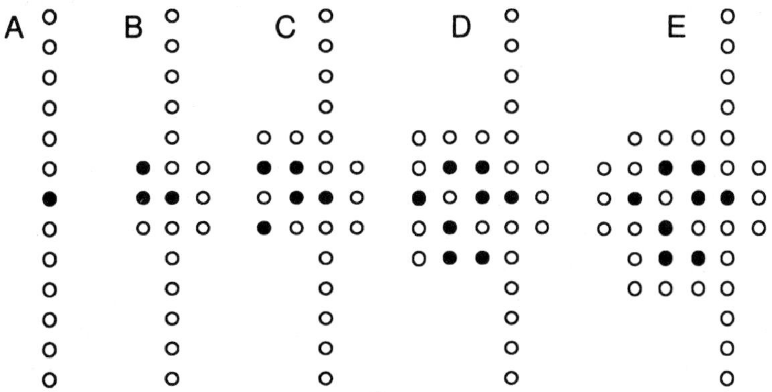

Sampling Space: Statistical Surveys   119

Figure 26. Example of adaptive sampling in a systematic survey by shovel tests or augering. Discovery of an artifact in one SST (black circle) in the first transect (a) leads to the addition of more SSTs in its neighborhood (b), and so on, until the new SSTs no longer produce any artifacts (e).

neighborhood. Discovery of one or more artifacts in any of these would lead to tests in its neighborhood too, gradually expanding the region tested until no more artifacts appear.

Adaptive sampling tends to be more efficient than simple random strategies only under particular circumstances. For cluster sampling, as in the case when the sample consists of quadrats or transects but sites are the analytical elements (see next section), adaptive sampling is well suited to populations of sites that are highly aggregated or clustered. It is also well suited to situations in which surveying in neighborhoods, rather than in dispersed units, reduces costs, such as the cost of travel or the cost of locating quadrat boundaries. It also depends on the cost of inspecting units that do not meet required conditions (e.g., ones without sites) being relatively low. On average, adaptive cluster samples also have relatively high discovery rates, which may make them useful for prospection (see chapter 7, section 1.8).

1.3 Cluster Sampling and Element Sampling

Most archaeological surveys and excavations involve spatial cluster samples (Judge et al, 1975; Mueller, 1975; Thomas, 1975). Whenever archaeologists sample a population of spatial units, such as quadrats or transects, but then proceed with analysis as though the population consisted of sites or artifacts, they are cluster sampling. In contrast to stratified sampling, which selects some observations in each stratum, cluster sampling is almost like taking one stratum and using every possible observation in it.

There is an important difference, however. Stratified sampling requires the assumption that each stratum is fairly homogeneous and different from others in some important respect, so that the elements within each stratum should be more similar to one another than to elements in other strata. A cluster sample, by contrast, involves the assumption that a single subset of the population is like a microcosm of the whole population. In other words, the members of the cluster sample should be quite diverse (have large variance) relative to the population as a whole. We would also expect two clusters from the same population to have very similar characteristics.

In a sense cluster sampling involves two kinds of populations. If N is the population of sampling elements (e.g., quadrats), there is also a population, M, of sites or artifacts, for example. The number of observations in the sample is n quadrats, but these sample quadrats contain m sites or artifacts.

Cluster sampling can be very efficient (i.e., have low sampling error) as long as the cluster sample is really well "mixed," so that it represents the population quite well. However, estimating some population parameters with cluster samples requires different estimators than with simple random samples. Cluster means and cluster proportions are essentially the same as with simple random samples, but standard deviations and standard errors are calculated differently. Drennan (1996:243-54) provides an excellent introduction to the use of well-behaved cluster samples.

Unfortunately, many archaeological cluster samples are not well behaved. Quite often, we cannot be confident that the cluster sample is "well mixed" or represents the whole population adequately. In such cases we would not expect it to provide good estimates of population parameters. This is often because spatial autocorrelation due to spatial patterning in cultural use of the landscape makes the sites in the sample more homogeneous than a "well mixed" sample would be. Ironically, it is often precisely this patterning that we are trying to detect in the first place, and is why stratified samples tend to work well. Spatial autocorrelation means that sites that are close together are more likely to be similar in their characteristics, and especially spatial or contextual characteristics, than ones found far apart. For example, sites that are close together have a high probability of being located near the same kinds of soil, geological outcrops, transportation routes, water sources and other features likely to be relevant to the sites' functions and economies. As a result, there is less variation (less variance) in the cluster than in the population, which likely includes sites associated with many kinds of soil and geological features that were excluded from the cluster sample.

Sometimes it is possible to avoid this problem by using analytical units that are identical to the sampling units. If the sample consisted of square quadrats, for example, rather than the numbers of sites occurred on each soil type or within 200 m of water sources, the data could include the total site area in each quadrat that occurred on each soil type, the area of each soil type in each quadrat, or the proportion of site total site area that lies within 200 m of a water source. Focussing on attributes of the quadrats that were the sampling elements results in an element sample rather than a cluster sample. A common practice to avoid cluster sampling in archaeology is to focus on artifact density (e.g., Thomas, 1975:65).

1.4 Sampling with Point Samples

Point sampling is most common where shovel-testing, divoting, coring, and augering are the detection methods, but it is also possible to use a sample of points as the centers of circular units for surface inspection.

The simplest way to select a random point sample is to impose a rectangular grid on the survey area and randomly select pairs of x- and y-coordinates. Stratified random samples simply involve selecting such random pairs within each stratum. Systematic point samples require selecting a kind of grid (e.g., rectangular or triangular) to use as a sampling frame, and the size of sampling interval (e.g., 5 m), then randomly selecting a point of origin and grid orientation. The resulting sample consists of all the grid intersections (see chapter 4, section 3.4.1).

Point samples are more common in intrasite survey, and especially intrasite geophysical survey, than in regional survey. Typically, points in systematic rectangular arrangements are used for resistivity or magnetic surveys, for example.

However, point sampling also describes many kinds of regional survey in areas where surface visibility is poor, such as unplowed parts of northern and eastern North America. These usually have shockingly low sampling fractions and very low probability of detecting many kinds of sites, yet typically few alternatives are available. Consequently, it is necessary to give careful consideration to the characteristics (particularly bias in site detection) of these kinds of samples in order to make realistic assessments of their results. In many cases, unfortunately, there is good cause to be pessimistic about these results, and to expect that "variance in our estimates due to small sample size overwhelms any variation attributable to behavioral and other variables!" (Wobst, 1983:72). The kinds of factors we need to evaluate in these surveys, as well as ways to optimize the distribution of observation points, are discussed in chapters 3 and 4, so will not be repeated here.

Chapter 4 mentioned the Czech-British project, Ancient Landscape Reconstruction in North Bohemia, that surveyed "polygons" that were selected by randomly locating points in space (Kuna, 1998:80). The difference between the units used for sampling (a sampling frame of point coordinates) and those actually surveyed leads to large polygons having a greater probability of being included in the sample than small ones. In some situations PPS (probability proportional to size) sampling could be undesirable, and it is easy to avoid it simply by randomly selecting the polygons directly (next section).

1.5 Sampling Geomorphic and Cultural Features or "Places"

As mentioned in chapter 4, the population for a statistical survey need not consist of a set of geometrical units. A population of hilltops, stream terraces, beaches, canal segments, or ancient fields is not only legitimate, but to be preferred when these elements are relevant to the distribution of material culture. Careful definition of a population along these lines can also allow you to avoid cluster sampling.

I illustrate this approach first with a simulated survey of a previously surveyed region of the lower Diyala basin, Iraq, where settlement occurred along canals, traces of which are visible in aerial photographs (Adams, 1981:195). The map in figure 27 shows canal traces, with the segments between canal intersections numbered.[1] These canal segments constitute the elements of the population. It is also possible to stratify the population. Although there are many ways to do this, there are reasons to suspect that central places and other large, important settlements will be on major canals, while small settlements, lower in the site hierarchy, could occur on both major and minor canals. The main canals, then, will be stratum 1, and the "branch" canals will constitute stratum 2. There are 52 segments belonging to the former and 92 to the latter stratum.

A proportionally stratified random sample, without replacement, of 30 canal segments (11 from stratum 1 and 19 from stratum 2) gave the results shown in table 2, using the published data on Seleucid-Parthian sites from the Diyala survey. These compare quite well with the results from the whole population, and the stratification seems to have been successful. Note, however, that sites' tendency to be located at the boundaries between canal segments causes pronounced edge effects and the raw data would require correction for the resulting bias in this case (see chapter 4, section 3.2).

In a real survey in Wadi Ziqlab, Jordan (Banning, 1996), the sampling frame consisted of a population of stream terraces demarcated by meanders in a deeply incised canyon. As the goals of the survey focussed on characteristics of Neolithic settlement systems, any terraces that were demonstrably too recent on geological grounds could be excluded. Terraces that were not excluded were subsampled with one or two test trenches, 1 m x 3 m in area and up to 2 m deep, to search for buried archaeological remains. This was necessary because colluvium deposited from the adjacent steep slopes could be expected to have buried some sites entirely, leaving no visible remains on the surface, while Neolithic features and artifacts were not expected to exhibit enough physical contrast with their environment for geophysical prospection to be successful.

The survey successfully detected Neolithic materials, and some of later age, on five terraces, including one where Neolithic artifacts were also visible in a road cut. One of these proved, on further excavation, to be a well preserved Neolithic farmstead (Banning et al., 1994), unlike any Neolithic site that had previously been discovered in Jor-

---

[1] To keep the map from being too crowded, this map only shows a subset of the canal traces, and thus exaggerates the density of sites belonging to the Seleucid-Parthian periods. More realistically, we would not know the dates in advance, and would have to sample the whole population of extant and visible canal traces.

Sampling Space: Statistical Surveys

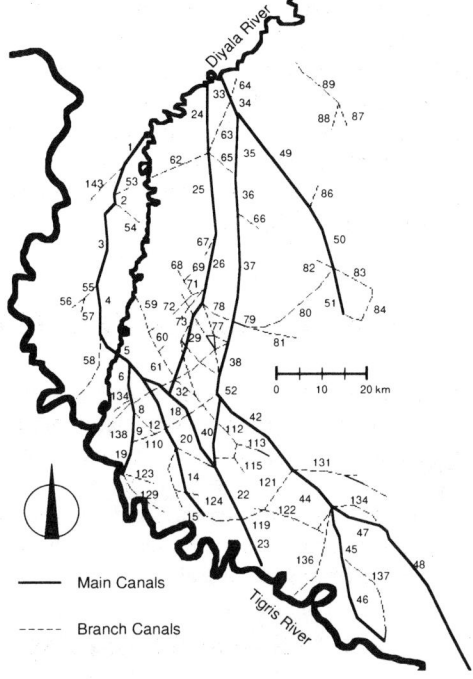

Figure 27. The population of main canals (stratum 1) and branch canals (stratum 2, dashed) of the Seleucid-Parthian period in the lower Diyala basin, Iraq (after Adams, 1981:195).

	Sample		Population	
Site Size	$n_1 = 11$	$n_2 = 19$	$N_1 = 52$	$N_2 = 92$
0 – 0.4 ha	2.3 ± 2.8	1.3 ± 0.8	1.8 ± 1.6	1.2 ± 0.8
4.1 - 10 ha	0.4 ± 0.5	0.5 ± 0.8	0.5 ± 0.8	0.4 ± 0.6
10.1 - 20 ha	0.09 ± 0.3	0.2 ± 0.4	0.2 ± 0.4	0.2 ± 0.4
20.1 - 40 ha	0.2 ± 0.4	0	0.1 ± 0.3	0.04 ± 0.2
40.1 – 200 ha	0.09 ± 0.3	0.05 ± 0.2	0.2 ± 0.4	0.09 ± 0.3
All sites	3.0 ± 2.9	2.0 ± 0.9	2.8 ± 1.9	1.9 ± 0.9

Table 2. Sample statistics (with standard deviations) and population parameters for the density of Seleucid-Parthian sites (sites per segment) along a population of canal segments in the lower Diyala valley, Iraq. Sites are classified by area in hectares. The figures shown here are not corrected for the bias due to edge effects.

dan, and the first to have a Neolithic cemetery with large grave cists. Thus the survey has helped to remedy a previous bias in our understanding of the Neolithic in the southern Levant by documenting a subpopulation (small, buried sites in valley bottoms) that previous surveys, all based on surface evidence, had overlooked (e.g., Banning, 1985; Banning and Fawcett, 1983). It is important to keep in mind, however, that the statistics of this sample are only relevant to the population of stream terraces in the valley. Drawing conclusions about some larger Neolithic population would require treating this population as a stratum in a stratified sample.

2. SAMPLE SIZE AND ESTIMATION

An important issue in survey design is the sample size that will be adequate for the survey's purposes. There is no "magic number" or cook-book sampling fraction that will guarantee useful results. The minimum sample size needed depends on interplay between the sampling element, the density of archaeological remains, the amount of sampling error that is tolerable, and the degree of confidence you would like to have in the results. All of these are specific to each project, so it makes no sense to copy a sample size from someone else's work.

2.1 Sample Size and Sampling Fraction

Sampling fraction is the proportion of the population that your sample includes (n/N). Although a sampling fraction close to 100% clearly provides better parameter estimates than one close to 10%, sampling fraction actually has a much less important role than sample size in the precision of your estimates.

Sample size is the actual number of observations in a sample (n) and, for most spatial samples, this means the number of quadrats, transects or auger holes, *not* the number of sites or artifacts. The fact that sample size is a major contributor to the size of sampling error should be obvious from the formula for the standard error of a population mean:

$$SE = \frac{\sigma}{\sqrt{n}}$$

The standard error is thus inversely correlated with the square root of the sample size. Consequently, if to halve a standard error, it is necessary to increase the sample size by a factor of four. To decrease the error by a factor of five, a sample size 25 times as large is necessary.

2.2 Fixed-sample Designs

The size of the error is only one of the factors relevant to sample size. First, the numerator in the equation for standard error, s, has a large effect. A population with twice the standard deviation would, then, also demand four times as large a sample to hold standard error constant.

Sampling Space: Statistical Surveys

Second, it is necessary to consider the desired degree of confidence in the result. Because even a well-behaved sample will sometimes provide an estimate that differs from the population parameter by a large amount, each time we accept or reject an estimate based on a sample we risk making an error. The error of rejecting a hypothesis (here the hypothesis that a statistic is a close approximation of a parameter) that is true is a Type I (or α) error. The error of accepting a hypothesis that is false is a Type II (or β) error. When we say that we are 95% confident in our result, we are taking a 5% chance on a Type I error, meaning that $\alpha = 0.05$.

McManamon's (1981) survey in Cape Cod is a good example of how we can use these factors to determine the sample size necessary to estimate a population parameter with desired precision.

To estimate a mean,

$$n = \frac{(\sigma t)^2}{(r\mu)^2}$$

where σ is the population standard deviation, t is the t-score for a t-test with the specified confidence level, r is the relative error (standard error divided by the mean), and μ is the population mean. For 95% confidence and large samples, for example, $t = 1.96$, but $t = 2.26$ for samples of ten. In archaeological cases, it is unlikely that the values of σ or μ would be known, making it necessary to substitute estimates for them. these could simply be guesses, perhaps based on previous experience, but it is more usual to substitute the sample mean and standard deviation from a small pilot sample:

$$\hat{n} = \frac{(st)^2}{(r\bar{x})^2}$$

To specify the absolute size of the acceptable error instead of the relative error,

$$\hat{n} = \frac{(st)^2}{d^2}$$

where d is the maximum difference between your estimate and the "true" value of the parameter that you are willing to accept.

Estimating sample sizes for estimating proportions, rather than means, is much the same (see also Asch, 1975). For example, to control for the absolute size (d) of the error in the proportion of some type of site in a cluster sample,

$$\hat{m} = \frac{t^2 p(1-p)}{d^2}$$

where m is the total number of sites, p is the proportion of the site type in a small pilot sample (our best estimate for the population proportion), and t is once again the t-score associated with the level of confidence we have selected. The worst-case scenario, which happens when the expected proportion is 0.5, requires the largest sample size. Assuming that the sample consists of spatial units (a cluster sample), dividing the estimate of m

by the estimated density of sites results in an estimate of n, the number of quadrats, transects, or other units.

When the population (i.e., number of quadrats or other spaces) is small, as often happens in archaeological survey (Read, 1975), it is best to use the finite population correction, so the estimated number of quadrats is,

$$\hat{n} = \frac{t^2 Np(1-p)}{(N-1)d^2 + p(1-p)}$$

where N is the number of spatial elements in the whole population.

Determining sample size is more complicated when it is necessary to estimate several proportions simultaneously, such as the proportion of sites that fall into each of several chronological categories (Thompson, 1987; 1992:39-40). A simpler approach is to calculate sample size for the worst-case scenario, which occurs when one proportion is 0.5 (van der Veen and Fieller, 1982:294).

It is easier to grasp how these equations work by working through an example. Using McManamon's data from Cape Cod, let us suppose we want to estimate the density of prehistoric sites in Stratum IA (the Nauset Bay area). In a 1% pilot sample, six units selected from a stratum of 125 units yielded an estimated density of 1.3 ± 0.74 sites per unit. The coefficient of variation here (0.57) is quite high; this small sample size does not allow a very precise estimate. McManamon (1981) decided to find out how large a sample would be necessary to reduce the relative error to 10% at a confidence level of 80% ($t = 1.28$):

$$\hat{n} = \frac{(st)^2}{(r\bar{x})^2} = \frac{(0.74 * 1.28)^2}{(0.1 * 1.3)^2} = \frac{0.897}{0.017} \cong 53$$

Where, as in this case, the resulting sampling fraction is rather large (53/125 = 0.42), we can reduce the sample size further as follows:

$$n = \frac{\hat{n}}{1 + (\hat{n}/N)} = \frac{53}{1.42} \cong 37$$

2.3 Optimal Allocation for Stratified Samples

To optimize precision of estimates based on stratified samples, it is possible to modify the above approach to determine the size of sample required for each of several strata.

Archaeologists using stratified sampling typically use proportional allocation. This simply means that they divide their survey effort among strata in proportion to the surface areas of those strata. Thus, if the sampling frame has N_i units in each stratum, for a total population of N units, the allocation to each stratum is:

$$n_i = N_i \frac{n}{N}$$

Sampling Space: Statistical Surveys   127

For example, if one stratum covers 20% of the survey universe, then they allocate 20% of their survey quadrats or transects to that stratum. Put another way, if the overall sampling fraction is 10% ($n/N = 0.1$), one-tenth of the N_i elements in each stratum are included in the sample. This is generally a simple and effective approach (with rounding to result in integer values for the n of each stratum), and probably should be used unless there is good reason to do otherwise.

However, it is possible to use disproportional stratified sampling to optimize allocation in a way that minimizes the overall variance on the estimate of important population parameters, such as site density or total site area (Deming, 1950:213-246; Orton, 2000:212). This may be useful in cases where the expected variance of a proportional design is very large or when the expected cost of surveying some strata is unusually high.

2.3.1 Neyman Allocation

One type of disproportional stratified sampling that is very efficient is called Neymann allocation. This varies the sampling fractions of the different strata so as to optimize the precision of estimates for a given overall sample size (Cochran, 1963:96; Neyman, 1934; Orton, 2000:30, 93, 212).

Where the cost of surveying in each stratum is constant, and it has already been decided what the total sample size will be, the sample size from each stratum that minimizes variance (i.e., maximizes precision) is

$$n_i = \frac{N_i \sigma_i n}{N}$$

where n_i is the number of elements in the sample to be selected from stratum i, n is the number of sample elements planned for the entire sample, N is the number of elements in the population, N_i is the total number of elements in stratum i, and s_i is the population standard deviation of some parameter for stratum i. What this means is that the elements allocated to each stratum, rather than being proportional only to N_i, are in proportion to the stratum standard deviations as well (i.e., to $N_i \sigma_i$). As in the last section, it is necessary to estimate (or guess) the value of the population standard deviation, usually on the basis of previous experience, expert opinion, or the sample standard deviation of a pilot sample. Fortunately, successful allocation does not depend on very accurate estimation of the σ_i values, and even rough guesses are usually sufficient (Deming, 1950:228-230). This is especially true as long as the estimated σ_i are approximately in the correct proportions, even if their absolute magnitudes are completely wrong.

In the common instance of having to estimate more than one parameter, each with different expected variance, it is conservative to use the largest estimated standard deviation for σ_i, as this will result in the largest sample size, or alternatively that of the parameter it is most critical to estimate precisely.

In many instances, it is unrealistic to assume that costs are identical across strata. Differences in stratum terrain, accessibility, travel time, visibility, and the prevalence of such obstructions as dense, thorny vegetation or barbed-wire fences can all lead to differences in the cost of thorough inspection. Fortunately, it is possible to determine optimal allocations that take these costs into account. Typically, the problem takes one of two forms:

a) Find the allocation for each stratum that will minimize overall variance within a fixed, budgeted cost, or

b) Find the allocation for each stratum that will minimize cost with a predetermined, acceptable variance (Deming, 1950:216).

2.3.2 Minimizing Variance on a Fixed Budget

The goal in this case is to detemine the values of $n_1, n_2, \ldots n_L$ that will result in the smallest expected variance for a given cost, C. Doing this requires first an estimate of the cost of surveying a single sample element in each stratum (c_i) and, as in previous examples, the variance of the parameter to be estimated in each stratum (σ_i^2). One can simply count the total number (N_i) of sample elements in each stratum, but must estimate the value of a constant, λ:

$$\lambda = \frac{\sum N_i \sigma_i \sqrt{c_i}}{C}$$

Then the sampling fraction for each stratum is:

$$\frac{n_i}{N_i} = \frac{\sigma_i}{\lambda \sqrt{c_i}}$$

Note that the sampling fraction for each stratum is directly proportional to its standard deviation, σ_i, but inversely proportional to the square root of its cost. We simply rearrange the terms of this expression to find the absolute number of sample units in each stratum:

$$n_i = \frac{\sigma_i N_i}{\lambda \sqrt{c_i}}$$

To illustrate this with an example, let us suppose that the cost of surveying with test pits in one stratum is 0.25 person-days per test pit, but 1.0 person-days per test pit in a second stratum that has very hard, clay sediment, and that the total budget is 150 person-days. Let us further assume that the sampling frame of the first stratum contains a total of 500 possible test-pit locations (i.e., $N_1 = 500$) and that of the second stratum contains 300 ($N_2 = 300$), and that we would estimate our variance on the estimates of the proportion of test pits to contain artifacts as $s_1^2 = 0.04$ and $s_2^2 = 0.09$. In that case, we would estimate λ as:

$$\lambda = \frac{500 * 0.2 \sqrt{0.25}}{150} + \frac{300 * 0.3 \sqrt{1}}{150} = \frac{50}{150} + \frac{90}{150} = 0.933$$

Then the estimated optimal allocations to the two strata become:

$$n_1 = \frac{0.2 * 500}{\frac{14}{15}\sqrt{0.25}} \cong 214 \quad \text{and} \quad n_2 = \frac{0.3 * 300}{\frac{14}{15}\sqrt{1}} \cong 96$$

This allocation of 214 and 96 contrasts with a simple proportional allocation that would have been 194 to the first and 116 to the second stratum.

Note that setting all the costs, c_i, to be equal results in the Neyman allocation of section 2.3.1:

$$\lambda\sqrt{c} = k, \text{ where } c_i = c, \text{ and } \frac{n_i}{N_i} = \frac{\sigma_i}{k}$$

2.3.3 Minimizing Cost for a Fixed Variance

This case works exactly like that of section 2.3.2, and with all of the same concepts.

The only difference is that the first thing to decide is what variance on the parameter estimate is acceptable. For example, a coefficient of variation of only 5%, or a standard deviation on a proportion of only 0.10 ($s^2 = 0.01$) might be desirable. In that case,

$$\lambda = \frac{s^2 + \sum N_i \sigma_i^2}{\sum N_i \sigma_i \sqrt{c_i}}$$

Since, as in section 2.3.2, it is possible to estimate all the values on the right side of this equation, and thus to determine the total minimum cost of achieving the desired variance, s^2, as:

$$C = \frac{\sum N_i \sigma_i \sqrt{c_i}}{\lambda}$$

The total sample size would be the sum of the allocations to each stratum:

$$n = \sum n_i$$

As before, let us illustrate this with an example. Given the same two strata used to illustrate section 2.3.4, but this time, instead of a fixed budget, a standard deviation on our estimate of the proportion of test pits containing artifacts fixed at 0.2. In that case, the estimate of λ is:

$$\lambda = \frac{0.2^2 + (500 * 0.04) + (300 * 0.09)}{(500 * 0.2\sqrt{0.25}) + (300 * 0.3\sqrt{1})} = \frac{0.04 + 20 + 27}{50 + 90} = 0.336$$

while the total cost is

$$C = \frac{(500 * 0.2\sqrt{0.25}) + (300 * 0.3\sqrt{1})}{0.336} = \frac{50 + 90}{0.336} = 416.67$$

or about 417 person-days, and the allocations for the two strata, using the same equation as in section 2.3.2, would be:

$$n_1 = \frac{0.2 * 500}{0.336 \sqrt{0.25}} = \frac{100}{0.168} \cong 595 \text{ and } n_2 = \frac{0.3 * 300}{0.336\sqrt{1}} = \frac{90}{0.336} \cong 268$$

Given the additional complications that arise from disproportional stratified sampling, it is often useful to compare their expected results with those of a simple proportional plan. If the gains in precision are very small, or the estimated costs are not especially accurate, it may not be worthwhile to pursue the more complex sample design. In some cases, even stratification itself may be unjustified.

2.4 Sequential Sampling

A different approach than deciding on a fixed sample size is simply to keep increasing sample size until it seems adequate, as measured by some criterion, such as relative error, standard error, confidence, or diversity. Ideally, sequential sampling makes it possible to optimize the balance between the cost of larger samples and the risk of obtaining poor estimates of population parameters, but it is not necessarily less costly than a well planned, fixed-sample design (Wetherill and Glazebrook, 1986:5).

The simplest kind of sequential sampling employs a "stopping rule." For example, the rule could be to continue adding observations (quadrats, for example) to the sample until the standard error on some estimate drops to a particular value, or until the number of site types increases to some value, or until each time period is represented by at least x sites. Truly optimal sequential sampling involves more complicated mathematics than most archaeologists want to absorb (e.g., Wetherill and Glazebrook, 1986:97-127), but a simple stopping rule is easy to put into practice. A stopping rule based on diversity or minimum numbers of sites or artifacts can produce biased estimates of the proportions of the taxa, however, because sequential sampling invests extra effort to record rare ones. Nonetheless, sequential sampling would often be a good solution in cases where certain minimum requirements must be met. It can also be a good compromise between statistical survey and prospection (chapter 7).

3. USING SAMPLES

Samples have become so routine in archaeological survey that there is a danger of forgetting their purpose. Samples are not intended to ensure the discovery of archaeological remains — in fact they may be poor at detecting some kinds of remains — but to allow us to estimate the parameters of some population. Here we will briefly review some kinds of estimation that well designed survey samples may facilitate.

3.1 Estimating the Density of Archaeological Materials

A common use of sampling is to estimate the number of sites/km^2 or the number of artifacts/m2 on some landscape or stratum (e.g., Thomas, 1975).

3.2 Estimating the Number of Archaeological Sites

Once reasonably accurate and precise estimates of the density of sites are available, it is straightforward to deduce what this means in terms of numbers of sites that must exist in the region sampled.

One danger in these estimates, however, is that uncritical observations of zero sites in some regions may be treated as evidence that no sites exist in those regions. Simply multiplying the apparent densities in different regions by some number, such as the reciprocal of apparent sampling fraction (e.g., 5 for a 20% sampling fraction), will leave the zero densities as zero sites, while exaggerating the importance of the non-zero observations (Wobst, 1983:64). It is better in these situations to work out the probability of having missed one or more sites in the spaces in which the survey detected none, and then calculate a threshold (e.g., "we estimate that there were no more than four sites").

Nance (1993) has shown, for example, that variation in visibility can have a significant impact on the estimate of site numbers. Correcting for these factors and making sure that the population sampled is really the one we are trying to characterize are critical to obtaining realistic estimates of this parameter.

Careful consideration of edge effects, sampling intervals, and other effects on the probability that the survey encountered different kinds of sites makes it possible to construct a graph of discovery probabilities with which to infer the number of sites of various kinds more accurately, including those sites that were not discovered (see chapter 3, section 2). Needless to say, estimates of the number of rare or very small sites are not likely to be very precise in most instances.

3.3 Estimating the Proportions of Archaeological Occurrences by Type or Period

This kind of estimation, which is extremely common in archaeology, entails all the problems encountered in estimating densities or numbers. In addition, it tends to suffer even more from small-sample effects. The more categories used to classify the sites or other targets, the more likely it is that "empty" categories or ones with only a few observations are simply ones for which the sample size is too small to provide reliable estimates. Although we can put limits on the density of sites of these types, if they cumulatively account for a fair proportion of sites, it could result in exaggerated estimates of the proportions of other site types.

In addition, when "type fossils" are used to date sites, we need to be aware that some periods, which lack highly diagnostic artifacts, may be under-represented in survey (Rutter, 1983).

3.4 Estimating the Proportions of Sites in Different Environments

Archaeologists with ecological interests, as well as ones attempting to construct predictive models for site location, typically want to detect associations between sites and various environmental factors. One simple way to do this is to see if the proportion of sites in different environmental circumstances differs significantly from what they would expect of a random distribution. Another is to look for correlations between site densities or site areas and the proportion of space taken up by specific environmental zones in survey quadrats or other units.

3.5 Estimating Changes in Regional Population or Settlement Area

Often archaeologists are interested in detecting rises or fluctuations in human population over region, and must depend on site numbers or settlement area as their main means to accomplish this.

One complicating factor, in addition to the ones common to estimating site numbers or site density, is time. If chronological resolution is coarse, as is usually the case, not all the sites that belong to the same period are likely to be contemporary. This could result in double-counting population. In addition, there is a risk in attributing all of a site's area to a particular period when in fact only a portion of it was occupied at any given time. These are issues that are difficult to assess, but require at least reasonable assumptions if the population estimates are to have any useful meaning.

3.6 Creating Locational Models

As mentioned briefly in section 3.4, sampling surveys can be used in the construction of predictive models of site location (or even "non-site" land use). The key, if such models are to be useful and reliable, is to ensure that the sample on which they are based is unbiased. Chapter 6, section 1.6, outlines procedures that help ensure that this is so.

4. CONCLUSION

Sampling in archaeological survey is appropriate whenever the goal is to draw inferences about a population of artifacts, sites, or spaces without having to study the population in its entirety. More specifically, it pertains to estimation of the parameters of that population, such as the proportion belonging to each of several classes, or how some parameters changed over time. It is also appropriate for building a predictive model for the distribution of archaeological materials, since such models typically involve specifying a variety of parameters.

In these cases, it is necessary to design a sample that represents the population closely enough to allow estimate of the parameters with sufficient accuracy and precision. This involves close attention not only to the overall sampling design, but also to sample size and, where appropriate, to the basis for stratification and allocation of effort to each stratum.

Chapter VI
Purposive Survey: Prospection

We may be looking for an object, and although we do not know where it is, we can reason out the chances of its being in various possible places. With a limited time to find it, where shall we look first and how long shall we look in each place? (Koopman, 1980:139).

The goal of some surveys is to discover particular kinds of archaeological materials or sites, including rare sites and evidence that can help to evaluate a specific hypothesis, rather than to estimate parameters of a more general archaeological population. Some archaeologists use the term "purposive survey" simply to describe haphazard surveys that lack careful design, but here I use the term in a more restricted way for surveys designed to optimize the probability of discovering particular kinds of archaeological materials with a given amount of search effort, or "prospecting."

Archaeologists have given far less explicit attention to the theory behind purposive survey than to surveys of the sampling type. Probably this is due to the widespread perception that surveys that do not employ statistical sampling are somehow "unscientific" (but see Asch, 1975). This has led, in turn, to the use of sampling as a prospecting tool when, in fact, it is usually quite poorly suited to the discovery of at least some kinds of archaeological "targets," and specifically sites. In fact, purposive search for particular kinds of archaeological evidence is a perfectly legitimate research goal that is implicit in much of the work that archaeologists do (Banning, 2002).

Prospectors use their experience, theoretical models, or hypotheses based on empirical data to predict where targets, such as settlement sites or shipwrecks, might be located or to restrict the amount of territory a survey must cover to provide satisfactory results. Sometimes this involves intentional bias in favor of locations most likely to exhibit the material culture of interest, or omitting areas where deposits of the appropriate age do not occur. Where prospecting must be combined with estimation, surveyors may favor disproportionate stratified sampling or adaptive sampling (chapter 6). Often, they use a suite of remote sensing methods, especially aerial ones, as well. Modern surveyors are also able to use Geographic Information Systems (GIS) and information from previous surveys to model the distribution of material culture in space and thus predict where certain kinds of materials are likely to be found. Not only can modelling improve the ability of surveys to find archaeological materials, purposive survey is also a way for us to test those models.

In prospecting for specific targets, such as particular shipwrecks or settlements known only from historical documents, some of the methods of Operations Research, including Bayesian analysis and the search patterns employed in search-and-rescue, can be helpful.

1. PROSPECTING

A few examples will suffice to illustrate some typical prospecting problems. Generally, the prospecting problem involves either targets that were previously known but whose location is uncertain, or ones that are suspected, but not known to exist. In addition, prospecting can be for a single target, or for multiple targets whose locations are assumed to be either independent or interrelated. The wreck of a single ship known to have sunk in a storm is a classic example of a single target known to exist, but whose location is uncertain. A fleet of such ships, however, would involve multiple, interrelated targets. In the case of the Chesapeake flotilla, for example, even the pattern (bow-to-stern) in which they were scuttled in the Patuxent River 1814 is known (Shomette and Eshelman, 1981). Unspecified archaeological sites, features, or artifacts accumulated over a long period in a small region might be effectively independent occurrences, meaning that we have no prior knowledge to suggest that the location of one target had an influence on the location of others. In many archaeological instances, however, there is reason to suspect that targets of approximately the same age were not independent. For example, artifact distributions are often clustered or sites show spatial autocorrelation, while settlements sometimes show fairly regular spacing. In addition, the locations of sites from one period of time sometimes influence the locations of succeeding settlements. In places like the Near East, this temporal autocorrelation has led to the creation of deeply stratified *tells*. Keeping these variations on the search problem in mind is important because the number of expected targets and whether or not their locations are independent can affect the strategy for finding them.

1.1 Surveying for Historically Documented Sites

Sometimes even a small amount of historical information can be a tremendous help in directing the search for a particular site, the precise location of which has been forgotten. For many years archaeologists have used historical information to narrow such a search, as in Schliemann's search for Troy. Yet, although recognizing the need for "a systematic approach to prospection, reducing the area of search and thereby incrementally increasing the probability of success" (Garrison et al. 1985: 302), searchers have rarely selected near-optimal strategies for this purpose, and sometimes even begin with a random sample that does not take advantage of prior information.

Purposive Survey: Prospection   135

Today, historical sources are often useful in the search for medieval and historic sites, including shipwrecks and specific buildings. Marine survey for wrecked ships typically relies heavily on historical evidence for the likely location of the wrecks. In some cases historic maps, historical documents, and ethnohistoric sources can provide important clues to the location of specific terrestrial sites as well, including medieval settlements in Europe and villages encountered by explorers and early settlers in North and South America.

In general, surveys of this type involve beginning the search in the area where prior information suggests the probability of finding the target (or targets) is highest, and then widening or intensifying the search in the light of information gained as survey progresses.

1.1.1 Location of Upper Creek Villages in Alabama

Lolley (1996) used a range of accounts by early travellers in Alabama and historic maps to predict the locations of many settlements that the Upper Creek Muskogees in the Coosa-Tallapoosa region of central Alabama reportedly occupied in the 17th, 18th and early 19th centuries. By focussing on the most useful maps, and especially those that show both villages and topographic features, and comparing the reported locations of villages on a large number of maps of varying date, Lolley was able to plot circles marking the predicted locations of those villages. Large circles indicate some uncertainty of location, while small circles indicate more precise locations. Lolley tested the predicted locations against site distributions known from previous archaeological investigations and found that many corresponded.

The obvious next step is to use the model to search predicted locations for sites that have not previously been documented.

1.1.2 Search for La Navidad

Historical information was useful to narrow the search for Columbus's settlement at La Navidad (Deagan, 1989). The sources limited the possible locations of this settlement to a particular area, and mentioned a number of geographical features and the settlement's relationship to a native village, which helped to narrow the possibilities further. Although this work did not make explicit reference to prospection theory, it followed many of the principles that that theory involves, and provides a good example of the search for a single terrestrial target.

1.1.3 Nautical Survey for *The Monitor*

The Monitor provides a good example of a single, specific target in survey at sea (Newton, 1975; Sheridan, 1979). This turreted ironclad of the Union Navy was lost off Cape Hatteras in December 1862, its exact location remaining unknown until a purposive survey employing side-searching sonar rediscovered it in 1973.

1.1.4 Search for the Submerged City of Helike

The discovery of Helike, a Greek city that disappeared into the Gulf of Corinth during an earthquake in 373 BC (Pausanias 7.24.3-7), is another case that calls for the principles of prospection. Schwartz and Tziavos (1979) report on their use of geological evidence to try and limit the area within which they must search for this lost city. They concluded that the site lay offshore somewhere between their boreholes 2 and 4, reducing the possible location of the site to a one-kilometer-wide band along the coast.

However, this is also a good example of how such reasoning often only identifies high-probability regions for further prospection, and how new information may alter those probabilities. Survey of the band that Schwartz and Tziavos identified was, in fact, unsuccessful because some of the assumptions on which it was based proved faulty.

Eventual discovery of the settlement inland, on the alluvial fan of the Helike River, was due to the realization that there had been uplifting of the fan that could have taken place after the city's destruction and burial. New boreholes on the delta showed a buried layer containing marine fauna as well as artifacts, and later test excavations finally revealed traces of the ancient city (Soter, 1998; Soter and Katsonopoulou, 1999; Soter et al., 2001).

1.2 Using Aerial Photography or Satellite Imagery

In some situations, certain kinds of archaeological phenomena, such as buried buildings, ditches, canals and roads, are much more obtrusive and visible from the air than they are to an observer on the ground. When aerial photographs or satellite images show traces that are suspected of being phenomena of interest, survey can then consist of *ground checks*, walking over the ground or conducting small test excavations at locations tagged during inspection of the photographs.

For example, during the first World War, O. G. S. Crawford and others noticed that aerial photographs from military reconnaissance missions in western Europe often showed unusual linear patterns that seemed to result from buried archaeological features (Crawford, 1929). In the areas where these features were observed, ditches and stone walls were not buried very deeply, and sometimes lay in shallow soil over chalky bedrock. During some periods, vegetation growing over these sites varied in color and height as a result of variations in soil depth and water availability. Grass growing over stone walls, for example, was stunted or yellowed, while grass growing over buried ditches was tall and green. When viewed from above, the color variations sometimes showed linear patterns. In addition, viewing the site in early morning or evening when sunlight struck the ground at a raking angle also caused taller vegetation to cast shadows.

North American archaeologists have less often relied on aerial reconaissance in their archaeological surveys, but in the Old World this method has had a great impact on archaeology. Over the past 80 years, aerial reconaissance has allowed archaeologists in western Europe to identify thousands of archaeological settlements and buildings, as well as whole field systems. Once a suspected site is detected in an aerial photograph, archaeologists on the ground can examine it and attempt to confirm the presence of archaeological remains and estimate their date and extent. In some cases, they follow up with geophysical methods.

Aerial photography is also very effective for archaeological prospecting in deserts (Kennedy and Riley, 1990; Poidebard, 1934). Here early-morning or late-afternoon raking light casts shadows across the micro-topography of ruined or slightly buried walls, making linear and circular features stand out against the natural background.

1.3 Exploiting Structure in Landscapes

Sometimes aerial photography, satellite imagery, or simply topographic maps, will show us not sites we can check out, but landforms or other landscape elements (Stafford, 1995) that might be associated with archaeological materials.

In one case, satellite imagery from the space shuttle was used to detect the buried traces of ancient watercourses in the Sahara Desert (McCauley, et al., 1982). Because we could expect prehistoric sites to be located near water sources in this arid region, knowledge of where these watercourses had been allowed archaeologists to narrow their search for sites.

Similarly, survey for ancient cities and towns in the Diyala and Uruk regions of Iraq depended on the assumption that these kinds of sites would always be located on canals (Adams, 1965; Adams and Nissen, 1972). Traces of the ancient canals are visible in aerial photographs taken in the 1950s and allow archaeologists to search along the canal banks for *tells* (mounds built up from settlement debris) and scatters of artifacts. In a way, the canals provided a sampling frame for the survey, even though this particular survey did not explicitly include a sampling design (see above, pp. xxx).

In a somewhat different vein, survey for submerged Paleoindian and Archaic sites on the continental shelf of Florida takes advantage of our knowledge of submerged watercourses and geological outcrops (Faught and Donoghue, 1997), and provides an example of multiple targets only suspected to exist. At the end of the Pleistocene, rising sea levels flooded large parts of what was once dry land in northwestern Florida. Archaeological sites that occurred in these areas now lie offhore. Finding underwater lithic scatters is quite a challenge, and the continental shelf is a very large area to search. As in terrestrial regions, however, we would expect prehistoric people in areas that were later engulfed by rising sea levels to have exploited rivers and chert sources that could be found in particular kinds of rock outcrop. Consequently, archaeologists concentrate their dives where they have identified relict (undersea) river channels, sinkholes, rock shelters and chert outcrops by aerial and diver survey, sonar or other methods. Focussing underwater survey in such locations, given the high cost and limited time of dives, makes more sense than trying to survey some large portion of the continental shelf. In the Apalachee Bay of northwestern Florida surveys of this type have documented more than 18 locations with prehistoric artifacts, three of which are probably habitation sites, along submerged river channels. Similar research on British Columbia's continental shelf has also shown success (Fedje and Christensen, 1999).

1.4 Exploiting Structure in Target Interrelationships

Sometimes the fact that site locations are not independent of one another can work to our advantage.

One kind of situation in which this happens is the search for the wrecks of ships that sank collectively, as in the case of the Chesapeake Flotilla (Shomette and Eshelman, 1981) or some cases of Spanish treasure fleets. In such cases, or whenever we expect the locations of several targets to be close together, discovery of any one of the targets provides the basis to refine our search for the others. In the case of the Chesapeake Flotilla, a contemporary account even reports that the ships were all scuttled in a row, bow-to-stern, and this information would narrow the search to a linear region once even two ships could be identified.

Another example in which the locations of archaeological targets are interdependent is the deployment of military installations. Attackers' siegeworks, for example, both respond to and influence the location of defensive walls, ditches, artillery, and sappers' tunnels.

1.5 Exploiting Exposures of Buried Deposits

One of the most serious shortcomings of surveys based on visual inspection of the modern surface is poor visibility. These surveys systematically overlook material culture that has been covered by colluvium, alluvium or modern construction. A sensible approach to prospecting for materials that, because of their age or preferred location, are likely to be buried is to search out places where eroded coastlines, erosion gullies, road cuts, pipeline trenches and foundation pits have exposed buried deposits.

For example, in parts of northern Jordan, Epipalaeolithic cultural materials can be expected to occur in particular kind of paleosols, some of which are buried by later colluvium (Edwards et al., 1996; Maher and Banning, 2001; Maher et al., 2001). Survey that takes advantage of outcrops of this paleosol in stream-cuts and road-cuts succeeds in discovering many Geometric Kebaran and Natufian sites, while conventional surface surveys typically find none.

1.6 Using Predictive Models and GIS

Where there has been enough thorough survey in a region to allow modelling the criteria for site location quite accurately, archaeologists can use the model to predict the most likely locations for particular kinds of sites in unsurveyed parts of the region. Today Geographical Information Systems (GIS) permit quite sophisticated modelling that can guide the search for archaeological materials (e.g., Carmichael, 1990; van Dalen, 1999; Maschner, ed., 1996; Warren, 1990b). Survey is also useful to test some kinds of hypotheses, to test the predictive model itself, or to focus archaeologists' energies on the most significant or even surprising kinds of sites (Altschul, 1990).

In the context of regional archaeological survey, predictive models (sometimes called "significance models") simply accumulate and formalize our prior knowledge about the locations of known archaeological materials in a way that generates expectations about where unknown ones should occur. As in Lolley's (1996) study of the settlement locations of Upper Creek Muskogees, such prior knowledge could come from historical sources, including maps. Typically, however, predictive models combine theoretical expectations (such as a formal, mathematical model of how a lithic raw material might fall away in frequency with distance from its source) with a large number of empirical generalizations based on previous archaeological work. Although it is possible to use modelling to predict various non-site distributions, such as artifact densities, most such models in archaeology are designed to predict the locations of sites. In addition, while it is possible and often sensible to create separate models for different kinds of sites, in many cases the site classifications of existing databases are too unreliable to allow this, leading to more generalized (and therefore less effective) models.

1.6.1 Early History of Predictive Modelling

Arguably intuitive kinds of predictive modelling have a long history in archaeology, but modern, quantitative approaches, particularly in the spatial context, owe their fluorescence to the availability of computers, which can handle the computational complexity typically required. Many modern applications owe their origins to the happy coincidence of the development of Geographical Information Systems and some archaeological surveys that took prediction as a tool for testing hypotheses.

The Reese River Project, already mentioned in chapter 1, made use of a fairly simple spatial model to predict where sites should be located if Steward's description of Shoshonean settlement and resource use were accurate. They then used ground survey to search locations both where the model predicted sites should occur, and where it predicted they should not occur (Thomas, 1972; Williams et al., 1973).

An early extension of this modelling approach to the management of archaeological resources was in south-central Arkansas (Scholtz, 1981; Parker, 1985). Parker used multivariate logistic regression to predict where sites should occur in unsurveyed regions near Sparta, Arkansas.

Ken Kvamme (1983a; 1984; 1985; 1992) advanced the use of logistic regression to model site-location criteria and apply them to the search for unknown sites. With empirical data on the environmental circumstances of sites found in previous archaeological work in Colorado, Kvamme was able to model site-location probabilities and use them to search for previously undocumented hunter-gatherer sites.

Predictive modelling also became common in Europe along with the spread of archaeological GIS there (Gillings and Wise, 1998; Lock and Stancic, 1995). Now predictive modelling is one of the research areas of the Virtual Institute for Spatial Technologies (VISTA), an international collaboration of archaeologists from University of Arkansas, University of Sydney, St. Cloud State University, University of Birmingham, University of Ljubljana, Ohio State University, and University of Southampton.

Other centers of innovation in the use of predictive modelling have been agencies involved in Cultural Resource Management, such as the Illinois State Museum (Warren, 1990b; Warren et al., 1987; Warren and Asch, 1996), the Minnesota Department of Transport, the US Federal Roadway Authority, and the US Department of Defence's Legacy Resource Management Program (Zeidler, 1995).

1.6.2 Assumptions of Predictive Modelling

For predictive models to be effective, and also to avoid making self-fulfilling prophecies, they must satisfy a number of important assumptions, aside from the ones common to any archaeological observations. What follows focusses on what some archaeologists call "inductive" models but, in principle, the models could be entirely theoretical (or "deductive" models).

Most of the predictive models that archaeologists currently use are site-based, and require the assumption that sites are fairly self-evident. As noted elsewhere in this book, it is not always obvious what is and what is not a site, while some archaeologists discount the relevance of sites generally. The creators of most current models, however, assume not only that sites exist, but that they can confidently distinguish spaces that contain sites from ones that do not. Clearly, this requires a very well conceived, reproducible, and discrete definition of "site," as it does not allow for any uncertainty in the recognition and correct identification of sites. However, it is possible to create models that do not require this assumption or that are not site-based.

Furthermore, creators of most of these models, as currently conceived, assume that they can partition the spatial population of interest into two categories: spaces that have been surveyed sufficiently to detect any sites or parts of sites that may lie within them, and unsurveyed spaces. In other words, they assume that, if someone has surveyed a space without finding any site in it, that space has no site. As noted in chapter 3 and elsewhere, this assumption requires extremely high levels of detectability — definite detection, in fact — that are probably almost never achieved. In addition, the previous surveys may have employed quite different methods and intensities, so that their pooled results may not accurately reflect variability in distribution of archaeological materials. In future, more sophisticated models will take detectability into account so that this assumption is unnecessary.

The models also depend on the assumption that the surveyed regions used to generalize to a larger population are representative of that population. In other words, the previous surveys should include reasonable proportions of the full range of both environmental variability and site types in the whole region to which the model will be applied. Sometimes, however, previous surveys may have seriously underrepresented certain environmental zones, so that we cannot be confident that the lack of sites reported from those zones indicates a real absence of sites (e.g., Altschul, 1990:230-231). Where this problem appears serious, it may be necessary to change the boundaries of the survey population to omit these zones, or to do a pilot survey to get more information from them. As we will see below, testing this assumption comes early in the process of model creation.

The models make use of many sources of environmental information, requiring some assumptions about the accuracy and scale of the environmental data. Often the critical assumption involves scale or resolution; we must assume that the environmental data is sufficiently fine-grained that an inaccurate impression of site locations does not result simply because the spaces are too large or the environmental maps are too generalized. One of the problems that spatial modelling can encounter, especially if the resolution of map data is coarse, is that different methods for interpolating between observations yield different results, and sometimes unrealistic reconstructions of landscapes (Kvamme, 1990; Warren 1990b). For example, data points that are too far apart may make rugged terrain appear smooth, or blend a flat site location into a slope. Where there are reasons to suspect this problem, it may be necessary to abandon some otherwise useful environmental variables.

It is also necessary to assume that the environmental variables used in the model do not covary. Keeping two or more correlated variables in the model could inflate its apparent power (Altschul, 1990:231). It is easy to test this assumption and reduce the number of variables, where necessary.

A very important assumption, however, is that the model uses the right environmental information in the first place. To create a model that predicts the locations of Late Pleistocene hunter-gatherer camps, for example, maps of modern environmental variables, or even topography, may be quite inappropriate. Valley incision or infill with colluvium or alluvium, changes in watercourses, climate, or sea level, and various other geological and botanical changes can all alter the landscape drastically over archaeological time scales. Where there is reason to believe that such changes have occurred since the abandonment of the sites of interest, we must make an effort to reconstruct the paleoenvironment, and use that reconstruction, rather than modern environmental maps, as the basis for our model.

As we will see in the next section, testing these assumptions is an important step in the use of predictive models.

1.6.3 Steps in the Use of Inductive Predictive Models

1.6.3.1 Creating Primary and Secondary Coverages

Following the assembly of data on environment and previous site locations, GIS processes the data to create "primary coverages," maps referenced to databases that document the value of any number of attributes at each space on the maps, and at a useful scale. Manipulating these, in combination with theoretical models, can create new variables that are archaeologically useful, such as slope or distance to nearest water. The new sets of variables constitute "secondary coverages."

1.6.3.2 Creating the Model

The next step is to analyse the secondary coverages to create logistic regressions. To begin this, modellers extract the subset of the spatial units that have been surveyed. They then statistically compare this subset with the remainder (unsurveyed spaces) to ensure that they are from the same population with respect to the relevant environmental parameters. If there are marked differences, it could be that the surveyed sample is not a good basis from which to predict site locations in the unsurveyed regions.

For exploratory analysis of the prior data, they usually take a subset the surveyed sample of spaces (holding back some of the data for later testing), and then subdivide it into spaces in which sites were found, and ones where no sites were found. They statistically compare these two subsets also. If, as seems likely, people had particular environmental circumstances in mind when they selected locations for settlement and other spatially restricted behaviors, there could well be statistically significant differences between the two subsets with respect to these environmental variables. A series of descriptive statistics and simple univariate statistical tests can usually help us identify the variables that most likely contributed to site selection (Warren, 1990a: 97).

Then modellers use computer software to find multivariate relationships, often by calculating logistic regressions, in a subsample of the surveyed sites. Generally, the software calculates the degree to which each variable contributes to the overall regression, or its predictive power, and selects the most powerful variables to create the regression. This takes the form of an equation that generates the probability that a site will occur in a particular space on the basis of that space's values for the most powerful variables.

1.6.3.3 Testing the Model

Basing a survey on the model generated in the last section entails the risk of overlooking important cultural material. Consequently, it is extremely important to test the model, especially if there are plans to use it to eliminate some areas from future survey altogether.

The first tests are of the model's internal accuracy. This begins by comparing the model's predictions with the data from the subset of spaces used to create the model. Because these data are not independent of the data, we would expect this comparison to provide optimistic estimates of the model's accuracy, so a failure to predict site locations very reliably at this stage would indicate that the model is far from adequate.

Assuming, however, that the model passes this test, the next step is to test it against data that were held back in the creation of the model. In other words, we try to predict site locations for the other subset of the surveyed spaces, which was not used up to now. The rate at which the model correctly classifies spaces in this subset gives a better idea of the model's effectiveness.

Next is a test of the model by field survey. A sample of thorough ground checks of previously unsurveyed spaces where the model predicts that sites should be present, as well as spaces where the model predicts they should not be present, permits testing the model more generally. Such a survey should use carefully planned prospection of the test spaces to ensure a high level of detectability, coming as close as possible to definite detection (see chapters 3 and 4). Compare the model's success at classifying these spaces correctly with a random allocation of spaces demonstrates how much better the model performs.

Only when the model performs well against these tests can anyone confidently use it to make decisions about how to distribute survey effort, or about "low-risk" or "low-sensitivity" areas that may not justify intensive survey in future. Otherwise, there is a risk of under-surveying areas perceived as unsuitable for human use. For example, most archaeologists do not expect marshlands to have great archaeological potential, yet research in wetlands has revealed that they are often the focus of important economic activities, such as hunting, fishing, and even habitation (Bernick, 1998; Coles and Lawson, 1987; Fairbanks, 1970; Fedick et al., 2000; Murphy and French, 1988; O'Sullivan, 1998, Rippon, 2000).

1.6.3.4 Applying the Model

When confidence in the model's validity is high, it is ready for application to particular survey situations. Generally this begins by selection of a cut-off probability. A simple possibility, assuming that all spaces have equal prior probabilities of containing sites or not, would be to select a cutpoint of 0.5. This would mean classifying any space that the model indicates as having a probability greater than 0.5 of containing a site as a "site" space, and any with lower probabilities as "non-site" spaces. However, this is not always the best approach.

There is always a trade-off between the error of misclassifying a space that contains a site as one that does not, and the error of misclassifying an "empty" space as one that contains a site. Depending on the risks associated with these two types of errors, one could select a conservative level of probability that minimizes the chance of incorrectly classifying a site as a non-site, which would likely lead to a more costly field survey, but fewer cases of overlooking sites. Alternatively, one could risk missing more sites to keep the cost of survey down, or select the cut-off probability that represents a compromise between the two types of error. This is the probability at the point where the two probability curves cross when graphed against cutpoint value.

In practical applications, especially in Cultural Resource Management, it is common to select more than one cutpoint to create an ordinal scale of "sensitivity." For example, spaces classified with site probabilities less than 0.5 might be assigned to a class of "low sensitivity," ones greater than 0.5 up to 0.6 as "moderate sensitivity," and ones with probabilities greater than 0.6 as "high sensitivity."

It is common for archaeologists to use the sensitivity model only to eliminate some areas from intensive survey, or to distribute survey effort among the different sensitivity classes intuitively. However, it is also possible to use the resulting probabilities to find the optimal allocation of prospection effort (see section 3), or the optimal allocation in disproportional stratified sampling (chapter 5, section 2.3).

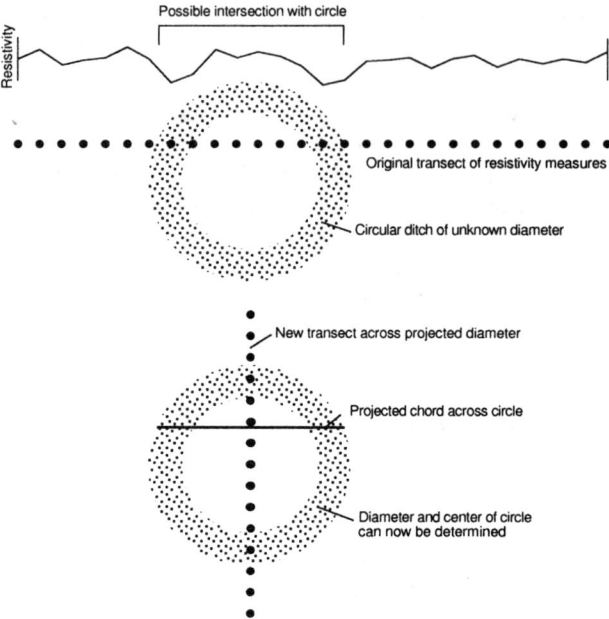

Figure 28. Selecting a perpendicular transect to search for a circular enclosure. When a first transect of resistivity observations intersects a possible enclosure in a broad search, a perpendicular transect is used as a contact investigation to detect the circle and determine its diameter (after Atkinson, 1953).

1.7 Using Geophysical Remote Sensing

As mentioned in chapter 3, archaeologists have found geophysical survey much more useful at the scale of individual sites than across regions, in part because, as with coring and augering, detection of anomalies on landscapes requires a closely-spaced grid of thousands of measurements. Consequently, where it has been used to search for sites, rather than features within sites, it has usually been to discover the exact location of sites that were known or suspected to occur in a relatively small area, or of larger and fairly obtrusive sites.

Atkinson (1953) took advantage of spatial structure in his attempt to locate circular ditch enclosures by resistivity surveying. He began with linear transects of resistivity measurements and, whenever one of these transects revealed the signatures of two ditches, he assumed that he had intersected a circle, and placed a new transect at right angles to the first where it bisected the cord of the circle (figure 28). If his assumptions were correct, the new transect would be along the circle's diameter. This was a very rapid way to identify the location and diameter of the enclosures without the need for high-resolution survey of the whole region. The spacing of the initial transects would need to be no greater than the likely circle diameter to make it reasonably certain that each circle was intersected by at least one transect but, where the circles are large, this prospecting technique would be much more efficient than a grid-based survey.

1.8 Adaptive Sampling Strategies

A sampling strategy that is relatively new to archaeologists, adaptive sampling, constitutes a rather satisfactory compromise between estimation and prospection (Orton, 2000:34-38, 93-98; Thompson and Seber, 1996:94-95). Adaptive cluster samples, on average, tend to discover greater numbers of sites, features, or artifacts than random or systematic samples, yet they still allow unbiased estimates of the densities of precisely those sites, features, and artifacts. This method is discussed in chapter 5, section 1.2.4.

2. PROSPECTION TO TEST MODELS OR HYPOTHESES

As Cowgill (1975) and Wobst (1983) have emphasized, probabilistic sampling is an inappropriate and inefficient tool in the evaluation of models or hypotheses that specify particular outcomes. To offer simple examples, a sample of 500 coin tosses might be an appropriate way to evaluate the *statistical* hypothesis that heads are as likely as tails, but sampling a whole region is a poor way to test the hypothesis that relict Pleistocene beach ridges tend to contain Paleoindian artifacts.

Survey of the Reese River Valley to test the hypothesis that site locations could be predicted from Shoshonean ethnography provides a good example of the use of survey to test particular predictions (Thomas, 1972; Williams et al., 1973). The model allowed researchers to predict which spaces should contain sites, and which should not, and the most efficient way to test these predictions is simply to survey a sample of spaces classified as "site" spaces, and ones classified as "non-site" spaces to see if the results met expectations (see section 1.6.3.3).

Unlike the logistic regression models that archaeological GIS currently favors, however, the Reese River project used a polythetic model. This type of model recognizes that combinations of certain characteristics improve the probability of a site being located in a space, but that we would not expect any space to combine all of these characteristics. Instead, we assume that each "site" space would exhibit some large number of the critical characteristics, but "non-site" spaces would exhibit only a few of them or none. In addition, we assume that each of the characteristics that are important for site location is shared by a large number of sites.

3. BAYESIAN PROSPECTION AND OPERATIONS RESEARCH

Since the Second World War, when the US Navy assembled mathematicians to work in its Anti-Submarine Warfare Operations Group (ASWORG), Operations Research has used the principles of probability to assist in the design of searches for sunken ships, enemy submarines, lost boaters, and mineral deposits (Cozzolino, 1972; Dobbie, 1968; Ellis and Blackwell, 1959; De Geoffroy and Wu, 1970; Harbaugh et al., 1977; Koopman, 1980, Richardson, 1989, Stone, 1989; Wignall and De Geoffroy, 1987). As it happens, the theory they have developed applies to many archaeological situations as well. Not surprisingly, the most obvious applications are to the search for old shipwrecks, but this theory deserves more general archaeological attention as well. Some archaeologists will immediately conclude that this section is yet another example of archaeological borrowing from a field of doubtful relevance to archaeology. However, it is important not to ignore research in other fields when it addresses exactly the same problems that archaeologists face. Archaeologists have wasted much time and effort rediscovering principles that had already been quite thoroughly investigated by colleagues in mathematical geology and Operations Research, as in connection with the optimal arrangement of point grids (chapter 4). Whether the goal is to discover buried Hohokam pit houses or buried ore bodies, many aspects of the problem are the same even though other aspects, such as scale, may differ.

The Bayesian approach uses prior probabilities based on existing information, analysis of expert opinion (Morris, 1977; Savage, 1971), or even educated guesses, to try to optimize the allocation of search effort over space (Koopman, 1980; Stone, 1975; 1989; see also Buck et al., 1996). It can also adapt to new information as survey progresses to refine the survey strategy.

Much as archaeologists have operated intuitively for decades, the Bayesian approach dictates that the search should concentrate on the place or places with the highest probability of containing the target. In the language of Bayesian analysis, survey starts in the region with the highest *prior probability*, as estimated from previous experience, historical evidence, or even experts' guesses. The exact values of these prior probabilities really do not matter very much. What matters is that, as in all Bayesian analysis, the probabilities change as we incorporate new information. In the search for a site of some kind, the longer someone searches an area without finding anything, the lower the *posterior probability* that the area contains that site. After a while, the area that initially had the highest prior probability of containing the site may end up with a posterior probability lower than the prior probability of some other area. In that instance, the surveyors abandon the search of the first area, and begin searching the second one. Search continues there until its posterior probability, perhaps, drops below the posterior probability of the first area or the prior probability of some other area, and the search is shifted accordingly or, alternatively, the search succeeds in finding its target.

Typically, a Bayesian search involves representing prior knowledge about targets' possible locations with a probability distribution over space. For example, the probability density of a bivariate normal distribution might represent the probable location of a potential shipwreck. In the worst-case scenario, it might assume a uniform distribution, with all parts of the survey space equally likely to contain the target or targets. In such instances, we end up with a strategy resembling the long-familiar sampling surveys

Bayesian search also assumes some constraint on search effort. Typically, an optimal search minimizes the expected effort invested up to the moment of detecting the target (Koopman, 1980:176). Some version of this approach is likely to be useful in CRM surveys that employ "sensitivity models" or "potential models" (above, section 1.6). Their most obvious application, however, is in the search for a particular entity, such as a specific shipwreck or an historic fort known from historical documents.

It also requires assuming a detection function. This is a function that specifies the probability of detecting a target with a certain amount of effort applied to a particular area of space, given that the target is present somewhere in that space. Common detection functions are the definite range law and the exponential detection function (see chapter 3, section 1.4, and Koopman, 1980).

Finally, Bayesian searches focus on the allocation of search effort to different parts of space.

3.1 Search Patterns

Many of the principles in chapter 4 were originally formulated in Bayesian Operations Research. This section will concentrate on situations in which the objective is to locate some very specific target. In that case, it is advantageous to use a search pattern that begins where previous experience or other information suggests that the probability of intersecting the target is highest, and then gradually widens. This is a procedure that most archaeologists have only used informally or intuitively, but it deserves more explicit attention.

As already noted in chapter 4, the size, shape and spacing of a search frame and its elements have a significant impact on the probability of intersecting an archaeological target. Most archaeological work on these effects has focussed on accounting for the bias they could cause in estimates of parameters, or on minimizing the risk of omitting small sites from a sample. Mathematical geologists have instead focussed on taking advantage of these effects in prospecting for ore bodies or petroleum reserves (e.g., Drew, 1979; Savinskii, 1965; Singer, 1975). The latter approach is equally applicable to prospecting for archaeological materials, and prospection by regular grids should use formulas presented in chapter 4 to optimize the recovery of sites or artifacts.

The classic Bayesian search literature focusses on the probability of intersecting a specific target, such as a shipwreck in a body of water or the remains of a historic fort buried on flat terrain. Where it is possible to estimate the target's most likely position, an *expanding square* centered on the *point of fix* is effective, and is now a standard search pattern in search-and-rescue efforts (Richardson and Discenza, 1980). The point of fix is the mode of a probability distribution extended over the survey space, and can often be approximated by a circular normal distribution, defined by the equation,

$$P(x, y) = f(x, y) = f(r) = \frac{e^{-r^2/2\sigma^2}}{2\pi\sigma^2}$$

where f(x, y) dx dy is the probability that the target is in the region (dx, dy), at some unknown point, (x, y), and at a distance r from the origin (0, 0) at the point of fix, and s is the standard deviation (Koopman, 1980:214). Note that this is also a formal description of the "fried-egg model" (chapter 1, section 3.1.4) for cases of small archaeological targets.

The expanding-square search is a set of transects beginning at the point of fix and, through a sequence of right-angle turns, gradually widening by the transect spacing, s (figure 17; Koopman, 1980:215-216). The value of s depends both on the standard deviation, s, of the probability distribution and the sweep width, W, which depends on the relationship between range and detection probability (the inverse-cube law, see pp. xx). In addition, in accordance with Bayes' theorem, if the first short transect fails to intersect the target, the posterior probability distribution is not normal, as the search has shown that the small region near the coordinates (0, 0) now has low probability of containing the target. Given some simplifying assumptions, the donut-shaped distribution that results has its ring of high probability a distance of $0.65\sqrt{W\sigma}$ from the original mode at (0, 0), and this indicates where the square should turn back on itself (Koopman, 1980:217):

$$s = 0.65\sqrt{W\sigma}$$

As it turns out, searching in a gradually widening spiral is also the minimax search trajectory for unbounded planes (see below, section 4.2.1).

For cases in which a different model of the prior probability of target location would be appropriate — for example, when there is reason to expect the site of interest to lie approximately 100 m from a river or a beach line — the same principles will help optimize the spacing of search transects running along mode of the probability distribution.

3.1.1 Search for the Chesapeake Flotilla

The Chesapeake Flotilla provides an example of how search patterns pioneered in Operations Research could aid in the discovery of shipwrecks. This was a fleet of 18 US warships and the merchant ships they were escorting that were scuttled in August of 1814 to prevent the ships' capture by the Royal Navy (Shomette and Eshelman, 1981). British Admiralty reports indicate that the ships were scuttled bow-to-stern in a single line extending some 1625 feet (500 m) in an area south of Spyglass Island. Work by the Maryland Department of Natural Resources to remove navigational hazards from the Patuxent River in the early 1970s resulted in the removal and destruction in burn boxes of many of these ships without any archaeological investigation. Subsequent work by the Calvert Marine Museum and Nautical Archaeological Associates, Inc., discovered one of the wrecks south of Spyglass Island. This information could contribute to establishing a line of fix for the survey.

We could model the prior probability of the wrecks' locations (ignoring the removal of some wrecks in the 1970s) as an elongated bivariate distribution that is normal perpendicular to, but that varies little parallel to, the long axis. Assuming a sweep width, W, based on the inverse-cube law for a magnetometer sweep of wrecks with iron guns in sediment some 3 m below the water surface, we can then use this model to plan a series of magnetometer transects along the river, beginning with the "ridge" of the prior probability density function. One advantage is that, because we know that the ships were scuttled end-to-end, once we precisely locate even two of the wrecks, the posterior probabilities change because we can then predict, within the errors introduced by current or sediment flow, the locations of almost all the other wrecks.

3.2 Optimal Allocation

One of the keystones of Bayesian searches is finding the optimal allocation of effort among a set of discrete spaces. These spaces could be groups of pixels in a GIS predictive model, zones defined by geomorphlogy or landform, or any discrete subsets of space, each with different area and probability of containing targets. This is much like finding the optimal allocations for disproportional stratified samples (chapter 5, section 2.3) except that, instead of minimizing variance, the goal is to maximize discovery probabilities for a given amount of search effort.

In that case, the optimum densities of search effort in these spaces equal the logarithms of quantities proportional to the probability densities of the spaces (Koopman, 1980: 149). When the search is for a single target, and it can only be in one of the spaces, all the probabilities sum to 1.0. In cases of search for a class of targets, and even the number of targets is unknown, the probabilities are independent. The total density of search effort (ϕ) in the i-th space of n spaces in a region of area A, is:

$$\varphi_i = \log \rho_i - \frac{1}{A}(A_1 \log \rho_1 + A_2 \log \rho_2 + ... + A_n \log \rho_n) + \frac{\phi}{A}$$

Here ρ_i is the probability density of space i (the prior probability that space i contains the target divided by the area of space i), n is the number of spaces in the search area, A_i is the area of space i, Φ = total search effort, expressed as area covered (for transects $\Phi = WL$), and ϕ_i is the density of search effort of area i:

$$\varphi_i = \frac{WL_i}{A_i}$$

where W and L are respectively the width and total length of transects. Φ/A, then, is the total density of effort (what archaeologist's have usually called "coverage" or "sampling fraction"). This can be expressed just as easily with the total area of test pits, augers or cores.

As it turns out, when the total amount of search effort is very small relative to the region surveyed, it is optimal to devote the entire search effort to the space or spaces with the highest probability density. This is much like what sometimes happens in use of predictive models in Cultural Resource Management. With middling amounts of search effort available, the expression above distributes it among the spaces. A simple test determines which spaces meet the threshold for allocation. If, for any two spaces,

$$\rho_1 \leq \rho_2 e^{-\Phi/A_1}$$

then no search effort is allocated to space 1 (Koopman, 1980: 149). When search effort is very large, however, the amounts of effort per unit area for all spaces become equal; this amounts to a simple, proportionally stratified sample, a type of survey strategy with which archaeologists are very familiar. Unfortunately, we usually do not have the luxury of nearly unlimited survey effort.

3.2.1 Simplified Examples of Optimal Allocation

To provide a more concrete example, let us assume a simple case with a survey region stratified into three spaces with areas of 3 ha, 2 ha and 1 ha, respectively. Let us furthermore assume that we are searching for a historic fort, but have no prior information about it other than that it should occur somewhere in the region we are surveying. A common archaeological plan is to divide search effort in proportion to the three areas, which amounts to assigning the three spaces prior probabilities of 0.50, 0.3333, and 0.1667. In that case, the value of ρ_i for every space will be the same: 0.1667, and most of the terms in the equation cancel out (Table 3a). Thus, the result is simply a proportionally stratified sample with equal coverage of each stratum; in other words, proportionally stratified samples assume equal probability densities. Let us assume, furthermore, that poor surface visibility and low expected artifact density leads us to survey with test pits, each 1 m² in size, and the amount of survey effort available (F) is 3000 m² (3000 test pits, or roughly 1500 person-days of effort [Zeidler, 1995:5.5]). Dividing this admittedly huge resource by the total survey area A, then gives us F/A of 0.05, or 5%, so that a total of 3000 test pits would be allocated as 1500, 1000, and 500 test pits, respectively.

An alternative, if there is no reason to think it more likely that the fort would occur in any one of these spaces is to assign them all equal prior probabilities. This may seem strange, but the practice in the last paragraph actually makes the untested assumption that large spaces are more likely to contain the fort even though we know that strategic locations for forts, such as hilltops or fords, often occupy very small proportions of space. Since the fort can only be in one place, the probabilities have to sum to 1.0, so the priors are all 0.3333. In that case, however, the probability density of the smallest space is so great relative to the others that we would allocate all search effort to it (Table 3b). Neither space 1 nor space 2 meets the threshold. Needless to say, assuming equal probabilities in cases where nothing is known except that the spaces vary considerably in size would be risky, so it makes sense to try to estimate probabilities more carefully (Banning, n.d.).

Sometimes statistics from previous surveys and background research provide a basis for estimating the fort's probability of being in various kinds of location. For example, a sample of a dozen similar forts in the broader region or information from historic maps might allow estimated prior probabilities of 0.45, 0.35, and 0.20, respectively

Purposive Survey: Prospection   151

Space	A_i (ha)	p_i	ρ_i	Φ/A	Φ (ha)	ϕ_i	No. Test Pits	Total
A								
1	3	0.500	0.167	0.05	0.3	0.05	1500	
2	2	0.333	0.167	0.05	0.3	0.05	1000	
3	1	0.167	0.167	0.05	0.3	0.05	500	3000
B								
1	3	0.33	0.111	0.05	0.3	0	0	
2	2	0.33	0.167	0.05	0.3	0	0	
3	1	0.33	0.333	0.05	0.3	1.0	3000	3000
C								
1	3	0.45	0.15	0.10	0.6	0.057	1706	
2	2	0.35	0.175	0.10	0.6	0.124	2476	
3	1	0.20	0.20	0.10	0.6	0.182	1818	6000
D								
1	3	0.45	0.15	0.05	0.3	0.007	206	
2	2	0.35	0.175	0.05	0.3	0.074	1476	
3	1	0.20	0.20	0.05	0.3	0.132	1318	3000
E								
2	2	0.35	0.175	0.02	0.12	0.021	413	
3	1	0.20	0.20	0.02	0.12	0.079	787	1200

Table 3. Examples of allocations to three spaces with unequal areas, proportional (A), equal (B) and unequal probabilities (C-E), and different amounts of total survey effort (Φ). Note that scenario A is equivalent to a proportionally stratified sample, and that in scenario B spaces 1 and 2 do not qualify for any survey at all (Banning, n.d.).

(Table 3d). In that case, dividing by their surface areas, the probability densities (ρ_i), are 0.15, 0.175 and 0.2 respectively. Note that the probability *densities* are ordered quite differently than the ordinary probabilities on which they are based. This results in a ϕ_1 of 0.007 (206 test pits spread over 3 ha), ϕ_2 of 0.074 (1476 test pits over 2 ha), and ϕ_3 of 0.132 (1318 test pits). A more generous, if unrealistic, total effort allocates a much greater number of test pits to areas 1 and 2 (Table 3c). Note, however, that if only enough resources are available to dig 1200 test pits (ca. 600 person-days), then the density of effort becomes 2% and space 1 no longer meets the threshold of probability density. Consequently, space 1 receives no effort in this allocation because its probability density of 0.15 is simply too low. Now only spaces 2 and 3 contribute to the calculation, so that f_2 becomes 0.021 (413 test pits), and f_3 becomes 0.0.079 (787 test pits)(Table 1e). Note how the proportions of effort change when the resources decrease, and how the greatest amount of effort, somewhat counter-intuitively, is concentrated in space 3, even though it had the lowest prior probability (but highest probability density).

It is important to keep in mind that adopting a strategy like this does not mean that the target is most likely to occur in space 3 — after all, there is a 45% chance that it is in space 1 — but only that looking in space 1 is more likely to be productive, given the resource constraints. Allocating a small amount of effort to such a large area as space 1, by contrast, is quite unlikely to find the fort even if it is there. We must remember that, in this case, the goal is to find the fort as quickly as possible and resources are limited. Had the goal been to characterize the three spaces, obviously the allocation would have been very different.

More realistic allocations are made incrementally, using information from a previous, unsuccessful search with effort Φ to plan the next increment with effort Φ' (Koopman, 1980:150).

3.3 Incrementally Optimal Searches

One of the key features of Bayesian approaches to any kind of research is the concept of updating probabilities in the light of new information (Buck et al., 1996). In addition, Kadane (1968) and Stone (1975:108-109) have shown that, for concave detection functions and continuous searching, any plan that always puts the next search in the space with the highest ratio of detection probability to search cost is also optimal for the total effort that results.

4. GAME THEORY AND LINEAR PROGRAMMING IN OPTIMAL SEARCHES

While the Bayesian approach to optimal search focusses on allocation of effort and on updating the search strategy in light of new information, some researchers use methods already familiar from Optimal Foraging Theory, such as the minimax approach and linear programming.

Game Theory treats a search as a two-person, zero-sum game between the searcher (the archaeologist) and the hider (the target or site)(Gal, 1980). This is like Optimal Foraging Theory's focus on foragers trying to optimize their encounters with prey (e.g., Paloheimo, 1971). Generally, the goal of the game is to find the trajectory or sequence of search spaces that will probably find the target most quickly. Sometimes, alternatively, it is to ensure against the risk of finding the target only at considerable cost, or of not finding the target at all. As in Optimal Foraging Theory, it uses a cost function to

Purposive Survey: Prospection

evaluate the risks and benefits of various strategies. Usually, it assumes that search consists of movement through a sequence of spaces or a continuous sweep of space, as in the transects that archaeologists typically use for surface survey by visual inspection.

The cost function, $C(S, H)$, represents the cost to the searcher for using strategy S, when the hider (in this case, the archaeological site) uses strategy H, usually represented in units of time to discovery. Since it is a zero-sum game, the cost to the searcher also represents the gain to the hider. The searcher's goal is to make $C(S, H)$ as small as possible.

Each pure search strategy (i.e., fixed trajectory) has a "value," $v(S)$, which represents the maximum cost that the searcher will incur from using the trajectory S. Clearly, the searcher wants to find the strategy that has the lowest value, indicating the shortest time to discovery of the target.

In addition, there are "mixed strategies" in which the searcher makes random choices from among the pure strategies. This often leads to better results, on average, than any pure strategy (Gal, 1989:35). Because they also make discovery time a random variable, mixed strategies cannot guarantee any fixed cost, but have expected costs denoted by $c(s, h)$.

Because the goal of search games is normally to minimize the time or cost up to the point of a single detection, archaeologists are only likely to find them useful in cases where they are searching for a single target that they expect to occur in some region, such as the case of the historic fort mentioned in section 3.2.1.

4.1 Discrete Search Games

Discrete search games begin, as with the Bayesian optimal allocation, with a set of discrete spaces. The target presumably occurs in one of the spaces, and the goal is to find the sequence of "looks" into these spaces that is likely to find the target most quickly. This is the class of search games that has the most obvious application to archaeology.

4.2 Continuous Search Games

The continuous version of the search game usually assumes a single target or "hider," and that the searcher begins at some point of origin, but is then free to follow any continous path inside the search space, subject to a constraint on speed. The search space can be a graph (i.e., a set of connected line segments or arcs, as in transects) or a region.

One also makes assumptions about the behavior of the hider. Since we do not expect archaeological sites to be actively evading detection, or even moving around, one possibility is to assume a random hiding strategy, which corresponds to a uniform distribution (Gal, 1989:37). In this case, the minimum expected search cost, $v(h)$, is at least $L/2$, where L is the total length of all the transects in a graph, so that the expected cost associated with this random strategy, h_R, when it is possible to move through all the transect endpoints without retracing steps, is

$$c(s, h_R) \geq \frac{L}{2g}$$

where g is the discovery rate.

Extending this from graphs to regions is straightforward, where it is reasonable to assume definite detection, by covering the region with transects of total length L spaced $2r$ apart, where r represents the discovery radius or lateral range. This amounts to tiling the region with strips with a width of $2r$, and allows a sweep of the entire region without retracing steps. Then if the searcher selects from the possible directions of sweep, starting at the origin, with equal probability (0.5), this will guarantee a value of $(1 + e)L/4r$. However, the uniform distribution for the hider implies that the discovery time will be at least $L/2g = L/4r$ (Gal, 1989:43-44).

The basic implication of continuous search games for archaeologists is that, when they are searching for a single target within a bounded region, and can anticipate its discovery radius, r, they should cover the region with transects spaced $2r$ apart and randomly select the direction in which to traverse a continuous tour of the transects. On average, this will minimize the time to detection of the anticipated target.

4.2.1 Exponential Spiral Search Trajectories

Much as with the expanding square (above, section 3.1), the minimax trajectory for sweeping an unbounded plane is an exponentially widening spiral (Gal, 1989:49-50). This assumes that the searcher will detect the target when the search radius intersects it, and that the distance of the trajectory from the origin, $X(q) = a \exp(bq)$, where a is a positive constant and b is the constant that minimizes

$$\exp(2\pi b)\sqrt{1 + \frac{1}{b^2}}$$

5. CONCLUSIONS

Prospection, or "purposive survey," is a legitimate and useful kind of survey, not a haphazard or dubious alternative to sampling space. It provides some kinds of information that sampling cannot, such as documenting the presence of rare sites, and can test hypotheses that make specific predictions about the locations of archaeological materials much more efficiently than sampling surveys (Cowgill, 1975: 260-261). Its tools also help minimize the risk that sampling surveys omit parts of the intended sample, creating bias, and allow us to evaluate the seriousness of such bias. Successful prospection depends on the combination of basic mathematical principles and archaeologists' experience and prior knowledge. By modelling the expected distribution of archaeological materials (Wobst, 1983: 62) or estimating the prior probabilities that particular kinds of targets occur in particular locations, prospection makes fruitful use of background research to increase the likelihood of detecting targets and to yield efficient survey designs.

Chapter VII
Surveying for Spatial Structure

This chapter will deal with situations in which most kinds of spatial sampling are inappropriate because missing data would undermine a survey's aims, and where what is sometimes called "total coverage" may be necessary. Chapter 4 already briefly introduced some kinds of analysis aimed at detecting spatial structure (Nearest Neighbor Analysis and Rank-Size Analysis). This chapter will cover the design of surveys intended for these kinds of analysis as well as isopleth mapping, landscape archaeology, Thiessen polygons, site-catchment analysis, trend-surface analysis, and Dimensional Analysis of Variance. The chapter will not go into details of the analytical methods themselves, but will show how missing data could undermine their results, and how to tailor survey to meet their assumptions (see also Kowalewski, 1990).

1. WHAT IS SPATIAL STRUCTURE?

Spatial structure involves both the pattern with which sites, buildings or artifacts are distributed in space, and the ways in which these entities are interrelated through historical ties, formation processes, and the movement of people, materials and information between them. At any given time, settlement can be dispersed or nucleated. Settlements may be fairly evenly spaced in settlement lattices, with large "central places" surrounded by smaller, subsidiary sites that are themselves surrounded by still smaller, less important sites that provide them with resources. Alternatively, settlements could be clustered, or distributed along river valleys in a dendritic pattern in such a way that some sites control the flow of goods and information to others. Within some kinds of sites, huts or pithouses could be scattered in a way that appears random, or houses could be arranged on a grid or some other regular pattern that has an impact on the way inhabitants interact with one another. In addition, non-settlement sites, such as burial monuments, agricultural or military earthworks, and other traces of land use may be interrelated in patterns that a spatial sample would fail to detect. Even varying artifact density over space that at first seems random could have meaningful patterning relevant to the way people cooperated or competed with one another. In addition, settlement systems have histories. People living in one settlement at one time may have lived in the same or a different settlement at a previous time, and patterns of mobility, including seasonality, nomadism, and colonization, entail the dimension of time as well as space.

1.1 Settlement Patterns and Settlement Systems

Some archaeologists have found it useful to distinguish between settlement patterns and settlement systems. Settlement patterns are static distributions of archaeological residues in space-time; settlement systems are dynamic and involve the human behaviors and cultural relationships that created the patterns.

Establishing the settlement pattern of a prehistoric human population involves determining the number, size, and spatial distribution of the full range of sites occupied by that population. Establishing the settlement *system* of a prehistoric human population involves the aditional, and much more difficult, task of determining the functional role of each site in the overall adaptive strategy of the human population. It involves determining the seasonality of occupation of different sites, as well as the political, kinship, and economic ties existing between groups occupying different sites. It also involves specifying and quantifying the movement of people, energy, and information between sites throughout the annual cycle (B. Smith, 1978:13).

The spatial and temporal evidence that Smith describes as settlement patterns involve estimating population parameters. Some of the parameters are site diversity (range of sites) and site size. Investigation of the natural and cultural factors involved in settlement systems is also largely a matter of parameter estimation.

Studying the political, economic and social relationships between sites, however, is definitely a matter of spatial structure. A random sample of sites or of small spaces is unlikely to provide the evidence to show where a particular village settlement had its quarries or hunting camps, or which villages supplied tribute to a particular chiefly center. Only a survey design informed by models of possible regional settlement systems, and with methods tuned to detection of the parts of those systems, will yield those kinds of results. Fortunately, there are some useful models that can guide this type of research.

Although previous chapters have referred to some kinds of models, it is important to recall what models are and what their role is. A model is a simplified depiction of what some reality might be like. It can even be a physical model, such as a scaled-down wooden model of a building. It can also be a mathematical model that we think might summarize the distribution of artifacts or sites, such as the Poisson encountered in previous chapters. A model can be any reasonably well defined hypothesis about some aspect of a problem.

Models help to focus research questions and interpret the results of analyses. Rather than collecting and scanning data haphazardly, it is useful to collect data in ways that make them comparable with the output of a number of competing models or hypotheses. The idea is not simply to assume that any model is "true," but to focus research in a way that allows us to evaluate and improve or reject models, or to see which of several models best fits a given case. It is sometimes reasonably certain that a particular model will not fit the data at all. For example, the Poisson distribution models random distributions of items in space-time, yet there are strong reasons to suspect that archaeologically significant remains are patterned, not random, in their distribution. Comparing those remains with the model helps measure the degree of certainty with which we can identify those patterns, which otherwise might be difficult to discern from randomness.

1.2 Central Places and Settlement Lattices

Johann von Thünen (1826) pioneered the concept that the use of territory around a city had a clear spatial structure, while Walter Christaller (1933) and August Lösch (1954) showed how similar spatial-economic principles fit these central places into regional networks or "lattices." Their work provides important models of settlement and land use that geographers and archaeologists can use.

1.2.1 The Central Place Model

Von Thünen was an economist who was interested in the principles that affected market prices and production decisions for agricultural goods. His model of the central place is one way to conceive of the way a city, at least in a modern state with a market economy, might be expected to exploit the land in its vicinity on the assumption that it is isolated from other major cities and occupies a fairly uniform landscape with only one kind of transport. Von Thünen assumed that in this situation the costs of travel time and transport (the "friction effect") would be an important influence on prices and agricultural practice. Not surprisingly, transport costs rise as a function of the distance that goods have to travel to the city. A farmer located a greater distance from the city, therefore, receives less return on his goods if he is competing with farmers closer to the city for sales in the market. This effect tends to restrict labor-intensive land uses and production of goods with a low price/weight ratio to land that is closer to the city, within a radius where costs of labor and transport are sufficiently lower than anticipated prices for the goods to yield a reasonable return at the market. The most highly valued land, with the greatest investments of labor and capital, would be within a very short distance of the city; land quite far from the city would only be used extensively, for such purposes as pasture. The result would be a concentric zonation.

There are many reasons why a particular city might depart in some respect from this highly idealized model. Sometimes topographic features, soil quality, the presence of a competing market, or the availability of better transport in some areas (roads or rivers) will cause distortion of the model or require us to consider a different model for the relationship between land uses and the costs and benefits of exploiting different kinds of land. Von Thünen in fact studied many of these effects as they applied to the situation in 19th-century Austria. In cases that anthropologists and archaeologists study, however, the poor fit of this model to real data may be because the central place is not involved in a market economy, and our assumptions about costs and benefits are wrong. For example, von Thünen was studying cities in which farmers were either paid laborers or entrepreneurs, in both cases motivated by prices and transport costs. In a medieval economy, by contrast, farmers would be peasants, or serfs, tied to the land, motivated instead by the requirement to pay tithes and rents, less likely to take the value of their own labor into account, and motivated more by the behavior of their feudal lords.

1.2.2 Hunter-gatherer Land-use Models

Prehistorians, whose focus is rarely on sites with market economies, have sometimes favored different versions of the Central Place model, sometimes based on ethnographic evidence. Not only is this because most of hunter-gatherers of archaeological interest had pre-market economies, but also because we might expect such social factors as marriage ties to be explicit in decisions about movement and location.

One economic model for hunter-gatherer settlement is that of the base camp with a variety of special-purpose camps. This is analogous to the classic Central Place model in that it involves activities and land uses dispersed around a central camp, and often takes costs and benefits into account through Optimal Foraging Theory, which, much like the economic theory behind von Thünen's work, uses decision theory (or "game theory") to evaluate the relative costs and benefits of competing foraging strategies. For example, special camp sites might be located in "patches" some distance away from a base camp where they are justified by the relative costs of search time and travel time and the anticipated value of a hunted animal or gathered resource.

Binford (1982), for example, envisages each residential base as surrounded by a "foraging radius," in which base residents can extract resources on a daily basis, in turn surrounded by a "logistical radius," in which special-purpose camps occur when it is necessary to stay away from the base for longer periods.

Although here I have characterized these models as appropriate to the study of hunter-gatherer settlement structure, versions of them are also appropriate for pastoral nomadic and some kinds of agricultural settlement systems.

1.2.3 Site-catchment Models

Another model that is a distant descendant of the Central Place Model is the site-catchment model (Higgs and Vita-Finzi, 1972). The classic variety of this model assumes, as von Thünen did, that there was a nearly circular zonation of land use around prehistoric and early historic sites. Users of this model attempt to infer what resources a base camp's residents would have found within one-hour, two-hour, and longer distances from base. They then try to use the distribution of these resources to infer why the site is located where it is.

1.2.4 Optimal Location Models

Alfred Weber (1909) pioneered the use of models for the way a place was located so as to minimize the costs of importing resources. Any site's location, under this model, is a compromise among the distances to the resources it needs, the weight of the resources brought from each place, and the effort or cost involved with movement. Although few archaeologists have made explicit reference to Weber's theory, as with von Thünen's, some of its principles are inherent in Optimal Foraging Theory (Clarke, 1977:23) and site-catchment models.

1.2.5 Settlement-lattice Models

Christaller (1933) and Lösch (Lösch, 1954) expanded on von Thünen's and Weber's work to show how various economic pressures can affect the organization of many central places, and their satellites, in cases where they are interrelated, rather than isolated. Their versions of the Central Place Model depend on the competitive aspects of market economies, in which producers can adjust their behaviors in relation to multiple potential markets for their goods, and centers can also adjust their behaviors to compete with neighboring centers.

Like von Thünen, Christaller made the simplifying assumption that the centers and their satellite sites were located on an undifferentiated plain, so as to investigate the relationships between distance, cost, price, and intensity of production. In addition, rather than consider only agricultural production, he looked at a range of goods and services and the behaviors of both suppliers and consumers. The central problem was determining the conditions that made some settlements become centers of supply for particular services and, when he considered many services simultaneously, the result was a hierarchy of major and minor centers.

Under the conditions that Christaller assumed, suppliers' attempts to locate as far as possible from their competition, so as to capture larger markets, results in an even spacing of suppliers that, once the density of suppliers is high enough, is hexagonal in its structure. The resulting hexagonal lattice maximizes the market areas for each supplier and also minimizes the distances consumers must travel to access goods and services. Goods and services of lower order (which enjoy more demand and therefore do not require large market areas) would also be spaced evenly and hexagonally, but with smaller distances between suppliers. As it turns out, the lattices of lower-order centers are nested within the higher-order ones, with major centers supplying goods and services of both higher and lower order and minor centers supplying only lower-order ones. The lower-order centers simply arrange themselves halfway between two higher-order ones.

Lösch recognized that these halfway points were not always optimum for suppliers and attempted to model a situation in which suppliers located themselves more precisely with respect to the size of market they needed to stay in business. This has the effect of allowing some higher-order centers to exist that do not offer lower-order goods and services, a situation that is unlikely to happen in real settlement systems (Smith, 1976:15).

Varieties of Christalleran models vary as a function of the amount of lower-level territory each higher-level center controls, summarized by a factor, K. Where K = 3, the center controls all of its own hexagonal territory plus one-third of each of its six neighboring hexagons. Where K = 4, the center controls its own plus one-half of its six neighboring territories. Where K = 7, it controls its own plus the equivalent of six other territories. These are the "classical" arrangements that Christaller discussed, but still higher K values are both possible and found to exist, where a center controls many hierarchical levels and correspondingly large numbers of lower-level territories. Christaller claims that K = 3 optimizes marketing functions by putting three service centers within easy reach of each settlement, while K = 4 optimizes for transportation between centers and higher orders facilitates administrative processes. Because they can interlock or overlap, just as different supply systems can be nested within one another, these systems are not mutually exclusive.

Several archaeologists have attempted to use models of the Christalleran type in the interpretation of archaeological settlement patterns. Johnson (1973; 1977) attempted to interpret distorted Christalleran lattices on an ancient Mesopotamian floodplain as evidence for administrative systems. Others have wrestled with the problem of how central places and their associated settlement lattices came into being (e.g., Cowgill, 1975; Flannery, 1972; Smith, 1976:44-51; Vance, 1970; Wright and Johnson, 1975).

1.2.6 Rank-size Models

Rank-size analysis is a method that some archaeologists have used in an attempt to identify urban settlement hierarchies (Cavanagh and Laxton, 1994; 1995; Falconer, 1994; Falconer and Savage, 1995; Johnson, 1980; Kowalewski, 1982; Moore, 1959; 1990; Savage, 1997). The method is based on a widely recognized pattern described by Zipf's Law (Zipf, 1949; Berry, 1961).

Zipf's Law is that the populations of settlements in hierarchical settlement systems are approximately inversely proportional to their rank. Mathematically, we can represent this as,

$$p_r = \frac{p_1}{r^k}, r = 1, 2, ...$$

where p_r is the population of the r-th ranked site and k is a constant close to 1.0. What it means is simply that (if k = 1) the second-rank settlement has a population about half that of the largest site, the third-rank settlement has one-third the population of the largest site, and so on. Thus, the sequence of population sizes will be,

$$p_1 > \frac{p_1}{2^k} > \frac{p_1}{3^k} > \frac{p_1}{4^k} > \frac{p_1}{5^k} > \frac{p_1}{6^k} > ... > \frac{p_1}{r^k}$$

Archaeologists who have used this model assume that site area is approximately proportional to settlement population, although recognizing that there are other influences on site size (Hirth, 1978). Their main interest in the Zipf relationship has been to see if the settlement data from survey are consistent with the model. Non-urban settlement systems do not fit this model, often because all the sites are very similar in size, as we would expect, for example, where small groups move repeatedly among a series of small campsites. Settlement systems in the very early stages of urbanism sometimes had very distorted rank-size relationships, often with an oversize central place and a dearth of middle-rank sites, and most sites hovering around a mode of fairly small size. Later, as urbanism became more entrenched, in some regions a few large centers size while many small settlements were abandoned and a few small ones ı middle size (Adams, 1965; 1981:70-75; Adams and Nissen, 1972:17-19).

1.3 Dendritic and Other Networks

In riverine environments or colonial frontiers, settlement systems sometimes have dendritic, rather than hexagonal, structure. In addition, the term "dendritic" has been applied to systems that occur in many poverty-stricken regions today, as well as some early states in which an unusually large center seems exclusively to control the distribution of goods to and collection of resources from an unusually large number of tributary sites (Johnson, 1970; Kelley, 1976). Although these aspects of dendritic systems are not mutually exclusive, here I use the term primarily in the former, more spatial, sense. Some classic examples would include Uruk and Old Assyrian networks with outposts on the peripheries of Mesopotamia (Algaze, 1993; Larsen, 1987), Hudson's Bay Company posts in the North American fur trade (Birk, 1994; Ewen, 1986), and the early mercantile economies of colonial America and Australia (e.g., Vance, 1970).

In dendritic systems, lower-order centers do not have access to two or more competing higher-order centers in which to buy and sell goods and services. Instead, they are tributary to a single higher-order center which is itself tributary to one of still higher order. Centers that are farther from the highest-order, controlling center are smaller in size and in the size of the territory they control. In this situation, there is no advantage for lower-order centers to locate themselves midway between higher-order ones, so hexagonal lattices do not form. Although the minor centers may compete with one another in access to a center of higher order, the major centers do not need to act competitively because they dictate the terms of exchange with their subsidiaries. This kind of system is very inefficient and disadvantageous, from the point of view of the minor centers and rural producers, but benefits the wholesalers or bureaucrats at the major centers, who dominate the system.

Note, for example, that in colonial America, it was illegal for colonists in New France to trade with England or Spain, or their colonies. Although smuggling did take place, the colonial powers expected their colonies to supply them exclusively with resources and to buy manufactured goods solely from the mother-country. This put the colonies at disadvantage and led to constant flows of cash out of the colonial economies, even in the face of exchange rates intended to prevent such outflow.

Sometimes a dendritic system may arise for physical-geographical reasons. Where settlements are strung out along the bottom of deep valleys or depend on irrigation by canal systems, settlements at one end of the river or canal network inevitably control access of water or other goods into and out of that network and thereby have power over ones farther down. In addition, travel or shipping from one end of the network to the other almost necessarily involves passing through intermediary centers of gradually increasing or decreasing size, each of which may be able to extract a tax or tribute. This leads to the "down-the-line" pattern of decreasing access to goods with increasing dis-

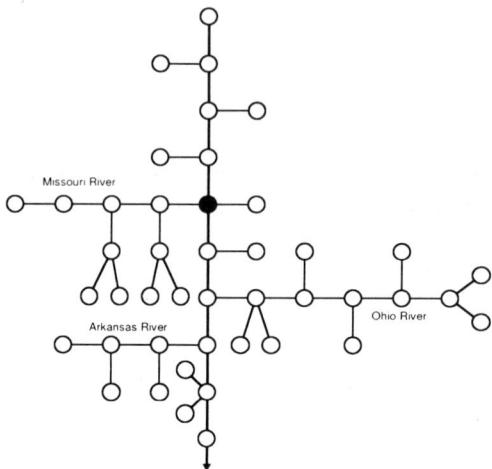

Figure 29. A model of the network of Mississippian settlement in the Middle Mississippi Valley (after Peregrine, 1991).

tance from their source (see Renfrew, 1975). Dendritic networks also tend to have more lower-level centers per major center than are found in Christalleran lattices. Consequently, their rank-size distributions may be concave, as in "primate" systems.

Network analysis provides a very useful way to analyse dendritic systems. This employs a model that represents important spaces (e.g., settlements or river segments) by circles, nodes or "vertices," and the communication routes between them as line segments or "edges." Euclidean space is ignored in favor of measuring distance by the number of steps or line segments one would have to traverse to get from one node to another. This is appropriate because, unlike centers in Christalleran lattices, centers in dendritic networks have no incentive to locate themselves midway between other centers, and the number of centers intervening between them and a major center is more important than distance in kilometers.

Peregrine (1991) applied this model to Mississippian settlement in the middle Mississippi valley. Here the rivers and their tributaries provided the links between settlements, a reasonable way to model communication where canoes were probably the principal mode of inter-site transportation (figure 29). Cases like this require confident knowledge of where the rivers flowed at the time the sites were occupied. In some cases, and particularly where many centuries have passed, river courses could have changed considerably.

Use of network models allows calculation of various measures that indicate how well interconnected the network is, while other measures indicate how well each site is integrated into the system, or the degree to which some sites control access to other sites or to resource locations (Hillier and Hanson, 1984).

In cases without rivers, canals, or tracks to show us the most likely connections between nodes of the network, site size, as it varies with distance from a frontier, or the high ratio of lower-order to higher-order centers may be the best clues to a dendritic network. Kelley (1976) has the advantage of historical documentation that reveals at least some of the wholesaling flows in the network of Navajo trading posts in the American Southwest prior to 1940. There, no more than four high-level centers supplied up to 140 trading posts at any time. Although only a few traders may have been literally compelled to deal with specific wholesalers, because of partnership or kinship with the wholesaler, for example, others were effectively tied to a single wholesaler through their dependence on credit and their high transport costs (Kelley, 1976:241-242).

1.4 Earthwork Patterns

In parts of Europe, a long history of archaeological investigation of rural landscapes has led to well developed methods for unravelling the sequence of landscape changes from sometimes confusing palimpsests of earthworks. Many kinds of earthworks are detectable on the landscape, including traces of agricultural fields, hedge rows, terraces, canals, ditches, fish ponds, mill ponds, roads, paths, abandoned rail lines, village mounds, farmsteads, burial monuments, fortifications, moats, lookouts, signal stations, windmills, bridges, dams, deer parks, quarries, mine shafts and spoil mounds, clay pits, woodlots, gardens, race tracks, and even rabbit warrens (Bowden, 1999; Brown, 1987; Everson and Williamson, 1998; Macready and Thompson, 1985; Taylor, 1973; 2000).

Although aerial photography and other kinds of remote sensing have long been a considerable aid to this type of research, these are no substitute for detailed observation, on the ground, of all preserved traces. The key is to understand how all parts relate to each other and to their environment. This is much like trying to decipher stratigraphic and other relationships in the excavation of a complex settlement site, and requires focus on alignments and intersection of different earthwork features. For example, does a settlement or a burial mound overlie a field system or are there indications that the fields were laid out so as to avoid these earthworks?

Archaeologists who have specialized in this kind of spatial structure on landscapes have developed principles and methods to decipher it (Bowden, 1999:73-96; Brown, 1987:65-88; Guy and Passelac, 1991:116-128; Zadora-Rio, 1991).

One approach is to treat the traces of field boundaries and other artificial features of the landscape in a quasi-grammatical manner, reducing them to sets of elementary units and deducing the relationships between them (Guy and Passelac, 1991). For example, given the field boundaries shown in figure 31, we can deduce a sequence of operations by which an original parcel of land was subdivided over time. We accomplish this through use of some principles or assumptions, such as:

- When one boundary (b) abuts a continuous boundary (a), a was probably in existence prior to the formation of b (figure 30; Guy and Passelac, 1991:117-118),

- When two continuous boundaries cross, without evidence that one cuts the other, their relationship is undetermined (figure 30d and e),

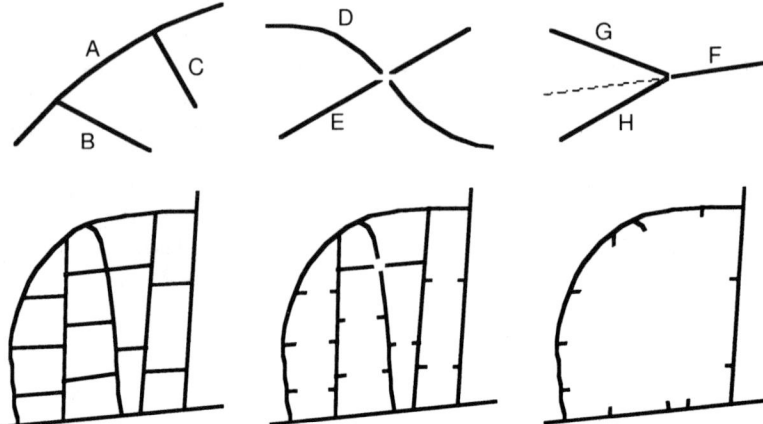

Figure 30. Chronological relationships among field boundaries. Wall (a) is probably older than (b) and (c), the relation between (d) and (e) is indeterminate, and that between (f), (g) and (h) is also undetermined. The lower register demonstrates the sequence of removing more recent features to deduce an earlier structure (modified from Guy and Passelac, 1991:118).

- However, when a long, continuous boundary crosses (i.e., cuts) others all along its length, with few or no cases of boundaries that abut one of its edges only, it is probably a recent feature, such as a modern road, placed without regard for the previously existing landscape structures (Guy and Passelac, 1991:117-118).

One variant of this kind of landscape archaeology even focuses on ancient woods, some of which have survived under human management for many centuries (Rackham, 1975; 1980; 1989). Woods may be enclosed by banks and ditches, but the character of trees and associated flora are also clues to their antiquity (Marren, 1990). "Coppiced" and "pollarded" trees, from which people have long removed wood while leaving the tree alive, can be many centuries old and have quite distinctive form. In addition, place names sometimes preserve the memory of woods that no longer survive.

1.5 Trend Surfaces, Clustering, and Isopleth Maps

Many applications of landscape archaeology, distributional archaeology, or "non-site" archaeology involve modelling the distribution of archaeological residues as continuous, undulating surfaces. The model thus looks like topography, and can be depicted either in three dimensions or as a kind of contour map. For artifact densities, for example, this is an "isopleth map," while for magnetic survey it is a magnetic susceptibility map. However, archaeological residues, in most cases, actually do not vary continuously in space, so that the topographic model is not entirely appropriate. It is only an approximation.

On true topographic maps, as on maps of the Earth's magnetic field strength and many other physical phenomena, it is always possible to interpolate between measurements to estimate quite accurately what unmeasured values will be. That is because the value, such as elevation above sea level, varies continuously over the intervening space. Because of this property, a contour map of topography or magnetic field strength will look closely similar no matter what the orientation or exact positioning of any systematic grid we use for observation. "Kriging" is a method for estimating a value at an unmeasured point in space on the basis of nearby measured spaces, and depends on this ability to interpolate.

Artifact distributions, by contrast, are not so amenable to this kind of map. Variations in the density of artifacts across the map are very sensitive to the orientation and position of the grid, just as the shapes of histograms are very sensitive to the boundaries between the graph intervals (Whallon, 1987:144-147). There can be very abrupt changes in density from one observation to the next, making it very difficult to see patterns or draw meaningful contours.

One solution is to use a smoothing or filtering function for this kind of data. The simplest smoothing function is to replace each value in the grid by the average of all neighboring values. In that case, we need to decide what consititutes each observation's "neighborhood," just as in adaptive sampling. In a rectangular grid, this could be the immediately adjacent four cells, or the eight cells that surround each cell, or the 24 cells within two intervals (figure 25). The greater the number of cells that contribute to the average, the smoother the surface will be.

Sometimes the goal is not simply to see how some measure, such as artifact density, varies over space, but explicitly to identify clusters or degree of clustering. Some of the methods for doing this, such as Nearest Neighbor Analysis and measures based on the variance-to-mean ratio, are extremely sensitive to edge effects and the size, shape, and positioning of observation units (Hodder and Orton, 1976).

1.6 Distributional Archaeology

Some archaeological research exploits the relationship between the scale of spatial clustering on the landscape and the scale of analytical units, rather than viewing this as a problem to be avoided.

Dimensional Analysis of Variance (DAV) (Schiffer, 1974; Whallon, 1973; Ebert 1992) is a method that detects the scale of clustering in dot patterns as the size of the basic observation quadrat is successively doubled. At each scale of quadrat, we calculate the variance/mean ratio, which should be close to 1.0 for a random (Poisson) distribution, and less than 1.0 for even distributions. We discover the scale of clustering by finding the quadrat size that yields the highest variance/mean ratio.

Some archaeologists (Ebert, 1992; Kvamme, 1998; Wandsnider and Ebert, 1986b) make use of this method in distributional archaeology. Ebert's and Wandsnider's teams use painstaking field methods to record the location of every artifact they encounter over fairly large areas, as well as some environmental attributes related to site-formation processes. This permits post-field analysis of those locations to determine the scale

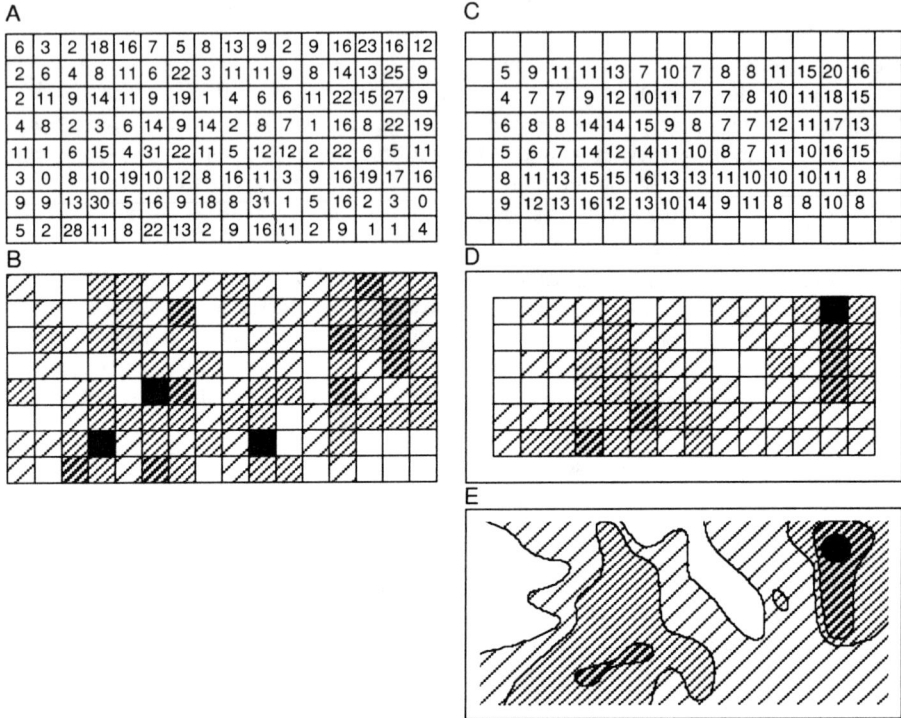

Figure 31. A data set of artifact counts (a) leads to a very patchy statistical surface (b), but smoothing the data, in this case by averaging over a neighborhood of four adjacent squares (c) leads to a smoother surface (d) and allows isopleth mapping (e).

of clustering of various classes of material. This reveals information about activities that were dispersed on the landscape, and which traditional survey methods would probably miss, but at a very high cost per unit area. Consequently, the "landscapes" to which this method has been applied are typically quite small, such as the 5.76 ha of the Grand Junction Survey (Kvamme, 1998).

Among the key requirements of DAV is a large, continuous, and regularly shaped tract of land. In fact, the survey region must not only be rectangular, but be proportioned in such a way as to allow the successive doubling of the quadrats within it. Typically, this involves a rectangle that is twice as long as it is wide. The Seedskadee Survey actually used a sample of 500 m x 500 m quadrats, which is actually not an optimal way to do distributional archaeology, because it makes it difficult or impossible to detect clustering at scales near or larger than this quadrat size.

2. THE CASE FOR "TOTAL SURVEY"

When a survey's goal is to study any of the spatial phenomena mentioned in the last section, a haphazard, probabilistic or systematic sample of a region is usually ineffective. These cases require thorough survey of a large enough area of contiguous space to reveal the kind of pattern that is the target of search. However, justification for "total survey" in the archaeological literature sometimes refers to quite different things.

2.1 The Definition of "Total Survey"

Most archaeologists who use the term, "total survey" or "total coverage," imply a 100% sampling fraction. This means a sample that includes every site, feature or artifact that was specified as the survey's target, in other words the whole population, or at least those members of the population that survive. In fact, archaeologists sometimes use the term to mean something rather different.

Most of the papers in Fish and Kowalewski's (1990) *The Archaeology of Regions* appear to consider surveys that cover contiguous areas, rather than samples of units scattered over space, as "total survey." They might look like virtually 100% sampling fractions, at least of the "visible" sites, but, in fact, the intensity of some of these surveys is not especially high. For example, transect intervals of 30 to 50m, or even more, are not uncommon (e.g., Parsons, 1990:11; Kowalewski, 1990: 36; Fish et al., 1990: 193). Consequently, while these surveys may include 100% of the spatial units (quadrats, for example) within their survey universes, we should not expect them to have detected 100% of the sites. In favorable circumstances, such surveys may detect 100% of the sites larger than the transect interval, and indeed survey of arid regions with unusually high visibility accounts for a large proportion of "total surveys." Yet the proportion of small, unobtrusive sites that such surveys detect could be quite low.

This would not be particularly disturbing except that claims for "total survey" at the regional scale can thus be misleading. They often simply involve sampling at a different scale. For example, some surveys will include 100% of the obtrusive sites above a certain size, and then sample within the sites to get estimates of their characteristics. Others will include all landscape features, or "places," in a region, and then carry out augering or test-pitting to sample the sediments in them. Most commonly, "total surveys" simply include every polygon in a gridded sampling frame, and then use a fairly high resolution of transects to cover each polygon. All these strategies are fine, but to assume that such surveys are recording a "total" inventory of archaeological traces involves the unrealistic assumption of 100% detectability.

All surveys, including high-resolution surveys that cover large, contiguous portions of space, need to make realistic assessments of their detection functions if anyone is to determine how many targets of various kinds the survey may have overlooked.

2.2 The "Presampling" and Large-site Bias Arguments

Some arguments for total survey are based on the view that the modern population being sampled already represents a mere sample of the population of interest. For example, Bar-Yosef and Goren (1980) argue that various geomorphological processes have altered the landscape in such a way that any population sampled on the modern landscape does not correspond with the prehistoric population of interest. However, it is not clear how "total survey" would alleviate this. A rational response in the sampling vein might be to sample the population of surviving landforms that date to the period of interest, such as the late Pleistocene.

In other cases, the argument for total survey is meant to alleviate past bias against small or unobtrusive sites, or simply to ensure a high intensity or resolution of survey. These are admirable goals, but achieving them does not necessarily entail total survey.

However, it remains true that some archaeological problems require examination of a reasonably large, contiguous region of space, and no kind of sample, in the usual sense of the word, would satisfy those requirements (see Kowalewski, 1990).

3. HOW TO SURVEY FOR SPATIAL STRUCTURE

Surveying in such a way that detection and interpretation of spatial structure is possible is difficult and can be costly, but sometimes purposive survey techniques (chapter 6) can narrow the search somewhat to reduce that cost. Models that predict likely site locations can be very useful in this context.

Although we should not expect any model to describe the actual distribution of material culture in space accurately and in detail, models such as those described in section 1 can help specify the kind and scale of units to use in a survey, the distribution of those units, the most effective search patterns, and the kinds of data crew members will need to collect.

3.1 Determining the Scale of Survey

After defining the survey's goals, the first thing that is necessary is to determine the appropriate scale of survey. It would be a waste of resources to survey a unit too small to contain a contiguous portion of the structure that is large enough to reveal its characteristics. This is where models and previous experience come in.

3.1.1 Surveying with Central Place Models

If the goal is to identify and interpret aspects of a Central Place model or to test competing varieties of Central Place model, details of the model help designers of surveys decide what scale the surveys need to have.

Surveying for Spatial Structure

For example, a Central Place model of an agricultural town surrounded by farmland where different agricultural activities took place, and with pastoral land uses in the outermost zone, will include information about the zones in which farmhouses, barns and other special agricultural sites are likely to occur. The distance of these zones from the center will vary, depending on whether or not the farmers had draft animals or wheeled transport, whether or not they may have participated in a market economy, and what kind of crops they were probably growing. When survey begins at a known central place, this assumption produces circular survey areas. Some archaeologists instead assume a one- or two-hour travel time between the town and its agricultural facilities. This will tend to result in irregularly shaped survey areas. In cases where the location of a central place is unknown, the details of the model will only tell us how large an area the survey must cover to include at least one central place and much of its hinterland with reasonable probability.

For Site Catchment models, Flannery (1976) recommends examining the finds from an excavated site to determine how large the site's catchment was likely to be. This is the best information available on the size and shape of the site's catchment, and is therefore to be prefered to radii based only on arbitrary distances or walking-times. As he points out, however, some resources we might find at a site, such as valuable obsidian, might be imported from very distant sources. Consequently, it is useful to distinguish between the catchment for such imports, probably far too large to survey in a meaningful way, and the everyday catchment for resources that were probably procured directly by the site's inhabitants. The latter would include items whose relatively low value or great bulk (and high transport costs) would mitigate against their import from distant or even neighboring centers.

3.1.2 Surveying for Settlement Lattices

In the case of settlement lattices, the key to selecting an appropriate scale is the likely distance between peer sites at or near the top of the settlement hierarchy. The intensively surveyed area should be broader than our upper estimate of this distance. The problem of setting the size of a survey region for this purpose is analogous to the problem of optimizing transect intervals (chapter 4, section 1.1.2). This case, however, requires reasonable certainty that all of at least one central place's hinterland will occur *between* the boundaries. This is almost like finding the spacing that has a low probability of intersecting the target, the reverse of the usual problem.

In a region in which the known central places are an average of 7 km apart, for example, this would imply an average distance between each central place and its most outlying settlements (at the hexagon corners) of about 4 km. Clearly any survey region less than 8 km wide will omit some part of a central place's hinterland. In a very unlucky case, it might even straddle the border between two or three hinterlands. As it turns out, even in a region 16 km wide there is a reasonably high probability that a particular circular hinterland will intersect one of the edges. Assuming that the survey region is square, the probability that the circle will intersect any of the four edges is

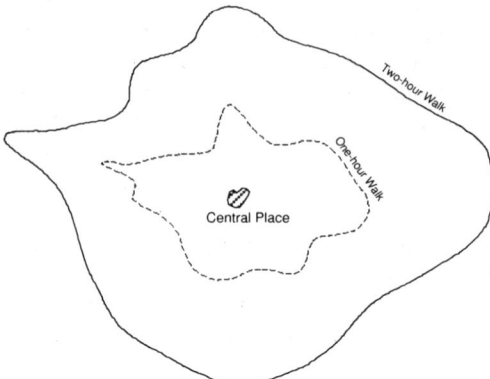

Figure 32. Survey regions defined by one- and two-hour walks from a known settlement site, as defined by walking radially arranged transects.

$$P(s) = \frac{d}{s}\left(2 - \frac{d}{s}\right)$$

where s is the width of the survey region and d is the diameter of the hinterland (McCammon, 1977:374). Consequently, a diameter of 8 km and $s = 16$ km yield a probability of 0.75. However, because the hinterlands are packed, a survey region of such a size should still include all of one hinterland.

In most cases, however, previous experience of the location of a central place and neighboring peer sites will be the best clue to placing useful boundaries. Drawing weighted or unweighted Thiessen polygons and then placing the survey boundary a short distance outside the polygon of interest is likely to include all of the territory of interest (see chapter 4, section 2.3).

Once these boundaries are established, it may be necessary to conduct a total survey within them, or at least within a portion that is large enough to establish the nature of the settlement lattice. If, for example, the survey area contains a central place in a classic hexagonal lattice, once its location is known, it will only be necessary to survey a little over one-third of its hinterland to determine the structure of the lattice, as long as the subsidiary sites are well preserved and have reasonably high detectability. Omitting parts of the survey area where recent development or geomorphological processes have probably destroyed or covered sites will also save time for survey in more productive parts of the settlement lattice.

3.1.3 Survey for Rank-size Analysis

One of the assumptions of rank-size analysis is that the sample of sites includes a central place and all its subsidiary sites, but no sites that do not belong to its settlement system. It is critical, therefore, to ensure that the survey includes a large enough territory to include the largest site or, in cases where we already know the location of this site, enough territory to include the second-largest, third-largest, fourth-largest, and fifth-largest sites. If it does, it will probably also include most of the smaller sites, although whether or not the survey succeeds in detecting them is a different matter. More difficult is the exclusion of sites from analysis that belong to different settlement systems. Including sites that do not really belong to the hierarchy of the large site can have a substantial effect on the shape of the rank-size distribution, especially if those sites are large, leading to incorrect conclusions about political complexity.

Trying to ensure that the survey only includes sites that belong to the largest site's settlement hierarchy is the greatest difficulty. This is really an issue of survey boundaries (chapter 4). Given incomplete information, at best, about the ancient boundaries of settlement systems, one solution to this problem is to use existing information, low-intensity survey, or aerial remote sensing to identify not only the central place of interest, but also its neighboring peer sites. As in the previous section, drawing Thiessen polygons and adjusting their boundaries slightly in response to major physical features, such as streams or mountains, establishes a reasonable hypothesis for the boundaries of the settlement system of interest. Although these boundaries will probably be far from perfect, they at least have a much higher probability of containing the appropriate sites than would some arbitrary boundary.

One aspect of Zipf's law for the rank-size relationship has important implications for the scale of survey. Cavanagh and Laxton (1994) have shown that the Zipf sequence entails *fractal* properties (Mandelbrot, 1982) with the fractal dimension of $1/k$, where k is the constant in the Zipf equation (see section 1.2.3). This means that the sequence shows *self-similarity*: any second-order level of the site hierarchy will show the same pattern as the first-order level, any third-order level will show the pattern of the second- and first-order ones, and so on. Consequently, it is not actually necessary to survey entire settlement systems in cases where Zipf's Law pertains. Instead, it is sufficient to survey a contiguous portion of the settlement system that includes a second- or third-order center, its satellites, and their satellites. Whatever pattern occurs in this portion should be the same as in other, unsurveyed, parts of the settlement system and of higher and lower parts of the hierarchy (Cavanagh and Laxton, 1994:63). However, this does not necessarily apply to cases that do not fit the Zipf sequence, as in hunter-gatherer settlement systems or the earliest state societies and, in fact, whether or not Zipf's law pertains is often the question we are trying to answer.

3.1.4 Surveying Dendritic Networks

Where the goal of survey is to detect or understand the structure of some dendritic networks, as in river drainages and irrigation systems, the physical scale of the river or canal systems themselves dictates the scale of survey. In short, it is necessary to survey contiguous segments of the network to determine the distances between sites at different levels of any site hierarchy.

For example, if the purpose of surveying the Diyala canal system were to determine the pattern by which sites of different size were interconnected by canals, fieldworkers could focus on a manageable and well-preserved portion of the canal networks and walk all the canals in this portion (or use other suitable discovery technique) to discover all the sites along them. They could then graph the network and calculate various measures of system interconnectedness and site integration (Hillier and Hanson, 1984).

Where a dendritic network does not follow physical, identifiable features, such as streams or canals, survey to detect the network is more difficult. In some cases, however, prior knowledge of the locations of some sites makes it possible to interpolate between them and select the regions in which intervening sites are likely to occur. For example, sometimes historical information suggests that two cities of the Roman era, or a city and an outlying fort, were connected by a road. Restricting survey to an elongated region between these two points allows intensive search for smaller settlements and waystops that probably occurred along the road. In other cases, some traces of paths or tracks persist (e.g., Wilkinson, 1993; Zamit, 1928).

3.1.5 Landscape Survey

Landscape surveys employ either arbitrary geometrical units or more meaningful landscape elements as their observational units but, in both cases, it is important for the scale of these units to be similar to the scale of the human behaviors the survey hopes to elucidate. For a survey aimed at discovering prehistoric hunter-gatherers' settlement strategy, for example, this means either quadrats or landscape elements small enough to reflect differences in food or other resources the hunter-gatherers may have exploited as well as variations in the attributes, such as drainage, aspect or slope, likely to affect the choice of one place over another as a "stopping point" or camp site (Binford, 1982; Schlanger, 1992; Stafford and Hajic, 1992).

A sensible approach, in this case, is to use as the survey unit landscape elements whose defining characteristics are closely related to the factors that were probably involved in the hunter-gatherers' choices of where to camp and forage.

3.2 Selecting Effective Search Patterns

Because most surveys for spatial structure aim for "total survey" of the target region with respect to some entity (artifact, artifact cluster, or site of some definition), it is critical to select a search procedure that minimizes the probability of omitting observations. Yet cost and other considerations may make it difficult to search the entire region with a fine-toothed comb. Where sub-surface remains are among the items of interest, a complete examination might literally involve sieving billions of cubic meters of sediment. Clearly, search strategies are required that make it possible to delineate the patterns of interest without such monumental, not to mention impossible, effort.

3.2.1 Surveying with Central Place and Site-catchment Models

Often, the goals of these surveys can be met with a radiating search pattern. In effect, this is usually a kind of sample because it may not be necessary to cover every square meter of the catchment, only to determine the distribution of archaeological remains and potential resources (soil types, chert sources, etc.) as a function of distance from the central place. One advantage of this type of survey, which involves walking outward from the central place, is that allows estimate of travel times to subsidiary sites and resources, and not only their map coordinates.

In cases where the catchment of a central place was probably very large, it may be possible to use prospecting techniques, such as aerial remote sensing, to identify candidates for the second- and third-order sites in the hierarchy and do ground-checks to see if the candidates are actually archaeological and belong to the appropriate time period. Finally, high-resolution survey around a sample of second- and third-order sites in different parts of the catchment would help to determine their function in the settlement system.

3.2.2 Surveying for Settlement Lattices

This kind of survey can be difficult, and may require total survey with high resolution of parallel transects in some large portion of the hinterland of a central place. However, there are alternatives that may work in some situations.

Sometimes knowing the locations of at least a few sites, or being able to spot likely site locations on aerial photographs, facilitates the use of purposive techniques to find the other sites in a settlement lattice. This takes advantage of the properties of settlement lattices to predict where sites should occur, and then uses intensive survey of small regions around the predicted locations to find them. For example, the model could predict a third-order site roughly halfway between each pair of second-order sites. Within each small search space, the expanding square search would probably find the site more quickly than traditional parallel transects.

In addition, this kind of strategy can be used to test the hypothesis that the sites fit a particular kind of settlement lattice. For example, the locations of a few known sites allow prediction of where second-order, third-order, and smaller settlements should occur if the K3, K4 or K7 Christaller model applies (see section 1.2.5). Surveying each of the predicted locations to see if sites do or do not occur there, and comparing the success of each model at predicting site locations serves as a test of the models.

3.2.3 Survey for Rank-size Analysis

The key to an accurate rank-size analysis is to ensure that any sample contains every single site larger than some minimum size that belongs to the site hierarchy, but none that do not. Any search pattern that samples in space will therefore be ineffective, but omitting very small sites poses much less problem because they have less effect on the shape of the rank-size curve.

Fortunately, the larger sites are generally the easiest to locate and detect. Therefore, a systematic search pattern with an interval small enough to intersect every site in the survey area larger than the size of the fifth- or sixth-ranked site will work as long as it is also possible to recognize sites once they are intersected. The constant spacing combined with good visibility and obtrusiveness will allow construction of a graph that relates site size to probability of discovery. Methods like Monte Carlo simulation (e.g., Falconer, 1994) can then be used to assess the effect of imperfect discovery for the smaller sites.

In addition, it is helpful to use prospecting techniques, such as aerial remote sensing followed by ground checks, to try and ensure that none of the large or medium sites are missing from the record.

3.2.4 Dendritic Networks

In cases where there is reason to expect that a communication network followed a physical one, such as the network of streams in a drainage basin or a system of canals, the obvious strategy is to use the segments of the physical system, such as both banks of each canal segment, as the units of survey.

Where there is no physical analogue for the network, but prior knowledge of the locations of at least some of the sites (possibly due to preliminary reconnaissance survey or aerial photographs), it is possible to use this information to allocate survey effort. For example, assuming a high prior probability that intervening sites will occur somewhere within a broad band running between two known sites (but not too close to the ends), helps to position a broad transect for the highest-priority survey. A band to either side of the first would contain regions of slightly lower prior probability. In addition, if survey begins fairly close to the two ends, discovery of any sites that were probably part of the network adds new information that allows surveyors to update their survey strategy, shifting the bands of high probability away from their initial, linear course. The result is a survey that locates the intervening sites in a network as quickly as possible, but that almost certainly omits sites that either were not part of the network, or were on its peripheries. Consequently it is a good idea to reserve some time to survey some regions where peripheral sites could occur.

3.2.5 Landscape Survey

Typical "non-site" or "distributional" surveys generally require extremely effective recovery of evidence within survey units. Archaeologists have developed a number of strategies to ensure this, particularly in survey for surface artifacts.

Ensuring total or nearly total collection of surface artifacts within a spatial unit involves careful inspection by teams of surveyors, whose members complement one another's observation strengths and weaknesses, walking across the unit in different directions at close intervals, and at different times of day (Ebert, 1992). Sometimes, the first team surveys the unit and flags artifacts on the surface, then a second team that records or collects the flagged artifacts also resurveys the unit for any artifacts the first team missed. This is a very time-consuming and costly strategy.

At other times, and particularly where it is necessary to use shovel-testing, augering or remote sensing as a discovery technique, it is necessary to sample within the observation units. In these cases, a systematic arrangement of observations in either a rectangular or hexagonal grid is typical. These arrangements allow reconstruction of variations in artifact density, magnetic susceptibility, or phosphate values over space through the use of data-smoothing filters (above, section 1.5). Note that this involves sampling within the landscape units that form the main units of analysis, not sampling at the scale of regions.

4. CONCLUSION

An important aspect of regional archaeological evidence is how it is structured in space. Most kinds of regional sampling are not designed to detect spatial structure. To learn something about settlement hierarchies or dispersed use of landscapes, it is necessary to employ intensive survey of contiguous space, rather than the spotty coverage that typical spatial samples provide. In addition, it is sometimes possible to take advantage of prior information and models of spatial structure to predict where undetected sites should occur. In some of these cases, survey constitutes a test of the models.

Chapter VIII
Cultural Resource Management and Site Significance

A common goal in modern archaeological survey is to assess the archaeological significance of an area that is experiencing, or is about to experience, the impact of development, often called an "Area of Potential Effects" (APE). Construction of new roads, pipelines, housing, office blocks, shopping malls, or water reservoirs is commonly the impetus for such survey. Often there is considerable pressure to complete the assessment quickly. Usually those who are funding the work have no specific research questions beyond determining what impact, if any, the development will have on archaeological resources, whether any of those resources is "significant," and what steps, if any, are necessary to mitigate the impact, preserve sites, or salvage information from them before their destruction. Some clients, in fact, may have no interest in heritage resources beyond satisfying minimal legal requirements. However, a good CRM survey will address gaps in archaeological knowledge and balance competing economic, social and cultural interests. In addition, modern CRM assessments often use predictive modelling to optimize their designs.

1. WHAT IS CULTURAL RESOURCE MANAGEMENT?

Cultural Resource Management (CRM) involves the documentation, assessment, management, and sometimes excavation or conservation, of irreplaceable cultural resources. These resources include heritage buildings, prehistoric sites, monuments, sites, and even landscapes deemed "significant" to the public and other communities, including historians, architects, and archaeologists. Not all CRM involves archaeological survey. Some involves assessment of known resources, such as historic buildings, or library research to establish whether survey is even desirable. Butler (1987:821) emphasizes that archaeologists are not cultural resource managers; they only make recommendations to such managers. Archaeological survey's role in CRM is to document and help managers assess cultural resources, and especially those that were previously unknown. In the jargon of environmental impact assessment and planning, to which CRM is closely related, archaeological survey is part of "Phase I" assessment.

1.1 The Objectives of Cultural Resource Management

The goals of Cultural Resource Management are varied and difficult to generalize. They can include, but are not limited to, the following:
- Detection and identification of unknown cultural resources
- Assessment of cultural resources to determine whether they are significant
- Planning the most appropriate long-term use of cultural resources
- Assessment of the risks to cultural resources
- Protecting significant heritage resources for the use or enjoyment of present and future generations
- Making recommendations as to how to manage, develop, or protect those resources
- Building and testing predictive models, sometimes called "potential models" or "sensitivity models," to provide a reliable basis on which to design future archaeological surveys or make planning decisions
- Recovering materials and data from cultural resources that are threatened or slated for destruction.

The remainder of this chapter will concentrate on those aspects of CRM that involve archaeological survey (often described as "Phase I" assessment, although sometimes extending into Phase II evaluation), but it is important to remember that survey is only a component, or a tool, that is useful in some instances and conceivably unnecessary in others.

1.2 The Responsibilities of CRM Professionals

There is considerable debate over whether the primary responsibility of the firms that do CRM work is to their clients (often developers who want to destroy or modify a heritage resource), to the public, to their own disciplines (archaeology, history), or to the heritage resources themselves. This is a complicated issue much like the one facing some other professionals, such as lawyers, real estate agents, and even police officers, who must balance the rights and needs of clients, the public, colleagues, employees, competitors, the law, and others. CRM archaeologists have generated much heat (and some light) debating this balance in such forms as ACRA. For the field to survive and thrive, it must counter the suspicions of some clients and members of the public that CRM is simply self-serving.

1.2.1 Responsibility to the Client

Clients pay for the CRM work and have some expectations as a result. Among these is often an expectation of confidentiality. Archaeologists, in the course of CRM work, are sometimes privy to confidential information about the client's development plans and are expected to keep this information private. Another expectation is that the CRM archaeologists will provide useful information that allows the client to avoid unecessary mitigation costs. For example, clients do not like to be surprised by an unexpected and highly significant site right in the path of their road or development project, and which a CRM survey failed to detect.

1.2.2 Responsibility to Archaeological and Other Heritage Resources

Archaeologists also have a responsibility to their profession and to the resources on which it depends. Usually, archaeologists are dedicated to the preservation of archaeological resources whenever it is reasonable and feasible. Archaeologists are often advocates for the preservation of heritage resources for the benefit of future generations, and consider publication of results a basic archaeological responsibility. However, protection of the resources sometimes requires keeping exact site locations confidential.

1.2.3 Responsibility to the Public

They also have a responsibility to the public, including indigenous groups. This entails not only helping to make some portion of heritage resources accessible, to further public enjoyment of heritage, and to protect resources that have symbolic or ideological significance to the community, but also not to impede unduly non-archaeological projects that are of public benefit. Unfortunately, this last responsibility sometimes conflicts with other archaeological responsibilities, because some highly beneficial projects have destructive impact on archaeological remains, and this makes some kind of balance necessary. In addition, the public is often also a client, and there is a responsibility to carry out public CRM work at a reasonable cost and in a timely manner.

1.2.4 Legal Obligations

In addition, CRM work is typically subject to regulation by government agencies and heritage organizations, and is often governed by heritage legislation. Although archaeologists may sometimes be free to exceed the standards set by these regulations, they must at least meet them. Regulations frequently set standards for aspects of background research, fieldwork, documentation, curation of artifacts, and reporting or publication. In some regions, consultation with indigenous people or local residents is also required, and in any case is advisable.

1.2.5 Responsibility to Personnel

Often, CRM archaeologists are also employers, and they have a responsibility to ensure the fair renumeration, and especially the health and safety, of their employees. Remuneration and other personnel issues are sometimes in the guidelines of CRM professional organizations (see section 4.2). Health-and-safety issues are discussed in Appendix 1.

2. REGIONAL IMPACT ASSESSMENTS BY FIELD SURVEY

It is a truism that, to assess potential impacts on heritage resources, managers must know or be reasonably able to predict where those resources are. Although some heritage surveys involve assessing known sites, such as historic buildings, common roles for CRM are to conduct regional survey to prospect for previously undocumented sites, assess the condition and significance of sites, and estimate various parameters of the archaeological record, such as site density or distribution by time period, in an impact area. CRM archaeologists typically carry these out through some combination of prospecting and spatial sampling. It is noteworthy, however, that it is sometimes possible to guide development in ways that will avoid negative archaeological impacts even without conducting expensive field surveys.

2.1 Goals of Impact Assessment

The purpose of cultural impact assessment is to provide information that decision-makers can use in the management of cultural resources or to balance the competing requirements of development and heritage preservation. Impact assessment is intended to document heritage resources or predict where they may occur, to estimate the probable effects of proposed development on them, and to recommend what action, if any, should be taken to mitigate these effects. Detailed cultural impact assessment typically has the following specific objectives:

- Identification of archaeological and historic resources in the area of probable impact,
- Evaluation of those resources' significance,
- Contributing to knowledge about the distribution of archaeological or historical resources,
- Estimate of the nature, magnitude and duration of probable impacts of the proposed development on the resources,
- Recommendations for viable alternatives or modifications to the development so as to minimize or avoid adverse impacts on the resources
- Recommendations for ways to recover or preserve signficant aspects of the heritage resources, should modifications to the development be impossible,
- Assisting with the design and planning of alternatives or mitigation, and
- Responsible collection of data from the resource that enhances public appreciation of the resource or is relevant to recognized research problems or future research needs that one can reasonably anticipate.

Cultural Resource Management and Site Significance

2.2 Satisfying Clients and Regulations

Unlike academic archaeologists, CRM archaeologists do not generally have the luxury of defining their own survey boundaries, objectives, or even major details of sampling strategy. Planning or development goals often dictate the project's scope and main objectives, while official guidelines often regulate the methods, sampling strategies, and survey intensity that will be acceptable. These guidelines vary from jurisdiction to jurisdication and typically become more specific and restrictive over time.

In addition, clients may announce projects with very short deadlines for proposals, while the deadlines for completion of background research, fieldwork, analysis, and presentation of results are also typically very tight. In the worst cases, this may lead to rushed work or adherence to "boilerplate" research plans rather than research designs tailored to particular requirements or contexts.

Financial constraints are also a major issue. Although the growth of CRM led to substantial increase in the funding of archaeological work overall, it also presents the risk of shifting the rationale for budgets away from research requirements toward financial expedience. The need to bid for contracts in a very competitive environment can lead to a downward spiral of budgeting at the sacrifice of expensive methods or intensive survey. As Wobst (1983:61) has noted, at least in the northeastern United States this has led to a negative correlation between the size of project areas and financial support per unit area, and thus also between project size and survey intensity.

We can also expect those charged with evaluating proposals for CRM work to be somewhat conservative. It might seem too risky to allow, let alone encourage, cutting-edge, experimental research designs. Instead, the tendency is to favor well established and easily understood methods and to encourage consistency between projects. Overall, this has led to minimum standards of performance rather than encouraging excellence or helping to tailor research to specific problems (Wobst, 1983:66), even if CRM practitioners sometimes rise above these standards and some jurisdictions do encourage sensible innovations.

We will return to some of the issues that regulation involves in section 4.

2.3 Use of Predictive Models in Phase I Assessment

It is increasingly common for the regulations governing CRM to call for the use of predictive models, sometimes called "sensitivity models" or "potential models," in the design of archaeological surveys at the Phase I or regional assessment level. The models that CRM uses are typically probability surfaces of some kind: more simply, they are maps that show how the probability of encountering archaeological materials is expected to vary over the landscape. The idea is that, if these models are accurate, we can use a different survey design in areas that have a high probability of containing significant archaeological material than in ones that have low probability. In some circumstances, planners may decide that the model is sufficiently well confirmed that low-probability areas can be targeted for development without any archaeological survey at all.

2.3.1 What Are Predictive Models and Sensitivity Models?

The predictive models typically used in CRM are essentially maps on which someone has assigned to different parts of the landscape some expectation that significant heritage materials will occur. In some cases, different landforms on the map are simply described as having "low," "medium," "indeterminate," or "high" probability of harboring archaeological or other heritage materials. These are sometimes called "sensitivity models" because they simply predict the sensitivity of each area to archaeological impact. More sophisticated models assign a probability value to different parts of the map, thus creating a probability surface. The models are created and tested with statistical surveys, and, once constructed, can be used to guide both purposive and stratified statistical surveys.

These models are built up from previous experience or statistical surveys. If, for example, many previous surveys have shown that 15% of the time when someone surveys one hectare of beach ridges that mark the edge of a former lake, they find Paleoindian artifacts, these one-hectare beach units would be assigned a probability of 0.15 (or a figure that has been adjusted for visibility and other influences on detectability) of having such materials. Some CRM managers are reluctant to make such probability estimates, fearing that they do not have enough information to be "exact." In fact, probability estimates are just that, estimates, and even fairly imprecise estimates are often more useful than the cruder ordinal scales (e.g., low, medium, high) more commonly encountered.

Today, probability modelling is widespread in CRM, is required in some jurisdictions, and now has quite a long track record. For example, Mitchelson (1984) developed a model based on a multivariate analysis of 3-acre (1.25 ha) spatial units in the region surrounding Fort Rucker, Alabama. The factors that contributed to his model included soil characteristics, distance to water sources, type of water source, and elevation above the water source.

A more recent example is the Archaeological Predictive Model of Minnesota's Department of Transport and the US Federal Roadway Authority. This is a GIS model of the entire state of Minnesota, whose pixels, each 30 m x 30 m in size, have been classified to eight levels of prior probability of containing archaeological materials.

Most of these predictive models rely heavily on environmental variables, such as distance to water, to predict site location. Where there has been little or no previous archaeological work with which to identify these factors, sometimes historical documentation, including old maps, and plausible expectations about the suitability of various geological and topographical areas for settlement or agricultural land use can contribute to the construction of a model. As already seen, Lolley (1996) developed such a model for the location of historic Upper Creek settlements in Alabama based on analysis of historic maps and ethnohistoric accounts. Some states, such as New Jersey (NJHPO, n.d.:3.3), explicitly require historical background information to contribute to Phase I predictive modelling in the case of historic sites.

2.3.2 Do Sensitivity Models Create Bias?

There is understandable cause for worry that use of such models can lead to "self-fullfilling prophecies" about the distributions of heritage resources (Wobst, 1983:59, 61), and this is a possibility that requires careful consideration.

Generally, the untested use of models to concentrate survey in areas of "high potential" and virtually ignore areas of "low potential" will indeed amplify any biases in our characterization of archaeological distributions. This has been a problem in the past wherever models have been presented and used without adequate justification and, especially, without adequate testing by thorough investigation of areas in which the model predicts there should *not* be archaeological materials. Unfortunately, it is all too easy to assume that regions where previous surveys have failed to detect sites have no archaeological resources, when in fact the failure is due to poor visibility, infinintessimal sampling fractions and sample sizes, or simple failure to assess the probability that those areas contain undetected resources on the basis of what is known about past surveys' intensity and other factors.

Another shortcoming of many models currently in use is that they only model one thing: whether or not heritage materials are likely to occur in various kinds of landscapes or at the juncture of various (usually geographical) circumstances. Better models also specify how the probabilities vary by the type of archaeological resource, estimate the likely characteristics of those resources, and evaluate the effects of visibility.

However, modelling what we think we know about archaeological distributions is an important step in designing efficient and informative CRM surveys. Anticipating the likely characteristics of these distributions need not lead to simple reaffirmation of the model. A well planned survey can test the model or increase its accuracy and precision. Often a statistical survey is useful in the initial specification of the model. As Wobst (1983:46, 49) and Cowgill (1975) point out, however, it is a mistake to assume that probabilistic sampling is the best procedure for testing the model after its formation. Typically the model makes quite specific predictions about where various kinds of archaeological materials should and should not be located, or about relationships among variables. Focussing survey effort by reference to these predictions is a much more efficient, less wasteful strategy than scattering random observations about in places that will contribute little improvement, or none at all, to the specification of the model. A very well-tested model will indeed contribute to the design of future surveys, which is not the same thing, however, as simply putting all effort into "high potential."

3. ASSESSING SIGNIFICANCE

Ideas on the matter range from the academic conviction that all sites were created significant (and are therefore worthy of eternal salvation) to the planners' view that sites were made to be "ranked" so that "expendable" ones can be consigned to the bulldozers while some of the "important" ones are preserved as monuments to their enlightened civic and ecological awareness (Moratto and Kelly, 1978:3).

Among the thorny issues in Cultural Resource Management are the grounds for assessing the significance of heritage resources (Hardesty et al., 2000; Tainter and Lucas, 1983). What is the basis for the claim that one site warrants preservation at all cost, another can be destroyed following excavation of a sample, while a third requires only basic documentation prior to its destruction? What makes someone decide to save pottery and lithics from a site, but sacrifice plant remains, while in another site recovering plant remains is paramount? Significance is the key concept for deciding such questions, and CRM agencies use a variety of criteria to measure it.

Significance decisions occur at a variety of scales ranging from spaces within sites, through sites, to landscapes. In addition, "just as the value of artifacts is determined by their context in a site, the significance of a site is best seen with respect to regional data potentials and research designs" (Moratto and Kelly, 1978:3).

3.1 Kinds of Significance

Typically, CRM archaeologists look at significance from a variety of perspectives. The following are not exhaustive, but illustrate the kinds of factors that may contribute to a framework for evaluating significance. They also overlap considerably. In addition, significance operates within a legal context; no matter what archaeologists may think about a property's worth, government regulators often have specific criteria for defining significance, as in the US National Register of Historic Places' "criterion d" (Butler, 1987). Archaeologists must justify their recommendations that a property qualifies for protection within such guidelines.

3.1.1 Scientific or Scholarly Significance

An important aspect of cultural impact assessment is evaluation of heritage materials' potential to contribute to the solution of research problems or further our understanding of past lifeways or cultural developments. Although the focus is usually archaeological or historical research, in some cases archaeological materials may also have potential to further research in other disciplines, such as geology, paleoenvironmental studies, or even private industry. Overall, argues Butler (1987), significance depends on potential contributions to theoretical and substantive knowledge.

It is not always easy to decide how to evaluate scientific significance, however. Sometimes archaeological materials that are rare or belong to periods or site types not previously documented in the area receive a high score for scientific significance. Alternatively, a site may be considered significant because it appears to be a good representative of a site type or reflects quite well the historical socioeconomic character of a neighborhood. In other cases, exceptionally good preservation of archaeological materials may lead to a high score. In still others, groups of sites in meaningful association, for example, when all aspects of an archaeological landscape are preserved, will be considered significant. In these cases, there is some blurring between scientific and public significance.

There are problems with using some of these criteria for scholarly significance. For example, it may seem reasonable to conclude that a type of resource that is extremely rare, or has never been documented before, should be preserved at all costs. However, this does not imply that resources that are relatively common are unworthy of preservation. Some kinds of sites may be poorly known because they are typically deeply buried, where archaeologists rarely encounter them, but, ironically, this could mean not only that many undetected ones exist, but that they are relatively well protected from development. Furthermore, sites of types that are rare or poorly known at present may be fairly well represented in the archaeological literature at some later date, or may only be rare by reference to a particular research interest of the moment. It is important to protect resources that may be uniquely suited to solving some kinds of research questions, but the definition of rarity, as with many other criteria of significance, may not be obvious.

Schiffer and House (1977) attempt to subdivide scholarly significance into four broad categories: substantive, anthropological, social scientific, and technical, methodological or theoretical significance. Substantitive significance is gauged against specific research questions in archaeology. Anthropological significance concerns the extent to which a cultural resource might be useful in investigating broad questions about human culture, cultural change, and cultural process. Social scientific significance is difficult to extricate from anthropological significance because it also has to do with broad issues about human society. Apparently the issues are broader still, and include major questions relevant to the disciplines of economics and sociology. In the last category are resources whose substance may not especially advance our scientific knowledge of the past or of human society, but that offer opportunities to make advances in method or theory.

In addition, cultural resources may have significance for disciplines outside the social sciences and humanities. For example, particularly at a time when the possibility of global warming is a major issue, many disciplines can benefit from archaeology's ability to offer data on climate change and human interactions with environmental changes over long time-frames (Dixon, 1977; Moratto and Kelly, 1978:8). In addition, archaeological studies of past land use have important implications for modern land management, such as planned irrigation schemes.

Clearly, although each archaeologist has his or her own research priorities, it is incumbant upon CRM archaeologists to try to transcend their own interests and recognize or anticipate the research needs of other scholars (Moratto and Kelly, 1978:7).

3.1.2 Public, Recreational, and Educational Significance

Public significance most often concerns the potential for a heritage resource to enhance the public appreciation of the past and emphasizes its educational and recreational aspects. Consequently, such attributes as ease of access, ownership, and aesthetics can be as important as the historic or anthropological attributes of the resource. Members of the public may value the authenticity (or perceived authenticity) or integrity (particularly architectural preservation) of a site or its prominence in local history or ethnic heritage. The spatial propinquity of several cultural resources in meaningful association may make them all more attractive for recreational use. In some cases, sites may have special symbolic significance for religious or national identity, such as the homes of past heads-of-state, battlefields from wars that contributed to nation-building, sites of religious pilgrimage, or the locations of major scientific discoveries. Consulting the community expected to use the resource is a key to its evaluation for public significance.

However, some kinds of public significance concern the resource's potential to make substantitive contributions to improving public welfare. For example, its contribution to understanding climatic change or the frequency of droughts or catastrophic events has an obvious application to planning for these eventualities. In addition, the presence of a well-preserved archaeological landscape might demonstrate the environmental stability necessary for the construction of a costly facility. Sometimes the evidence of ancient agricultural systems may even provide surprisingly useful guidance for modern land use.

3.1.3 Historical Significance

Many properties are considered significant and become protected because of the widespread perception that they are connected with important individuals or events in the historical development of communities and nations. More broadly, some resources may be historically significant because they illustrate cultural patterns associated with those individuals or events (Scovill et al., 1972). As with public significance, the kinds of resources that tend to be accorded historical significance are those associated with nation-building or national mythology, and tend to represent only the most flattering or most prestigious facets of historic communities, such as stately bank buildings or the homes of the wealthy (Hickman, 1977; King and Hickman, 1973). However, there is an increasing tendency to represent underprivileged or oppressed groups, such as slaves and poor immigrant communities, and less flattering aspects of people's lives. The highly successful Jorvik Viking Museum in York, for example, even attempts to replicate the rather foul odors of a Viking town.

3.1.4 Economic Significance

Some kinds of archaeological and historic sites have economic value, typically through their touristic potential. In these cases, impact assessments should include estimates of the likely economic benefits that could result from development of the site as a recreational or educational attraction. This requires assessing public or tourist demand for similar sites and the willingness of potential users to pay admissions to the site or to spend money in the community in which the site is found. A survey of potential users may help to establish this.

Some CRM practitioners have also tried to evaluate the monetary worth of archaeological resources in terms of the cost of mitigation (Scovill et al., 1972). For example, one might compare the economic benefit of a development with the cost of a complete excavation and data analysis for a site that the development would destroy. The trouble with this kind of assessment is that, although it is possible to estimate the cost of total data recovery in the framework of current methods, theory, and research priorities, it is less easy to assess future data requirements or evaluate the cultural evidence, itself, in monetary terms. Furthermore, putting a price on the artifacts contained in archaeological sites potentially contributes to driving up the market for illicit artifacts, and putting other cultural resources at risk of pot-hunting.

Although financial realities are relevant to the establishment of a resource's significance, most CRM practitioners would argue that they are secondary to other criteria for significance, such as scientific and public value (House and Schiffer, 1975b:182; Moratto and Kelly, 1978:18; Raab and Klinger, 1977).

3.1.5 Ethnic Significance

Some cultural resources have symbolic significance for particular ethnic groups, whether for religious, spiritual, nationalistic, or linguistic reasons. In the United States and Canada, for instance, some ethnic groups, such as native Americans and decendents of Chinese immigrants, are underrepresented in documentary history. Sites such as Chinese railroad camps are therefore significant as tangible evidence of the depth of ethnic histories and as symbols of group identity. Ethnically significant resources "have at least a potential role to play in the maintenance of a community's integrity, in the maintenance of some group's sense of place and cultural value, or in the advancement of human knowledge" (King et al., 1977:96).

If evaluations of significance do not explicitly take ethnic significance into account, there is a risk that the decisions about which properties to preserve will favor ones that illustrate mainly the histories of dominant groups, such as relatively wealthy Americans of European origin. Given that many CRM evaluators are also members of dominant groups, it is worthwhile to include relevant ethnic groups in the process of evaluating resources.

3.1.6 Significance in Land Claims

Some kinds of archaeological evidence are significant for the evidence they provide for aboriginal territories, duration of habitation, and land use that can contribute to the adjudication of land claims by indigenous people and compensation for treaty violations.

3.2 Measuring Significance

Even if we could agree on the aspects of archaeological materials that contribute to their significance to scholars and the public, it would not be obvious how to decide whether one site was more or less significant than another. How can one measure significance in ways that make cultural occurrences as different as Paleoindian scatters and brick farmhouses comparable?

One argument is that archaeologists should simply refuse to rank cultural resources on any kind of scale. Inherent in any scoring or ranking system for these resources is the risk that developers and planners will treat only the resources with the highest rankings as worthy of protection, and will interpret relatively low scores as a recommendation for site destruction. A standard scoring system also glosses over the very different factors, already discussed in section 3.1, that contribute to the score. A cultural resource could score extremely high on its historical significance but low, for example, on economic or scientific significance. Does this justify a total score somewhere in the lower middle of the pack, which some will interpret as little cause for protection? Even ranking sites for their scientific significance, something at which we might expect archaeologists to excel, depends heavily on individual researchers' interests, theoretical orientations, and experience (McMillan et al., 1977:32; Schiffer and House, 1977). In addition, for some purposes, such as elibibility for listing on the National Register of Historic Places, properties are either significant or they or not (Butler, 1987).

Ranking cultural properties, as a response to developers' needs, is a planning device basically incompatible with archaeological ideals. We are asked to generate simple models (ranked lists) from complex realities (diverse cultural resources) for the ultimate purpose of destroying some resources and preserving others (Moratto and Kelly, 1978:23).

Yet, at the same time, there is a need for archaeologists to translate their expertise about the significance of cultural resources into language that planners will understand. As Thompson (n.d.:5) observes, it is better for archaeologists, themselves, to develop a reasonably objective way to set priorities for archaeological resources in ways that are "consistent with sound archaeological principles." The alternative, letting planners measure significance, is much worse. Distasteful though it might seem to prioritize these resources, only archaeologists are likely to place some kinds of sites, such as low-density lithic scatters, anywhere but the bottom of the list.

In the United Kingdom, "scheduling" of sites on the basis of their national significance has been rather subjective, but is guided by criteria published by the Secretary of State (Wainwright, 1989:165-166). These include the condition of the resource at the time of assessment and its fragility or vulnerability. Some sites that currently preserve a great deal of their ancient structure, but are nonetheless at risk of destruction from a single agricultural plowing, warrant a high priority on their protection. The period of the resource is also a factor, the ideal being to preserve examples of all kinds of monuments that characterize each period. This is not to be confused with giving greater priority to older sites, and sites as recent as the 1940s have been scheduled as monuments. The rarity of the resource is also a factor: some kinds of resource are so rare that any examples that preserve any archaeological potential warrant protection. This, however, does not discount the importance of preserving typical or common types of resource to characterize a period and more accurately represent the distribution of sites. Diversity of features is a factor to be considered, but some sites are significant for a single important attribute. The guidelines also assign greater signficance to sites that have been recorded in previous archaeological investigations or historical documents. They also give weight to groups of associated sites, such as a settlement with its associated cemetery or field systems, which enhance one another if jointly protected.

Some surveyors have attempted to construct scoring systems that result in a quantitative measure, such as a score ranging from 0 to 100. Technically these scores, even though they look like ratio-scale measures, are summaries of several ordinal-scale estimates. The weight given to the various ordinal measures that contribute to the overall score has a substantial effect on the result, and can only be decided by careful consideration of the factors that should have more weight in planning or policy.

Bell and Gettys (n.d.) developed a system based on 18 weighted factors that they related to some aspect of significance for CRM projects in Arkansas. The factors, including such things as site size, depth, type, rarity, and estimated cost of fieldwork, were scored and summed to provide an overall estimate of significance that could be used to rank sites. Thompson (n.d.) similarly suggested 20 factors, including ones concerning chronology, ethnicity, and potential for public interpretation.

In Jordan, the Wadi al-Hasa Survey and the Wadi Ziqlab Survey instituted an "inventory rating" to score the significance of sites they encountered from 1979 to 1982 (Banning, 1985, 1988; MacDonald et al., 1980). The score ranged from 0 to 100 and consisted of the sum of scores for a number of academic, preservation, accessibility, and economic or recreational criteria. Subsequently, a version of this system was adopted by JADIS (Jordan Antiquities Database and Information System), the Jordanian Department of Antiquities' main tool for cultural resource management. The score gave greatest weight to academic priorities, such as the likelihood that a site can contribute new information, fill gaps in knowledge, or help solve current academic debates, but did also include such factors as touristic potential and practicability of excavation.

Apart from other objections raised above, one could argue that these assessments have a relatively short "shelf life." What is an academic priority or gap in knowlege one year, may be quite well investigated some time later. However, they do help make planning and academic decisions for about a decade, and periodic review of the criteria and their weighting can help keep them current.

4. ADMINISTRATIVE, ETHICAL, AND LEGAL ASPECTS OF CRM

Although the design of CRM surveys, like those of academic archaeologists, must balance research goals with cost and practicality, they are also constrained by legislation, contractual obligations and reporting requirements in ways that academic archaeologists largely escape. Government agencies and development clients often have very specific guidelines or regulations that govern the way contracted firms must carry out surveys and report their results. Another difference is that, while academic archaeologists must write research proposals to apply for funding, CRM firms must bid on contracts. A successful bid, furthermore, is based on quite different criteria, in some cases, than those that govern success in research funding. Sometimes government regulations seem excessively rigid; in other cases the lack of firm guidelines may make it too easy for a spiral of underbidding to erode the quality of work or undermine its rationale.

4.1 Government and Institutional Regulation of Surveys

Governments and institutional clients often have very specific, detailed requirements for archaeological survey of the properties they control. These help to ensure consistency in and comparability of results, and create a "level playing field" for the firms bidding on CRM contracts. However, they may also impose a rigid structure or minimum standard that does not facilitate good outcomes (Wobst, 1983). In particular, they sometimes specify the intensity of survey, the methods survey can employ, whether sampling should be used and, if so, what sampling fraction is required, without any reference to the characteristics of the population to be sampled. In other cases, they allow considerable flexibility in these decisions.

4.1.1 US Federal Legislation and State Guidelines

The United States has a long history of legislation relevant to the preservation of cultural heritage. It includes the Act for the Preservation of American Antiquities of 1906, the Historic Sites Act of 1935, the Historic Sites Preservation Act of 1966, the National Environmental Policy Act of 1969, and the Archaeological and Historical Preservation Act of 1974 (King, 1998; King et al., 1977; McGimsey, 1972; Moratto, 1977). In addition to legislation, executive orders and recommendations by the President's Advisory Council on Historic Preservation are relevant to the preservation of archaeological resources. Notably, Executive Order 11593 of 1971 broadened federal interest in cultural resources to non-federal lands that were affected by projects that were federally funded or licensed, and required federal agencies to inventory eligible sites in their jurisdictions and nominate them for the National Register of Historic Places.

One of the most important pieces of regulatory legislation for CRM in the United States is Section 106 of the National Historic Preservation Act (NHPA), which requires all Federal agencies to identify and assess the effects of Federal activities on historic resources (King, 2000). Under this legislation, Federal agencies must take into account, during the planning of their projects, the views of State and local officials, indigenous groups, and members of the public concerning the projects' likely effects on historic resources and the importance of preserving those that are deemed significant. Section 106 applies to projects that have any Federal involvement, including licensing or the granting of permits or funding, and that could affect any property listed, *or eligible for listing*, in the National Register of Historic Places. The Advisory Council on Historic

Preservation is charged to oversee the Section 106 review process. In some States, assessing whether or not a site qualifies for listing in the National Register is the major goal of Phase I survey.

However, it is usually the State Historic Preservation Officer (SHPO) who sets the guidelines that CRM firms must follow in carrying out work triggered by Section 106, although Tribal Historic Preservation Officers and the Federal agencies themselves can also be involved.

It is not surprising, therefore, that there is considerable variation from state to state in the nature of these guidelines (e.g., CHSOAHP, 1998; FBHP, 1990; GCPA, 2001; NJHPO, n.d.; 2000; SCSHPO, 2000; TDEC, 1997; WAS, 1997). The SHPOs or, in some cases, State professional organizations that cooperate with them, specify their own guidelines for proposals, personnel qualifications, fieldwork, documentation, curation, and reporting.

For example, one of the debates in the CRM world of the United States has focussed on the standards for subsurface survey in areas where the surface visibility of archaeological resources is poor. As noted in preceding chapters, even substantial efforts devoted to well designed subsurface survey can only be expected to detect a tiny fraction of the archaeological materials that occur in a region. Consequently, these standards are very important. Yet in some regions, especially in the South, shovel-test intervals of 30 m are typical, while 10 m or even 5 m intervals are required elsewhere. In South Carolina, for example, shovel tests are at 30 m intervals in "high-probability" areas but at intervals of up to 60 m in "low-probability" ones (SCSHPO, 2000:13). Minimum shovel-test areas, and minimum intervals for systematic pedestrian transects also vary substantially. Although CRM firms are at liberty to use sampling intensities greater than the regulated standards, the economic realities make it difficult for them to do so, as shrinking the interval increases the costs of survey exponentially.

In future, perhaps, standards will address the precision of estimates for a variety of parameters, such as artifact density, rather than setting arbitrary observation intervals.

4.1.2 English Legislation

In the United Kingdom, the legislative and administrative responsibilities for portable artifacts and heritage (roughly the UK term for CRM) *on the ground* are separate. In England, which will serve as an example of the situation in the United Kingdom, the former, which historically often came under the terms of *treasure trove*, are the responsibility of national and local museums, while the latter falls under the terms of the Ancient Monuments and Archaeological Areas Act of 1979 and, for historic buildings, the Town and Country Planning Act of 1971. From 1908, the Royal Commission on Ancient and Historical Monuments of England (RCAHME) and parallel institutions in Wales and Scotland, took responsibility for building a national record of archaeological and historic sites (the National Monuments Records) and recently for surveying sites to be shown on the Ordnance Survey maps as well. Under the National Heritage Act of 1983, a new agency, the Historic Buildings and Monuments Commission (or English Heritage), assumed responsibility for heritage management, including public presentation and commercialization of heritage (Saunders, 1989). In addition, it is important to keep in mind the important place that the Ordnance Survey has held in the documentation of archaeological landscapes, especially in the first half of the 20th century.

The 1979 Act supercedes the Ancient Monuments Protection Act of 1882, which governed the preservation of ancient and medieval monuments that were not currently used for residential or ecclesiastical purposes. The criterion for "scheduling" of monuments, that they are judged to be of "national importance," has tended to limit this protection rather severely to a tiny proportion of the archaeological landscape. Furthermore, the standard of recording of the Royal Commission on the Historical Monuments of England has also led to documentation of only a fraction of known sites (Drewett, 1999:31).

The Town and Country Planning Act follows on powers first claimed in 1947 over currently inhabited buildings of historic and architectural importance. It calls on local planning authorities to identify buildings or neighborhoods of architectural or historical significance and to designate them as conservation areas, in order to preserve or enhance their character. The Secretary of State for the Environment is responsible for approving the criteria by which buildings or areas or so listed, and a very large number of buildings in England have been listed or are eligible for listing.

Under the National Heritage Act, English Heritage is responsible for the preservation of ancient monuments and historic buildings in England, for enhancing the character of English conservation areas, and for promoting public appreciation and enjoyment of ancient monuments and historic buildings in England. Parallel bodies exist in Wales and Scotland. In addition to responsibilites for managing various historic properties and providing funding for the enhancement of properties to be preserved or mitigation of ones to be destroyed, English Heritage is actively involved in research on and publication of archaeological heritage sites. It tends to focus on work that does not fall under the planning regulations, such as archaeological resources threatened by coastal erosion or intensified agriculture.

Although there are many English laws and several institutions that pertain to archaeological heritage, these only protect a fraction of that heritage and help to slow down the destruction of a somewhat larger fraction. Scheduled monuments on private land are under the control of their owners, who can apply for permission to alter or destroy them following a public enquiry.

Most of the CRM surveys in England, however, are conducted by professional archaeologists in "units" attached to particular towns or counties, and supported by a mix of central and local government funding and, in some instances, contracts from developers. A large percentage of CRM work falls under the terms of planning documents (PPG-13, etc.), which tend to emphasize urban areas and built environment.

The legal separation of portable artifacts and archaeological sites or monuments has important implications because, unlike monuments, the artifacts cannot be scheduled. With the exception of finds of gold or silver that can be determined to meet certain requirements that fall under the Crown's prerogative of Treasure Trove, any artifacts found in the ground on private property belong to the landowner, who can dispose of it

Cultural Resource Management and Site Significance   193

as he or she wishes (Saunders, 1989). This can lead to some problems for CRM survey unless landowners can be pursuaded to give up their rights over this property, and makes it all the more important for CRM firms to maintain good relationships with the public.

4.1.3 Canadian Legislation

In Canada, legislation and other regulations affecting heritage resources occur at the federal, provincial, and municipal levels.

At the federal level, most CRM work arises from the activities of Parks Canada, the Crown Corporation responsible for Canada's national parks and a number of monuments and historic forts, and the Archaeological Survey of Canada (ASC), which is responsible for CRM work arising from construction or other potentially destructive activities on other federal properties, such as harbours, canals, and airports.

Much CRM work takes place as a result of provincial legislation, such as the Ontario Heritage Act of 1974 and Environmental Assessment Act of 1975 in Ontario (Ferris, 1998; Pearce, 1989). As in the United States, legislation and guidelines for survey work vary considerably from province to province, but some provinces allow a fair amount of discretion in such things as the balance between sampling and prospection, or in the use and interval of subsurface tests. In Newfoundland's guidelines, for example, the intensity and nature of fieldwork depend on the expected impact of the proposed development the size of the APE, and the extent of prior knowledge about the location of sites (Newfoundland Museum, n.d.). The guidelines express preference for sampling approaches that provide representative samples, and outline some goals for the results, but are not especially restrictive, apart from the statement that units of 40 cm by 40 cm are "generally appropriate" for subsurface tests. British Columbia's guidelines, by contrast, provide "recommended sampling strategies," ranging from total survey for initial inspection of unknown areas (a very conservative and costly approach where some low-intensity initial reconnaissance might be helpful), to random and stratified sampling, and specify what kinds of field observations various combinations of visibility, slope, topography, and drainage would require (BCRIC, 2000).

4.1.4 Summary

Regulations that specify the nature of sampling and especially sampling fraction can be frustrating because, as discussed in chapter 6, no single sampling design can satisfy all situations and sample size should depend on the anticipated density of archaeological remains and the amount of precision required for parameter estimates. It would be better, in fact, if clients and regulators specified levels of precision or probabilities of missed sites rather than sample sizes or sampling fractions.

Some jurisdictions have guidelines with enough flexibility for a well-argued research design, tailored to specific contexts and objectives, to be attractive, while others are more rigid. Even where there is some flexibility, however, the need to compete for contracts can discourage archaeologists from proposing designs that go beyond minimum standards, while the need to maintain a level playing field encourages a certain amount of rigidity also. Balancing these needs with good practice is possible but not always easy.

4.2 Professional Organizations and Self-regulation

In addition to government regulations, guidelines and codes of conduct that archaeologists themselves have formulated influence the character of archaeological surveys. The following is just a sample of organizations that promote guidelines for professional practice in archaeology and cultural resource management. Most of them have web sites with links to similar organizations at the regional level or in other countries.

4.2.1 The American Cultural Resources Association (ACRA)

The American Cultural Resources Association is a relatively young organization that promotes professionalism in and represents the interests of professionals in a variety of disciplines who are involved in heritage management and preservation. This includes archaeologists, architects, conservators, and planners. Its aims include supporting the business needs of member CRM firms, promoting awareness of cultural resources in government and among the public, encouraging high standards of professional conduct, promoting workplace safety and good relations between employers and employees in the CRM field, and lobbying and monitoring government with regard to heritage policies. The association publishes a list of member CRM firms and heritage architects, and members agree to abide by the associations Code of Ethical and Professional Conduct. This code outlines members' responsibilities to their clients, employees, and colleagues or competitors.

4.2.2 The Register of Professional Archaeologists (RPA)

The RPA grew out of the Society of Professional Archaeologists, which went dormant once the RPA was formed in 1998. The register is jointly sponsored by the Society for American Archaeology, the American Institute of Archaeology, and the Society for Historical Archaeology to promote universally high standards of professional archaeological practice and to publish a directory of professional archaeologists who agree to abide by a code of conduct. The RPA provides a grievance procedure, whereby anyone may complain formally about the behavior of any archaeologist on the register who does not comply with the code. Meanwhile, archaeologists on the register may display the RPA logo as evidence that they have agreed to abide by this code.

The RPA Code of Conduct and Standards of Research Performance outlines RPA archaeologists' responsibilities to the public, colleagues, employees, students, employers, and clients. Unlike some of the other codes mentioned in this section, it goes on to list standards for archaeological research, making RPA archaeologists responsible for ensuring that they and their work meet the criteria of adequate qualifications, preparation, scientific research design, staffing and support, and curatorial facilities. It calls on

Cultural Resource Management and Site Significance   195

them to meet legal requirements, to make economical use of the heritage resource (i.e., to destroy or alter it as little as possible), and to meet minimum standards for the survey or excavation, documentation, analysis, and storage of finds, and dissemination of results. These standards are not, however, very stringent.

4.2.3 The Institute of Field Archaeologists (IFA)

The Institute of Field Archaeologists (IFA), headquartered at the University of Reading, is the United Kingdom's principal organization representing the interests of CRM archaeologists and promoting ethics and high standards in professional archaeological heritage work. All members are expected to adhere to the IFA Code of Conduct, which governs not only ethical and responsible use of archaeological resources and their presentation to the public, but also the safe and fair working conditions of CRM employees. Failure to comply with this code can lead to censure, suspension, or expulsion from the Institute. Like ACRA in the United States, IFA publishes a list of member CRM firms so that potential clients may confirm that these firms meet professional standards.

4.2.4 The Canadian Association of Professional Heritage Consultants (CAPHC)

The CAPHC Code of Professional Conduct and Ethics specifies the qualifications of heritage consultants and outlines their responsibilities to the public, clients, employers and other members. Notably, the code specifically refers to the requirement to bill clients appropriately, with fair compensation to employees, a clear (although not entirely successful) attempt to prevent a spiral of underbidding on contracts. The association publishes a directory of members in good standing, which, as with ACRA, include professionals from a number of heritage-related disciplines outside archaeology.

4.3 Development Pressures on Surveys

As mentioned in section 1.2, developers are commonly the clients who actually pay for CRM work and to whom CRM firms have at least some responsibility. In other cases, members of the public pay for cultural resource management through their governments. Not surprisingly, these clients have an interest in minimizing the cost of cultural resource management. In addition, they want to implement their projects, which sometimes involve destruction or alteration of heritage resources, as quickly and with as little modification as possible. Not surprisingly, CRM firms sometimes find themselves under considerable pressure to minimize interference with projects and to avoid delays in their implementation. In addition, clients who have spent substantial sums on survey can reasonably expect to avoid the surprise of encountering important archaeological occurrences after their construction or other impact has begun.

4.4 Reporting Requirements

Most of the guidelines discussed in section 4.1 also refer to reporting and publication of results. In many instances, they specify the format and type of content of the reports in considerable detail (e.g., NJHPO, 2000; SCSHPO, 2000:18-24). Importantly, these reports should present, not only summaries of results and recommendations, and the usual scholarly apparatus, but also explicit details of the survey's research design and methods. These include good estimates of the density of search effort, discussion of possible bias in parameter estimates, any changes in methods made during the course of survey, and detailed documentation of coverage, such as maps showing as precisely as possible the locations of transects or subsurface tests. In other words, it should be possible to evaluate the survey's detection function, and variation in this function over space that such factors as visibility may have imposed, and any effects such variations may have had on generalizations based on the survey. Preferably, the report should include such evaluations rather than leaving them to others.

In addition, the guidelines often require illustration of reports by maps, drawings and photographs, sometimes in specific formats, and may specify details of the database that should result from the survey. For example, many jurisdictions maintain centralized site databases, and insist on receiving files that they can import easily into them.

5. CONCLUSION

The regional assessment phase of Cultural Resource Management typically includes some combination of prospection and statistical survey. Although it is possible to design sophisticated CRM surveys that are sensitive to the characteristics of the resources, there are typically also many constraints on survey design that legislation, heritage guidelines, or clients impose. CRM archaeologists also have to operate within a highly competitive economic climate.

Key concerns for CRM surveyors, besides survey design itself, are assessing the significance of archaeological resources and finding ways to make recommendations that are both fair to clients and the public and as benign as possible for the heritage resources. Ideally survey should detect and recognize all significant sites early enough that development plans can change to accommodate them.

Chapter IX
Surveying Sites and Landscapes

Although the overall design of regional survey has been the focus of this book, it is necessary to say something about the kinds of observations archaeologists make during regional survey, and especially about the way they document the "sites" or landscapes they encounter. This is also integral to the process of research design.

As mentioned in chapter 3, not all surveys employ the concept of site, and those that do define sites in various ways. Most often, however, sites are conceived either as nearly discrete clusters of material culture, thought to correspond in some way with settlements or the locations of past clusters of human activities, or as high-density clusters of cultural material on a low-density background. Sometimes natural processes or recent cultural activities have distorted these clusters or created new ones, however.

Where surveys do not use sites as recording units, it is necessary instead to record the attributes of polygons in space, including information about artifacts found within them, or to record the locations of individual artifacts directly.

1. FIELDWALKING AND SURFACE SURVEY

There are many conditions in which fieldwalking is not a practical discovery technique and more invasive methods, such as divoting or test-pitting, is necessary. Because fieldwalking and visual search of the surface for artifacts is the most common kind of archaeological survey, however, it is appropriate to emphasize some points relevant to its success.

Once the sampling frame or some strategy for purposive survey or ground checks has been worked out, most surveys involve some consistent procedure for walking over the surface and inspecting it for artifacts.

As noted in chapter 1, some of these procedures were already somewhat formalized by the early 1920s. Typically, they involve distributing team members some regular distance apart and having them walk parallel transects across a quadrat, field or natural topographic feature, often after the ground has been plowed. Along each transect, each surveyor either collects artifacts or marks their locations with pinflags.

1.1 Locating Transects and Staying on Course

The first challenge in fieldwalking is locating the beginning of the first transect. Today, the availability of accurate GPS makes this much easier; the crew only needs to enter the coordinates of the place sought and the GPS will lead you to it. In the past it was usually necessary for one of the crew members to be proficient in map-reading and triangulating position with a Brunton compass, in order for this starting-point to be found within 30 m or so. Aerial photographs are also very helpful, whether GPS is available or not, as they often show considerable detail, such as the positions of individual trees, that helps to pin down location.

Once the crew has reached this starting-point, team members distribute themselves in a line with the appropriate distance between them. Typically, the transect spacing is between 3m and 50m but, as noted in chapter 4, the spacing between these transects warrants careful consideration.

Team members usually walk straight-line transects, which makes it easier to stay on course. When the inter-transect spacing is fairly large or the transects are long, each team member should use a compass to identify a landmark near the horizon that has the appropriate bearing. Since transect orientation is largely arbitrary in most of these surveys, there is no particular reason why they should be oriented to North, however, and there are practical advantages to using an orientation that puts high ground with many possible landmarks on the horizon, as long as this orientation is used consistently in the survey. The important point is that team members should remember and aim for the distant landmark, rather than making frequent reference to the compass. The latter would lead to considerable cumulative error in course, while the former is self-correcting. Sighting on the horizon allows surprisingly accurate and evenly spaced transects unless trees or buildings obstruct the horizon's visibility.

In surveys that require high intensity or greater precision in the location of artifacts, as in some varieties of non-site survey, it is instead necessary to divide blocks of the survey area into fairly small units in which crew members walk closely spaced transects with little error. For example, in the Grand Junction Survey in Colorado, survey teams walked sets of four transects across each 4 m x 4 m quadrat placed by transit and tape (Kvamme, 1998:130). Typically such surveys mark the four corners of a quadrat, then run tapes between the corners to place stakes or pin-flags along at least two opposite sides of the quadrat to mark the intervals between transects. Crew members would then follow a string or tape run between the pin-flags. If the survey method involves a second pass with transects at a different orientation, such as 90° or 45°, pin-flags are also necessary along the other two sides.

Marking out intervals along the sides works equally well, and actually more easily, with equilateral triangles, because you do not need to set right angles. Crew members need only stretch three tapes horizontally so that they intersect at equal distances, such as 10 m, place stakes or pin-flags to mark the corners of the triangle, then place pin-flags along two sides of the triangle spaced at the appropriate interval. For example, they could place four pin-flags at intevervals of 2 m along each side and then run strings between the pin-flags on opposite sides (see chapter 4, section 1.4.1).

Surveying Sites and Landscapes

An excellent preparation for fieldwalking, especially if transects are long and there are not frequent stakes or flags to guide the route, is to provide each team member, in advance, with a copy of an aerial photograph, covered with a clear acetate sheet, on which the planned transect route has been marked. Note that this will not necessarily look straight on the aerial photograph because, in hilly terrain, there are parallax effects that distort spatial relationships somewhat. Establishing the route on the photo in these cases requires that someone carefully matches features on the photos, such as stream meanders, buildings, and intersecting roads, with ones on topographic maps. Knapp and Johnson (1994), for instance, found that supplying team members with aerial photographs at approximately 1:5000 scale led to surprisingly small errors in the placement of transects in the Sydney Cyprus Survey Project. They used a hand scanner to scan a 3-inch wide strip centered on each transect route and then printed out the scanned images on pages with plenty of room for notes in the margins. These pages with scanned portions of the aerial photographs became the principal recording instrument for the location of transects, sample plots, and sites.

1.2 Intertidal Surveys

Intertidal surveys are able to take advantage of most of the methods of terrestrial fieldwalking by scheduling fieldwork for periods of low tide. The special circumstances of the foreshore, however, do influence survey strategies, leading Wilkinson and Murphy to characterize intertidal archaeology as a "guerrilla technique":

One advances with the retreating tide; all relevant natural or cultural exposures are cleaned, recorded, and sampled for paleoecological material and artifacts; then one retreats with the advancing tide (Wilkinson and Murphy, 1986:179).

The need to advance and retreat with the tide has implications for the kind and orientation of transects that surveyors cover. Orienting transects parallel to the shore allows gradual advance and retreat in time with the tide. Yet, unless the intertransect spacing is very small, it is usually better for each team member to do a winding survey of a separate stretch of beach, rather than walking side-by-side. The irregular shape of some intertidal zones will force departures from this ideal arrangement, while more detailed recording will instead require repeated visits to small blocks or lanes of the foreshore (see section 3.7).

1.3 Facilitating Evaluation of Survey Results

Whatever strategy a survey employs to cover the ground, other researchers can really only evaluate the survey's results if they have detailed information about the routes travelled and factors, such as visibility, that may have affected detectability and other attributes of the survey universe.

The use of aerial photographs mentioned in the last section is a particularly effective aid in this respect. Although most surveys publish a set of site locations (or a map of quadrats in distributional survey), they rarely publish detailed information on the day-to-day procedures of the survey. It is an excellent idea to publish an appendix of aerial photographs that show the exact routes of surveyors, as nearly as that can be established, including any errors in transect placement that may have occurred. This allows others to make rational assessments of the likelihood that the survey missed certain kinds of material, and helps them relocate sites for future investigations. One caution regarding this degree of divulgence is that it might, in some cases, increase the risk of site damage through pot-hunting or other vandalism. However, this is a risk that any publication of field data entails.

In addition, reporting estimated errors, based perhaps on control samples or resurvey, and information pertinent to detectability, is critical if others are to make profitable use of the survey results. Reporting a set of site sizes or artifact densities is not useful if there is no basis for comparing them with other surveys or even to make meaningful comparisons within a single survey. A little honest reporting of the survey's reliability can go a long way.

2. COMMON ATTRIBUTES OF SITES

In addition to the map location and some way of identifying each site, including sometimes a modern name, archaeologists typically record a number of conventional attributes that they expect to be useful to their colleagues. Today, site location is often determined by Global Positioning Systems (GPS).

In many surveys, crews' time available for recording site attributes is very limited because of the need to continue surveying the territory allocated to them. Consequently, it is important to adopt practices that help to make this recording more efficient. Such practices can include use of recording forms that anticipate many observations with check-boxes that obviate lengthy written descriptions, and ensuring that team members have equipment and supplies that facilitate measurements, and know how to use them. In some surveys, there are separate detection and recording crews, so that the recording process does not slow down detection (e.g., Ebert, 1992).

2.1 Site Size

In site-oriented survey, measuring or estimating site size is one of the most common activities. It is particularly important in surveys whose goals include documenting changes in regional population size or shifts in land-use pattern over time. It is also critical for surveys that use rank-size analysis as a tool in understanding the form of settlement systems.

Some of the methods archaeologists have used to estimate site size are discussed in section 3.1.

Surveying Sites and Landscapes   201

2.2 Site Function and Site Hierarchies

As seen in chapter 7, understanding settlement systems requires that we go beyond the simple documentation of where sites occur and attempt to understand how they may have operated in a settlement system. At a minimum, this usually means gaining some sense of the site's function.

A carefully designed recording system for artifacts found at the site may facilitate reasonably rapid and consistent assignment of sites to broad activity-based categories. As with non-site survey (below, section 3.3), attributes of stone tools, such as predominant stage in the reduction sequence and modal edge angle, can help to identify sites that had a focus on stone quarrying, tool manufacture or tool use in hunting, butchering or food processing activities. High artifact diversity, corrected for sample size, is frequently interpreted as evidence for habitation sites. The important thing is to prepare, in advance, a recording system that ensures collection of the kinds of data considered useful for classification of site function. Simply copying a lithic or ceramic coding system that was designed for quite different purposes will not be satisfactory.

In some regions, particular classes of material culture might also be clues to a site's position in a regional settlement hierarchy. For example, Johnson (1973) assumes that colored clay cones that were used to decorate the walls of Sumerian temples consistitute evidence as to which sites were central places rather than simpler, dependent villages. In other instance, certain classes of portable art might be so much more common on central places than other sites as to constitute good evidence for a site's position in a settlement hierarchy.

In very fortunate circumstances there may also be architectural evidence visible at the surface that helps us to classify a site by its function or place in a settlement system. For example, some might have fortifications, grain silos, or evidence of house walls (see below, section 2.4).

2.3 Site Chronology

Most site-based surveys consider evidence for the period or periods in which each site was used or occupied to be quite important. In particular, many of these surveys include among their goals identification of changes in population density, settlement pattern, or land use over time. "Diagnostic" artifacts or "type-fossils" are commonly the main grounds for assigning sites to particular periods, but other methods are sometimes applicable to survey data as well.

2.4 Site Features or Topography

Small topographic variations, earthworks, or architectural traces can be important clues to the structure and even chronology of sites.

Some sites have earthworks, such as ditches, mounds, house pits, or fortifications, that, even in an eroded state, are detectable in their microtopography. Often these features are easier to detect from the air or with raking light, but sometimes they are more obvious and warrant careful documentation.

For example, on the Northwest Coast of North America, the sites of former plankhouse villages frequently show series of shallow depressions that mark the locations of former house pits and slight mounds over former middens. Careful attention to these details, which may extend in some cases to a complete topographic map of the site by theodolite or electronic distance meter (EDM), makes it possible to determine how many houses were in the village, the approximate sizes of those houses and, indirectly, the approximate size of the village's maximum population in the past, on the assumption that the house pits were used contemporaneously.

More broadly, Portugali (1982) notes that some Middle Eastern *tells*, or village mounds, are stepped or terraced, with material of different date sometimes occupying different portions of these more complex mounds. This may help us discern cases where an ancient settlement grew in size by adding a "lower town" on one side or where a larger settlement shrank into a smaller, citadel-like area of the site. Surveyors who are careful to record the shape and profile of such mounds, as well as locations of surface collections (e.g., Whallon, 1979), provide important evidence with which to evaluate those collections.

2.5 Site Environment

Archaeological surveys frequently record both information about the modern environment and evidence that might help us reconstruct what the site's environment may have been like at the time or times the site was occupied.

Among the factors of the modern environment that interest archaeologists are ones that could have affected the survey's results, and especially site detection. For example, some surveys record a visibility score at each site, or for each transect segment, so that they can correct site detection probabilities, as in the Hvar Survey in Croatia (Gaffney, et al., 1991). Other surveys simply record information about vegetation cover, current agricultural or other use, probable depth of colluvium or alluvium, and presence of tarmacs or modern buildings, that could impede visibility by visual inspection.

Collecting information tht might be relevant to the probable ancient environment often focusses on factors that might have encouraged settlement at a particular place, or were relevant to economy, site function, or the site's relationship to other sites. Commonly cited attributes include proximity to springs or other good sources of fresh water, position on defensible hilltops with commanding views of the surrounding country, and relationship to chert outcrops, soil types, and drainages.

2.6 Site Preservation

It is also important to record information about the probable preservation of sites, especially when there is evidence either that they have already suffered recent damage or that they are endangered in some way. A common example is a riverbank or some construction activity that is cutting into the site and has already removed some unknown portion of its deposits or surface area. In that case, it is sometimes possible to estimate the amount that is missing, so that site-size estimates can be adjusted. Another too-common example is evidence for recent pot-hunting or tomb-robbing. Modern agricultural activities often also have adverse impacts on archaeological materials, so it is useful to record the incidence of terracing, ditches, deep-plowing, stone-clearance, and other such impacts.

3. EXAMINING SITES AND COLLECTING OR RECORDING ARTIFACTS

In some archaeological surveys, a team of archaeologists invests considerable time at each site they encounter, perhaps preparing maps, making a large collection of artifacts found on the surface, or even conducting small-scale, test excavations. In others, each site may receive a fairly cursory examination, or the team may spend enough time to draw or photograph artifacts on-site, and leave the artifacts where they were found. In any of these scenarios, there are many possible strategies for examining a site or cluster of material culture.

In intertidal survey, even under ideal conditions, the periods when tides are low enough for survey to take place are no more than a few hours, leaving little continuous time to record artifacts or features. In spite of these difficulties, surveyors often manage to record them in great detail.

3.1 Estimating Site Size

It is important to anticipate what consititutes reasonable precision for this measurement. For a variety of reasons, including the fact that the boundaries of many kinds of site are far from obvious, we can usually expect rather little consistency between different surveyors' estimates of site size. As noted later in this chapter, repeated survey by five different crews in the Black Mesa Survey led to substantial differences in this measurement, and a standard deviation of some 30% of the mean (Plog, et al., 1978). If the survey's research goals demand precise information about site sizes, achieving sufficient precision could be costly and time-consuming. On the other hand, some research goals may only require assigning each site to an ordinal size category, which a properly trained crew can usually accomplish much more quickly unless poor visibility is a factor. In general, published estimates of site size that give the impression of extreme precision warrant some suspicion.

Attempts to estimate site size in pedestrian surface survey are often rather impressionistic. Members of the survey team walk a series of transects across an apparent cluster of elevated artifact density or walk outward from the cluster's approximate center. In the course of walking these transects, they either flag the locations of artifacts (in cases of relatively low artifact density) or simply flag the regions of each transect where artifact density appears to fall off to "background" levels. Once the site boundaries are approximately determined, team members typically pace the length and width of the site with two transects at right angles, unless the site has an unusual shape or surface features that warrant more complicated mapping. Note that, although 30m or 100m tapes can be used to measure the site axes, the error in establishing the site boundary is usually much greater than the error introduced by small variations in pacing. Consequently, measuring these axes to the nearest centimeter is usually unecessary and could lead to a misleading impression of precision. However, as long as chaining the site goes quickly and the result is accompanied by a realistic estimate of error, there is no harm in careful measurement. It is then possible to round the final result to an appropriate number of significant digits (Banning, 2000:12-13). For surveys of most kinds of large site, there is little reason to expect better precision than $\pm$ 5 m on each of the length and width, and probably no site warrants more precision than $\pm$ 1 m.

Surveys that demand more detailed documentation, especially if that involves gridding the site at a reasonable level of detail (see below, section 2.1), may permit more accurate determination of site boundaries. For example, a grid of systematic surface collections or systematic augering can provide the data for high-resolution mapping of artifact densities or chemical concentrations. Spatial analysis of this data set may then allow determination of boundaries between "high" and "low" regions with a relatively high degree of confidence (e.g., Buck et al., 1996:256-291).

In some jurisdictions, the guidelines for Cultural Resource Management specify methods for determining site size. In some cases where subsurface survey is the detection method, for example, it is necessary to place a series of more closely spaced tests radiating in four directions from each place of contact (discovery of artifacts in a unit). The guidelines go on to specify how to base site boundaries on the distribution of finds in these additional units.

A complication occurs when site size may have varied over a site's lifetime. In that event, overall site size in the present reflects, not the size of some settlement or work area at any time in the past, but the accumulation of material culture over a long time. If the survey's research goals require information on how settlement size has changed over time, achieving these goals could be costly, ranging from careful search of the surface for variations in the distribution of material culture diagnostic of different periods through intensive coring, augering or test-pitting in different parts of the site to identify differences in stratigraphic sequence in different parts of the site (see section 1.3, below).

3.2 Site Chronology

A common way to "date" sites is by "type-fossils." There are, however, some problems with their use. Even where some classes of artifact have a high degree of chronological distinctiveness, the presence of these artifacts can only lead to a rather high probability that a site was used or occupied during the time when this artifact type was made, used, and discarded. The main problem involves the use of negative evidence; just because a survey finds no artifacts diagnostic of some other period does not ensure that the site was unoccupied during that period. Many "type fossils" can be expected to be rare (they have a very low expected density, λ). Consequently, even in a fairly large sample of spatial units there is a high probability that these rare items will not be observed. In fact, some sites with fairly low artifact densities will probably yield no "diagnostic" artifacts at all.

Because most surveys that rely on diagnostic "type fossils" for chronology do not need to quantify the abundance of different artifact types — they assume that the presence of a type fossil is sufficient to conclude that the site was used during a particular period — it is not strictly necessary to employ any formal or statistical sampling strategy on site. Instead, members of the survey team seek out as wide a variety of type fossils as possible in the hope that they will omit no period in which the site was occupied. This biases the sample in favor of rarer items, but this is actually desirable when the goal is to prevent the omission of some time periods. Some surveys will use ordinal categories to distinguish classes of material that are common or rare on the site, in which case it may be useful to estimate the degree of this bias. How much harder did crew members have to look to find the rare item than to find the more common ones?

In cases where it is reasonable for most sites, or at least most sites of a particular kind, to have been occupied only for short periods of time, seriation or a similar method can help sort artifact assemblages from the surfaces of the sites into a probable chronological order. In such cases, it is important to collect or record in the field a large enough sample of artifacts with "useful" attributes for seriation to be possible. In contrast with the collection of type fossils, this should be a sample that is representative of the population of artifacts in the site, or at least on its surface, usually a probabilistic cluster sample.

Some archaeologists have conceived of quantitative methods for dating survey materials chronometrically on the basis of artifact samples. Many of these employ regressions on artifact attributes that appear to have changed in a near-linear fashion over time. One such method employs patterned change in the diameter of pipestems to date North American historic sites (Heighton and Deagan, 1971). Another approach exploits the changing proportions of different types of glass trade beads to date Iroquoian sites in the early contact period (Rumrill, 1991; M. Smith, 1983). Plog and Hantman (1990) use a multiple regression on the proportions of three design elements to estimate the date of sites with a standard error of about 20 years. The relationships between the values of artifact attributes and time upon which these methods are based can only be established by reference to an independent dating method, such as tree rings or historical evidence. Such methods can be useful in cases where type fossils are too rare to offer useful dating evidence or are able to provide only very coarse periodization. As with seriation, the samples upon which the date is based should be representative of the population from which they are drawn.

In cases where site chronology is particularly important, more costly and intrusive examination of the sites may be necessary, even including augering or test excavations, to obtain stratigraphic information and possibly even material for radiocarbon dates. In intertidal survey, for example, the frequent occurrence of wooden remains makes dendrochronology attractive whenever it is feasible, but ironically most waterlogged wood is not suitable for this. Furthermore, since many of the finds are structural features without artifacts or without clear association with the artifacts, it is necessary to rely heavily on radiocarbon dating (Tyson et al., 1997:85).

3.3 Documenting Site Features

In many surveys, one can only estimate the probability that features or structures lie below the artifact scatters we find (e.g., Powell and Klesert, 1980). In some regions, however, it is fairly common for surveys to encounter traces of ancient earthworks, features, or architecture on the modern surface. For example, the tops of stone walls or their foundations may be visible, stone cairns or caches my lie unburied, or depressions may still outline the locations of ditches or house pits. Furthermore, intertidal surveys routinely uncover obtrusive rows of boulders or wooden posts or outlines of sunken ships that require detailed mapping, particularly when they are in danger of destruction by wave action.

Where this type of evidence is anticipated, survey crews should have the skills and equipment necessary to produce at least reasonably accurate sketch maps of the architecture. A team of three people with three 30m tapes, one drawing compass, a clipboard, paper and pencil can draw quite an accurate architectural map by triangulation in a very short time as long as they have adequate training. In other cases, surveyors use total station theodolites that can download their data to a computer for Computer-Aided Design (CAD) plotting.

Drawing by triangulation is accurate and quite easy, although some people find it somewhat counter-intuitive at first. The key is to have at least two fixed points, a known distance apart, which could be two corners of a building or pins pushed into some convenient places in the ground or in the masonry of ruined structures. The first step is to measure the distance between these two datum points as accurately as possible and then use an architect's rule to mark that distance, at the appropriate scale, on paper that has been mounted on a large clipboard or plastic drafting board. Then hook two tapes to the two nails (or have someone hold the ends of the tapes to the known points) and pull the tapes taught and horizontally so that they cross at the point, such as the corner of a room, you wish to plot. Read the two distances and, for each, open a drawing compass the required distance by reference to the architect's rule. Then use the compass to draw arcs originating on the two datum points on the drawing. The new point is where the two arcs cross. With some practice, crew members can do this quite quickly for each room corner and any other important points, and then join the dots to complete a quite accurate building plan. To expand the drawing to cover new areas, or if the original data points are no longer conveniently located (triangulation does not work well if the angles are too obtuse), pull tapes to triangulate onto one or two new datum points, and repeat the process, or establish a web of datum points across the whole area you will map (e.g., Robertson, 1993:67-68). To orient and locate the triangulated map correctly in space, it is necessary to locate each triangulation datum, either by triangulation from a theodolite, by taking compass readings on landmarks such as buildings, communication towers, or lighthouses, or, minimally, with GPS for location and compass for finding magnetic North.

For very large structures, such as major fortifications or earthworks, GPS readings may be sufficient to map their important features. Since 2000, when the military security error was lifted, GPS horizontal accuracy has been remarkably good, on the order of only 1-2 m when enough satellites can be sighted. This is quite sufficient for planning mounds and ditches, for example, even though the vertical accuracy of the GPS is much poorer. In cases that warrant greater precision and accuracy, documentation of the architecture may require returning to the site with a theodolite, EDM, or total station.

Sometimes surveys reveal well-preserved features with thousands of artifacts, stones, or timbers that warrant accurate mapping. Where it is necessary to accomplish this quickly, as in intertidal survey, a total station is nearly essential. It is important to tie the total station's readings to at least two permanent benchmarks (above the high-tide line for intertidal survey). Datum pins driven deeply into the intertidal sediments so that they will resist tidal displacement can be helpful, much as in the triangulation method mentioned above, but are not permanent enough to allow later researchers to relocate the site.

Photogrammetry can also be useful in cases where detailed recording of timbers or artifact scatters is desirable. In that case, it is necessary for each picture to have several well-marked benchmarks at known locations, and it is useful to have a bipod or some similar means to elevate a camera well above the features to be recorded (Patias and Karras, 1995; Turpin et al., 1979).

3.4 Sampling or Stratifying the Site

Many surveys attempt to characterize sites with observations from a spatial sample. As we have seen, representative samples are necessary for seriation or chronology based on the regression of artifact attributes, for example.

A common approach, once a site is detected, is simply to make some transects across it, often at right angles, to scan the surface for variations in artifact density while estimating the site's length and width.

A still more thorough and more time-consuming approach is to subdivide the site into sampling strata, such as four quadrants of a circular or elliptical site, and then either search each quadrant thoroughly for artifacts or sample within it. If the quadrants are established by running two tapes at right angles along the axes of the site, it is possible to use coordinates measured along these tapes to establish the locations of sample points or areas within each quadrant. An expedient that some surveys have employed to save time is to make arbitrary "pseudo-random" selection of sample locations in each quadrant. For example, crew members could toss a trowel or some other item in the air and use the spot where it falls as the center of a sampling circle. Where vegetation cover is sparse and the ground not too hard or stony, it is easy to scribe a circle of standard size around this point if each crew member has two nails tied together with a standard length of string. For example, a 5 m^2 sampling unit should have a radius-string that is 1.26 m long. Alternatively, some surveyors subdivide two transects at right angles to one another into square-meter intervals, and then collect these intensively (e.g., Whallon, 1979).

Particularly when a site is large, or seems to have distinct subdivisions, it is useful to examine each part that might differ from the rest in some relevant respect. A site may constitute a cluster of somewhat distinct artifact clusters, for example, separated by areas with somewhat lower artifact density. In that case, it is useful to examine each cluster in case it differs from the other chronologically or in some functional characteristic. In other cases, the topography of the site may suggest different areas that require attention, such as upper and lower parts of a stepped mound (Portugali, 1982). In some cases, these sub-areas can serve as the strata for a stratified sample of the site (see section 2.2).

Another thing that is quite important is to search out parts of the site where some process, such as erosion, well-digging, trenching, or construction activity, may have exposed buried deposits. On stratified sites this is particularly important, and surveyors may be able to determine the approximate depth of cultural material or identify features or components they would have overlooked if they depended only on surface remains. One of the most common complaints about survey — that it failed to recognize an early (buried) component — is often due to omission of this step. Looking carefully for erosion gulleys, tree throws or even rodent burrows is more likely to yield exposures of buried deposits.

3.5 To Collect or Not to Collect

Some surveyors make a conscious decision not to collect artifacts from the surface of sites, while others make substantial collections. The latter need to consider how much it is reasonable to collect.

Non-collectors may want to preserve the evidence for future researchers, accommodate the cultural or spiritual beliefs of people who claim a connection with the site, or avoid the cost of curating a large collection. In other cases, non-collection may be a requirement of an archaeological licence. Furthermore, if collection favors, for example, decorated pottery or retouched stone tools, future attempts to resample the site or region would lead to highly biased estimates of assemblage characteristics. Particularly if the survey plans do not entail a detailed analysis of the collected materials, it is arguably wasteful to collect at all.

To document the site adequately without collection requires careful documentation of artifacts in the field, including, at a minimum, photographs of artifacts observed on the surface, and measurement of basic attributes, such as size and artifact type. Some teams draw the artifacts or take useful measurements on a sample of artifacts. All of this takes time, so a non-collecting survey needs to have a large enough team with the requisite skills to carry out this documentation, and enough time to survey only a few sites per day, their number depending on the density of material. Simply making a few verbal comments about the most "typical" artifacts seen at the site and providing an estimate of its date and significance is generally insufficient. Without detailed documentation, backed up by illustrations or photographs, colleagues will not be able to evaluate the results without revisiting the site.

Surveying Sites and Landscapes

In cases where the site is likely to be destroyed by development or erosion, where the density of artifacts is high, or resource constraints or the kinds of analysis the survey's goals require make on-site analysis and documentation of artifacts impractical, archaeologists collect samples of artifacts from the sites they encounter. In addition, some archaeologists argue that collection is a scientific responsibility, to ensure replicability of data (Butler, 1979; 1987). Collecting samples also allows more time and flexibility to analyse them, and in some cases makes it possible to apply analytical techniques that require specialized laboratory facilities. A well-designed sample of artifacts, furthermore, can provide reliable estimates of population parameters.

Surveys that collect artifacts need to document the artifact find-spots in ways that are relevant to the survey frame and to carry the artifacts in ways that do not cause unreasonable damage or loss of contextual information. In cases where it is necessary to carry bags of artifacts several kilometers in backpacks, for example, plastic bags can burst open, or lithics can cut their way through them. Artifacts that spill out of the bags may then have lost their contextual information. Jostling artifacts around in bags can also cause breakage and edge damage. Generally heavy cloth bags are better in these situations, or aritfacts can be divided up among a fairly large number of small bags to minimize these effects.

In addition, surveys that involve collection require careful thought about how much to collect. Sometimes there is a temptation to make large collections where they really are not necessary to accomplish the survey's goals. Particularly if collection is haphazard and no one will ever carry out a detailed analysis of the material, there is no point to making such large collections. It is especially wasteful if the artifacts will be discarded after a very preliminary or even cursory analysis in the field, as sometimes happens. Even where there are plans for a detailed and careful analysis of collections, it is responsible to use a sample size that is sufficient for the problem at hand but not larger than necessary. The same principles used for determining the sample sizes in space (chapter 5, section 2) can be used to help decide on the size of collections (see also Banning, 2000; Orton, 2000).

3.6 Test Excavations

Some survey goals, especially where stratified, multi-component sites are anticipated, call for subsurface testing. This is more costly and more destructive than surface survey but has the advantage of providing information on buried deposits and stratigraphic sequence that is otherwise only available if a road-cut or erosion gully has intersected the site. Although sometimes coring or augering is sufficient to test for buried cultural deposits, a common approach is to excavate a sample of 1m x 1m squares or small trenches, or to use a backhoe to cut trenches across the site.

3.7 Cleaning Intertidal Deposits

Intertidal survey frequently blurs the distinction between excavation and survey (Tyson et al., 1997:93-95). In addition to including test excavations in many instances, it routinely involves removal of shallow sediments to clean off features and reveal artifacts. At the Stumble in Essex, for example, surveyors used squeegees to clean sediment in lanes prior to planning the soilmarks and features and collecting artifacts and sediment samples on a 1 m x 1 m grid (Wilkinson and Murphy, 1988). In spite of surveyors' best efforts to clean off new mud that obscures the areas that they survey, however, each tide will redeposit it, making erection of caissons useful wherever work, such as test excavation, must continue over several tides.

4. DOCUMENTING "NON-SITE" OR "OFF-SITE" MATERIAL CULTURE

Where material culture is not conceived as clustered into more-or-less discrete sites, the approaches to documentation necessarily differ somewhat from the preceding.

"Non-site" or distributional approaches tend to use arbitrary spatial units, such as quadrats, within which they document every artifact encountered on the surface. Documentation of each quadrat involves, at a minimum, counting items belonging to various classes of material to facilitate calculation of densities. Many non-site surveys also measure attributes of individual artifacts that are relevant to economic or technological systems.

For example, Thomas (1972) attempted to convert his observations of artifact attributes into TKUs or "tool kit units." Such attributes as edge angle were grouped into "sets of functional attribute states" and then used to classify 500 m x 500 m quadrats with respect to their likelihood of having been inhabited or used for various hunting, butchering, or plant-processing activities mentioned in the ethnographic record.

The Seedskadee Survey (Ebert, 1992; Wandsnider and Ebert, 1986b) and the Grand Junction Survey (Kvamme, 1998) provide good examples of the procedures that may be involved in distributional survey. The survey frame for Seedskadee was a grid of 500 m x 500 m quadrats, from which Ebert drew a sample of 30 quadrats. Survey of these quadrats took place in several distinct steps. The survey near Grand Junction, Colorado, by contrast, examined 3600 4m x 4m quadrats over an area of 5.76 ha.

4.1 Artifact Discovery

On the Seedskadee Survey, a "discovery crew" of five people first had to locate each target quadrat, marking first one corner with a stake, and then using a magnetic compass and 100 m tapes to find and mark the approximate locations of the other three corners, while also placing pinflags at 25m intervals along each quadrat edge.

The team of five then traversed each quadrat with systematic transects at 5m intervals, using the pinflags at 25m intervals as a guide. While walking along a transect, each team member marked every artifact seen with an orange pinflag and counted it with a tally counter (Ebert, 1992:161-162).

On the Grand Junction Survey, it was similarly necessary to locate the survey quadrats on the landscape. A team of two surveyors laid out the grid of 4m squares in blocks of 40 m x 40 m with transit and tapes, using pinflags to mark the grid corners.

A two-person crew then searched each 4 m quadrat by "saturation" survey. The two team members started in opposite corners of a square and each walked four transects with a notional width of 1 m. They then repeated the process with transects at right angles to the first set, so that each quadrat was actually surveyed four times, in four different directions. Kvamme views this set of transects as ensuring total coverage of the artifacts, defined as lithics at least 5 mm in size, in each quadrat.

4.2 Quadrat Mapping

Subsequently, the Seedskadee "mapping crew" of two or three people recorded the three-dimensional point location of all the artifacts that the discovery crew had flagged with an electronic distance-measuring theodolite (EDM). Unless they had already been numbered by the artifact recorders, this crew numbered the artifacts (actually their pinflags) sequentially while mapping them in, the rodman communicating with the instrument person by radio over distances as great as 1.7 km. Where artifact density was high, point provenience was sacrificed in favor of recording artifacts to the nearest 1m x 1m square within the larger quadrat (Ebert, 1992:162). The mapping team also recorded the actual locations of the marked quadrat corners, which were prone to a certain degree of error due to their having been placed by tape and compass.

Unlike the Seedskadee Survey, the discovery crews of the Grand Junction Survey did not flag or point-plot the artifacts detected. With the exception of a 20m x 20m control block, which was point-plotted, surveyors recorded artifact provenience only to the 4m quadrat. This helps to reduce the cost of the survey by making the EDM survey unecessary while, in the case of this part of Colorado, providing sufficient spatial control for the scale of prehistoric activities and formation processes expected (Kvamme, 1998:130-131). As it happens, it also naturally provides data in the form of observations per unit area, making them amenable to modelling by the Poisson model and to isopleth or GIS mapping.

Similarly, many European surveys attempt to count or collect every artifact in each of a large number of contiguous quadrats. This then allows them to plot artifact densities across survey plots (e.g., figure 33 and Davies and Astill, 1994).

4.3 Artifact Recording

In addition, the Seedskadee Survey had a recording crew, consisting of three experienced lithic analysts who visited the quadrat before or after the mapping crew. They numbered the pinflags if the mapping crew had not already done so, and used red pinflags to mark any unflagged artifacts that they noticed. Most importantly, they examined each artifact and recorded some of its attributes on a coding form. For this particular survey, the attributes were ones expected to provide information of reduction stage, edge treat-

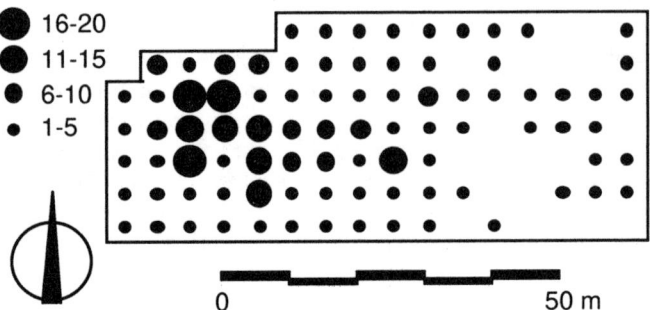

Figure 33. Density distribution of medieval pottery in plot H145 of the 1986 East Brittany Survey (after Davies and Astill, 1994:86).

ment, functional tool type, artifact use, wear, breakage and recycling (Ebert, 1992:171). Ebert's focus is on the scale of clustering of various classes of material.

The Grand Junction Survey was also a non-collecting one, and field observations of artifact attributes included ones relevant to stage and intensity of flaking activity, as well as to post-depositional effects, such as lithic size and presence of cortex (Kvamme, 1998:130-135).

4.4 Recording Geographical Information and Formation Processes

Meaningful interpretation of surface finds, and not only research with ecological goals, requires documentation of evidence for the geological and other formation processes that have contributed to the artifact distributions (Ebert, 1992:165-170). Often archaeologists make do with existing geological maps at a scale much greater than the one used for archaeological observation, but it is possible for a geomorphological crew to visit each quadrat or to include someone with geomorphological expertise on the discovery, mapping or recording crew. In some cases, however, aerial photography or other remote sensing data are sufficient to allow classification of all survey quadrats to one of several geomorphological types, and it is only necessary to groundcheck a sample of quadrats to confirm these assignments and describe in detail the processes associated with each landform type.

In the Grand Junction Survey, the discovery crew also recorded vegetation cover, soil type and geological observations in each quadrat (Kvamme, 1998:130).

4.5 Recording Influences on Visibility and Detectability

Some formation processes, such as colluviation or alluviation, not only contribute to the shape of archaeological distributions, but can enhance or obscure visibility. It is useful for one of the survey crews to record information on any conditions, such as vegetation cover or stony surface conditions, that may make it difficult to detect artifacts, even if they are laying on the surface.

Some surveys use a numerical estimate of visibility that can be used to help correct for differences in detectability (Gaffney, et al., 1991). In these cases, it is important either to have the same person always score visibility or to ensure, as much as possible, that different crew members have clear and agreed criteria by which to score visibility, generally on an ordinal scale.

5. INTERTIDAL SURVEYS

The special circumstances of the foreshore influence practical planning of intertidal surveys. As noted above, tides and currents affect the visibility and accessibility of intertidal archaeological materials. It is additionally necessary to pay particular attention to scheduling, weather, transport of equipment and samples, and crew safety.

Intertidal survey is most useful where the foreshore has little slope and the difference between low and high tide levels is at least several meters. Yet even here the periods when tides are low enough for survey to take place are no more than a few hours.

Generally, the best conditions for intertidal survey are in midsummer when long daylight hours correspond with very low tides (Tyson et al., 1997:83), although seasonal variations in sediment accretion may sometimes offer better visibility at some other time of year, in spite of the shorter hours of good light. Repeated visits to the same stretch of shore allows identification of newly exposed surfaces, especially after storms.

Adverse weather conditions are particular impediments to intertidal survey. Speed and direction of wind and currents can affect the exact timing of the returning tide, or can cause it to rise from unexpected directions. Close attention to weather reports and availability of a boat, for safe removal in an emergency, are critical.

Since intertidal zones often lie far from any road access, a boat is very useful for transporting more fragile equipment and samples, as well as for crew safety. Large wire cages left on site are useful for storing heavier equipment that is less vulnerable to seawater, such as hoses and hoes, right on the foreshore, but bad storms can carry away even heavy, well-anchored cages (Godbold and Turner, 1993:6; Tyson et al., 1997:84).

6. CONTROLS AND DATA QUALITY

Factors discussed in chapter 3 and in previous sections of this chapter can lead to various kinds of errors, including missing data, bias on measurements and estimates, and misclassification of discoveries. The following will not concentrate on statistical errors because these are integral to the sampling issues discussed in chapter 6. Instead, brief consideration of some ways to make it easier to assess the quality of survey measurements is warranted.

As mentioned in chapter 1, an effective research designs include consideration of analytical procedures, what measurements are necessary for achievement of research goals, and the reliability of procedures and measurements. Consequently, some archaeologists have built experimental controls into their survey designs. Such controls are also important in the evaluation of survey results (chapter 10).

The Seedskadee Survey, for example, had controls with which to assess the accuracy and reliability of artifact detection and attribute measurement, and the influence of geomorphological processes (Ebert, 1992:163-170; Wandsnider and Ebert, 1986a).

6.1 Control for Artifact Detection

While survey crews are in the field, there are at least two ways to check for interobserver error and each crew's detection function.

The Seedskadee Survey controlled for imperfect artifact detection by "seeding" survey units with a known number of modern artifacts. In one unit, for example, 202 washers and nails, some of which were painted a color similar to that of the surface sediment while others were painted flat black, were distributed and mapped with an EDM (Ebert, 1992:164). Two days later the survey crew assigned to that unit was instructed to flag washers and nails in addition to prehistoric artifacts. The crew succeeded in detecting 70% of the washers and 61% of the nails, and 60% of the buff-painted but 71% of the black items. There was a strong relationship between detection probability and degree of object clustering (see also pp. 49-50).

An alternative way to control for artifact detection would be to repeat survey of the same units (e.g., Shott, 1995). In the Seedskadee Survey, for example, after each crew flagged artifacts, a recording crew could map the flags and them remove them to prepare the unit for resurvey by another crew. For this to work well, it might be necessary to have a surface that is fairly compact, so that footprints of previous workers are not obvious. It may also be necessary for the time intervals between resurveys to be short and variations in weather and lighting conditions to be minimized. Then a statistical analysis of the results would allow us to place realistic confidence intervals on the reported artifact densities.

For example, when the Black Mesa Project (Plog, 1986:42-48; Plog et al., 1978:414) had five crews independently measure site size and ceramic density in the same areas during an archaeological survey in northeastern Arizona, the crews disagreed substantially in their measurements, indicating fairly poor precision. Their averages were probably reasonably accurate estimates, but a broader test of intercrew variation (see chapter 10), to identify bias, requires more controls, such having the crews survey places with known or simulated parameters.

Observations on continuous scales, such as artifact density, are always approximations, while errors of misclassification of artifacts are also possible. Citing estimated errors provides an honest assessment of how reliable interval measurements are, and repeated survey of a sample of areas is one way to assess consistency between crews, with control for weather or lighting conditions.

6.2 Control for Accuracy of Artifact Attributes

As in any archaeological research that involves measuring attributes of artifacts, measurements will differ somewhat from observer to observer, and even between repeated measurements by the same observer (Banning, 2000:21; Fish, 1978). It is particularly important to control for this type of error in surveys that do not collect artifacts, but instead record their attributes in the field.

The Seedskadee Survey, again, attempted to control for interobserver error by having each of its lithic recorders code the same control set of 200 items, including both lithics and several non-artifactual, angular rocks (Ebert, 1992:166). The results showed high reliability for continuous ratio-scale measurements, such as flake thickness, but poor reliability for discontinuous ones, such as number of striking platforms, or nominal-scale measurements.

Adams attempted to measure the reliability of nominal-scale measures on Nubian pottery with a similar process, having each recorder code the same sherds. He measured the degree of misclassification by the error rate (Adams and Adams, 1991:238), which is simply the proportion of sherds that were misclassified. The approach treats all misclassifications as though they are equally serious (Nance, 1987:258-67). More sophisticated measures of misclassification may recognize some kinds of error as more serious than others, or even account for the costs or risks of misclassification (Hand, 1997). For example, to record something as "unknown" may be less serious than assigning it to the wrong category.

6.3 Control for Accuracy and Precision of Site and Spatial Attributes

Much as with artifact attributes, variation between teams or team members can lead to errors in the characterization of sites and other spatial or geographical units.

For example, when the Black Mesa project (Plog, 1986:42-48; Plog et al., 1978:414) had five crews independently measure ceramic density, they also assessed reliability of measurements of site size and estimates of the percentage of sites less than 100 m^2 in size. Their comparison implies that we should not be very confident, in this case at least, of differences between site areas of less than about 30%. Again, the standard deviation on the averages of these measurements gives some idea of precision, but testing for systematic differnces between crews would be necessary to check for bias.

While one should not generalize from the Black Mesa results — differences in visibility, crew, and site characteristics will lead to different reliability on different surveys — carrying out similar evaluations makes it possible to assess the reliability of measures on any survey.

As with artifact attributes, it is possible to analyse differences between teams statistically on a variety of important site or spatial data categories, by resurveying the same areas with different teams. In that case, it helps to keep the composition of crews constant. Alternatively, in a simple analysis of differences between teams' regular work, it is important to control for other sources of difference that might lead to the false impression that one team was inaccurate. For example, if one team surveyed a higher than average proportion of some landform type where sites were typically smaller or more specialized, it would record very different site attributes even if there were no differences between teams' recording habits.

7. CONCLUSION

Detecting sites or other archaeological phenomena is only one step in the process of archaeological survey. In addition to detection, and understanding the factors that affect detectability, surveyors must accurately record the location and other attributes of sites, artifacts or artifact clusters and the environments in which they are found.

Chapter X
Evaluating Surveys

A key step in a survey is to evaluate its success at detecting materials of interest and achieving the other goals the surveyors set. A related issue is to evaluate the results of previous surveys, usually ones that others have conducted, sometimes a long time ago. Only through such evaluation can researchers confidently draw conclusions from the surveys' results.

1. ASSESSING DETECTION PROBABILITIES

A crucial element in making use of survey data is determining how likely it is that the survey missed targets of interest and, if so, what proportion of these are included in the sample or data set. Many claims for "100% survey" would fail to meet a test of that claim through careful evaluation of the surveys' intersection and detection probabilities. For sampling surveys, failure to account for variations in detection probability usually leads to biased estimates, such as overestimate of average site size or underestimate of the proportion of small sites or the total number of sites (Miller, 1989; Nance, 1983).

Chapters 3 and 6 dealt with detection probabilities at length, but in the context of survey planning. Ideally survey designers should determine the detection functions of surveys before most of the fieldwork has begun, but often lack sufficient reliable information to do this. Once survey is complete, and especially in light of any changes to the survey plan, we are in a better position to evaluate the actual detection probabilities of a survey.

1.1 Estimating Detection Probabilities of Systematic Surveys

Most modern surveys employ systematic or other formal designs for which it is relatively easy to measure survey intensity. For any intensity it is then possible to estimate intersection probabilities for a range of site sizes and shapes or discovery radii. the next step is to multiply intersection probabilities by estimates of the conditional probability of detecting targets, given that they are intersected (e.g., Krakker et al., 1983:479). This last probability is largely a function of target visibility for the method or methods of survey or, for sub-surface survey, of artifact density and clustering. Alternatively, surveyors can include visibility and other factors in their estimates of discovery radius.

For example, the discovery radius of a teepee ring by pedestrian visual survey might be 25 m on fairly flat terrain with sparse vegetation, but only 4 m on rocky terrain and only 2 m where there is tall grass.

The estimate of detection probabilites for cases of this type is discussed in Section 2 of chapter 3. In the simple case of definite detection of various kinds of target within a discovery radius, R, it is easy to measure the area swept for each of these targets (taking care to exclude overlaps in coverage), and then to divide this by the total area of survey to obtain estimates of the detection probabilities for each. If, as in the examples from the Wadi Hasa Survey (figure 10), survey employed nested subsampling, had anomalies in coverage due to inaccessibility or innacuracy in unit placement, or employed some non-systematic survey design, the resulting graph of the relationship between detection probability and discovery radius will have breaks in slope.

If the estimates of discovery radius are reasonable, and take such factors as visibility into account, the graph of detection probabilities makes it possible to estimate how many sites of a given size and obtrusiveness the survey may have missed.

1.2 Assessing the Impact of Visibility, Intensity, and Other Specific Factors

Some archaeologists have studied specific factors that probably affected their surveys' detection of archaeological materials. Visibility is the factor that has attracted the most interest.

Wherever surveyors have employed some reasonable and reproducible way of quantifying visibility, it is straightforward to see if there is a correlation between visibility and the probability that the survey found sites or any other targets. For example, Terrenato (2000) drew scatterplots of the percentage of high-visibility surface area in each quadrat against the number of sites found in each quadrat, and found that there was a fairly strong correlation. This is a very simple way to assess whether or not visibility has had an important impact on a survey's results, and Terrenato's attempt to account for it involved maps plotting the ratio of site density to the proportion of each space with high visibility. Testing for spatial autocorrelation between sites and regions of high visibility is a good way to check for visibility's impact. An alternative, in cases where surveyors have estimated a visibility score for each site, is to test statistically for significant differences between the scores for sites and those for randomly distributed non-site locations in the survey area.

The most important thing is to detect any factors, such as visibility, that have had a significant impact on the survey's results. Superimposing site distributions on a visibility map is also a good idea, even though such maps can be difficult to interpret (Terrenato, 2000:66).

Evaluating Surveys

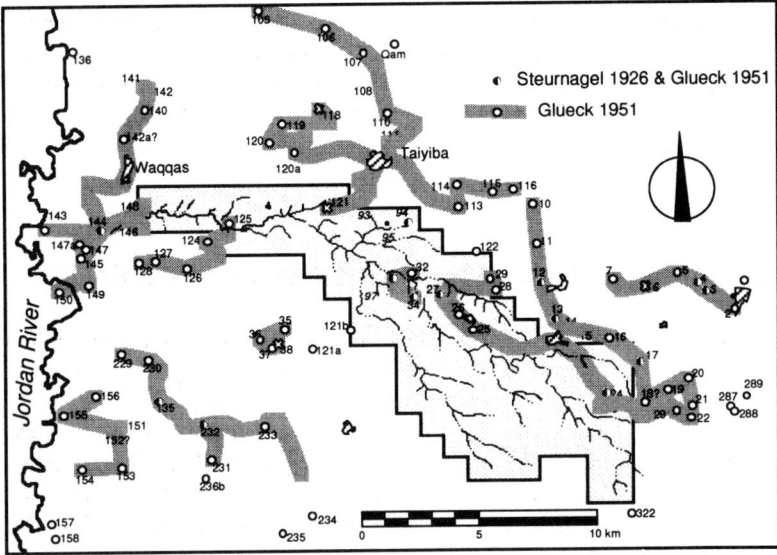

Figure 34. Map of Nelson Glueck's probable routes of survey through part of al-Kura, northern Jordan, in 1942, overlaid on the survey universe of the 1981 Wadi Ziqlab Survey (light shading).

1.3 Estimating Detection Probabilities of Informal Surveys

In evaluating more informal surveys that lack a regular sampling frame, one can begin by estimating intensity. Even a rough estimate of the area the survey covered, divided by the survey region's total area, can be useful. For example, in the 1940s, Nelson Glueck (1935; 1939; 1951) conducted an extensive survey of Transjordan, mainly by horseback. In those days, archaeologists did not typically discuss their survey methods in detail, but we can still estimate his survey's coverage and intensity.

Fortunately, it is possible to reconstruct his itinerary, as revealed by site numbers and dated observations (figure 34). Glueck appears to have travelled on horseback along roads and tracks to modern settlements, where local informants could direct him to some of the surrounding antiquities. In addition, he recorded observations of sites he noticed on the way, which permits, for example, estimate of the detection probabilities for the portion of Glueck's survey that fell within Wadi Ziqlab's drainage basin. Most of Glueck's trips in al-Kura region of northern Jordan, where Wadi Ziqlab is found, took place from 15 to 21 June 1942 and on 12 October 1942. On these days he recorded 36 sites. If he had travelled along the shortest routes between the sites he described on these trips, the transects' total length would be 25 km. Let us assume that Glueck would have detected any site, by his definition (i.e., ruined villages and fairly obtrusive remains), that was within 100 m of his path. The actual distance would have varied with topography, visibility and obtrusiveness, but 100 m seems reasonable from horseback on hilly terrain with mainly sparse vegetation in most areas. Then his coverage would be 5 km^2. As a proportion of the survey area of the Wadi Ziqlab Project in this same region (Banning, 1985), this represents a density of effort of 0.043, or less than 5%. Consequently, his survey's estimated detection probability for village sites is 0.05, albeit with a fairly large margin of error.

Section 2 will present other ways to evaluate this survey.

2. ASSESSING THE "EXHAUSTION" OF A REGION

Sometimes, before beginning work in a region or allocate significant amounts of effort to research there, surveyors need some sense of how thorough previous surveys have been. Can we assume that they have found most of the sites, or only a small fraction of them? In exploration geology this problem is called determining the "exhaustion" of the region. It is useful to know if the previous work has been distributed in such a way as to ensure that targets of interest could not have escaped detection, or if the survey left conspicuous "gaps" where some targets could lie undetected. The exploration history of a region can allow us to determine a "physical exhaustion sequence" for that region (Singer and Drew, 1976:646-647).

Some archaeologists have grappled with something like this concept. Schiffer (1987: 340-41, 344-45) makes the sensible assumption that, as survey continues in a region, the cumulative number and variety of detected sites should level off as the region becomes exhausted. In other words, new surveys will find less and less that is new because most of the sites have already been discovered.

For example, more than a century of archaeological survey in Wadi Ziqlab, northern Jordan, as figure 35 shows, suggests that Wadi Ziqlab is not exhausted. The cumulative frequency curve rises fairly gradually until about 1970, then rises abruptly when the more intensive Wadi Ziqlab Survey adds new sites in 1981. In addition, the Wadi Ziqlab survey claimed a detection probability of less than 20% for most kinds of sites that could be discovered by surface examination. A much slower and less intensive survey for buried sites added a few observations up until the early 1990s, and then purposive survey in the late 1990s added several more, even though the survey was not very intensive. Even the small plateau in cumulative frequency around 1985 reflects a slowing in the pace of survey work, not an exhaustion of the region's sites.

Estimates of changes in the diversity (here richness) of sites known also supports this interpretation. Buckingham (1821) mentions only one site, a tomb. Several later writers vaguely mention *khurub* or "ruins," probably ruined settlements, increasing site diversity to 2. Oliphant (1880) mentions a dolmen field and scattered sarcophagi, bringing richness up to 4. Schumacher and Steuernagel mention ruined and inhabited settlements with evidence of ancient architecture (*khurub*), dolmen fields, large caves, and clusters of cisterns, as well as graves, increasing the richness of sites to 6 (Schumacher, 1890; Steuernagel, 1925; 1926). Although Schumacher mentions vineyard walls, towers and winepresses, he does not specifically describe individual examples. Glueck (1951) adds simple sherd scatters, increasing richness to 7. The Wadi Ziqlab Project added lithic scatters, field walls, wine presses, aqueducts and a rock-carved game board in

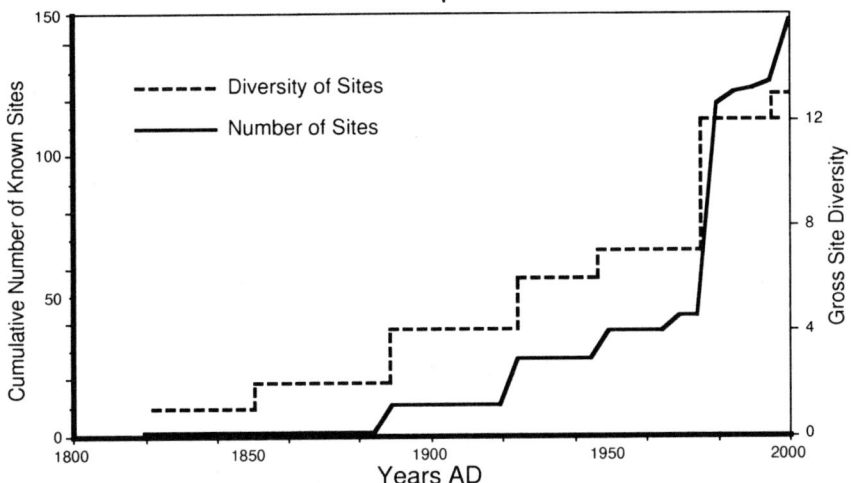

Figure 35. Increases in both number and diversity of known sites in Wadi Ziqlab, northern Jordan, show no sign of levelling off, suggesting that this region is not exhausted.

1981 (Banning, 1985), while subsequent work added flour mills, increasing diversity in gross site type to 13. Glueck recorded sites he dated to 12 distinct time periods, ranging from Early Bronze I to Medieval. The Wadi Ziqlab Project added sites of the Middle and Upper Palaeolithic, and subsequent work from 1986 to 2001 has added sites of the Kebaran, Geometric Kebaran, Pre-Pottery Neolithic B, Late Neolithic, and Chalcolithic. This relatively sudden increase in chronological diversity also suggests that the region is far from exhausted.

The estimated proportion of large and obtrusive settlement sites among all kinds of site may also be instructive. Again turning to the history of survey in Wadi Ziqlab, the proportion is 0.75 for the Schumacher-Steurnagel reports, 0.68 for Glueck (1951) and 0.79 for Mittmann, but only 0.13 for the 1981 Wadi Ziqlab Survey, indicating a much greater emphasis on small sites and non-settlements in the last. This also indicates that the degree of exhaustion of earlier surveys really only applies to the largest and most obtrusive sites.

Where the distrubution of survey is well documented, and especially when the survey employed systematic grids of points or transects, it is possible to evaluate exhaustion much more effectively. Section 1 showed how to use this information to estimate the discovery probabilities for targets with various discovery radii. But even where allocation of previous survey effort has been very uneven or unsystematic, one can actually prepare maps that show which areas are exhausted (i.e., have no chance of containing undetected targets) and which are effectively unexplored (i.e., might well contain undetected sites).

Singer and Drew (1976) discuss a method that maps exhaustion for targets of various size or obtrusiveness (in other words, with varying discovery regions), on the assumption that the targets are either circular or elliptical and that survey was by coring.

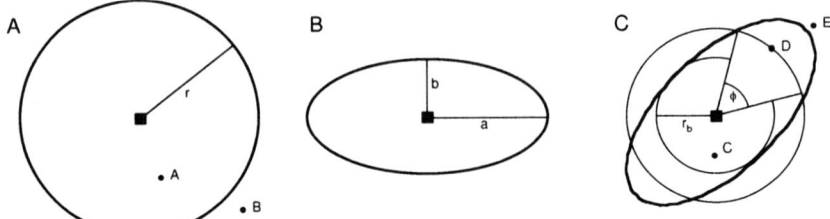

Figure 36. For a subsurface test (black square), intersection of a circular target is certain if its center is within radius r (point A), but impossible outside r (point B). For an elliptical target (b), with semimajor axis a and semiminor axis b, intersection is certain within radius r_b (point C), impossible at point E, and at point D has a probability of ϕ /180 (after Singer and Drew, 1976:643).

The principles are the same as those for estimating detection probabilities for different arrangements and spacings of point grids (see section 1), and can be extended to transect surveys as well.

Singer and Drew (1976) depend on the definite detection law — they assume that intersection equals detection — but it is possible to avoid this assumption. For point surveys (e.g., shovel tests or auger holes), given a sensing method and assuming definite detection, around each point, a circle of radius r (the radius of a circular target), or r_b (the semiminor axis of an elliptical target), defines the area in which no target could have occurred without being detected (i.e., the circles are totally exhausted), while undetected targets could exist anyplace outside of r or r_b (figure 36). However, between r_a (equal to the semimajor axis of an elliptical target) and r_b the probability of undetected targets increases, so that the degree of exhaustion decreases. That is because the orientation of any elliptical targets that might exist is unknown; sometimes it is possible to detect them within r_a, but at other times only within r_b, and usually at some intermediate distance.

The equation for the probability of intersecting an elliptical target (chapter 4, section 3.1.1) determines the area within which any observation point should have intersected targets of various sizes (or the discovery regions of obtrusive targets) with a certain probability, such as 0.8, for example. This also applies to arrays of many points or for sets of transects, taking care to deal with overlaps (Singer and Drew, 1976:644). The orientation within which two points could intersect an ellipse, for example, is the sum of the possible hit angles (ϕ_1 and ϕ_2) minus the angles of multiple intersections (ϕ_0).

The final step is to create physical exhaustion maps of the survey region. Each of these resembles a contour map and shows the predicted degree of exhaustion by survey for targets of a particular size and shape. Since the degree of exhaustion is equal to the probability of detection by the completed survey, the implication is that undetected targets, of the given size and shape, could occur anywhere this value is low on the map. Wherever survey was by transects, exhaustion maps will show distinctly linear contours, but spotty or less systematic survey, especially taking irregular topography and the discovery regions of obtrusive sites into account, will lead to quite irregular exhaus-

Evaluating Surveys

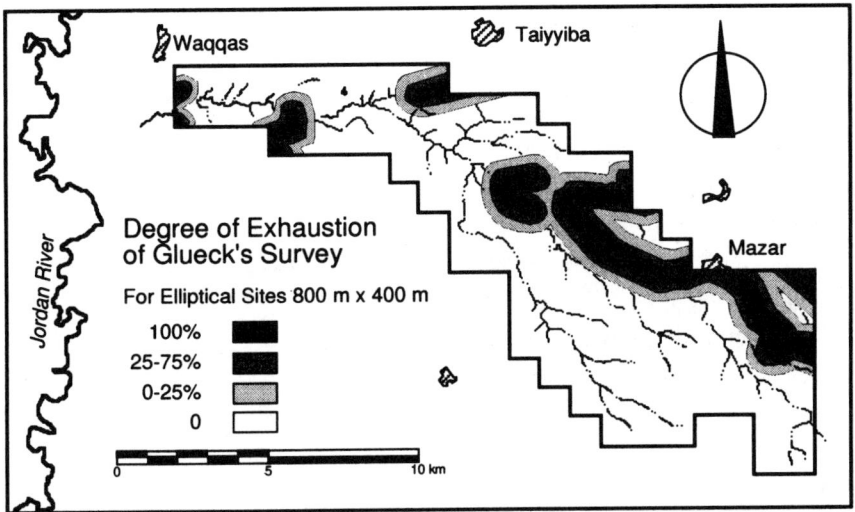

Figure 37. Exhaustion map for elliptical targets 800 m x 400 m in Nelson Glueck's 1942 survey within the boundaries of the Wadi Ziqlab drainage.

tion maps. The example (figure 37) of the estimated exhaustion for Nelson Glueck's survey in part of al-Kura, Jordan, in 1942, provides a more realistic idea of that survey's thoroughness than does the estimated detection probability in section 1.2, above.

Exhaustion maps graphically highlight which parts of the survey region are most likely to contain undetected targets, and thus they can prove extremely useful for the design of future surveys, including purposive ones. In that case, overlapping the exhaustion map on a model of "high probability" regions (chapter 6, section 1.6) would highlight the regions that are most likely to yield new discoveries. Singer and Drew (1976:645) recommend subtracting the exhaustion values from 1.0, and then multiplying the results by the model's "sensitivity" values to create an *exploration potential map* of the region.

3. EVALUATING THE EFFECTIVENESS OF SAMPLING

Whenever completing a statistical survey, it is important to evaluate the precision of its parameter estimates and the effectiveness of any stratification the survey employed.

Chapter 5 dealt with some of the methods with which to set sample sizes, so as to meet certain goals of precision on estimates. Once the survey is complete, it is necessary to compare the actual variances or coefficients of variation with the ones predicted for the sample size.

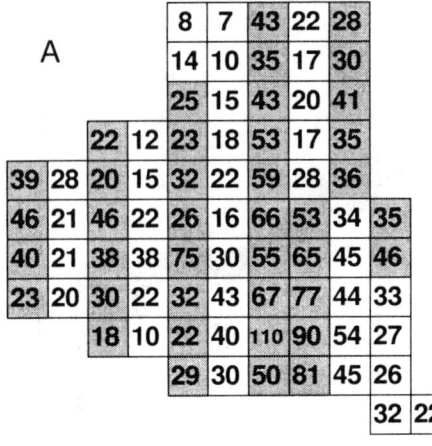
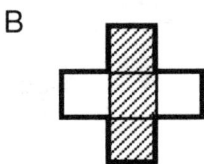

Figure 38. Data (a) on the number of lithic artifacts collected in each meter square at Dakhleh locality 216TP, Egypt, by collector A (white squares) and collector B (shaded)(after Hawkins, 2000), and (b) adjacent squares collected by the same (hatched) and different collectors.

For stratified samples, it is important to evaluate the usefulness of strata once survey is complete. If the grounds for stratification are meaningful, then the parameters of at least some strata should differ. If, on the other hand, the strata do not seem to differ with respect to the parameters of interest, then the stratification has failed, in the sense that it yielded results no better than what a simple random sample would have provided. In addition, one should compare the precisions of estimates that resulted from the stratified plan with those that would have resulted with no stratification at all. After all, the whole point of stratification is to increase the precision of estimates.

4. ASSESSING THE RELIABILITY OF CREW OBSERVATIONS

As noted in chapter 3, crew members naturally vary in their abilities and inclinations to record different kinds of observations, such as site size and artifact density. Confidence in these observations requires evaluating their data quality.

As noted in chapter 9, Section 5, the Black Mesa Project and Seedaskee Survey used repeat survey to assess the reliability of crew observations. These controls make post-survey evaluation much simpler, but it is often necessary to evaluate surveys for which no such controls are available.

Since the survey designs of most surveys do not anticipate the need for data-quality controls, it is often necessary to try to detect inter-observer variability or biases in detection rate after the fact. In the Dakhleh Oasis Prehistoric Survey, for example, Hawkins (2000:535-541) noticed that quadrats and transects in which different crew members collected artifacts systematically differed in artifact density. It was a reasonable hypothesis that the differences were due to the crew members' differing detection abilities and small differences in search time between them.

One simple way to test this hypothesis is by a statistical comparison of mean artifact densities by crew member. However, the problem is complicated by the fact that there could be real differences in artifact density that just happen to be correlated with the distribution of collectors. A way to take this real spatial variation into account is to compare each collection quadrat with neighboring quadrats collected by the same and by different team members, taking advantage of spatial autocorrelation.

If there were no inter-observer differences, we would expect that, on average, there should be no significant difference between the two sets of adjacent units. If, however, there are inter-observer differences, we would not only expect the two sets to differ, but we would expect each unit to be more similar in artifact density to adjacent units collected by the same person than to adjacent units collected by different people.

Turning to data from locality 216 TP (figure 38), for example, Hawkins compared the mean of the absolute differences between the densities of same-collector units with that of dfferences between each unit and adjacent units collected by different people. In this case, there were two collectors and, for the most part, they collected alternate rows of quadrats, although with some distortion. Hawkins did not take the direction of differences into account, even though she thought she could detect the direction of bias. For 132 boundaries between units, the mean absolute difference in density between adjacent squares collected by the same person was 11 ± 11 artifacts, while that between adjacent squares collected by different people was 19 ± 14, a difference that is significant at the 0.05 significance level.

Another way to attack this problem is to recognize that collector B, on average, collected more artifacts than collector A. In that case, the research hypothesis is that adjacent squares collected by person B will, on average, have higher densities than adjacent squares collected by person A (only considering each square's neighbors, rather than its own density). Analysing the data for locality 216 TP in this way indicates that the average density for adjacent squares by collector B is 45.6 ± 18.6, while that for collector A is only 26.3 ± 10.7. More importantly, adjacent squares by collector B al- most always show higher densities than those by collector A, so that the mean difference between the two sets of adjacent squares is 19.3 ± 14.1. These differences are significant in a paired, one-tail test at the 0.001 significance level. If collector B represents the standard of "complete" detection, then we would estimate that collector A was under-reporting artifacts, with a detection probability of only about 0.58 ± 0.33. This could be used to adjust collector A's counts upwards (by a factor of $1/0.58 = 1.7$) to provide more realistic density estimates with appropriate margins of error.

Alternatively, using the Wilcoxon two-sample (or Mann-Whitney U) test with correction for tied values avoids assuming a normal distribution. In that case, the difference between collectors for pairs of nearby squares is also significant.

In some cases, more complicated statistical analyses of interobserver variation may be warranted. For example, where there is concern that one team member may have over-reported lithics and under-reported pottery, a multivariate analysis might reveal if the suspect team member's presence or absence has a statistically significant association with the likelihood that lithics or pottery will be reported, or with the amount that will be reported.

5. ASSESSING BIAS IN THE CHARACTERIZATION OF FINDS

Even when a survey had very good detection probabilities, corrected for visibility and site size, and crews did an excellent job of estimating artifact densities and so on, sometimes the very nature of the archaeological evidence can lead to completely incorrect conclusions about the relative abundance of various items, if we are not careful.

For example, perception of the relative abundance of sites of different periods often depends on the relative abundance of diagnostic artifacts, which itself is not independent of the periods of interest. As Rutter (1983) points out, for example, surveys quite readily identify periods represented by highly distinctive ceramics of types that detailed and extensive stratigraphic excavations have documented and dated. However, these same surveys will underrepresent periods for which the material culture is not very distinctive, whose material culture awaits serious and detailed study, or for which nearby stratigraphic excavations have yet to provide good collections of well-dated examples of local wares. Sometimes the archaeological distinctiveness of wares is a function of greater standardization of production in certain periods (Malone and Stoddart, 2000). Attempting to date small rural sites on the basis of the same diagnostic ceramics as large town sites assumes that these radically different site types will show the same kinds of pottery assemblages, even when we know they would have had different access to manufactured goods (Banning et al., 1994:159). In addition, surveys can sometimes underrpresent periods of short duration relative to very long periods.

Rutter (1983) suggests a way to assess this problem, in the case of pottery, by compiling lists of the ceramic classes that are supposed to be diagnostic of each period and attempting to estimate on the basis of excavated assemblages how common each class is. Comparing this information with statements about the alleged rarity or even absence of some periods in the survey evidence then suggests whether differences in ceramic "visibility" (not to be confused with usage of this term elsewhere in this book) might account for it.

In addition, although archaeologists tend to think of ceramic sherds as nearly indestructable, sherds from surface survey are frequently battered and worn. Some kinds of pottery, notably poorly fired prehistoric pottery, does not withstand this battering very well, often being quite fragile and unable to survive very long on the surface (Banning et al., 1994:154; Malone and Stoddart, 2000; Stoddart and Whitehead, 1991). Processes such as wet-dry cycling can decrease the structural strength of sherds, making them more susceptible to trampling and abrasion (Schiffer, 1987:161-162). A greater tendency for sites of some periods to be located in areas where such processes are likely to occur can then lead to reduced obtrusiveness (Banning et al., 1994).

6. ASSESSING VARIATIONS IN COLLECTION METHOD

Sometimes it is necessary to vary the methods for artifact collection or other kinds of observations, or variation may be part of an experiment in survey design. The Keban Reservoir survey, for example, experimented with several different means for making surface collections, including collection along transects consisting usually of 3 m x 4 m squares ("gridded strips"), collection in concentric bands, and simple random sampling, usually of four-meter squares over the site (Whallon, 1979). Evaluation of the results demonstrated the importance of attuning the area of the collecting unit to artifact density (i.e., ensuring large enough value of λ) and of selecting sampling methods that provided fairly even coverage of sites.

Comparing differences in collection method is very similar to testing for inter-observer error. The principal problem, however, is that in most cases it is difficult to unravel differences due to collecting method from real differences between sites or regions. The only way to get around this is either to test different methods on exactly the same site, or to conduct experiments with artifical "sites" seeded with modern artifacts in ways that simulate the character of the sites of interest.

7. CONCLUSION

A very important step in any archaeological survey is to evaluate its results. One cannot simply assume that any survey has found all, or even most, of the sites or other targets in the survey area, and it would be naïve to convert survey results into population estimates or to detect settlement patterns without first giving some consideration to data quality.

As already pointed out in chapter 3, a great many factors affect the number and kind of archaeological remains that fieldworkers will find with a given amount of survey effort. Rather than be too dismayed by the fact that finding 100% of the sites that exist now, let alone the ones that may once have existed, is unrealistic, archaeologists should concentrate on how to recognize and compensate for the potential distortion that omissions could cause.

Various quantitative methods, not to mention common sense, can help us recognize where shortcomings in survey results lie. There are then many tools with which to compensate for these shortcomings. Some involve additional fieldwork, such as purposive prospection or more intrusive survey methods in regions of poor visibility. Others involve quantitative compensation for the effects, for example, by recognizing that the survey's detection function varied over space in a predictable way. Much as Terrenato (2000) compensates for visibility effects, the ratio of site density to detection probability, rather than raw site numbers, might reveal patterns in the distribution of sites, for example.

Finally, realistic evaluation of previous survey results helps archaeologists plan future research. Does a "hole" in a site distribution represent a real absence of sites? Or is it simply an artifact of past survey history? Evaluating the "exhaustion" of a region is the key to making efficient and productive use of our limited resources in future surveys.

Chapter XI
Surveying the Future

As this book began with a brief survey of the history of archaeological survey, it now seems appropriate to speculate about its future prospects and point out the problems that require further research. Among the areas where new developments are likely are survey's role in understanding the past, investigation of less accessible landscapes, survey method and technology, and theoretical and mathematical aspects of survey design. These take on particular importance in the context of the rapid pace of urban and industrial development, which is destroying and degrading archaeological landscapes at an alarming pace.

1. SURVEY'S EXPANDING ROLE

A few decades ago, most archaeological surveys had little explicit purpose other than identifying sites that would yield good results from excavation. Increasingly, however, archaeologists have exploited the unique ability of archaeological survey to investigate the spatial dimension of past cultures, a trend that the recent resurgence of landscape archaeology has accelerated. In addition, archaeological survey has become an integral aspect of environmental assessment, a role that will become even more important in future.

Half a century after Gordon Willey's landmark Virù Valley survey, there is still some way to go to ensure that surveys allow archaeologists to identify and understand the workings of settlement systems, rather than simply to recognize certain aspects of settlement patterns. For much of the intervening time, surveys have been so focussed on sampling homogenized and ill-defined populations that there is much work to do to design surveys that are effective at detecting settlement hierarchies, identifying the form of settlement structure, or determining how, or even if, sites and offsite areas were functionally or culturally related. Speculations about changes in hunter-gatherer use of landscapes and later development of regional polities will not become convincing or testable theories until we develop the methods we require.

Interest in such issues and others will increasingly depend on innovative survey designs specifically tailored to solve problems and test for particular kinds of spatial structure. Recent resurgence of interest in investigating ancient canals, roads and pathways that people used to move water, themselves, their goods and livestock over the landscape and between settlements is an encouraging step in this direction (e.g., Mabry, 1996; Mathien, 1991; Pavlidis et al., n.d.; Trombold, 1991; Wilkinson, 1993; 1998). Aerial remote sensing will be a useful tool in this development.

Cultural Resource Management now accounts for the lion's share of archaeological surveys in most developed countries, typically with a focus on mitigating the impacts of modern development on archaeological and historic heritage. In the near future, this role will continue to be important, but archaeological survey will also become increasingly useful for its ability to monitor long-term environmental change or stability. Archaeologists and colleagues in other disciplines will be integrating evidence for changes in the distribution of past communities in Arctic regions, for example, into models of climate change, thus assisting efforts to understand global warming. Archaeological features along eroding coastlines are already important for monitoring coastal erosion in the United Kingdom, and we can expect this practice to spread to other coastal regions. No one will want to place a nuclear power plant, for example, in a location where the archaeological evidence shows that it will be vulnerable to coastal erosion in the forseeable future. Discovery of Neolithic fish weirs on the nearby intertidal zone, however, might suggest a long period of coastal stability.

2. INVESTIGATING "HIDDEN" AND NEGLECTED LANDSCAPES

Already archaeologists have begun to expand greatly the range of landscapes, including ones of very low visibility, that are subject to archaeological survey, and we can expect this trend to continue. In the 1970s, most of the great advances in archaeological survey were in arid regions, such as the Middle East, the American Southwest, and central Mexico, where visibility and accessibility were unusually good. Yet, even then, some researchers had begun to develop methods for investigating the much less visible landscapes in forested regions. By the 1980s, other archaeologists had begun serious efforts to investigate intertidal zones and landscapes that were buried too deeply for simple surface survey to detect (e.g., Stafford, 1995; Wilkinson and Murphy, 1986). Yet difficulties still remain, and the expansion of archaeological survey effort into new and more challenging environments has barely begun.

2.1 Subsurface Survey and Geoarchaeological Approaches

In general, our best-protected archaeological resources are also those most difficult to detect: the ones that are deeply buried. Current methods, such as augering and digging small test pits, intersect buried paleosols over such tiny areas, and at such great cost, that we cannot expect them to be very successful at intersecting them. Yet modern construction tends to be much more intrusive than most archaeological efforts; more massive buildings with ever deeper foundations can expunge important residues of our most poorly understood, early predecessors.

To detect these buried deposits efficiently before construction efforts destroy them will require further development of theory and method specifically devoted to this problem. Random sampling will not be the solution; we will require surveys explicitly designed to maximize the probability of detecting buried archaeological remains. No doubt this will require both predictive modelling and the cooperation of geomorphologists who can help us identify the deposits and paleosols most likely to yield archaeological material, and to reconstruct the shapes of prehistoric landscapes. We may also see increased use of geophysical remote sensing methods, such as Ground-Penetrating Radar (GPR) (e.g., Conyers and Cameron, 1998), greater use of opportunistic exposures, such as wells and road cuts, and the cooperation of the geotechnical engineers who evaluate the soil mechanics of development sites.

2.2 Wetland Survey

Although there have been great advances in this type of survey in the last two decades, its use is still very limited. Even in northwestern Europe, where intertidal and lake survey are most common, archaeologists have investigated only a tiny proportion of the drowned and intertidal landscapes that are likely to harbor important archaeological vestiges. Furthermore, the methods for carrying out these surveys efficiently are still in their early stages of development, and many practical difficulties remain.

Future expansion of archaeological efforts in marshes and foreshores may benefit from increasing accessibility that small hovercraft would afford (Tyson et al., 1997:85), and from advances in aerial and space-borne remote sensing (Cox, 1992; Custer et al., 1986; Dahlin and Pope, 1989), but the principal change will be more widespread recognition that wetland surveys are worthwhile.

2.3 Marine Survey

Relative sea levels in some regions are so much higher today than in the early Holocene that subtidal, and not merely intertidal, archaeology is critical to our understanding of such issues as colonization of the New World and the spread of agricultural communities into Europe. So far, efforts to investigate drowned landscapes below the tide level have been limited to a few regions, such as Florida and the Black Sea (Ballard et al., 2001; Dunbar et al., 1989; Faught and Donoghue, 1997), and most underwater archaeology has focussed on shipwrecks.

Recent advances in the development of ROVs (Remotely Operated Vehicles), small, unmanned submersibles, deep-water photography, and sonar imaging will become more widely available to archaeologists. Detection and investigation of shipwrecks, inundated settlement sites, and other underwater archaeological features will come to depend less on scuba divers and dredging equipment and more on remote observation of the sea floor. Increase in the role of underwater remote sensing (e.g., Blake, 1991) will continue.

3. SURVEY METHOD AND TECHNOLOGY

Already GPS, GIS, total stations, and aerial remote sensing are having significant impacts on the speed, accuracy, and efficiency with which we can carry out archaeological surveys. No doubt further technological advances will continue to improve our effectiveness as surveyors.

Improved technology for detecting archaeological materials, especially where they are buried or underwater, will assist survey at the regional scale, rather than being largely restricted to the scale of individual sites. Already we are headed in this direction, with rapidly improving resolution in available satellite imagery, and increasing utility of the non-visible parts of the spectrum by using, for example, AIRSAR (AIRborne Synthetic Aperture RADAR), Thermal Infrared Multispectral Scanner (TIMS), and Airborne Oceanographic Lidar (El-Baz, 1997; Fassbinder and Irlinger, 1999; Ferguson et al., 1987; Fowler, 1995; Miller et al., 1991; Scollar et al., 1992). They will also provide better detail and sensitivity. New software and methods for image analysis and pattern recognition will increase our ability to distinguish archaeologically important materials from false targets quickly.

We must temper our enthusiasm for these new technologies with realism, as there are some kinds of false targets that we will probably never be able to distinguish from archaeological targets without careful groundtruthing, often including excavation. Yet we can probably still expect improved remote sensing to speed up prospection and make our surveys more efficient.

New technologies for survey documentation will also become more widespread. Active GPS tracking of crew members, a technology already applied to tractors in high-tech agriculture, will document transect routes accurately, leading to better estimates of survey detection functions. Digital video and hand-held or wearable computers will increase the speed and detail of archaeological documentation (Ryan and van Leusen, n.d.; Ryan et al., 1997), and in future it may be possible to integrate GPS, internet access, and data logging in a single device. More sensitive GPS and Electronic Marker Systems (EMS), which involve inserting inexpensive passive antennas with polyethylene shells ("cyberstakes") into site deposits, will allow later researchers to relocate previously surveyed points easily and accurately (Topouzi et al., n.d.; Whitlam, 1998).

4. MATHEMATICAL APPROACHES TO SURVEY THEORY AND EVALUATION

Increasing attention to mathematical aspects of survey design, beyond the basic statistics of sampling, could have considerable impact in the years to come and especially in improving the productivity of surveys. Principal effects will be to optimize the distribution of survey effort with respect to surveys' goals and to allow more realistic evaluation of survey results.

4.1 Optimizing Surveys

Although there has been some progress in this area, especially in subsurface survey, up to now most archaeological surveys have been far from optimal in their balance between survey effort and discovery probability. In some cases discovery probabilities are vanishingly small, and slavish adherence to standardized sampling designs ignores the results of prior research and effectively wastes effort that could be invested more productively. In others, surveyors eschew sampling in favor of what they perceive as "total survey," failing to recognize the diminishing returns of increasing survey intensity or to realize that total survey of one small sector of space often results in no survey at all in some adjacent and equally important sector. One way or another, we will always "miss" some archaeological materials; the point is to detect and successfully recognize as many of them as possible given our restricted survey resources, or at least to make accurate assessments of any bias that remains.

Adapting and further developing some of the optimal search mathematics that researchers in other fields have introduced, along the lines of chapter 7 above, should improve our application of predictive modelling and allocation of survey effort to the large spaces we must survey in the shadow of urban development. We can be certain that Geographic Information Systems (GIS) will take on even more importance as our predictive models and survey designs become more sophisticated (Cardinali et al., 1997; Jacoli and Carrara, 1996).

The most fully developed approaches currently available come from operations research and depend heavily on Bayesian methods to make optimal allocation of effort. In future, we may not only find ourselves regularly applying these methods, where appropriate, but exploring other approaches to survey optimization, such as game theory, examining issues other than allocation and density of survey effort, and developing some theory of our own.

4.2 Evaluating Survey Results

At present, the result of most archaeological surveys is either a report on and interpretation of the archaeological materials actually found, or a set of estimates based on a subset of some target population. The problem with the first approach is that it gives us no inkling at all of how many or what kind of archaeological remains might remain undetected, while the problem with the second is that the estimates are often quite unrealistic.

In both cases, this presents the danger that development will proceed unhindered in areas "certified" as free of significant archaeological resources, not to mention that we will have unrealistic ideas about settlement pattern and other aspects of spatial structure and biased estimates of attributes of the archaeological record.

A critical development that must take place in future is for surveys routinely to include evaluation of their own results and methods, and not only of the archaeological resources themselves. As emphasized in chapter 10, it is only through evaluation of their detection probabilities — really detection functions — that we can provide accurate estimates of the parameters of archaeological populations or ensure that any spatial patterns we identify are not just artifacts of our survey methods. Simply multiplying the number of discovered sites by the reciprocal of the nominal sampling fraction, for example, provides only a naïve and optimistic underestimate. Many methods for improving the accuracy of these estimates are already available, and archaeologists should be using them.

5. CONCLUSION

Archaeological survey is uniquely suited to investigation of archaeological distributions over regions and past use of landscapes. It is also our prime weapon in the fight to protect and manage archaeological heritage. It behooves us to develop it as a method to the fullest of its potential.

Over the last two decades, there have been steps toward applying survey more intensively, in more kinds of environments, and with new technologies, yet there has been little *theoretical* advance in archaeological survey since the 1970s. Now is the time for us to redress this imbalance.

Appendix 1
Health, Safety, and Practical Matters in Field Survey

Like any fieldwork, archaeological survey entails many logistical and practical considerations, not least of which are the health and safety of survey team members.

1. HEALTH AND SAFETY IN FIELD SURVEY

Fieldwork can be exhilarating, tiring, uncomfortable, and amusing. It can also be dangerous. Survey teams should be prepared for all reasonable contingencies and trained to avoid hazards (Mercer, 1985; Poirier and Feder, 2001).

1.1 Notifying Landowners and Relevant Authorities or Agencies

Prior to beginning a survey, team leaders should ensure that relevant authorities and agencies, such as the local Police, Coast Guard, Park Rangers, mountain rescue, marine rescue and local hospitals are aware of the surveyors' presence. Police or search-and-rescue services should know in what area the survey will take place. A local hospital or doctor should be aware of any special health risks that may affect any of the team, such as allergies.

In addition, team members' presence should not be a surprise to landowners or agricultural workers who find them walking across their fields. It is a good idea to use local publicity, such as newspapers or radio stations, to alert people to the survey and keep them informed as it progresses. Where surveyors need to work on private property, the team leader should seek the owners' permission. If there is any possibility of game hunting (even out-of-season) where the survey takes place, it is critical that potential hunters are aware that archaeologists are present. Survey during hunting season is out of the question in these cases.

In some survey regions, there may even be a danger of wandering into military restricted zones. Here it is essential to alert military authorities to surveyors' presence, and it may be necessary to seek security clearance before beginning the survey. Probably this will also affect the boundaries of the survey by making some areas inaccessible.

1.2 Educating Team Members

Team members should be instructed in the safe use of all equipment and materials with which they will come into contact, and should be informed of the risks associated with the survey, such as the risk of snake-bite in some areas, hunters, falls, or twisted ankles in others. Teams should stick closely to planned survey routes but, in the event that anyone gets lost, everyone should have a compass and know some highly visible local landmarks. It pays to agree on advance on where to meet should anyone get separated.

1.3 First-Aid

At least one member of each survey team should carry a First-Aid kit and all team members should know how to use it, and preferably should have some formal First-Aid training. Surveyors should try to anticipate what kinds of injuries are most likely to occur and be ready for them. Sprains and abrasions from falls are commonly among these; broken bones are less common but they do happen.

1.4 Communication

Team members should not work alone, but in pairs or groups. If possible, each group should have a cellular phone or radio unless the survey is in an area where telephones and transportation are readily available. Where this is impossible or impractical, issuing whistles is a good idea. The telephone numbers of a local hospital, police station, and the project base camp or house should accompany cell phones.

1.5 Preparation for Weather

Unless surveyors are prepared for it, bad weather can result in both illness and poor morale. All crew members should have adequate rain gear or warm clothing where rain and cold can be expected. At the other extreme, in hot, sunny weather, crew members should carry and drink large quantitites of water and wear hats and sun screen to protect themselves from sunburn. Most archaeologists underestimate their risk of dehydration, sunstroke or heat prostration and rarely drink enough water. Where high ultraviolet levels are a risk, make sure sunglasses that team members wear are adequate. In intertidal and underwater survey, crew members need to be particularly watchful for storms, and should have reliable means for making their escape and calling for assistance should a sudden storm come on.

Health, Safety, and Practical Matters 237

1.6 Risk of Encountering High-voltage Lines, Toxic Waste or Explosives

In some regions, survey planning must anticipate the possibility of encountering dangerous materials, especially if the survey involves sub-surface testing of some kind. Particularly in or near urban centers, contacting utility companies should precede any sub-surface testing, whether by augering or test excavations, to avoid accidental interception of high-voltage lines or gas pipes. In addition to the health hazard that such encounters would entail, cutting a power line or gas line would lead to costly penalties or litigation. The project director should telephone the utilities and ask them to flag any buried lines that might occur in the area he or she plans to survey.

In some cases buried toxic waste is also a possibility and, unfortunately, this will not necessarily be documented. Illegal waste dumps can occur in unexpected locations, but the current or past presence of a chemical industry near the survey area is a clue that illegal dumping or industrial contamination could have taken place some time in the past.

Even the presence of unexploded ammunition or mines is a possibility you sometimes need to anticipate. If surveying in a former war zone or on a military base, you will need to find out from local military authorities whether there is any risk of encountering explosives.

1.7 Risks from Animals or Disease

In some regions, there is real risk of animal attack or encountering disease vectors. In Alaska and northern Canada, for example, bear attacks are a real possibility, and so survey crews must carry appropriate firearms to protect themselves from attack. In tropical and desert regions, venomous snakes, scorpions, spiders, and centipedes are potential risks. Crew members need to be prepared to minimize their chance of bites, as well as to deal with bites should they occur. Furthermore, some regions where archaeological surveys take place pose risks of malaria or other diseases that use mosquitoes or ticks as vectors. Where ticks, for example, are a risk and survey involves walking through thick or high vegetation, team members should check themselves frequently for ticks.

1.8 Risk from Hunters or Military Activity

When surveying forested regions where deer, for example, are hunted, crew members need to be cautious and wear bright clothing that will make it easier for hunters to distinguish them from prey. Even if survey does not take place during hunting season, surveyors need to anticipate the possibility of illegal hunting.

In some regions, there could even be danger of gunshot injuries if surveyors accidentally wander into restricted areas where there are military exercises, or when survey takes place in a region with a history of political unrest. Wars can break out with very little warning, but using a radio to keep informed of local news, and making sure the embassay (for out-of-country surveys) is aware of the project, can help to ensure that crew members can get out before the survey area becomes a war zone. The best way to avoid wandering onto rifle ranges or other restricted areas is to ensure that military authorities are aware of the survey plans.

1.9 Insurance

Even when every precaution has been taken, accidents and illness can happen. That is why it is necessary to insure the project for liability unless it is already covered through an insured sponsoring institution, such as a university or CRM company. It is also a good idea for team members to sign waivers after being informed of the survey's anticipated risks to show that they understand the survey conditions and undertake to avoid unnecessary risks.

2. OUTFITTING THE SURVEY CREW

We shold not expect team members to do good surveys if they are ill-equipped for it, and planning ahead for their needs can save much time in the field.

2.1 Personal Gear and Bad-weather Gear

It is important to ensure that team members have clothing and other gear adequate to the circumstances they can expect to encounter, and especially to protect their health and safety. Footwear is obviously important in pedestrian survey, and team members should select boots that help protect ankles from sprains in rough terrain or from snakebite where that is a risk. Survey in hot, arid climates usually requires sunscreen and other protection from sunburn, such as hats, as well as UV protection for the eyes. Where serious rainstorms, sandstorms, or even snowstorms are a possibility, teams should be prepared for them and have contingencies for sudden weather changes that force them to quit survey early. It is also important to be able to protect equipment and records from bad weather.

2.2 Mapping and Recording Instruments

A large variety of tools and supplies can facilitate survey. Search teams require means for locating themselves in space, such as Global Positioning Systems (GPS) or at least compasses and maps, as well as someone proficient in their use. They may also require pin-flags or stakes to lay out transects, and tapes or "chains" to set the intervals between transects. Survey recording teams usually must have cameras, notebooks or hand-held computers, maps in waterproof map pages, and tapes for measuring features or sites. All survey teams would find it useful to carry some pin-flags, large nails or something similar to pin down the end of a tape while taking measurements.

2.3 Sampling Equipment and Supplies

Collecting teams at the very least need sturdy bags, such as cloth ones that sharp lithics will not cut through, small plastic "zip-loc" bags for individual artifacts, and tags or some other means (e.g., bar codes) for labelling collected samples.

Subsurface surveys require excavation equipment to remove sod and leaf litter or to penetrate buried deposits. They usually also require screens with which to sieve removed sediments in search of small or unobtrusive artifacts.

In addition, surveys that collect sediments, such as cores or thin-section samples, require excavation, augering or coring equipment and appropriate holders for the samples. For example, Kubiena boxes (small metal boxes) may be necessary for small blocks of sediment that you will later use for thin sections.

2.4 Safety Equipment

Each survey team should carry or be close to a First-Aid kit. Bandages, tensor bandages, and disinfectant are the items that tend to be most in demand. Some survey circumstances entail risks that call for specific safety preparations. Survey on construction sites or some kinds of industrial areas may require steel-toed boots, hard-hats or even fire-retardant clothing. Today, a cell-phone is invaluable as a safety tool in regions with cell coverage, allowing calls for medical help from quite remote areas in many cases.

In regions where bear attacks are a possibility, at least one team member needs to carry a shotgun and be trained to use it properly and safely. In most places, this team member also needs a licence to carry it.

3. CREW TRAINING AND ORIENTATION

As noted already in chapter 3, crew members who lack adequate training or experience, or who do not understand project goals, are not likely to carry out good surveys.

At the beginning of each field season or whenever new crew members join a project, an orientation meeting can go a long way toward ensuring that a survey works well. Everyone should know their own and others' roles in the project and to whom they should turn should they need advice or encounter a problem. It should be clear how to resolve differences of opinion over procedures or other issues. Importantly, everyone should know what the project goals are and be at least somewhat familiar with any previous work, such as an earlier survey of the same region, that might be relevant.

New team members usually require training in the methods and equipment that the project will use. This can include training in practical matters, such as the use of a GPS receiver or the proper way to lay out quadrats or transects. It might also include some basic statistical training, such as ways to generate random samples or to estimate the size of collections they should make at sites. In some cases it might involve basic First-Aid training, the safe handling of firearms, or the operation of a vehicle.

Importantly, team members must also be familiar with the materials they are expected to find and, if possible, the environmental circumstances of the places they will survey. Showing new team members what kinds of artifacts they are likely to encounter, and training them how to recognize important attributes on them, will usually improve their recovery of these items. It is also useful to show them non-artifactual items that could be confused with artifacts. Going over maps and aerial photographs or briefing them so that they know what kinds of topography, sediments, and vegetation to expect is also very helpful. One of the nice things about survey is that there are always surprises, but a good familiarity with the usual lie of the land makes it easier to notice surprising landforms, some of which might be cultural in origin.

Bibliography

Aberg, A., and Lewis, C., eds., 2000. *The Rising Tide: Archaeology and Coastal Landscapes.* Oxbow Books, Oxford.
Adams, R. McC., 1965. *Land Behind Baghdad: A History of Settlement on the Diyala Plains.* University of Chicago Press, Chicago.
— 1981. *Heartland of Cities: Surveys of Ancient Settlements and Land Use of the Central Floodplains of the Euphrates.* University of Chicago Press, Chicago.
Adams, R. M., and Nissen, H. J., 1972. *The Uruk Countryside: The Natural Setting of Urban Societies.* University of Chicago Press, Chicago.
Adams, W. Y., and Adams, E. W., 1991. *Archaeological typology and Practical reality, A Dialectical Approach to Artifact Classification and Sorting.* Cambridge University Press, Cambridge.
Agocs, W. B., 1955. Line-spacing effect and determination of optimum spacing illustrated by the Marmora, Ontario, magnetic anomaly. *Geophysics* B20:870-885.
Aikens, C. M., Loy, W. G., Southard, M. D. and Hanes, R. C., 1977. *Remote Sensing: A Handbook for Archeologists and Cultural Resource Managers.* Cultural Resource Management Division, National Park Service, Washington, DC.
Aitken, M. J., 1974. *Physics and Archaeology.* Oxford University Press, Oxford.
Alexander, D.A., 1983. The limitations of traditional surveying techniques in a forested environment. *Journal Of Field Archaeology* 10:177-186.
Algaze, G., 1993. *The Uruk World System. The Dynamics of Expansion of Early Mesopotamian Civilization.* University of Chicago Press, Chicago.
Allen, J. R. L., and Fulford, M. G., 1986. The Wentlooge Level: A Romano-British saltmarsh reclamation in southeast Wales. *Britannia* 17:91-117.
Allen, M. J., 1988. *Archaeological and environmental aspects of colluviation in south-west England.* In Man-Made Soils, edited by w.Groenman-van Wateringe, and M.Robinson, pp. 67-92. British Archaeological Reports, Oxford.
— 1991. *Analysing the landscape: A geographical approach to archaeological problems.* In Interpreting Artefact Scatters: Contributions to Ploughzone Archaeology, edited by A.J. Schofield, pp. 39-57. Oxbow Books, Oxford.
Almgren, O., 1914. De pågående undersökningarna om Sveriges första bebyggelse. *Fornvännen* 9:1-16.
Altschul, J. H., 1990. Red flag models: The use of modelling in management contexts. In *Interpreting Space: GIS and Archaeology*, edited by K. M. S. Allen, S. W. Green, and E. B. W. Zubrow, pp. 226-238.
Ammerman, A. J., 1981 Surveys and Archaeological Research. *Annual Review of Anthropology* 10:63-88.
— 1985. Plow-Zone Experiments in Calabria, Italy. *Journal of Field Archaeology* 12:33-40.

Ammerman, A. J., and Bonardi, S., 1981. Recent developments in the study of Neolithic settlement in Calabria. In *Archaeology and Italian Society*, edited by G. Barker and R. Hodges, pp. 335-342. BAR International Series 102. British Archaeological Reports, Oxford.

Arnold, B., 1986. *Cortaillod-Est: Un Village du Bronze Final, No. 1: Fouille Subaquatique et Photographie Aérienne*. Éditions Ruau, Sainte-Blaisé.

Asch, D. L., 1975. On sample size problems and the uses of nonprobabilistic sampling. In *Sampling in Archaeology*, edited by J. W. Mueller, pp. 170-191. University of Arizona Press, Tucson.

Ashmore, P. J., 1994. *Archaeology and the Coastal Erosion Zone: Towards a Historic Scotland Policy*. Historic Scotland, Edinburgh.

Atkinson, R. J. C., 1953. *Field Archaeology*. Methuen, London.

Ballard, R. D., Hiebert, F. T., Coleman, D. F., Ward, C., Smith, J., Willis, K., Foley, B., Croff, K., Major, C., and Torre, F., 2001. Deepwater Archaeology of the Black Sea: The 2000 Season at Sinop, Turkey. *American Journal of Archaeology* 105:607-623.

Bakkevig, S., 1980. Phosphate analysis in archaeology — problems and recent progress. *Norwegian Archaeological Review* 13:1-100.

Banning, E. B., 1982, The research design of the Wadi Ziqlab Survey, 1981. *American Schools of Oriental Research Newsletter* 8:4-8.

— 1985. *Pastoral and Agricultural Land Use in the Wadi Ziqlab, Jordan: An Archaeological and Ecological Survey*. Ph. D. thesis, University of Toronto.

— 1988. Methodology. In *The Wadi el Hasa Archaeological Survey 1979-1983, West-Central Jordan*, edited by MacDonald, B., pp. 13-25. Wilfred Laurier Press, Waterloo, Canada.

— 1996. Highlands and lowlands: Problems and survey frameworks for rural archaeology in the Near East. *Bulletin of the American Schools of Oriental Research* 301:25-45.

— 2000, *Archaeological Laboratory Analysis*. Plenum/Kluwer Academic Press, New York.

— 2002, Archaeological survey as optimal search. In *Archaeological Informatics: Pushing the Envelope. CAA2001 Computer Applications and Quantitative Methods in Archaeology Proceedings of the 29th Conference, Gotland, April 2001*, edited by G. Burenhult and J. Arvidsson, pp. 341-350. BAR International Series S1016. Archaeopress, Oxford.

Banning, E. B., and Fawcett, C., 1983. Man-land relationships in the ancient Wadi Ziqlab: Report of the 1981 survey. *Annual of the Department of Antiquities of Jordan* 27:291-309.

Banning, E. B., Rahimi, D., and Siggers, J., 1994. The Late Neolithic of the southern Levant: Hiatus, settlement shift or observer bias? The perspective from Wadi Ziqlab. *Paléorient* 20:151-164.

Bartlett, M. S., 1954. Processus stochastique ponctuels. *Annales de l'Institut Poincaré* 14:35-60.

— 1963. The spectral analysis of point processes. *Journal of the Royal Statistical Society* B25:264-281.

— 1964. The spectral analysis of two-dimensional point processes. *Biometrika* 51:299-311.

Bar-Yosef, O., and Goren, N., 1980. Afterthoughts following prehistoric surveys in the Levant. *Israel Exploration Journal* 30:1-16.

BCRIC, 2000. *British Columbia Archaeological Inventory Guidelines*. Archaeology Branch, Culture Task Force, Resources Inventory Committee, Ministry of Small Business, Tourism and Culture, Government Publications Centre, Victoria. [http://www.for.gov.bc.ca/ric/Pubs/Culture/arch/index.htm].

Bell, M., 1983. Valley sediments as evidence of prehistoric land-use on the South Downs. *Proceedings of the Prehistoric Society* 49:119-150.

— 1993. Intertidal archaeology at Goldcliff in the Severn Estuary. In *A Spirit of Inquiry: Essays for Ted Wright*, edited by J. Coles, V. Fenwick, and G. Hutchinson, pp. 9-13. Warp, Exeter.

Bell, M., Caseldine, A., and Neumann, H., 2000. *Prehistoric Intertidal Archaeology in the Welsh Severn Estuary.* CBA Research Report 120, Oxbow Books, Oxford.

Bell, R. E., and Gettys, M., n.d. A consideration of the archaeological and historical resources involved in the Mid-Ark project. Manuscript on deposit, Arkansas Archaeological Society, cited in Moratto and Kelley, 1978.

Bellerby, T. J., Noel, M., and Brannigan, K., 1992. Recent developments in thermal archaeological prospection. In *Geoprospection in the Archaeological Landscape*, edited by P. Spoerry, pp. 101-111.

Bernick, K., ed., 1998. *Hidden Dimensions: The Cultural Significance of Wetland Archaeology.* University of British Columbia Press, Vancouver.

Berry, B. J. L., 1961. City size distribution and economic development. *Economic Development and Cultural Change* 9:573-588.

Bewley, R. H., and Rackowski, W., eds., 2001. *Aerial Archaeology, Developing Future Practice.* NATO Science Series I.337. IOS Press, Amsterdam.

Binford, L. R., 1964. A consideration of archaeological research design. *American Antiquity* 29:425-444.

— 1982. The archaeology of place. *Journal of Anthropological Archaeology* 1:5-31.

Birk, D., 1994. When rivers were roads; Deciphering the role of canoe portages in the western Lake Superior fur trade. In *The Fur Trade Revisited: Selected Papers of the Sixth North American Fur Trade Conference, Mackinac Island, Michigan, 1991*, edited by J.S.H Brown, W.J. Eccles, and D.P. Heldman, pp.359-376. Michigan State University Press and Mackinac Island State Park Commission, East Lansing, MI.

Blackham, M., 2000. Distinguishing bioturbation and trampling using pottery sherd measures, Tell Fendi, Jordan. *Geoarchaeology* 15:469-497.

Blake, V. S., 1991. Remote sensing in underwater archaeology.*Science and Archaeology* 33:3-17.

Bloemaker, J. D., and Oakley, C. B., 1999. The firebreak plow and subsurface site discovery. *Journal of Field Archaeology* 26:75-82.

Boismier, W. A., 1991. the role of research design in surface collection: An example from Broom Hill, Braishfield, Hampshire. In *Interpreting Artefact Scatters: Contributions to Ploughzone Archaeology*, edited by A. J. Schofield, pp. 11-25. Oxbow, Oxford.

Borlase, W., 1753. Of the great alterations which the Islands of Scilly have undergone since the time of the ancients. Philosophical Transactions of the Royal Society 48:55-67.

— 1756. *Observations on the Ancient and Present State of the Islands of Scilly, and their importance to the trade of Great-Britain.* Fletcher, Clements, and Parker, Oxford.

Bowden, M., ed., 1999. *Unravelling the Landscape, An Inquisitive Approach to Archaeology.* Tempus Publishing, Stroud, Gloucestershire.

Bowden, M., Ford, S., Gaffney, V. L., and Tingle, M., 1991. Skimming the surface or scraping the barrel: A few observations on the nature of surface and sub-surface archaeology. In *Interpreting Artefact Scatters: Contributions to Ploughzone Archaeology*, edited by A. J. Schofield, pp. 107-113. Oxbow, Oxford.

Boyd-Dawkins, W., 1872. Ancient geography of the west of England. *Proceedings of the Somersetshire Archaeological and Natural History Society* 1:27-30.

Brooks, I. A., Levine, L. D., and Dennell, R. W., 1982. Alluvial sequence in central west Iran and implications for archaeological survey. *Journal of Field Archaeology* 9:285-299.

de la Broquiere, B., 1457. *Le Voyage d'Outremere de Bertrandon de la Broquiere,* edited by C. Schafer. Ernest Leroux, Paris, 1892.

Brown, A., 1987. *Fieldwork for Archaeologists and Local Historians.* Batsford, London.

Buck, C. E., , and Cavanagh, W. G., and Litton, C. D., 1996. *Bayesian Approach to Interpreting Archaeological Data.* John Wiley & Sons, New York.

Buckingham, J. S., 1821. *Travels in Palestine, Through the Countries of Bashan and Gilead, East of the River Jordan: Including a Visit to the Cities of Geraza and Gamala in the Decapolis.* Longman, Hurst, Rees, Orme, and Brown, London.

— 1825. *Travels among the Arab Tribes Inhabiting the Countries East of Syria and Palestine, Including a Journey from Nazareth to the Mountains Beyond the Dead Sea, and from thence through the Plains of the Hauran to Bozra, Damascus, Tripoly, Lebanon, Baalbeck, and by the Valley of the Orontes to Seleucia, Antioch, and Aleppo.* Longman, Hurst, Rees, Orme, Brown, and Green, London.

Buckley, V. M., and Sweetman, P. D., 1991. *Archaeological Survey of County Louth.* Dublin.

Burckhardt, J. L., 1822. *Travels in Syria and the Holy Land.* John Murray, London.

— 1829. *Travels in Arabia.* Henry Colburn, London.

Butler, W. B., 1979. The no-collection strategy in archaeology. *American Antiquity* 44:795-799.

— 1987. Significance and other frustrations in the CRM process. *American Antiquity* 52:820-829.

Cardarelli, R., 1924. Confini fra orbetello e Marsiliana; fra Port' Ecole e Monte Argentario (28 dicembra 1508-2 marzo 1510). *Maremma* 1:131-142, 155-186, 205-224.

— 1925. Confini fra orbetello e Marsiliana; fra Port' Ecole e Monte Argentario (28 dicembra 1508-2 marzo 1510). *Maremma* 2:3-36, 75-128, 147-213.

Cardinali, M., Carla, R., Carrara, A., Jacoli, M., and Verardi, G., 1997. Remote sensing, GIS technology and predictive models in investigating archaeological sites: The case studies of western Nepal and southern Italy. *Proceedings of the Third Annual Meeting of the European Association of Archaeologists, Ravenna, Sept. 24-28, 1997.*

Carmichael, David L. 1990. GIS predictive modelling of prehistoric site distributions in central Montana. In *Interpreting Space: GIS and Archaeology*, edited by K. M. S. Allen, S. W. Green, and E. B. W. Zubrow, pp. 216-225. Taylor and Francis, New York.

Carr, C., 1982, *Handbook on Soil Resistivity Surveying: Interpretation of data from Earthen Archaeological Sites.* Illinois Center for American Archeology, Evanston, IL.

— 1985. Introductory remarks on regional analysis. In *For Concordance in Archaeological Analysis: bridging Data Structure, Quantitative Technique, and Theory*, edited by C. Carr, pp. 114-127. Westport, Kansas City.

Cavanagh, W. G., Hirst, S., and Litton, C. D., 1988. Soil phosphate, site boundaries, and change point analysis. *Journal of Field Archaeology* 15:67-83.

Cavanagh, W. G., and Laxton, R. R., 1994. The fractal dimension, rank-size, and the interpretation of archaeological survey data. In *Methods in the Mountains: Proceedings of UISPP Commission IV Meeting, Mount Victoria, Australia, August 1993*, edited by I. Johnson, pp. 61-64.

— 1995. The rank-size dimension and the history of site structure from survey data. *Quantitative Archaeology* 5:327-58.

Chapman, J. C., 1981. *The value of Dalmatian museum collections to Dalmatian settlement studies.* In The Research Potential of Anthropological Museum Collections, edited by A.M. Cantwell, J.B. Griffin, and N.A. Rothschild, pp. 529-555. New York Academy of Sciences, New York.

Cherry, J. F., 1983. Frogs round the pond: Perspectives on current archaeological survey projects in the Mediterranean region. In *Archaeological Survey in the Mediterranean Area*, edited by D. R. Keller and D. W. Rupp, pp. 375-416. BAR International Series 155:375-416. British Archaeological Reports, Oxford.

— 1984. Common sense in Mediterranean survey? *Journal of Field Archaeology* 11:117-120.

Christaller, W., 1933. *Die zentralen Orte in Süddeutschland: eine okonomisch-geographische Untersuchung über die Gesetzmassigkeit der Verbreitung und Entwicklung der Siedlungen mit stadtischen Funktionen*. Translated by C. W. Baskin as *Central Places in Southern Germany*. C. W. Baskin, Englewood Cliffs, NJ, 1966.

CHSOAHP, 1998. *Colorado Cultural Resource Survey Manual 1, The Steps*. Colorado Historical Socielty, Office of Archaeology and Historic Preservation.

Chung, C. F., 1981. Application of the Buffon needle problem and its extensions to parallel-line search sampling schemes. *Journal of Mathematical Geology* 13:371-390.

Clark, A. J., 1977. Geophysical and chemical assessment of air photographic sites. *Archaeological Journal* 134:189-193.

Clarke, W. G., 1922. *Our Homeland Prehistoric Antiquities and How to Study Them*. The Homeland Association, London.

Clay, R. C. C., 1927. Some prehistoric ways. *Antiquity* 1:54-65.

Cliff, A. D., and Ord, J. K., 1973. *Spatial Autocorrelation*. London.

Cochran, W. G., 1963. *Sampling Techniques* (2nd ed.). John Wiley, New York.

Codrington, T., 1869. the superficial deposits of South Hampshire and the Isle of Wight. *Quarterly Journal of the Geological Society* 26:528-548.

Coles, J. M., and Lawson, A. J., eds., 1987. *European Wetlands in Prehistory*. Clarendon Press, Oxford.

Conder, C. R., 1889. *The Survey of Eastern Palestine: Memoirs of the Topography, Orography, Hydrography, Archaeology, etc.*, volume 1. Committee of the Palestine Exploration Fund, London.

Conyers, L. B. and Cameron, C.M., 1998. Ground-penetrating Radar techniques and three-dimensional computer mapping in the American Southwest. *Journal of Field Archaeology* 25:417-430.

Cook, S. F., and Heizer, R. F., 1965. *Studies on the Chemical Analysis of Archaeological Sites*. University of California Press, Berkeley.

la Cour, V., 1927. *Sjællands ældste Bygder*. Copenhagen.

Cowgill, G., 1975. A selection of samplers: Comments on archaeo-statistics. In Mueller, J. W. (ed.), *Sampling in Archaeology*. University of Arizona, Tucson: 258-274.

Cox C., 1992. Satellite imagery, aerial photography and wetland archaeology: An interim report on an application of remote sensing to wetland archaeology: The pilot study in Cumbria, England. *World Archaeology* 24: 249-267.

Cox, E. W., 1894. Traces of submerged lands on the coasts of Lancashire, Cheshire and North Wales. *Transactions of the Historical Society of Lancashire and Cheshire* 110:42-49.

Cozzolino, J. M., 1972. Sequential search for an unknown number of objects of nonuniform size. *Operations Research* 20:293-308.

Crawford, O. G. S., 1927. Lyonesse. *Antiquity* 1:5-14.

— 1929. *Air-photography for Archaeologists*. Ordnance Survey, H.M. Stationery Office, London.

— 1953, *Archaeology in the Field*. London.

Curwen, E. C., 1927. Prehistoric agriculture in Britain. *Antiquity* 1:261-289.

Cushing, F. H., 1890. Preliminary notes on the origin, working hypotheses and preliminary researches of the Hemenway Expedition. In *Seventh International Congress of Americanists*, pp. 151-194. Berlin.

Custer J.F., Eveleigh T., Klemas V., and Wells I., 1986. Application of LANDSAT data and synoptic remote sensing to predictive models for prehistoric archaeological sites: An example from the Delaware coastal plain. *American Anthropologist* 51:572-588.

Dabas, M., Delétang, H., Ferdière, A., Jung, C., and Zimmermann, W. H., 1998. *La Prospection*. Éditions Errance, Paris.

Dahlin, Bruce H. and Pope, Kevin O., 1989. Ancient Maya wetland agriculture: New insights from ecological and remote sensing research. *Journal of Field Archaeology* 16:87-106.

Van Dalen, J., 1999. Probability modelling: A Bayesian and a Geometric example. In *Geographical Information Systems and Landscape Archaeology*, edited by M. Gillings, D. Mattingly, and J. van Dalen, pp. 117-124. Oxbow Books, Oxford.

Dancey, W. S., 1998. The value of surface archaeological data in exploring the dynamics of community evolution in the middle Ohio Valley. In *Surface Archaeology*, edited by Sullivan, A. P., pp. 3-19. University of New Mexico Press, Albuquerque.

Darwin, C., 1882. *The Formation of Vegetable Mould, through the Action of Worms with Observations on their Habits.* John Murray, London.

Dassié, J., 1978. *Manuel d'Archéologie Aerienne.* Editions TECHNIP, Paris.

Davies, W., and Astill, G., 1994. *The East Brittany Survey: Fieldwork and Field Data.* Aldershot, Hampshire.

Deagan, K. A., 1989. The search for La Navidad, Columbus' 1492 settlement. In *First Encounters: Spanish Explorations in the Caribbean and the United States, 1492-1570*, edited by Milanich, J. T., and Milbrath, S. , pp. 41-54. University of Florida Press, Gainesville

Deming, W. G., 1950. *Some Theory of Sampling.* Dover Publications, New York.

Department of the Environment, 1980. Fieldwalking as a Method of Archaeological Research. Occasional Paper 2. HMSO, London.

Deuel, L., 1969. *Flights into Yesterday.* Macdonald, New York.

Dobbie, J. M., 1968. A survey of search theory. *Operations Research* 16: 525-537.

Drennan, R. D., 1996. *Statistics for Archaeologists: A Commonsense Approach.* Plenum Press, New York.

Drew, L. J., 1967. Grid-drilling exploration and its application to the search for petroleum. *Economic Geology* 62:698-710.

— 1979. Pattern drilling exploration: Optimum pattern types and hole spacings when searching for elliptical shaped targets. *Mathematical Geology* 11:223-254.

Dixon, K. A., 1977. Applications of archaeological resources: Broadening the basis of significance. In *Conservation Archaeology: A Guide for Cultural Resource Management Studies*, edited by M. B. Schiffer and G. J. Gumerman, pp. 277-290. Academic Press, New York.

Drewett, P. L., 1999. *Field Archaeology, An Introduction.* UCL Press, London.

Dunbar, J. S., Webb, S. D., Faught, M., Anuskiewicz, R. J., and Stright, M. J., 1989. Archaeological sites in the drowned Tertiary karst region of the eastern Gulf of Mexico. In *Underwater Archaeology*, edited by Arnold, J. B., pp. 25-31. Proceedings of the Society for Historical Archaeology Conference, Baltimore, Maryland.

Dunnell, R. C., 1988. Low-density archaeological records from plowed surfaces: Some preliminary considerations. *American Archaeology* 7:29-38.

Dunnell, R. C., and Dancey, W. S., 1983. The siteless survey: A regional scale data collection strategy. *Advances in Archaeological Method and Theory* 6: 267-287.

Dyson, S. L., 1978. Settlement patterns in the *Ager Cosanus*: The Wesleyan University Survey, 1974-1976. *Journal of Field Archaeology* 5:251-268.

Ebert, J. I., 1984. Remote Sensing Applications In Archaeology. *Advances in Archaeological Method and Theory* 7:293-353.

— 1992, *Distributional Archaeology.* University of New Mexico Press, Albuquerque, NM.

Ebert, J. I. and Lyons, T. R., 1976, *The role of remote sensing in a regional archaeological research design: a case study.* In Remote Sensing Experiments in Cultural Resource Studies, edited by Lyons, T. R., pp. ?? University of New Mexico, Albuquerque.

Edwards, P. C., Macumber, P. G., and Head, J., 1996. The Early Epipalaeolithic of Wadi al-Hammeh. *Levant* 28:115-130.

Eidt, R. C., 1973, A rapid chemical field test for archaeological site surveying. *American Antiquity* 38:206-210.
— 1977, Detection and examination of anthrosols by phosphate analysis. *Science* 197:1327-1333.
— 1984. *Advances in Abandoned Settlement Analysis: Application to Prehistoric Anthrosols in Columbia, South America.* Center for Latin America, University of Wisconsin, Milwaukee, WI.
El-Baz F., 1997. Space age archaeology. *Scientific American* 277 (2):40-45.
Ellis, R. M., and Blackwell, J. G., 1959. Optimum prospecting plans in mineral exploration. *Geophysics* 24:344-358.
Everson, P., and Williamson, T., eds. 1998. *The Archaeology of Landscape. Studies Presented to Christopher Taylor.* Manchester University Press, Manchester.
Ewen, C. R., 1986. Fur Trade Archaeology: A Study of Frontier Hierarchies. *Historical Archaeology* 20:15-27.
Fagan, B., 1988. *Archaeology: A Brief Introduction.* Scott Foresman and Co., Glenview.
Fairbanks, C. H., 1970. Archeology and history of coastal Georgia. In *Conference on the Future of the Marshlands and Islands of Georgia,* edited by D. Maney, F. Marland, and C. West, pp. 35-45. Atlanta.
Falconer, S. E., 1994. Village economy and society in the Jordan Valley: A study of Bronze Age rural complexity. In *Archaeological Views from the Countryside: Village Communities in Early Complex Societies,* edited by G. M. Schwartz and S. E. Falconer, pp. 121-142. Smithsonian Institution Press, Washington.
Falconer, S. E., and Savage, S., 1995. Heartlands and Hinterlands: Alternative Trajectories of Early Urbanization in Mesopotamia and the Southern Levant. American Antiquity 60:37-58.
Fassbinder, J. W., and Irlinger, W., eds., 1999. *Archaeological Prospection: Third International Conference on Archaeological Prospection.* Arbeitsheft, Bayerisches Landesamt für Denkmalpflege. Bayerisches Landesamt für Denkmalpflege, Munich.
Fasham, P. J., Shadla-Hall, R. T., Shennan, S. J., and Bates, P. J., 1980. *Fieldwalking for Archaeologists.* Andover, Hampshire.
Faught, M., Donoghue, J. F., 1997. Marine Inundated Archaeological Sites and Paleofluvial Systems: Examples from a Karst Controlled Continental Shelf Setting in the Apalachee Bay, Northeastern Gulf of Mexico. *Geoarchaeology* 12:417-458.
FBHP, 1990. *The Historic Preservation Compliance Review Program of the Florida Department of State Division of Historical Resources: A guide to the Historic Preservation Provisions of State and Federal Envrionmental Review Laws.* Bureau of Historic Preservation, Division of Historical Resources, Florida.
Fedick, S. L., Morrison, B., Andersen, B., Boucher, S., Acosta, A., and Matthews, J., 2000. Wetland manipulatin in the Yalahau region of the northern Maya Lowlands. *Journal of Field Archaeology* 27:131-152.
Fedje, D. W., and Christensen, T., 1999. Modeling paleoshorelines and locating early Holocene coastal sites in Haida Gwaii. *American Antiquity* 64:635-652.Fedje, D. W., and Christensen, T., 1999. Modeling paleoshorelines and locating early Holocene coastal sites in Haida Gwaii. *American Antiquity* 64:635-652.
Felgate, M., 2002. A Roviana ceramic sequence and the prehistory of Near Oceania: Work in progress. In *The Archaeology of the Lapita Dispersal in Oceania: Papers from the 4th Lapita Conference, June 2000, Canberra, Australia,* edited by G. R. Clark, A. J. Anderson, and T. Vunidilo, pp. 39-60. terra australis 17. Pandanus Press and Research School of Pacific and Asian Studies, Australian National University, Canberra.

Ferguson K.P., Tanis F.J., and Tyler W.A., 1987. SPOT Bathymetric image for archaeological investigations. In *Proceedings of the 21st International Symposium of Remote Sensing of the Environment*, edited by xxx, pages 863-866. Ann Arbor, Michigan.

Ferris, N., 1998. "I don't think we're in Kansas anymore...": The rise of the archaeological consulting industry in Ontario. In *Bringing Back the Past: Historical Perspectives on Canadian Archaeology*, edited by J. Smith and D. Mitchell, pp. 225-247. Mercury Series 158. Canadian Museum of Civilization, Hull, Québec.

Field, J., and Banning, E. B., 1998. Hillslope processes and archaeology in Wadi Ziqlab, Jordan. *Geoarchaeology* 13:595-616.

Fish, P. R., 1978. Consistency in archaeological measurement and classification. *American Antiquity* 43:86-89.

Fish, S. K., Fish, P. R., and Madsen, J. H., 1990. Analyzing regional agriculture: A Hohokam example. In *The Archaeology of Regions: A Case for Full-Coverage Survey*, edited by S. K. Fish and S. A. Kowalewski, pp. 189-218. Smithsonian Institution Press, Washington, DC.

Fish, S. K., and Kowalewski, S. A., eds., 1990. *The Archaeology of Regions: A Case for Full-Coverage Survey*. Smithsonian Institution Press, Washington, DC.

Flannery, K. V., 1972. The cultural evolution of civilizations. *Annual Review of Ecology and Systematics* 3:399-426.

— 1976. Empirical determination of site catchments in Oaxaca and Tehuacán. In *The Early Mesoamerican Village*, edited by K. V. Flannery, pp. 103-117. Academic Press, New York.

Foley, R. A., 1977. Space and energy: A method for analysing habitat value and utilization in relation to archaeological sites. In *Spatial Archaeology*, edited by D. L. Clarke, pp. 163-187. Academic Press, London.

— 1980. Archaeological research in the Amboseli basin. *Nyame Akuma* 17:16-17.

— 1981a. Off-site archaeology: An alternative approach for the short-sited. In *Patterns of the Past: Studies in Honour of David Clarke*, edited by Hodder, I., Isaac, G., and Hammond, N., pp. 157-183. Cambridge University Press, Cambridge.

— 1981b. A model of regional archaeological structure. *Proceedings of the Prehistoric Society* 47: 1-17.

Fowler, M.J., 1995. High-resolution Russian satellite imagery. *AARGnews* 11:29-32.

Frescobaldi, L. di Niccolo, ca. 1390. *Viaggio di Lionardo di Niccolo Frescobaldi fiorentino in Egtitto e in Terra Santa*. In *Visit to the Holy Places of Egypt, Sinai, Palestine and Syria in 1384*, edited and translated by T. Bellorini, E. Hoade, and B. Bagtatti, pp. 29-90. Franciscan Press, Jerusalem, 1948.

Fulford, M., Champion, T., and Long, A., eds., 1997. *England's Coastal Heritage, A Survey for English Heritage and the RCHME*. Archaeological Report 15. Royal Commission on the Historical Monuments of England and English Heritage, London.

Gaffney, V. L., Bintliff, J., and Slapsak, B., 1991. Site formation processes and the Hvar Survey Project, Yugoslavia. In *Interpreting Artefact Scatters: Contributions to Ploughzone Archaeology*, edited by A. J. Scholfield, pp. 59-77. Oxbow, Oxford.

Gal, S., 1980. *Search Games*. Academic Press, New York.

— 1989. Continuous search games. In *Search Theory: Some Recent Developments*, edited by D.V.Chudnovsky, and G.V.ChudnovskyChudnovsky, pp. 33-53. Marcel Dekker, Inc., Basel.

Gallagher, J. P., 1977. Contemporary stone tools in Ethiopia: Implications for archaeology. *Journal of Field Archaeology* 4:407-414.

Garrison, E. G., Baker, J. G., and Thomas, D. H., 1985. Magnetic prospection and the discovery of Mission Santa Catalina de Guale, Georgia. *Journal of Field Archaeology* 12:299-313.

GCPA, 2001. *Georgia Standards and Guidelines for Archaeological Surveys*. Georgia Council of Professional Archaeologists.

de Geoffroy, J., and Wu, S. M., 1970. Design of an optimal sampling plan for regional geochemical surveys. *Economic Geology* 65:340-347.
Gillings, M., and Wise, A., 1998. *GIS Guide to Good Practice*. Arts and Humanities Data Service Guides to Good Practice. University of York (http://ads.ahds.ac.uk/project/goodguides/gis/).
Glueck, N., 1935. *Explorations in Eastern Palestine II*. American Schools of Oriental Research, New Haven.
— 1939. *Explorations in Eastern Palestine III*. American Schools of Oriental Research, New Haven.
— 1951. *Explorations in Eastern Palestine IV*. American Schools of Oriental Research, New Haven, CT.
Godbold, S., and Turner, R., 1993. *Second Severn Crossing: Archaeological Response Phase 1 — The Intertidal Zone in Wales, Final Report*. Blaenavon.
Goodyear, A. C., Raab, M. L., and Klinger, T. C., 1978. The status of archaeological research design in Cultural Resource Management. *American Antiquity* 43:150-173.
Green, E. L., 1973. Location analysis of prehistoric Maya sites in northern British Honduras. *American Antiquity* 38:279-293.
Gucci, G., ca. 1390. *Pilgrimage of Giorgio Gucci to the Holy Places*. In *Visit to the Holy Places of Egypt, Sinai, Palestine and Syria in 1384*, edited and translated by T. Bellorini, E. Hoade, and B. Bagtgatti, pp. 93-156. Franciscan Press, Jerusalem, 1948.
Guernsey, S. J., and Kidder, A. V., 1921. *Basket-maker Caves of Northeastern Arizona: Report on the Explorations, 1916-17*. Papers of the Peabody Museum of American Archaeology and Ethnology. Harvard University, Cambridge.
Gumerman, G. J., and Euler, R. C., eds., 1976. *Papers on the Archaeology of Black Mesa, Arizona*. Southern Illinois University Press, Carbondale.
Guy, M., and Passelac, M., 1991. Prospection aérienne et télédétection des structures de parcellaires. In *Pour une Archéologie Agraire*, edited by J. Guilaine, pp. 103-129.
Hand, D. J., 1997. *Construction and Assessment of Classification Rules*. John Wiley & Sons, New York.
Harbaugh, J. W., Doveton, J. H., and Davis, J. C., 1977. *Probability Methods in Oil Exploration*. John Wiley & Sons, New York.
Hardesty, D. L., Little, B. J., and Fowler, D., 2000. *Assessing Site Significance: A Guide for Archaeologists and Historians*. Heritage Resource Management Series. Altamira Press, Walnut Creek, CA.
Haslegrove, C., Millet, M., and Smith, I., eds., 1985. *Archaeology from the Ploughsoil: Studies in the Collection and Interpretation of Field Survey Data*. Department of Archaeology and Prehistory, University of Sheffield, Sheffield.
Hawkins, A., 2000. *Getting a Handle on Tangs: Defining the Dakhleh Unit of the Aterian Technocomplex — A Study in Surface Archaeology from Dakhleh Oasis, Western Desert, Egypt*. PhD thesis, University of Toronto.
Hayes, P. P., 1991. Models for the distribution of pottery around former agricultural settlements. In *Interpreting Artefact Scatters: Contributions to Ploughzone Archaeology*, edited by A. J. Schofield, pp. 81-92. Oxbow Books, Oxford.
Heidenreich, C. E., and Konrad, V. A., 1973. Soil analysis at the Robitaille Site, part II: A method useful in determining the location of longhouse patterns. *Ontario Archaeology* 20:33-62.
Heidenreich, C. E., and Navratil, S., 1973. Soil analysis at the Robitaille site, part I: Determining the perimeter of the village. *Ontario Archaeology* 20:33-62.
Heighton, R. F., and Deagan, K. A., 1971. A new formula for dating kaolin pipestems. *The Conference on Historic Site Arogy Papers* 6:220-229.

Hester, T. R., Shafer, H. J., and Feder, K. L., 1997. *Field Methods in Archaeology.* Mayfield Publishing, Mountain View, CA.
Hickman, P. P., 1977. Problems of significance: Two case studies. In *Conservation Archaeology: A Guide for Cultural Resource Management Studies,* edited by M. B. Schiffer and G. J. Gumerman, pp. 269-275. Academic Press, New York.
Higgs, E. S. and Vita-Finzi, C., 1972. *Prehistoric economies: a territorial approach.* In Papers in Economic Prehistory, edited by E.S.Higgs, pp. 27-36. Cambridge University Press, Cambridge.
Hillier, B., and Hanson, J., 1984. *The Social Logic of Space.* Cambridge University Press, Cambridge.
Hirth, K. G., 1978. Problems in data recovery and measurement in settlement archaeology. *Journal of Field Archaeology* 5:125-131.
Historic Scotland, 1996. *Coastal Zone Survey.* Archaeology Procedure Paper 4. Historic Scotland, Edinburgh.
Hobler, P. M., 1978. The relationship of archaeological sites to sea levels on Moresby Island, Queen Charlotte Islands. *Canadian Journal of Archaeology* 2:1-13.
Hodder, I., and Orton, C., 1976. *Spatial Analysis in Archaeology.* Cambridge University Press, Cambridge.
Hope-Simpson, R., 1983. The Limitations of Surface Surveys. In *Archaeological Survey in the Mediterranean Area.,* edited by D. R. Keller and D. W. Ruppe, pp. 45-48. BAR International Series 155. British Archaeological Reports, Oxford.
— 1984. The Analysis of Data From Surface Surveys. *Journal of Field Archaeology* 11:115-117.
House, J. H., and Schiffer, M. B., 1975a. Archaeological survey in the Cache River basin. In *The Cache River Archaeological Project,* edited by M. B. Schiffer and J. H. House, pp. 37-53. Research Series 8. Arkansas Archaeological Survey, Fayetteville.
House, J. H., and Schiffer, M. B., 1975b. Significance of the archaeological resources of the Cache River Basin. In *The Cache river Archeological Project, An Experiment in Contract Archeology, edited by M. B. Schiffer and J. H. House, pp. 163-186.* Research Series 8. Arkansas Archaeological Survey, Fayetteville.
Ibn Jubayr, A.H.M.A., 1185. *The Travels of Ibn Jubayr,* translated by R.J. C. Broadhurst. Jonathan Cape, London, 1952.
Isaac, G., 1981. Stone Age visiting cards: Approaches to the study of early land use patterns. In *Pattern of the Past: Studies in Honour of David Clarke,* edited by I. Hodder, G. Isaac, and N. Hammond, pp. 131-156. Cambridge University Press, Cambridge.
Ives, J., 1982. Evaluating the effectiveness of site discovery techniques in boreal forest environments. In *Directions in Archaeology: A Question of Goals,* edited by P.Francis and E. Poplin, pp. 95-114. University of Calgary, Calgary, Alberta.
Jacobson, T., 1981. Forward. In *Land Behind Baghdad: A History of Settlement on the Diyala Plains,* by R. McC. Adams. University of Chicago Press, Chicago.
Jacoli, M., and Carrara, A., 1996. GIS-based multivariate models for identifying archaeological sites, Calabria, Southern Italy. *Proceedings of the International Congress on Science and Technology for the Safeguard of Cultural Heritage in The Mediterranean Basin,* Catania Nov. 26-Dec. 2, 1995.
Johnson, E. A. J., 1970. *The Organization of Space in Developing Countries.* Harvard University Press, Cambridge, MA.
Johnson, G. A., 1973. Local Exchange and Early State Development in Southwestern Iran. Anthropological Papers of the Museum of Anthropology 51. University of Michigan, Ann Arbor.

— 1977. Aspects of regional analysis in archaeology. *Annual Review of Anthropology* 6:479-508.
— 1980. Rank-size convexity and system integration: A view from archaeology. *Economic Geography* 56:234-247.
Judge, W. J., Ebert, J. I., and Hitchcock, R. K., 1975. Sampling in regional archaeological survey. In *Sampling in Archaeology*, edited by J. W. Mueller, pp. 82-123. University of Arizona Press, Tucson.
Kadane, J. B., 1968. Discrete search and the Neyman-Pearson lemma. *Journal of Mathematical and Analytical Applications* 22:156-171.
Keller, F., 1866. *The Lake-Dwellings of Switzerland and Other Parts of Europe* (J. E. Lee, trans.). Longmans, London.
Kelley, K. B., 1976. Dendritic central-place systems and the regional organization of Navajo trading posts. In *Regional Analysis I, Economic Systems*, edited by C. A. Smith, pp. 219-254. Academic Press, New York.
Kendall, M. G., and Moran, P. A. P., 1963. *Geometrical Probability*. Charles Griffith, London.
Kennedy, D. L., 1995a. Southern Hauran Survey 1993. *Levant* 27:39-73.
— 1995b. Water supply and use in the Southern Hauran, Jordan. *Journal of Field Archaeology* 22.3:75-90
— 1996. Aerial archaeology in the Middle East. *Aerial Archaeology Research Group News* 12:11-15.
Kennedy, D. L., and Gilbertson, D. D., 1984. An archaeological reconnaissance of water-harvesting structures and wadi walls in the Jordanian desert north of Azraq Oasis. *Annual of the Department of Antiquities of Jordan* 28:51-62.
Kennedy, D. L., and Riley, D. N., 1990. *Rome's Desert Frontier from the Air*. Batsford, London, and University of Texas Press, Austin, TX.
Kimes, T., Haselgrove, C., and Hodder, I., 1982. A method for the identification of the location of regional cultural boundaries. *Journal of Anthropological Archaeology* 1:113-131.
King, T. F., 1998. *Cultural Resource Laws and Practice: An Introductory Guide*. AltaMira Press, Walnut Creek, CA.
— 2000. *Federal Planning and Historic Places: The Section 106 Process*. Altamira Press, Walnut Creek, CA.
King, T. F., Hickman, P. P., and Berg, G., 1977. *Anthropology in Historic Preservation: Caring for Culture's Clutter*. Academic Press, New York.
Kintigh, K. W., 1988. The effectiveness of subsurface testing: A simulation approach. *American Antiquity* 53:686-707.
— 1989. Sample size, significance and measures of diversity. In *Quantifying Diversity in Archaeology*, edited by R. Leonard and G. Jones, pp. 25-36. Cambridge University Press, Cambridge.
Knapp, A. B., and Johnson, I., 1994. Quantifying survey data from Cyprus: the use of aerial photos for field recording and GIS input. In *Methods in the Mountains: Proceedings of UISPP Commission IV Meeting, Mount Victoria, Australia*, edited by I. Johnson, pp. 157-164. Sydney University Archaeological Methods Series 2. The University of Sydney, Sydney.
Kolesar, P., 1982. On searching for large objects with small probes: A search model for exploration. *Journal of the Operational Research Society* 33:153-159.
Koopman, B. O., 1980. *Search and Screening: General Principles with Historical Applications*. Pergamon Press, New York.
Kowalewski, S., 1982. The evolution of primate regional systems. *Comparative Urban Research* 9:60-78.

— 1990. Merits of full-coverage survey: Examples from the Valley of Oaxaca, Mexico. In *The Archaeology of Regions: A Case for Full-Coverage Survey,* edited by S. K. Fish and S. A. Kowalewski, pp. 33-85. Smithsonian Institution Press, Washington.

Krakker, J. J., Shott, M. J., and Welch, P. D., 1983. Design and evaluation of shovel-test sampling in regional archaeological survey. *Journal of Field Archaeology* 10:469-480.

Kuna, M., 1998. Method of surface artefact survey. In *Space in Prehistoric Bohemia*, edited by E. Neustupny, pp. 77-83. Institute of Archaeology, Academy of Sciences of the Czech Republic, Prague.

Kvamme, K. L., 1983a. Computer-processing techniques for regional modeling of archaeological locations. *Advances in Computer Archaeology* 1:26-52.

— 1983b. *A Manual for Predictive Site Location Models: Examples from the Grand Junction District, Colorado*. Submitted to the Bureau of Land Management, Grand Junction District, Colorado.

— 1984. Models of prehistoric site location near Pinyon Canyon, Colorado. In *Papers of the Philmont Conference on the Archaeology of Northeastern New Mexico*, edited by C. J. Condie, pp. 349-370. New Mexico Archaeological Council.

— 1985. Determining empirical relationships between the natural environment and prehistoric site loctions: A hunter-gatherer example. In *For Concordance in Archaeological Analysis: Bridging Data Structure, Quantitative Technique, and Theory*, edited by C. Carr, pp. 208-238. Westport, Kansas City.

— 1990. Predictive modelling of archaeological site location: A case study in the Midwest. In *Interpreting Space: GIS and Archaeology*, edited by K. M. S. Allen, S. W. Green, and E. B. W. Zubrow, pp. 201-215.

— 1992. A predictive site location model on the High Plains: An example with an independent test. *Plains Anthropologist* 37:19-38.

— 1998. Spatial structure in mass debitage scatters. In *Surface Archaeology*, edited by A. P. Sullivan, pp. 127-141. University of New Mexico Press, Albuquerque.

Langdon, S. J., 1987. Traditional Tlingit fishing structures in the Prince of Wales Archipelago. In *Fisheries in Alaska's Past: A Symposium*. Alaska Historical Commission Studies in History 227. Office of History and Archaeology, Anchorage.

Larsen, M. T., 1987. Commercial networks in the ancient Near East. In *Centre and Periphery in the Ancient World,* edited by M. Rowlands, M. T. Larsen, and K. Kristiansen, pp. xxx. Cambridge University Press, Cambridge.

Lewarch, D. E., and O'Brien, M. J., 1981. The expanding role of surface assemblages in archaeological research. *Advances in Archaeological Method and Theory* 4:297-342.

Lewis, S. A., 1837. *A Topographical Dictionary of Ireland*. S. Lewis, London.

Lightfoot, K. G., 1986. Regional surveys in the eastern United States: The strengths and weakness of implementing subsurface testing programs. *American Antiquity* 51:484-504.

— 1989. A defense of shovel test sampling: A reply to Shott. *American Antiquity* 54:413-416.

Linden, R. H., and Shurer, P. J., 1984. Results of a sub-bottom acoustic survey in a search for the Tonquin. *International Journal of Nautical and Underwater Exploration* 13.4: 305-309.

Lock, G., and Stancic, Z., eds., 1995. *Archaeology and Geographic Information Systems: A European Perspective*. Taylor and Francis, London.

Lolley, T. L., 1996. Ethnohistory and archaeology: A map method for locating historic Upper Creek Indian towns and villages. *Journal of Alabama Archaeology* 42: 1-81.

Lösch, A., 1954. *The Economics of Location*, translated by W. F. Stolper. Yale University Press, New Haven, CT. (Originally *Die raumlishe Ordnung der Wirtschaft*, 1940.)

Lovis, W. A., 1976. Quartersections and forests: an example of probability sampling in the northeastern woodlands. *American Antiquity* 41:364-372.

Lynch, B. M., 1980. Site artifact density and the effectiveness of shovel test probes. *Current Anthropology* 21:516-517.
Lyons, T. R., and Avery, T. E., 1977. *Remote Sensing: A Handbook for Archeologists and Cultural Resource Managers*. Cultural Resource Management Division, National Park Service, Government Printing Office, Washington, DC.
Mabry, J. B., ed., 1996. *Canals and Communities: Small-Scale Irrigation Systems*. Arizona Studies in Human Ecology. University of Arizona Press, Tucson.
MacDonald, B., Banning, E. B., and Pavlish, L. A., 1980. The Wadi el Hasa survey 1979: A preliminary report. *Annual of the Department of Antiquities of Jordan* 24:169-183.
Macready, S., and Thompson, F. H., eds., 1985. *Archaeological Field Survey in Britain and Abroad*. Society of Antiquaries of London, Occasional Papers (New Series) 6, London.
Maher, L., and Banning, E.B., 2001. Geoarchaeological Survey in Wadi Ziqlab, Jordan. *Annual of the Department of Antiquities of Jordan* 45:61-70.
Maher, L., Lohr, M., Betts, M., Parslow, C., and Banning, E.B., 2001. The Middle Epipalaeolithic in the southern Levant: The view from Wadi Ziqlab. *Paléorient* 27:5-19.
Malone, C., and Stoddart, S., 2000. The current state of prehistoric ceramic studies in Mediterranean survey. In *Extracting Meaning from Ploughsoil Assemblages*, edited by R. Francovich and H. Patterson, pp. 95-104. The Archaeology of Mediterranean Landscapes 5. Oxbow Books, Oxford.
Mandelbrot, B. B., 1982. *The Fractal Geometry of Nature*. Freeman and Co., San Francisco.
Marren, P., 1990. *Woodland Heritage*. David and Charles, Newton, Abbott.
Maschner, H. D. G., ed., 1996. *New Methods, Old Problems. Geographic Information Systems in Modern Archaeological Research*. Occasional Paper 23. Southern Illinois University Center for Archaeological Investigations, Carbondale.
Matérn, B., 1960. Spatial variation. Stochastic models and their application to some problems in forest surveys and other sampling investigations. *Meddelanden frn Statens Skogsforskningsinstitut* 49:5.
Mathiassen, T., 1948. *Studier over Vestjyllands Oldtidsbebyggelse*. Nationalmuseets Skrifter Arkæologiskhistorisk Række 2. Copenhagen.
— 1959. *Nordvestsjællands oldtidsbebyggelse*. Nationalmuseets Skrifter Arkæologisk-historisk Række 7. Copenhagen.
Mathien, F. J., 1991. Political, economic, and demographic implications of the Chaco road network. In *Ancient Road Networks and Settlement Hierarchies in the New World*, ed.ited by C. D. Trombold, pp. 99-110. Cambridge University Press, Cambridge.
McCammon, R. B., 1977. Target intersection probabilities for parallel-line and continuous-grid types of search. *Journal of the International Association for Mathematical Geology* 9:369-382.
McCauley, J. F., Schaber, G., Breed, C., Grolier, M., Haynes, C. V., Issawi, B., Elachi, C. and Blom, R., 1982. Subsurface valleys and geoarchaeology of the eastern Sahara revealed by Shuttle radar. *Science* 218:1004-1020.
McGimsey, C. R., 1972. *Public Archaeology*. Seminar Press, New York.
McIntosh. J., 1986. *The Practical Archaeologist*. Facts on File, New York.
McManamon, F. P., 1980. *Site discovery: past and future directions*. In Discovering and Examining Archaeological Sites: Strategies for Areas with Dense Ground Cover, edited by F.P.McManamon, and D.J.Ives, pp. University of Missouri, Columbia.
— 1981. Probability sampling and archaeological survey in the Northeast: An estimation approach. In *Foundations of Northeast Archaeology*, edited by D. R. Snow, pp. 195-227. Academic Press, New York.
— 1984. Discovering sites unseen. *Advances in Archaeological Method and Theory* 7:223-292.

McMillan, B., Grady, M., and Lipe, W., 1977. Cultural Resource Management. In *The Management of Archaeological Resources: The Airlie House Report*, edited by C. R. Mcgimsey III and H. A. Davis, pp. 25-63. Society for American Archaeology, Washington, DC.

Mercer, R., 1985. A view of British archaeological field survey. In *Archaeological Field Survey in Britain and Abroad*, edited by S. Macready and F. H. Thompson, pp. 8-24. The Society of Antiquaries of London, London.

Miller, C. L., 1989. Evaluating the effectiveness of archaeological surveys. *Ontario Archaeologist* 49:3-12.

Miller, W.F., Sever T.L., and Lee D. , 1991. Applications of ecological concepts and remote sensing technologies in archaeological site reconnaissance. In *Applications Of Space-age Technology in Archaeological Site Reconnaissance*, edited by C.Behrens and T.Sever, pp. 121-136. NASA Space Center, Stennis.

Mills, N., 1985a. *Sample bias, regional analysis and fieldwork in British archaeology*. In Archaeology from the Ploughsoil: Studies in the Collection and Interpretation of Field Survey Data, edited by C.Haselgrove, M.Millett, and I.Smith, pp. 39-47. Sheffield University Press, Sheffield.

— 1985b. *Geomorphology and settlement studies in archaeology*. In Paleoenvironmental Investigations: Research Design, Methods and Data Analysis, edited by N.R.J.Fieller, D.D.Gilbertson, and N.G.A. Ralph, pp. 175-206. British Archaeological Reports, Oxford.

Mitchelson, R. L., 1984. The predictive model. In A Cultural Resource Survey of Fort Rucker, Alabama, edited by C. O. Braley and R. L. Mitchelson, pp. 72-93. Report submitted to the National Park Service, Interagency Archeological Services, Atlanta. Cited in Ensor and Largent, 1997.

Moore, T., 1959. A note on city size distributions. *Economic Development and Cultural Change* 6:465-466.

Moratto, M. J., 1977. A consideration of law in archaeology. In *The Management of Archaeological Resources: The Airlie House Report*, edited by C. R. McGimsey and H. A. Davis, pp. 8-24. Society for American Archaeology, Washington.

Moratto, M. J., and Kelly, R. E., 1978. Optimizing strategies for evaluating archaeological significance. *Advances in Archaeological Method and Theory* 1:1-30.

Morris, P. A., 1977. Combining expert judgments: A Bayesian approach. *Management Science* 23: 679-693.

Morse, P. M., and Kimball, G. E., 1951. *Methods of Operations Research*. MIT Press.

Mortensen, P., 1974. A survey of prehistoric sites in northern Luristan. *Acta Archaeologica* 45:1-47.

— 1979. The Hulailan survey: a note on the relationship between aims and method. In *Akten des VII. Internationalen Kongresses für Iranische Kunst und Archäologie, München 7.-10. September 1976*, pp. 3-8. Dietrich Reimer Verlag, Berlin.

Moyal, J. E., 1962. General theory of stochastic population processes. *Acta Mathematica Scandinaviae* 108:1-31.

Mueller, J. W., 1975. Archaeological research as cluster sampling. In *Sampling in Archaeology*, edited by J. W. Mueller, pp. 33-41. University of Arizona Press, Tucson.

Munro, R., 1882. *Ancient Scottish Lake-Dwellings or Crannogs; with a Supplementary Chapter on Remains of Lake-Dwellings in England*. D. Douglas, Edinburgh.

— 1890. *The Lake-Dwellings of Europe*. Cassell, London.

Murphy, P., and French, C., eds., 1988. *The Exploitation of Wetlands*. BAR British Series 186. British Archaeological Reports, Oxford.

Nadel, D., 1993. Submerged archaeological sites on the shores of Lake Kinneret, Israel. *'Atiqot* (English series) 22:1-12.

Nance, J. D., 1979. Regional Subsampling and Statistical Inference in Forested Habitats. *American Antiquity* 44:172-176.
— 1983. Regional sampling in archaeological survey: The statistical perspective. *Advances in Archaeological Method and Theory* 6:289-356.
— 1987. Reliability, validity, and quantitative methods in archaeology. In *Quantitative Reserch in Archaeology, Progress and Prospects*, edited by M. S. Aldenderfer, pp. 244-93. Sage Publications, Newbury Park, CA.
— 1993. Statistical sampling, estimation, and analytic procedures in archaeology. *Journal of Quantitative Anthropology* 4:221-248.
Nance, J.D., and Ball, B. F., 1986. No surprises? The reliability and validity of test pit sampling. *American Antiquity* 51:457-483.
— 1989, A Shot in the dark: Shott's comments on Nance and Ball. *American Antiquity* 54:405-412.
NJHPO, n.d. *Guidelines for Phase I Archaeological Investigations: Identification of Archaeological Resources.* New Jersey Historic Preservation Office, New Jersey Department of Environmental Protection, Division of Parks and Forestry, Trenton [http://www.state.nj.us/dep/hpo/1identify/arkeoguide1.htm].
— 2000. *Guidelines for Preparing Cultural Resources Management Archaeological Reports.* New Jersey Historic Preservation Office, New Jersey Department of Environmental Protection, Division of Parks and Forestry, Trenton.
Newfoundland Museum, n.d. *Stage 2 Detailed Impact Assessment, 2A, Introduction and Objectives.*
Newton, J. G., 1975. How we found *The Monitor. National Geographic* 147(1):48-61.
Neyman, J., 1934. On the two different aspects of the representative method: The method of stratified sampling and the method of purposive selection. *Journal of the Royal Statistical Society* 97:558-625.
— 1939. On a new class of contagious distributions applicable in entomology and bacteriology. *Annales de la Mathématique Statistique* 10:35-57.
Neyman, J., and Scott, E. L., 1958. Statistical approach to problems of cosmology. *Journal of the Royal Statistical Society* B20:1-43.
O'Brien, M. J., and Lewarch, D. E., 1981. *Plowzone Archaeology: Contributions to Theory and Technique.* Vanderbilt University Publications in Anthropology 27. Nashville, TN.
Odell, G. H., and Cowan, F., 1987. Estimating tillage effects on artifact distributions. *American Antiquity* 52:456-484.
Oliphant, L., 1880. *The Land of Gilead.* Wm. Blackwood and Sons, London.
Orton, C., 2000. *Sampling in Archaeology.* Cambridge University Press, Cambridge.
O'Sullivan, A., 1998. *The Archaeology of Lake Settlement in Ireland.* Discovery Programme Monograph 4. Royal Irish Academy, Dublin.
— 2001. *Foragers, Farmers and Fishermen in a Coastal Landscape: An Intertidal Archaeological Survey of the Shannon Estuary.* Discovery Programme Monograph 5. Royal Irish Academy, Dublin.
Paloheimo, J. E., 1971. On a theory of search. *Biometrika* 58:61-75.
Parker, S. C., 1985. Predictive modeling of site settlement systems using multivariate logistics. In *For Concordance in Archaeological Analysis: Bridging Data Structure, Quantitative Technique, and Theory,* edited by C. Carr, pp. 173-207. Westport, Kansas City.
Parsons, J. R., 1990. Critical reflections on a decade of full-coverage regional survey in the Valley of Mexico. In *The Archaeology of Regions,* edited by S. K. Fish and S. A. Kowalewski, pp. 7-31. Smithsonian Institution Press, Washington, DC.
Patias, P., and Karras, G., 1995. *Contemporary Photogrammetric Methods Applied to Architecture and Archaeology.* Thessaloniki, Greece.

Pausanias. *Pausaniae Graeciae Descriptio.*
Pavlidis, L, Fraser, C., and Ogleby, C., n.d. The application of high-resolution satellite imagery for the detection of ancient Minoan roads on Crete. In *Archaeological Informatics — Pushing the Envelope. Proceedings of CAA 2001, Computers and Quantitative Methods in Archaeology Conference 2001, Visby, Sweden*, edited by G. Burenhult and J. Arvidsson. In press. BAR International Series, Oxford.
Pearce, R. J., 1989. Cultural Resource Management at the federal, provincial, municipal and corporate levels in southern Ontrio, Canada. In *Archaeological Heritage Management in the Modern World*, edited by H. Cleere, pp. 146-151. Unwin Hyman, London.
Pepper, G., 1902. The ancient basketmakers of southeastern Utah. *American Museum Journal* 2(4).
Peregrine, P., 1991. A graph-theoretic approach to the evolution of Cahokia. *American Antiquity* 56:66-75.
Petraglia, M. D., and Potts, R., 1994. Water flow and the formation of early Pleistocene artifact sites in Olduvai Gorge, Tanzania. *Journal of Anthropological Archaeology* 13:228-254.
Plog, F., 1974. *The Study of Prehistoric Change.* Academic Press, New York.
Plog, S., 1978. Black Mesa research design. In *Excavation on Black Mesa, 1977: A Preliminary Report,* edited by A. L. Klesert, pp. 21-42. Center for Archaeological Investigations Research Paper 1. Southern Illinois University, Carbondale.
Plog, S., ed., 1986. *Spatial Organization and Exchange: Archaeological Survey on Northern Black Mesa.* Southern Illinois University Press, Carbondale.
Plog, S., and Hantman, J. L., 1990. Chronology construction and the study of prehistoric culture change. *Journal of Field Archaeology* 17:439-456.
Plog, S., Plog, F., and Wait, W., 1978. Decision making in modern surveys. *Advances in Archaeological Method and Theory* 1:384-421.
Plog, S., and Powell, S., eds., 1984. *Papers on the Archaeology of Black Mesa, Arizona, Volume II:* Center for Archaeological Investigations. Southern Illinois University Press, Carbondale.
Poidebard, A., 1934. *La Trace de Rome dans le Désert de Syrie; Le Limes de Trajan à la Conquête Arabe, Récherches Aeriennes (1925-1932).* Geuthner, Paris.
Poirier, D. A., and Feder, K. L., 2001. *Dangerous Places: Health, Safety, and Archaeology.* Bergin & Garvey, Westport, Connecticut.
Portugali, Y., 1982. A field methodology for regional archaeology (the Jezreel Valley Survey, 1981). *Tel Aviv* 9:170-188.
Powell, S., and Klesert, A. L., 1980. Predicting the presence of structures on small sites. *Current Anthropology* 21:367-369.
Prag, K., 1984. Continuity and migration in the south Levant in the late third millennium: A review of T. L. Thompson's and some other views. *Palestine Exploration Quarterly* 116:58-68.
Proudfoot, B., 1976. The analysis and interpretation of soil phosphorus in archaeological contexts. In Geoarchaeology: Earth Science and the Past, edited by D. A. Davidson and M. L. Shackley, pp. 93-113. Westview, Boulder, CO.
Provan, D. M., 1971. Soil phosphate analysis as a tool in archaeology. *Norwegian Archaeological Review* 4:37-50.
Raab, L. M., and Klinger, T. C., 1977. A critical appraisal of "significance" in contract archaeology. *American Antiquity* 42:629-634.
Rackham, O., 1975. *Hayley Wood, Its History and Ecology.* Cambridge and Isle of Ely Naturalists Trust, Cambridge.
— 1980. *Ancient Woodland: Its History, Vegetation and Uses in England.* Edward Arnold, London.

— 1989. *The Last Forest: The Story of Hatfield Forest*. Dent, London.
Read, D. W., 1975. Regional sampling. In *Sampling in Archaeology*, edited by J. W. Mueller, pp. 45-60. University of Arizona Press, Tucson.
— 1957. *A Theoretical Evaluation of Various Search/salvage Procedures for Use with Narrow-path Locators, Pt. II, Locating an Object Whose Apparent Presence and Approximate Position are Known*. Bureau of Ships, Minesweeping Branch Technical Report 118.
Redman, C. L., 1973. Multistage fieldwork and analytical techniques. *American Antiquity* 38:61-79.
— 1974. *Archaeological Sampling Strategies*. Addison-Wesley Modular Publications in Archaeology 55. Addison-Wesley, Reading.
— 1975. Productive sampling strategies for archaeological sites. In *Sampling in Archaeology*, edited by J. W. Mueller, pp. 147-154. University of Arizona Press, Tucson.
Redman, C. L., and Anzalone, R. D., 1980. Discovering architectural patterning at a complex site. *American Antiquity* 45:284-290.
Reeve, R., 1989. Recent work on the prehistory of the Western Solomons, Melanesia. *Bulletin of the Indo-Pacific Prehistory Association* 9:44-67.
Remote Sensing Society, 1984. *Satellite Remote Sensing — Review and Preview*. Remote Sensing Society, London.
Renfrew, C., 1975. Trade as action at a distance: Questions of integration and communication. In *Ancient Civilization and Trade*, edited by J. A. Sabloff and C. C. Lamberg-Karlovsky, pp. 3-59. University of New Mexico Press, Albuquerque.
Richardson, H. R., 1989. Search theory. In *Search Theory: Some Recent Developments*, edited by D. V. Chudnovsky and G. V. Chudnovsky, pp. 1-12. Marcel Dekker, Inc., Basel.
Richardson, H. R., and Discenza, J. H., 1980. The United States Coast Guard computer-assisted search planning system (CASP). *Naval Research Logistics Quarterly* 27:659-680.
Ringrose, T. J., 1993. Diversity indices and archaeology. In *Computing the Past. Computer Applications and Quantitative Methods in Archaeology, CAA92*, edited by J. Andresen, t. Madsen, and I. Scollar, pp. 279-285. Aarhus University Press, Aarhus.
Rippon, s., 2000. *The Transformation of Coastal Wetlands: Exploitation and Management of Marshland Landscapes in North West Europe during the Roman and Medieval Periods*. Oxford University Press, Oxford.
Robertson, P., 1993. Searching for the Seven Sisters. *Sussex Archaeological Society Newsletter* 70:11.
Robinson, E., 1856. *Later Biblical Researches in Palestine and the Adjacent Regions: A Journal of Travels in the Year 1852*. John Murray, London.
Roper, D. C., 1976. Lateral displacement of artifacts due to plowing. *American Antiquity* 41:372-375.
Rumrill, D. A., 1991. The Mohawk glass trade bead chronology ca. 1560-1785. *Beads* 3:5-45.
Rupp, D., n.d. Evolving strategies for investigating an extensive terra incognita in the Paphos district by the Canadian Palaipaphos Survey Project and the Western Cyprus Project. In *Archaeological Field Survey in Cyprus: Past History, Future Potentials*, in press. British School at Athens, London.
Ruppe, R.J., 1966. The archeological survey: A defense. *American Antiquity* 31:313-333.
Rutter, J. B., 1983. Some thoughts on the analysis of ceramic data generated by site surveys. In *Archaeological Survey in the Mediterranean Area*, edited by D. R. Keller and D. W. Rupp, pp. 137-142. BAR International Series 155. British Archaeological Reports, Oxford.
Ryan, N. S., and van Leusen, M., n.d. Educating the field-work assistant. In *Archaeological Informatics — Pushing the Envelope. Proceedings of CAA 2001, Computers and Quantitative Methods in Archaeology Conference 2001, Visby, Sweden*, edited by G. Burenhult and J. Arvidsson. In press. BAR International Series, Oxford.

Ryan, N. S., Pascoe, J., and Morse, D., 1997. FieldWorker Advanced 2.3.5 and FieldWorker Pro 0.91. *Internet Archaeology* 3.

Sampson, C. G., 1985. *Atlas of Stone Age Settlement in the Central and Upper Seacow Valley.* National Museum Memoirs 18. National Museum, Bloemfontein.

— 1988. *Stylistic Boundaries among Mobile Hunter-Foragers.* Smithsonian Series in Archaeological Inquiry. Smithsonian Institution Press, Washington.

Sanders, W. T., Parsons, J. R., and Santley, R. S., 1974. *The Basin of Mexico: Ecological Processes in the Evolution of a Civilization.* Academic Press, New York.

Saunders, A, 1989. Heritage management and training in England. In *Archaeological Heritage Management in the Modern World*, edited by H. Cleere, pp. 152-163. Unwin Hyman, London.

Savage, L. J., 1971. Elicitations of personal probabilities and expectations. *Journal of the American Statistical Association* 66: 783-801.

Savage, S. H., 1997. Assessing departures from log-normality in the rank-size rule. *Journal of Archaeological Science* 24:233-244.

Savinskii, I. D., 1965. *Probability Tables for Locating Elliptical Underground Masses with a Rectangular Grid.* Consultants Bureau, New York.

Schiffer, M. B., 1974. On Whallon's use of dimensional analysis of variance at Guila Naquitz. *American Antiquity* 39:490-492.

— 1987, *Formation Processes of the Archaeological Record.* University of New Mexico Press, Albuquerque, NM.

Schiffer, M. B., and House, J. H., eds., 1975. *The Cache River Archeological Project, An Experiment in Contract Archeology.* Research Series 8. Arkansas Archeological Survey, Fayetteville.

Schiffer, M. B., and House, J. H., 1977. An approach to assessing scientific significance. In *Conservation Archaeology: A Guide to Cultural Resource Management Studies*, edited by M. B. Schiffer and G. J. Gumerman, pp. 249-257. Academic Press, New York.

Schiffer, M. B., Sullivan, A. P., and Klinger, T. C., 1978. The design of archaeological surveys. *World Archaeology* 10:1-28.

Schlanger, S. H., 1992. Recognizing persistent places in Anasazi settlement systems. In *Space, Time, and Archaeological Landscapes*, edited by J. Rossignol and L. Wandsnider, pp. 91-112. Plenum Press, New York.

Schlezinger, D. R., and Howes, B. L., 2000. Organic phosphorus and elemental ratios as indicators of prehistoric human occupation. *Journal of Archaeological Science* 27:479-492.

Schofield, A. J., 1989. Understanding early medieval pottery distributions. *Antiquity* 63:460-470.

Schofield, A. J., ed., 1991. *Interpreting Artefact Scatters: Contributions to Ploughzone Archaeology.* Oxbow Monographs 4. Oxbow, Oxford.

Scholtz, S. C., 1981. Location choice models in Sparta. In *Settlement Predictions in Sparta*, edited by R. Lafferty, J. Otinger, S. Scholtz, W. F. Limp, B. Watkins, and R. Jones, pp. 207-222. Research Series No. 14. Arkansas Archaeological Survey, University of Arkansas, Fayetteville.

Schumacher, G., 1890. *Northern 'Ajlun, "Within the Decapolis".* Alexander P. Watt, London.

Schwartz, M. L., and Tziavos, C., 1979. Geology in the search for ancient Helice. *Journal of Field Archaeology* 6:243-252.

Schwimmer, B., 1976. Periodic markets and urban development in southern Ghana. In *Regional Analysis I, Economic Systems*, edited by C. A. Smith, pp. 123-145. Academic Press, New York.

Scollar, I., Tabbagh, A., Hesse, A.,and Herzog, I., 1992. *Archaeological Prospecting and Remote Sensing*, Cambridge.

Scovill, D. H., Garland, J. G., and Anderson, K. M., 1972. *Guidelines for the Preparation of Statements of Environmental Impact on Archeological Resources*. Arizona Arceological Center, National Park Service, Tucson.

SCSHPO, 2000. South Carolina Standards and Guidelines for Archaeological Investigations. South Carolina State Historic Preservation Office, South Carolina Institute of Archaeology and Anthropology and Council of South Carolina Professional Archaeologists.

Sharer, R. J., and Ashmore, W., 1996. *Discovering Our Past: A Brief Introduction to Archaeology*, 2nd ed. Mayfield Publishing, Mountain View, CA.

Shennan, S., 1997. *Quantifying Archaeology*, 2nd ed. Edinburgh University Press, Edinburgh.

Sheppard, P., and Aswani, S., 1997. *New Georgia Archaeological Survey (NGAS), Roviana Lagoon, Year 2*. Annual Report to Solomon Islands Government. Centre for Archaeological Research, University of Auckland.

Sheridan, R. E., 1979. Site charting and environmental studies of *The Monitor* wreck. *Journal of Field Archaeology* 6:253-264.

Shomette, D. G., and Eshelman, r. E., 1981. A developmental model for survey and inventory of submerged archaeological resources in a riverine system: The Patuxent river, Maryland. In *Underwater Archaeology: The Challenge Before Us*, edited by g. P. Watts, pp. 159-171. Fathom Eight, San Marino, CA.

Shott, M., 1985. Shovel-test sampling as a site discovery technique: A case study from Michigan. *Journal of Field Archaeology* 12:457-468.

— 1989. Shovel-test sampling in archaeological survey: Comments on Nance and Ball, and Lightfoot. *American Antiquity* 54:396-404.

— 1995. Reliability of archaeological records on cultivated surfaces: A Michigan case study. *Journal of Field Archaeology* 22:475-490.

Shurygin, A. M., 1976. Discovery of deposits of given size by boreholes with pre-selected probability. *Journal of Mathematical Geology* 8:85-88.

Sinclair, A. J., 1975. Some considerations regarding grid orientation and sample spacing. In *Geochemical Exploration 1974*, edited by I. L. Elliot and W. K. Fletcher. Elsevier, Amsterdam.

Singer, D. A., 1972. Elipgrid, a FORTRAN IV program for calculating the probability of success in locating elliptical targets with square, rectangular and hexagonal grids. Geocom Programs, London.

— 1975. Relative efficiencies of square and triangular grids in the search for elliptically shaped resource targets. *United States Geological Survey Journl of Research* 3:163-167.

— 1976. RESIN, a FORTRAN IV program for determining the area of influence of samples or drill holes in resource target search. *Computers and Geosciences* 2:249-260.

Singer, D. A., and Drew, L. J., 1976. The area of influence of an exploratory hole. *Economic Geology* 71:642-647.

Singer, D. A., and Wickman, F. E., 1969. *Probability Tables for Locating Elliptical Targets with Square, Rectangular and Hexagonal Pointnets*. Pennsylvania State University Mineral Science Experiment Station Special Publication 1-69.

Sjoberg, A., 1976. Phosphate analysis of anthropic soils. *Journal of Field Archaeology* 4:447-454.

Smith, B., 1978. *Prehistoric Patterns of Human Behavior: A Case Study in the Mississippi Valley*. Academic Press, New York.

Smith, C. A., 1976. Regional economic systems: Linking geographical models and socioeconomic problems. In *Regional Analysis I, Economic Systems*, edited by C. A. Smith, pp. 3-67. Academic Press, New York.

Smith, I. F., 1955. Late Beaker pottery from the Lyonesse surface and the date of the transgression. *Bulletin of the London Institute of Archaeology* 11:29-42.

Smith, M. T., 1983. Chronology from glass beads: The Spanish period in the Southeast, c. A.D. 1513-1670. *Proceedings of the 1982 Glass Bead Conference*, edited by C. F. Hayes, pp. 147-158. Research Records 16, Rochester Museum and Science Division, Rochester, NY.

Soter, S., 1998. Holocene uplift and subsidence of the Helike Delta, Gulf of Corinth, Greece. In *Coastal Tectonics*, edited by I. Stewart and C. Vita-Finzi, pp. 41-56. Geological Society Special Publication 146. London.

Soter, S., Blackwelder, P., Tziavos, C., Katsonopoulou, D., Hood, T., and Alvarez-Zarikian, C., 2001. Environmental analysis of bore hole cores from the Helike Delta, Gulf of Corinth, Greece. *Journal of Coastal Research* 17:95-106.

Soter, S., and Katsonopoulou, D., 1999. Occupation horizons found in the search for the ancient Greek city of Helike. *Geoarchaeology* 14:531-563.

Squier, E. G., and Davis, E. H., 1848. *Ancient Monuments of the Mississippi Valley*. Smithsonian Contributions to Knowledge 1. Smithsonian Institution, Washington.

Stafford, C. R., 1995. Geoarchaeological perspectives on paleolandscapes and regional subsurface archaeology. *Journal of Archaeological Method and Theory* 2:69-104.

Stafford, C. R. and Hajic, E. R., 1992, *Landscape scale: Geoenvironmental approaches to prehistoric settlement strategies*. In Space, time, and Archaeological Landscapes, edited by Rossignol, J. and Wandsnider, L., pp. Plenum Press, New York

Stein, J., 1991. Coring in CRM and archaeology: A reminder. *American Antiquity* 56:138-142.

Steinberg, J., 1996 Ploughzone sampling in Denmark: Isolating and interpreting site signatures from disturbed contexts. *Antiquity* 270:368-392.

Steuernagel, D. C., 1925, Der Adschlun. *Zeitschrift des deutschen-Palästinavereins* 48:1-144, 201-392.

— 1926, Der Adschlun. *Zeitschrift des deutschen-Palästinavereins* 49:1-167.

Stewart, A., Friesen, T. M., Keith, D., and Henderson, L., 2000. Archaeology and oral history of Inuit land use on the Kazan River, Nunavut: a feature-based approach. *Arctic* 53:260-278.

Stoddart, S., and Whitehead, N., 1991. Cleaning the Iguvine stables: Site and off-site analysis from a central Mediterranean perspective. In *Interpreting Artefact Scatters, Contributions to Ploughzone Archaeology*, edited by A. J. Schofield, pp. 141-148. Oxbow Books, Oxford.

Stone, G.D., 1981 On artifact density and shovel probes. *Current Anthropology* 22:182-183.

Stone, L. D., 1975. *Theory of Optimal Search*. Academic Press, New York.

— 1989. *Theory of Optimal Search*, 2nd ed. Operations Research Society of America, Arlington, VA.

Storck, P. L., 1978. Some Recent Developments in the Search for Early Man in Ontario. *Ontario Archaeology* 29:3-16.

— 1982. Palaeo-Indian Settlement Patterns Associated with the Strandline of Glacial Lake Algonquin in Southcentral Ontario. *Canadian Journal of Archaeology* 6:1-31.

— 1984. Glacial Lake Algonquin and Paleo-Indian Settlement Patterns in Southcentral Ontario. *Archaeology of Eastern North America* 12:286-298.

Sullivan, A. P., 1978. Inference and evidence in archaeology. *Advances in Archaeological Method and Theory* 1:183-222.

— 1996. Risk, anthropogenic environments, and Western Anasazi subsistence. In *Evolving Complexity and Environmental Risk in the Prehistoric Southwest*, edited by Tainter, J. A. and Tainter, B. B., pp. 145-167. Addison-Wesley, Reading, MA.

Sullivan, A. P., ed., 1998. *Surface Archaeology*. University of New Mexico Press, Albuquerque.

Synenki, A. T., 1984. Understanding the relationship between surface and subsurface remains: An approach to isolating potential sources of variation. In *Papers on the Archaeology of Black Mesa, Arizona, volume II*, edited by S. Plog and S. Powell, pp. 14-38. Center for Archaeological Investigations. Southern Illinois University Press, Carbondale.

Bibliography

Tainter, J. A., and Lucas, G. J., 1983. Epistemology of the significance concept. *American Antiquity* 48:707-719.

Taylor, C., 1973. *The Cambridgeshire Landscape: Cambridgeshire and the Southern Fens*. Hodder & Stoughton, London.

— 2000. *Fields in the English Landscape*, 2nd ed. Sutton Publishing, Stroud.

TDEC, 1997. Tennessee State Archaeological Permits, Standards and Guidelines for Archaeological Permit Applications. Tennessee Department of Environment and Conservation, Division of Archaeology. [http://www.mtsu.edu/~kesmith/TNARCHNET/Permit.html].

Terrenato, N., 2000. The visibility of sites and the interpretation of field survey results: Towards an analysis of incomplete distributions. In *Extracting Meaning from Ploughsoil Assemplages*, edited by R. Francovich and H. Patterson, pp. 60-71. Oxbow Books, Oxford.

Terrenato, N., and Ammerman, A. J., 1996. Visibility and site recovery in the Cecina Valley, Italy. *Journal of Field Archaeology* 23:91-109.

Theodericus, ca. 1172. *Libellus de Locis Sanctis*, trans. By A. Stewart. Italica Press, New York, 1986.

Thomas, C., 1894. *Report of the Mound Explolrations of the Bureau of Ethnology*. Smithsonian Institution, Washington.

Thomas, D. H., 1972. A computer simulation model of Great Basin Shoshonean settlement patterns. In *Models in Archaeology*, edited by D. L. Clarke, pp. 671-704. Methuen, London.

— 1975. Nonsite sampling in archaeology: Up the creek without a site? In *Sampling in Archaeology*, edited by J. W. Mueller, pp. 61-81. University of Arizona Press, Tucson.

Thompson, H. R., 1954. A note on contagious distributions. *Biometrika* 41:268-271.

— 1955. Spatial point processes with applications to ecology. *Biometrika* 42:102-115.

Thompson, R. H., n.d. Letter to C. Silvestro, Chairman of the Advisory Council on Historic Preservation, 1977, cited in Moratto and Kelly, 1977.

Thompson, S. K., 1987. Sample size for estimating multinomial proportions. *The American Statistician* 41:42-46.

— 1992. Sampling. John wiley & Son, New York.

Thompson, S. K., and Ramsey, F. L., 1987. Detectability functions in observing spatial point processes. *Biometrics* 43:355-362.

Thompson, S. K., and Seber, G. A. F., 1994. Detectability in conventional and adaptive sampling. *Biometrics* 50:712-724.

— 1996. *Adaptive Sampling*. John Wiley and Sons, New York.

von Thünen, J. H., 1826. *Der isolierte Staat*. Translated by C. M. Wartenberg and edited by P. Hall as *Von Thünen's Isolated State*, Pergamon Press, Oxford, 1966.

Topouzi, S., Tripolitsiotis, A., Sarris, A., Mertikas, S., and Soetens, S., n.d. Errors and inaccuracies in repositioning of archaeological sites. In *Archaeological Informatics — Pushing the Envelope. Proceedings of CAA 2001, Computers and Quantitative Methods in Archaeology Conference 2001, Visby, Sweden*, edited by G. Burenhult and J. Arvidsson. In press. BAR International Series, Oxford.

Trombold, C. D., ed., 1991. *Ancient Road Networks and Settlement Hierarchies in the New World*. Cambridge University Press, Cambridge.

Turpin, S.A., Watson, R.P., Dennett, S., Muessig, H., 1979. Stereophotogrammetric documentation of exposed archaeological features. *Journal of Field Archaeology* 6:329-xxx.

Tyson, H. J., Fulford, M. G., and Crutchley, S., 1997. Survey and recording in the intertidal zone. In *England's Coastal Heritage, A Survey for English Heritage and the RCHME*, edited by M. Fulford, T. Champion, and A. Long, pp. 74-102. English Heritage and the Royal Commission on the Historical Monuments of England, London.

Valentine, K. W. G., Fladmark, K. R. and Spurling, B. E., 1980, The description, chronology, and correlation of buried soils and cultural layers in a terrace section, Peace River Valley, British Columbia. *Canadian Journal of Soil Science* 60:185-197.
Vance, J. E., 1970. *The Merchant's World:Geography of Wholesaling.* Prentice-Hall, Englewood Cliffs, NJ.
Wainwright, G. J., 1989. The management of the English landscape. In *Archaeological Heritage Management in the Modern World*, edited by H. Cleere, pp. 164-170. Unwin Hyman, London.
Wandsnider, L., and Camilli, E. L., 1992. The character of surface archaeological deposits and its influence on survey accuracy. *Journal of Field Archaeology* 19:169-188.
Wandsnider, L., and Ebert, J. I., 1986a. Accuracy in archeological surface survey in the Seedskadee Project area, southwestern Wyoming. In *The Seedskadee Project: Remote Sensing in Non-Site Archeology*, edited by D. L. Drager and A. K. Ireland, pp. 211-226. Southwest Region, National Park Service, Albuquerque, NM, and Upper Colorado Region, Bureau of Reclamation, Salt Lake City, UT.
— 1986b. Distributional archaeology: Survey, mapping, and analysis of surface archaeological materials in the Green River Basin, Wyoming.In *The Seedskadee Project: Remote Sensing in Non-Site Archeology*, edited by D. L. Drager and A. K. Ireland, pp. 227-242. Southwest Region, National Park Service, Albuquerque, NM, and Upper Colorado Region, Bureau of Reclamation, Salt Lake City, UT.
Warren, R. E. 1990a. Predictive modelling in archaeology: A primer. In *Interpreting Space: GIS and Archaeology*, edited by K. M. S. Allen, S. W. Green, and E. B. W. Zubrow, pp. 90-111. Taylor and Francis, New York.
— 1990b. Predictive modelling of archaeological site location: A case study in the Midwest. In *Interpreting Space: GIS and Archaeology*, edited by K. M. S. Allen, S. W. Green, and E. B. W. Zubrow, pp. 201-215.Taylor and Francis, New York.
Warren, R. E., and Asch, D. L., 1996. *A Predictive Model of Archaeological Site Location in the Eastern Prairie Peninsula, Illinois.* Illinois State Museum, Springfield.
Warren, R. E., Oliver, S. G., Ferguson, J. A., and Druhot, R. E., 1987. *A Predictive Model of Archaeological Site Location in the Western Shawnee National Forest.* Technical Report 86-262-17. Quaternary Studies Program, Illinois State Museum, Springfield.
Warren, S. H., Piggot, S., Clark, J. G. D., Burkitt, M. C., Godwin, H., and Godwin, M. E., 1936. Archaeology of the submerged land-surface of the Essex coast. *Proceedings of the Prehistoric Society* 9:178-210.
WAS, 1997. *Guidelines for Public Archeology in Wisconsin.* Wisconsin Archaeological Survey.
Washburn, A. R., 1981. *Search and Detection.* Operations Research Society of America, Arlington, VA.
Weber, A., 1909. *Über den Standort der Industrien.* Tübingen.
Wetherill, G. B., and Glazebrook, K. D., 1987. *Sequential Methods in Statistics.* Chapman and Hall, London.
Whallon, R., 1973, Spatial analysis of occupation floors I: the application of dimensional analysis of variance. *American Antiquity* 38:266-278
— 1979. *An Archaeological Survey of the Keban Reservoir Area of East-Central Turkey.* Memoirs of the Museum of Anthropology, University of Michigan, 11. Ann Arbor.
— 1987. Simple statistics. In *Quantitative Research in Archaeology, Progress and Prospects,* edited by M. S. Aldenderfer, pp. 135-50. Sage Publications, Newbury Park, CA.
Whitlam, R. G., 1998. Cyberstaking Archaeological Sites: Using Electronic Marker Systems (EMS) for a Site Datum and Monitoring Station. *SAA Bulletin* 16(2):xxxx.
Wickler, S., 2001. The prehistory of Buka: A steppling-stone island in the Northern Solomons." *Terra Australis* 16:17, 21-28.

Wignall, T. K., and De Geoffroy, J., 1987. *Statistical Models for Optimizing Mineral Exploration.* Plenum Press, New York.
Wilkinson, T. J., 1982. The definition of ancient manured zones by means of extensive sherd-sampling techniques. *Journal of Field Archaeology* 9:323-333.
— 1989. Extensive sherd scatters and land-use intensity: Some recent results. *Journal of Field Archaeology* 16:31-46.
— 1993. Linear hollows in the Jazira, upper Mesopotamia. *Antiquity,* 67:548-562.
— 1998. Water and human settlement in the Balikh Valley, Syria: Investigations from 1992-1995. *Journal of Field Archaeology* 25: 63—87.
Wilkinson, T. J., and Murphy, P., 1986. Archaeological survey of an intertidal zone: The submerged landscape of the Essex coast, England. *Journal of Field Archaeology* 13:177-194.
— 1988. *Hullbridge Basin Survey 1987.* Interim Report 8. Chelmsford.
— 1995. *The Archaeology of the Essex Coast, Volume 1: The Hullbridge Survey.* East Anglian Archaeological Reports 71. Chelmsford.
Willey, G. R., 1953. *Prehistoric Settlement Patterns in the Virù Valley, Peru.* Bureau of American Ethnology Bulletin 155. Smithsonian Institution, Washington, DC.
Williams, L., Thomas, D. H. and Bettinger, R., 1973, *Notions to numbers: Great Basin settlements as polythetic sets.* In Research and Theory in Current Archaeology, edited by Redman, C. L., pp. 215-237. John Wiley and Sons, New York.
Wobst, H.M., 1983. We can't see the forest for the trees: Sampling and the shapes of archaeological distributions. In *Archaeological Hammers and Theories,* edited by J. Moore and A. Keene, pp. 32-80. Academic Press, New York.
Wood-Martin, W. G., 1886. *The Lake-Dwellings of Ireland or Ancient Lacustrine Habitations of Erin Commonly Called Crannogs.* Dublin.
Woods, W. I., 1977. The quantitative analysis of soil phosphate. *American Antiquity* 42:248-252.
Wright, H. T., and Johnson, G. A., 1975. Population, exchange, and early state formation in southwestern Iran. *American Anthropologist* 77:267-289.
Yorston, R. M., Gaffney, V. L. and Reynolds, P. J., 1990, Simulation of artefact movement due to cultivation. *Journal of Archaeological Science* 17:67-83
Zadora-Rio, É, 1991. Les terroirs médiévaux dans le Nord et le Nord-Ouest de l'Europe. In *Pour une Archéologie Agraire,* edited by J. Guilaine, pp. 165-192.
Zamit, T., 1928. Prehistoric cart-tracks in Malta. *Antiquity* 2:18-25.
Zarky, A., 1976. Statistical analysis of site catchments at Ocós, Guatemala. In *The Early Mesoamerican Village,* edited by K. V. Flannery, pp. 117-130. Academic Press, New York.
Zeidler, J. A., 1995. *Archaeological Inventory Survey Standards and Cost-estimation Guidelines for the Department of Defense.* US Army Corps of Engineers Research Laboratories Special Report 96/40.
Zipf, G. K., 1949. *Human Behavior and the Principle of Least Effort.* Harvard University Press, Cambridge, MA.
Zubrow, E., and Harbaugh, J. W., 1978. Archaeological prospecting: Kriging and simulation. In *Simulations Studies in Archaeology,* edited by I. Hodder, pp. 109-122. Cambridge University Press, Cambridge.

Index

Accessibility, 63–65, 76
Adaptive sampling
   spatial sampling, 118
Aerial reconnaissance,
   4, 41, 54, 136, 137
Airborne oceanographic LIDAR, 232
AIRSAR, 232
Allocation
   Neymann allocation, 127
   optimal allocation, 149
   stratified samples, 126–130
Amboseli Basin, 8
American Cultural Resources Association 194
American Southwest, 6
Ancient Landscape Reconstruction in North Bohemia, 87, 94, 121
Anthropic soil horizons, 43
Antisite survey, 12
Apalachee Bay, 137
Archaeological distributions, 11, 75
Archaeological populations, 30
Archaic, 137
Area of Potential Effects (APE), 177
Artifact clusters, 59
Artifact density, 6, 81, 109
Artifact displacement, 73, 73–74
Attrition, 10
Augers, 40, 69
Augering, 14
Autocorrelation
   spatial, 65, 117
   temporal, 134

Background, 50
Basin of Mexico Project, 6
Bayes' theorem, 148
Bayesian analysis, 134
Bias, 89, 183, 224-227
Binford, Lewis, 20
Bioturbation, 54, 73
Black Mesa Project, 7, 214, 224
Borlase, William, 8
Boundaries
   of survey area, 76
   of sites, 6
Broad searches, 67
Buried landscapes, 11

Cache River, 92
Caissons, 210
Canadian Association of Professional Heritage, 195
Canals, 90
Catchments, 78–79
Cecina survey, 48
Celtic fields, 4
Chemical signatures, 55
Chemical surveys, 43
Chesapeake flotilla, 134, 148
Christaller, Walter, 157
Circular sites, 99
Circular targets, 97
Clarke, W. G., 3
Cluster means, 120
Cluster proportions, 120
Clustered distributions, 53

Clustering 52, 53
Clusters, 50
Coin distributions, 79
Collecting artifacts, 208–209
Colluvium, 41
Communication routes, 34
Community patterns, 5
Concave distributions, 80
Conclusive contact investigation policy, 67
Conic distribution, 17
Consistency, 36
Constituents, 49, 54
   constituent removal, 54
Construction, 47
Contact investigation, 67
Contagious distributions
   Neyman type A distribution, 17
   negative binomial distribution, 17
Continuous distributions
   mapping of, 34
Continuous search games, 153
Contrast, 48, 49
Controls and data quality, 213
Coppiced trees, 164
Cosa, 78
Cost, 24, 86, 95, 109
   balancing with benefits, 109
   cost function, 153
   of data collection, 62
   fixed, 102
   minimizing, 129
      for a fixed variance, 129
   of mitigation, 103
   of survey, 102
Coverage, 61, 63
Crannogs, 9
Crawford, O. G. S., 136
Crews, 65–67
Crop marks, 4, 49
Cultural Resource Management, 37, 76, 143, 177-196, 230

Data quality, 213–216
Decision theory: *see* Game Theory
Definite detection, 57–58, 107, 222

Definite range law, 57, 69, 70
Dendritic networks, 174
Dendritic structure, 161
Density of effort, 60–62
Detectability, 40, 74, 82
   in artifact detection, 214
Detection functions, 38, 217, 227
Detection probabilities, 70, 217-220, 227-228
Dimensional Analysis of Variance (DAV), 155, 165
Discovery radius, 69, 70
Discovery regions, 70
Discrete search games, 153
Discrete sites, 75, 197
Disproportional stratified samples, 149
Distance from target to sensor: *see* Range
Distributional survey, 12, 37, 165, 199, 210-212
Distributions, 75
   clustered, 53
   of coins, 79
   concave, 80
   conic, 17
   contagious, 17
   continuous, 34
   convex, 80
   random, 32
   surface, 11
Diyala River, 5, 122, 137
Drainages, 77

Earthwork patterns, 163
Edge effects, 80, 83, 85–86, 111
   on parameter estimates, 85
Effective site detection area, 84
Effective visibility, 108
Electromagnetic (EM) surveys, 44
Electronic Marker Systems (EMS), 232
Ellipse orientation, 99
Elliptical targets, 82, 99, 222
Environmental zones, 32, 132
Erosion, 73
   gullies, 46

Index

Error of measurement, 71
Estimation
    of artifact attributes, 32
    of densities of artifacts, 31, 130
    of densities of sites, 30
    of human population sizes, 32, 132
    of number of archaeological sites, 131
    of parameters, 27
    of population parameters, 30–33
    of proportions of site types, 31
    of proportions of sites by environmental zone, 32
    of range or diversity, 33
Evaluation, 72, 233
    of bias, 224-226
    of differences in collection method, 227
    of detection probabilities, 217–218, 217–220, 219–228
    of exhaustion of a region, 220–223
    of intensity, 218
    of reliability of crew observations, 224–225
    of sampling, 223–224
    of survey results, 199–200
    of visibility, 218
Exhaustion, 220-223
    exhaustion maps, 222
Expanding-square searches, 108, 147, 148
Expected reward, 104
Exploration potential map, 223
Exploratory analysis, 142
Exponential spiral search, 154

False targets, 67–72, 232
    false-target density, 68
Features, 206–207
Fertilizers, 75
Fieldwalking, 3, 4, 197
Filtering data, 110
Finite population correction, 126
Fire-cracked rock, 3, 50
Fixed-sample designs, 124
Flakes, 50

Fluvial transport, 75
Foley, Robert, 8
Foraging radius, 158
Forests, 63
Fractal properties, 171

Game theory, 152
    continuous search games, 153
    discrete search games, 153
Geoarchaeology, 11, 122-124, 230–231
Geographic Information Systems (GIS) 29, 233
Geographical Information Systems (GIS) 138, 139
Geometry of sites, 59
Geomorphic features, 122–124
Geomorphological processes, 11
Geophysical remote sensing, 24, 55
Geophysical survey, 55
Global Positioning System (GPS), 207, 232
Global Positioning Systems (GPS), 13
Glueck, Nelson, 219–228, 220–228
Goals of survey, 27–38
    multiple goals, 35
Government regulation, 190
Grand Junction Survey, 210
Gridded strips, 227
Grids, 88
    equilateral, 98
    hexagonal, 88, 99
    isoceles, 98
    Optimal spacing, 101–105
    rectangular, 91, 98
    square array, 98
    squares, 88
    systematic point grids, 97
    triangular, 97
Gross detection return, 104
Ground checks, 29, 136, 142
Gulf of Corinth, 136

Hawkins, Alicia, 224
Helike, 136
Heritage resources, 179, 184

Histograms, 34
Historic forts, 64, 150
Historical-political boundaries, 78
Historically documented sites, 134
History of survey, 2
Hunter-gatherers, 7
Hvar survey, 48
Hypothesis tests
  evaluation of models, 145

Inaccessibility, 64, 76
Indigenous groups, 179
Institute of Field Archaeologists (IFA), 195
Intensity, 60–62
Internal accuracy, 142
Intersection probabilities, 39, 60, 68, 69, 82, 105, 109
Intertidal surveys, 8, 65, 199, 209, 213, 230
Intrasite surveys, 121
Inverse-cube law, 58, 70
Isopleth maps, 15

Judgment samples, 64

Kriging, 165
Kvamme, Ken, 139

La Navidad, 135
Lake-bottom survey, 8
Landowners, 63
Landscape archaeology, 4
Landscape elements, 87
Landscape survey, 172
Landscape systems, 34
Lateral range: *See* Range
Law of clean sweep, 57–58
Law of definite detection. *See* Definite range law
Legislation
  Canadian, 193
  English, 191-193
  US, 190-191
Linear programming, 152

Linear targets, 99
Localities, 19
Locating transects, 198
Locational models, 132
Logistic regressions, 142
Logistical radius, 158
Lolley, 135, 139
Lösch, August, 157
Lynchets, 4

Magnetic anomalies, 55
Magnetometer surveys, 44
Mann-Whitney U test, 225
Marine surveys, 231–233
Mathematical geologists, 147
Mathiassen, Therkel, 4
McManamon, F., 55
Medium of propagation, 48
Method of inspection, 40
  aerial reconnaissance, 41
  coring, 42
  divoting, 43
  pedestrian survey, 41
  subsurface survey (SST), 38-39, 42–43, 68, 70, 88, 108-110, 150-152, 209, 230-231
  test-pitting, 42-43, 150-152, 209
  underwater, 45-47
  visual, 40–41
Methodological significance: *See* technical significance
Military bases, 64
military security, 76
mineral prospecting, 39
Minimax, 152
Models, 12-22
  bulls-eye: *See* modal
  central-place, 157
  distributional, 20
  earthwork model, 13
  fried-egg model, 13
  locational, 132
  modal, 15
  monument model, 13, 75
  negative binomial, 15, 53

Index   269

non-site: *See* Distributional Model
paleolandscape, 22
palimpsest, 18
place, 20
Poisson distribution, 50, 68, 109
polythetic, 145
potential, 147, 181
predictive, 138–140
    deductive, 140
    inductive, 140-141
    sensitivity, 147, 181
    significance, 139; *see also* predictive
sinusoidal, 17
    bimodal normal distribution, 17
    testing, 145
    uniform, 13, 75
Monitor, 135
Monitoring environmental change, 230

National Historic Preservation Act (NHPA), 190
National Register of Historic Places, 190
Nearest Neighbor Analysis (NNA), 80
Nested survey areas, 80
New Archaeology, 7
Non-geometrical units, 86–88
Non-response, 64
Non-site spaces, 143
Non-site surveys, 7, 11, 198, 210–213; *see also* structural survey

Obtrusiveness, 43, 48–56, 74
    in aerial reconnaissance, 54
    of artifact scatters, 49–54
    in chemical surveys, 55–56
    in geophysical surveys, 55
Off-site surveys: *See* non-site surveys
Offsite approach, 8
Operations Research, 63, 146, 147, 148
Optimal foraging theory, 152
Optimization, 233
    of allocation, 126-130, 149, 150-152
    of arrangement, 96-101

of densities of search effort, 149
incrementally optimal searches, 152
of location, 158
of spacing, 101-108
of unit size, 108-110

Paleoindians, 137
Paleolandscape model, 22
Paleolandscape survey, 42
Paleolandscapes, 230, 230–231
Paleosols, 138, 231
Palimpsest model, 18
Parameter estimates, 110
Parameters, 30, 113-132
Pastoralism, 19
Pattern recognition, 38, 155
Patternless distribution, 32
Pedestrian survey, 3-6, 40-41, 89-91
Phosphates, 55–56
Photogrammetry, 207
Physical exhaustion maps, 222
Physical exhaustion sequences, 220
Physical-geographical boundaries, 77
Place models, 20
Places, 87
Plank-house villages, 202
Plog, Fred, 7, 39, 83-84
Plog, Steve, 39, 83-84, 203-204, 214-215
Plow-zone distributions: *See* Surface distributions
Point elements, 83
Point of fix, 92, 147
Points, 83, 88-89
Poisson distribution, 13, 50, 68, 109
Poisson process, 52
Political-economic boundaries, 78
Pollarded trees, 164
Polygonal survey units, 94
    optimal arrangement, 100–101
    size, 108
Polythetic models, 145
Population size, 5
Post-depositional factors, 72–73
Post-depositional processes, 12
Posterior probabilities, 146

Potential models, 147, 181
Precision, 203
Predictive models, 138-140
  deductive, 140
  inductive, 140-141
Preservation, 9
Primary coverages, 141
Prior information, 135
Prior probabilities, 146, 150
Probability densities, 151
Probability proportional to size, 121
Problem domains, 23
Proportional allocation, 126
Proportional stratification, 115
Prospecting: *see* Prospection
Prospection 27–29, 88, 134, 137, 231
  Bayesian, 146
Purposive survey, 5, 28-29, 133, 154, 231

Quadrats, 8, 83, 84, 95, 117
  size of, 88, 108

Range, 56, 56–59, 69
Rank-size distributions, 80, 160
Rare phenomena, 28
Raw-material procurement, 19
Reaves, 4
Recording, 203–210
  artifacts, 211
  detectability, 212
  find spots, documenting, 209
  formation processes, 212
  procedures, 25
  provenience, 3
  site size, 203
  visibility, 212
Recovery theory, 29
Reese River Valley, 8
Regional survey, 10
Register of Professional Archaeologists (RPA), 194
Regulation
  Canadian, 193
  English, 191

US, 190-191
Remote sensing, 44
  aerial reconnaissance 54
  geophysical, 55, 144
  Ground-Penetrating Radar (GPR), 45, 231
  phosphates, 55–56
  resistivity, 44
  seismic, 45
  thermal, 45
    aerial infrared thermography, 45
    direct-contact thermography, 45
    Thermal Infrared Multispectral Scanner, 232
  underwater, 232
Remotely Operated Vehicles (ROVs), 231
Research design, 22-25
  multi-stage, 24
Research strategies,
  standardized, 37
Resolution, 43, 51, 53, 62–63
Resource extraction, 22
Retiring-square, 108, 147-148
Richness, 33
Roads, 90

Safety, 235-239
  equipment, 239
Sahara Desert, 137
Salt damage, 73
Sampling, 33, 113, 207–208
  adaptive, 118, 145
  cluster, 111, 117, 119–120
  element, 119
  equipment and supplies, 239
  fraction, 63, 124
  frame, 5, 81, 95
  point, 121
  probabilistic, 145
  random, 113–114
    with replacement, 114
    without replacement, 114
  representative, 27
  sample size, 124

Index

sequential, 130
spatial, 34
stratified, 33, 113, 115–116, 207–208
  cross-cutting stratification, 118
stratified random, 122
subsampling, 94
systematic, 113, 116–117
systematic, stratified, unaligned, 117
Satellite imagery, 136
Saturation survey, 211
Scale, 52, 94-111
Scientific significance, 184
Search patterns, 88-94, 147-149, 154
Search time, 60, 152-153
Secondary coverages, 141
Sediment load, 47
Sediments, 56
Seedskadee Survey, 210, 224–225
Self-similarity, 171
Sensitivity, 116
Settlement hierarchies, 229
Settlement lattices, 34, 169
Settlement patterns, 4, 156
Settlement structure, 229
Settlement systems, 156
Sheetwash, 47
Shovel-testing, 14, 68
Signal-to-noise ratio, 49, 55
Significance
  anthropological, 185
  assessing, 183
  economic, 186
  ethnic, 187
  historical, 186
  public, 185
  scholarly, 185
  scientific, 184
  social scientific, 185
  substantitive, 185
  technical, 185
  theoretical, 185
  Site hierarchies 31
site preservation 202
site-formation processes 8

Sites 12, 81–83
  attributes of, 200
  chronology of, 201, 204–206
  elliptical, 82
  catchments of, 93, 155
  differentiation of, 7
  environments of, 202
  features of, 201–202
  frequency of, 31
  functions of, 5, 201
  orientation of, 82–83
  preservation of, 202–203
  settlements, 12
  shapes of, 82–83
  size of, 82–83, 200, 203
Size
  of polygons, 108
  of quadrats, 108, 110
  of SSTs, 109
  of units, 95–96
    optimizing, 109
Sociopolitical organization, 5
Soils, 56
Sonar, 45
Sorting by erosion, 73
Spacing, 96-110
  systematic, 96
  optimal, 108
    of point grids, 101-105
    of transects, 105-107
  in retiring square, 108
  transects within polygons, 107-108
Spatial organization, 11
Spatial patterns, 72–73, 110
Spatial structure, 28, 34, 55, 155
Springs, 93
Standard deviations, 120
Standard errors, 120, 124
Standardization in CRM, 38
  of research strategies, 37
State Historic Preservation Officer, 191
Statistical surveys, 28, 30, 113-132
Steward, Julian, 8
Stopping rule, 130
Strata, 115

Stratification, 224
  optimal allocation in, 126-130
Stratified samples
  disproportional, 115
  proportional, 115
Streams, 92
Structural survey, 28
Substantitive significance, 185
Subsurface survey: *see* Subsurface testing
Subsurface testing (SST) 7, 38-39, 42–43, 68, 70, 88, 108-110, 118, 150-152, 209, 230–231
  augering, 40, 49, 52, 69
  coring, 14, 42
  divoting, 43
  shovel-testing, 14, 68
  sondages, 42-43, 150-152
  test excavations, 209
  test-pitting, 42-43, 150-152, 209
Surface distributions, 11
Survey units, 67, 76, 81-96
  equilateral triangles, 198
  geometrical, 83-86
  landscape elements, 87
  non-geometrical, 86-88
  points, 83, 88-89
  polygons, 94
  sites, 13, 81-83
  size, 95–96
  transects, 6, 41, 57, 83-86, 89-91, 100, 105-108, 117, 198, 232
  quadrats, 41, 83-86, 108
  undulating, 41, 91
Sweep width, 108
Systematic survey, 62

Targets, 39, 42, 44
  distance of, 96-59
  false, 67-72, 232
  intersection of, 222
  obtrusiveness of, 49
  orientation of, 82, 222
  value of, 103
Team composition, 66

Team motivation, 66
Technology 232
Tells, 64, 137, 202
Territories, 77, 78
Testing hypotheses, 27
Thiessen polygons, 78
Thomas, David Hurst, 8
Tool kit units (TKU), 210
Total coverage, 61, 155, 167
Total station theodolites, 206
Total survey 61, 155, 167
Training, 65–67, 66
Trampling, 54, 73
Transects, 6, 41, 83-86, 89-91, 117, 198, 232
  continuous parallel transects, 100
  diagonal 91
  discontinuous transects 100
  expanding square 92
  intersecting transects 90
  locating transects, 198
  non-adjacent transects 90
  optimal arrangement 100
  optimal spacing 105–108
  parallel transects 57, 89–90, 197
  random transects 90
  retiring square 92
  systematic transects 90
  undulating 91
Travel time, 95
Trend surfaces, 155, 164
Triangulation, 206
Type fossils, 131, 205
Type I errors, 125
Type II errors, 125

Underwater lithic scatters, 137
Underwater survey 45
Units: *see* Survey units
Universe, 30
Upper Creek Muskogees, 135, 139
Upper Seacow Valley, 79
Uruk, 5, 137

Value, 102-107, 153

Variance
    minimizing for fixed budget, 128
Variance-to-mean ratio, 52, 53
Vegetation, 47, 64
Virtual Institute for Spatial Technologies
    (VISTA), 139
Virù Valley, 4, 229
Visibility, 46-48, 72, 74, 121, 131, 212
Von Thünen, Johann, 157

Wadi Ziqlab, 122, 220
Waste disposal, 19
Weber, Alfred, 158
Wet-dry cycling, 73
Wetland survey, 231
Wilcoxon two-sample test, 225
Willey, Gordon, 4, 229
Windscreen surveys, 40

Zipf's Law, 160